A History of Women and Ordination

A History of Women and Ordination: Volume 1: The Ordination of Women in a Medieval Context, by John Hilary Martin, O.P. Edited by Bernard Cooke and Gary Macy.

A History of Women and Ordination: Volume 2: The Priestly Office of Women: God's Gift to a Renewed Church, Second Edition, by Ida Raming. Edited by Bernard Cooke and Gary Macy.

A History of Women and Ordination

Volume 2
The Priestly Office of Women: God's Gift to a Renewed Church, Second Edition

Ida Raming

Edited and Translated by
Bernard Cooke and Gary Macy

The Scarecrow Press, Inc.
Lanham, Maryland • Toronto • Oxford
2004

SCARECROW PRESS, INC.

Published in the United States of America
by Scarecrow Press, Inc.
A wholly owned subsidiary of
The Rowman & Littlefield Publishing Group, Inc.
4501 Forbes Boulevard, Suite 200, Lanham, Maryland 20706
www.scarecrowpress.com

PO Box 317
Oxford
OX2 9RU, UK

First edition © 1976 by Ida Raming as *The Exclusion of Women from the Priesthood: Divine Law or Sex Discrimination?*, Metuchen, N.J.: Scarecrow Press. 0-8108-0957-5

British Library Cataloguing in Publication Information Available

Volume 1 of this series was catalogued by the Library of Congress as follows:

A history of women and ordination.
p. cm.
Includes bibliographical references and index.
Contents: v. 1. The ordination of women in medieval context / edited by Gary Macy and Bernard Cooke.
ISBN 0-8108-4327-7 (alk. Paper)
1. Ordination of women—History. I. Macy, Gary. II. Cooke, Bernard, J.

BV676.H57 2002
262'. 14'08209—dc21

2002020090

This edition is A History of Women and Ordination, Volume 2: The Priestly Office of Women: God's Gift to a Renewed Church, Second Edition. ISBN 0-8108-4850-3.

The paper used in this publication meets the minimum requirements of American National Standard for Information Sciences—Permanence of Paper for Printed Library Materials, ANSI/NISO Z39.48-1992.
Manufactured in the United States of America.

Contents

Acknowledgments

First and foremost, the editors would like to thank Dr. Ida Raming, who graciously allowed us to edit the second edition of her work and to translate the extensive references in her dissertation. Her patience, helpful critiques and prompt replies to our numerous requests made the project a pleasure.

We would also like to thank the editors of *Orientierung* for granting us permission to reprint the three articles that are appended to Dr. Raming's dissertation. We are especially grateful to John Wijngaards, who allowed us to use the English translation of two of Dr. Raming's articles as the basis of our own translation. Ms. Gisela Werner-Jones gave generously of her time by translating the introduction to the second edition of Dr. Raming's book. Without their cooperation, this project would have been impossible. Even more importantly, we would like to thank Scarecrow Press and particularly Shirley Lambert and Melissa Ray, whose consistent optimism, support and amiability carried us through the sometime tedious project of editing. We also want to thank Scarecrow for allowing us to use the original English translation of Dr. Raming's dissertation, which they first published in 1976.

Several people were indispensable in preparing this volume for publication. Mrs. Eugenia Navas scanned much of the material for us. Ms. Lucinda Jacobs and Ms. Michelle Bruns both did an amazing job of cleaning up the scanned materials and tracking down obscure references for the editors. Mrs. Evi Quinn, Dr. John Fendrick and Dr. Russel Fuller all deserve our thanks for checking the German translations.

We would be remiss as well if we did not acknowledge the many feminist scholars who over the years encouraged us to pursue the history of women in Christianity. To name a just a few of the most important, Dr.

Evelyn Kirkley, who first suggested to us that a study of women's ordination would be valuable, Dr. Pauline Turner, who kept us focused on the value of a feminist approach. Also, Dr. Joann Wolski Conn, Sr. Vera Chester and Dr. Jane Via, who for so many years provided invaluable insights and correctives to our inevitable male approach.

Finally, we wish to thank all those who encouraged us again and again to make the sources on women's ordination available to as wide an audience as possible. Members of Call to Action, and of WomenChurch, in particular, wished to have easier access to the history and sources of the continuing historical debate on women's ordination. Our hope is that this volume serves as an answer to those needs.

Introduction to the Series

Bernard Cooke
and Gary Macy

During the past half century, few issues have been more prominent and disputed in religious circles than has the ordination of women. This has been most acutely felt in the Roman Catholic, Orthodox and Anglican Churches, but other Christian groups, as well as Judaism, have not been completely exempt. Beginning in 1975 with the first national conference on women's ordination in Detroit, a meeting that drew national attention and eventuated in formation of the Women's Ordination Conference, there has been a continuing and vocal demand by increasing numbers of Catholics that there be a reconsideration and reform of women's status in the Church. Basically, this has been a demand for full equality for women, but ordination to both diaconate and presbyterate has consistently been seen as the key symbolic recognition of such equality.

The Detroit conference drew more than national attention. Within a few months the Vatican responded with a letter on the nonordination of women, a document that was widely criticized but did much to frame debate on the topic. Without detailing its line of argument, one of its principal points was that the long-standing tradition of the Church has always seen women as incapable of ordination. Ordination today would be contrary to this tradition and so, while Church officials appreciated the important role of women in the Church, their equality as members, and the depth of their faith and commitment, extending this to ministerial ordination lay outside the authority and power of Church officials. Change was not only inadvisable, it was impossible. For the moment, debate centered on the question of whether such a long-standing tradition should prove an obstacle, and in the absence of accurate historical knowledge, the impression in many circles was that the question of women's ordination was a very recent phenomenon, an outgrowth of the contemporary feminist movement.

Careful top-level theological, historical, and biblical examination of the Papal argumentation disagreed with it and concluded that there did not appear to be any intrinsic block to the ordination of women. But that did not alter the Papal position nor close off the discussion. The Women's Ordination Conference has continued in existence. Several other women's organizations have emerged to further urge the issue, an attempt of the U.S. bishops to skirt the question by a pastoral letter on women's role in the church foundered on women's organized objection, and support for women's ordination has gradually grown in most parts of the worldwide Church.

Meanwhile the Anglican Churches throughout the world have confronted the question and, despite strong objections from some quarters, have officially moved to ordination. In the United States this was triggered by the extra-legal ordination of some women in 1974, a move that was first declared invalid but then accepted within a year as illicit by the Episcopalian House of Bishops. But the deed was done. Since then, Anglican ordination of women has become common. A few women have even been ordained as bishops; and some members, including clergy, have left the Anglican Church and "gone to Rome" in protest.

In Roman Catholic circles as well as in the Eastern Orthodox Churches, the official position remains firmly in opposition to women's ordination. Attempting to quell growing popular support and ongoing pressure from women's groups, the Vatican attempted to suppress discussion of the issue. In 1998, a document was promulgated that forbade further debate of the question, since presumably it had been definitively decided by Papal decree. Not surprisingly, this statement proved counterproductive: To deny responsible dissent from Papal teaching on the topic was widely recognized as unenforceable and discussion was probably intensified by this move.

While all this was happening as a high-profile and rather acrimonious event, another question that was inseparably bound up with women's ordination was emerging almost unnoticed. This was the question regarding ordination itself: What was the intrinsic character of ordination in the Christian Churches? What was the actual historical origin of episcopal and presbyteral ordination in Christianity? And what did ordination effect and how did it change those who were ordained?

In Roman Catholicism, these questions were affected by the stance of Vatican II. Above all, the council's recognition of the ministerial responsibility and empowerment of all members of the Church, the people of God, raised questions about the role and power of the ordained. If the faithful were empowered by baptism to undertake most of what had come to be a clerical monopoly of ministry, what was left to the ordained as distinctively theirs? The response seemed clear: Only the ordained were empowered to perform the sacramental actions, most importantly as celebrants of the Eucharist, but that was not as clear as it looked.

Implicit in both debates—about women's ordination and about the role of the ordained clergy—was the same assumption, that "ordination" had always meant what it has come to mean in recent centuries and means for people today. Scholarly research, above all, by Yves Congar, had uncovered evidence that only in the 12th century had "ordination" come to indicate an action that produced in the ordinand two intrinsic powers, the power to absolve sins and the power to change bread and wine in the Eucharist. Prior to that time, "ordinare" had quite a different meaning: To "ordain" a person was a matter of assigning that individual a social/ecclesiastical status and role.

How accurate are the "new" understandings mentioned here? Is there responsible scholarly study that supports them? The answer is that for some decades there has been such study, but it has been largely unrecognized, sometimes arrogantly rejected as marginal by mainstream academe, and scarcely known by those engaged in the debates we have mentioned. It is to remedy this lack, to bring to public attention, to help clarify the truth about historical development in the thinking of Christianity that this series is published. Bringing again to people's notice the evidences of what actually was thought and done regarding ministerial ordination of both men and women will, we hope, help to make discussion of these issues more fruitful.

Translators' Preface

Bernard Cooke
and Gary Macy

This present volume is an English translation of the second German edition of Dr. Raming's important study, *The Exclusion of Women from the Priesthood: Divine Law or Sex Discrimination?* In her second edition, Dr. Raming reproduced the original study, her doctoral dissertation, under the title, *The Priestly Office of Women: God's Gift for a Renewed Church.* To the original study, Dr. Raming added a new introduction, newly edited versions of three of her articles, which had appeared subsequently to her original study, and an extensive bibliography for the women's ordination movement in Europe. This volume is an English translation of that second edition. The editors felt that they did not need to add anything to Dr. Raming's fine new introduction but did think that a few words regarding their translation would be appropriate.

In order to make the material in these studies more accessible to a wide range of readers, the Latin notes in Dr. Raming's study have been translated into English. Every translator is also a traitor, as the old saying goes, and this translation is no exception. Several editorial decisions needed to be made which affect the kind of English that appears in the translations. First, the academic Latin of the Middle Ages consisted mostly of class notes of one kind or another. They are not polished prose, and so neither is the English translation. The decision was made to stick as closely to the original structure and presentation of the Latin as decent (or at least acceptable) English would allow. The editors decided to err on the side of literal accuracy at the expense of literary elegance.

Secondly, specific Latin words offered difficulties in translation. The clearest example of this is the Latin word *sacramentum*. In general, the word can be translated as "symbol," but in certain circumstances, *sacramentum* more clearly means "ritual" or "sacrament" in the English sense of that word. In order to aid the reader in following this ambiguity, the editors have placed the Latin word *sacramentum* in parentheses following the English translation of the word as "symbol," "ritual" or "sacrament." The medieval authors would have, of course, understood the word as having the overtones of all three of the English words, probably not distinguishing as carefully between the three as modern English speakers. Similarly, the Latin word *homo* usually means human being, but as Dr. Raming points out in her study *homo* can sometimes mean "male." In those instances where *homo* clearly means "male," we have so indicated in the translation. *Vir* is always translated as "male" and not "man" so as to avoid confusion with the English "mankind." The one exception to this rule occurs in those instances where *vir* means "husband." Again these passages are clearly marked.

As in the first volume in this series, the editors have attempted in all cases to provide clear and precise references to the original Latin sources for those readers who wish to read the original for themselves. The editors certainly encourage readers to do so. Another language creates another world that even the best translation cannot capture.

The original translation from the German of Dr. Raming's dissertation by Norman R. Adams has been retained, except when changes were necessitated by changes in the Latin translation. The numbering of the notes has also been changed to correspond with the German original. The translations of two of Dr. Raming's articles are based on the translations by Mary Dittrich for the womenpriests.org website. The changes which Dr. Raming made to the originally published articles for the second edition of her book have been included with one exception. In the revised version of the article "A Definitive 'No' to the Ordination of Women?" Dr. Raming shortened the article, referring readers to the longer exposition found in the article "The Twelve Apostles Were Men . . . " The editors have retained a more extended version of "A Definitive 'No'" for those readers who might wish to read only this article. Whenever possible, the English version of documents and articles are provided in place of the German sources used by Dr. Raming. With these few exceptions, the authors have attempted to maintain a faithful rendering of the second German edition of Dr. Raming's groundbreaking study.

A History of Women and Ordination Volume 2 The Priestly Office of Women: God's Gift to a Renewed Church, Second Edition

Ida Raming

Introduction to the Second Edition of *The Exclusion of Women from the Priesthood* (1973)

Translated by Gisela Werner-Jones

"Now is the Time: A Celebration of Women's Call to a Renewed Priesthood in the Catholic Church"—this was the motto under which the international network Women's Ordination Worldwide (WOW) organized the First International Conference on the issue of the ordination of women from June 29 to July 1, 2001. About 350 men and women from 26 countries and all 5 continents, representatives of the numerous national sub-organizations of WOW as well as several guests from the ecumenical movement, congregated in Dublin, Ireland. In one declaration and eleven resolutions,[1] they unanimously expressed their determination to actively promote the access of women who have a calling to the ordained offices of the church, e.g., by continuously keeping the issue of women's ordination in the public and by supporting the education of women for the deaconate and priesthood. The assembled men and women will not allow themselves to be discouraged by threats and bans from the Vatican—which burdened the conference in Dublin before it even started. Instead, they want to create a path for the ordination of women in the church, trusting in the power of God's spirit.

This conference is an important milestone on the way to the ordination of women in the Roman Catholic Church. It is an occasion to look back at the development since the Second Vatican Council and also to look into the future. From this perspective, this reprint of the dissertation (from 1973), which takes an in-depth look at this issue, is published at the right time.

Doctrinal Development since the First Printing

The time period between the Second Vatican Council (1962-1965) and the present (2001) within the church is marked by the fact that a large number of members of the church have repeatedly asked for several reforms. Not the least of them is the call for a position for women in keeping with the times, that is their complete equality in the structures of the church.

Several women took the initiative on the grass root level in 1962 and 1963 and were supported by some bishops during the Council. Their attempt was a small one that found surprising and strong support in the Encyclical *Pacem in terris* (1963) by the Council Pope John XXIII. In this encyclical for the first time in the history of the Catholic Church, the women's emancipation movement was regarded as positive, as a "sign of the times" that deserved attention.

In the period immediately following the Council, there was an increasing number of publications (articles and books) about the issue "Women in the Church," among others the first printing of this dissertation (1973), which is now available as a reprint. The special character of this work was undoubtedly that it contains a critical analysis of the basis for the exclusion of women from the priesthood, especially of the relevant legal sources and dogmatic positions. At the time the issue was taboo, and it was only the second dissertation in German-speaking countries that dealt with this issue.

It is thanks to the professor of legal history of law and canon law at the Catholic Theological Department at the University of Muenster at the time, Professor Doctor P. J. Kessler, who died in 1988, for guiding and supervising this work competently and without censoring the author. This is especially worth mentioning because at the time—and possibly still today—it was (and is) very rare that a professor at a Catholic Theological Department would support with his name a research project which was (and is) basically detrimental to his reputation but important for the development of the church.

In the postconciliar period, the scientific and journalistic treatment of the issue, along with synodal processes at the national as well as church-wide levels, including a vote for the deaconate of women and a continuing discussion of the priesthood for women, had a widespread impact.

On the other hand, however, as a reaction to this, the powers within the church that are oriented towards inertia and the conservation of the status quo, which had already been noticeable during the final phase of the Council, organized. The conflict between those trends in the church that are oriented towards reform and those that want to preserve the existing situation intensifies dramatically in the attitude towards the ordination of women. In this sense, the issue of the ordination of women is a crucial question—because the answer to this question decides if real equality of women in the church is wanted or rejected.

After the Council, the "No" from the Vatican about the ordination of women has been expressed in several pronouncements. On the other hand, this might be seen as a sign that the responsible authorities at the Vatican that are oriented towards the preservation of patriarchy in the church can only react with means of power and pressure because they find themselves more and more on the defensive, due to the growing movement on the grassroots level that is urging for a reform of the position of women, and due to the results of theology that is critical of patriarchy.

Only four years after the first printing of this dissertation, in 1977, during the pontificate of Paul VI, the first official document against the admission of women to the priesthood was published: the declaration of the Congregation for the Doctrine of the Faith *Inter insigniores*.[2] It caused critical reactions worldwide, not only from Catholic women's groups, but also from theologians, and even from members of other institutions of the Vatican (the Secretariat for Christian Unity, especially the Biblical Commission) who felt left out when the document was drafted.

The latter had declared in a vote in 1976 that there was no decision about the ordination of women to the priesthood in the New Testament, that therefore the ban of female priests could not be deduced from the New Testament, and furthermore that Christ's plan of salvation was not violated or falsified by the admission of the ordination of women.[3] With regard to the theological standing of the declaration *Inter insigniores*, it can be said that while it is an "authentic declaration of the Roman magisterium," it is not an "infallible" statement—it does not mention that its doctrine is based on divine revelation.[4] The declaration itself qualifies the "dogmatic obligation of church practice . . . as unmistakably small" and clearly limits the "implications of the arguments from scripture and tradition."[5]

During the pontificate of John Paul II, the restraint and self-restriction of the magisterium that still exists in the declaration *Inter insigniores* is given up completely. In speeches and written announcements, the pope repeatedly expressed his rejection of the priesthood of women, sometimes even under threat of sanctions.[6] The pressure of the church leadership on the opposite opinion grew considerably during the pontificate of John Paul II and lasts until today.

In the Apostolic Letter *Mulieris Dignitatem*[7] (*On the Dignity and Vocation of Women*), the pope expresses formally his opposition to the priesthood of women, with reference to the declaration of the Congregation for the Doctrine of the Faith *Inter insigniores* (No. 26). His rejection is embedded in an anthropological "meditation" about gender relations, which is interpreted as a symbolic relationship between "groom" and "bride." This way, a "polarized image of humans"[8] and antiquated roles of men and women are propagated (man as priest, "Vicar of Christ" —woman as representative of the "bride" church or lay church). Immediately after the publication of this Apostolic Letter, there were again many critical voices around the world—the widening gap between the magisterium on the one hand and a growing number of members of the church on the other hand was already obvious.

This growing dissent could not be overcome by the pope's apostolic letter *Ordinatio Sacerdotalis*[9] either, published in 1994. The explicit purpose of this letter is to end the ongoing discussion of the ordination of women with a papal word of authority. This letter was supposed to make a binding doctrinal decision against the admission of women to priesthood which was to be "*definitively* held by all the Church's faithful" (no. 4; emphasis by author). But this use of authority by the magisterium, until then the strongest of its kind against the ordination of women, also remained without results because its decision was based on theological views that could not withstand a scientific, theological examination: "Well-founded counter arguments to the doctrinal position with regard to the ordination of women cannot be settled by the use of authority,"[10] as could be clearly observed in the diverse critical reactions to it.[11]

Contrary to the intention of the papal letter, the discussion of this issue gained even more widespread impact. The demand for the ordination of women became stronger, for example through a church petition for a referendum in Austria, Germany and other countries. As a reaction to this, the Vatican used their "last resort" to force the ongoing discussion to stop and to force the demand for the ordination of women to be abandoned: In "On '*Ordinatio Sacerdotalis*' *Responsum ad Dubium*" (October 28, 1995) the Congregation for the Doctrine of the Faith declared it was part of the deposit of faith and therefore demanded "definitive consent."[12] On the basis of this classification, the doctrine of the exclusion of women from ordination and priesthood belongs to the new "category of a 'definitive doctrine'" developed by the Roman magisterium, which was not mentioned by the Second Vatican Council or by any other ecumenical Council, nor was it the result of an extensive consultation of all bishops, nor was it "the result of critical discussions of the theologians."[13] Nevertheless, it was added to church law.[14] However, even this—so far the most severe—action by the church leadership, working in a centralist way—without the inclusion of the College of Bishops—will not be able to achieve adoption and acceptance of the pope's decision against the ordination of women with most members of the church. The continuing dissent between the magisterium and a growing number of the church's faithful in this question shows that this is a "case of theological non-reception".[15]

About the Development of Church Law (since 1973)

According to the principle that canonical law follows the official Church teaching, the rejection of the ordination of women was also reflected in church law, in the *Codex Iuris Canonici* (hereafter *CIC*) of 1983. Canon 1024 of the "new" codex repeats verbatim from the corresponding canon of the codex from 1917 (c. 968 § 1): "Only a baptized man can validly receive sacred ordination." While this rule is not qualified as divine law, it still found its way into church law through the new category of a "definitive doctrine" (cf. *CIC*, c. 750 § 2), after it was formulated in the Apostolic Letter *Ordinatio Sacerdotalis* (1994) as a "definitive" doctrine about ordination being reserved for men, which was confirmed in *Responsum ad dubium* (1995) of the Congregation For the Doctrine of the Faith. Its binding character is explicitly stressed (the doctrine is "to be recognized and observed") and is made a punishable offense (cf. c. 1371, n. 1).[16]

This means that women in the Roman Catholic Church continue to be excluded from the diaconate and allegedly "definitively" from the priesthood and the episcopate. The far reaching consequences for the position of women in the church are obvious: Women are denied, for example, the independent and personally responsible practice of pastoral care. Since they are not ordained and cannot have any ecclesiastical jurisdiction (*potestas iurisdictionis*), but can only participate as lay persons in its practice according to the law (cf. *CIC*, cc. 129 § 1; 274 § 1), they are also denied any influence (within the framework of a religious office) on the obligatory doctrines of faith and morals as well as on the church legislature. Some examples can show how this legal position affects actual church practice. Despite the growing lack of priests, women cannot head the Eucharist. Even a female religious community whose members are often well educated in theology needs a man as priest and pastor. Women are excluded from the official teaching of doctrines, e.g., during councils. Correspondingly the existing code of canon law has been written by a committee of men alone.

In view of these drastic legal restrictions, the programmatic words of the church constitution of the Second Vatican Council *Lumen Gentium* (No. 32): "In Christ and *in the church* there is no inequality because of race and ethnicity, social status or *gender* (emphasis by author) (cf. Gal. 3, 28)" seem like a hollow phrase, because the fundamental right for equality (cf. *CIC*, c. 208), which results from the membership with God's people, is considerably limited for women because of their gender. This, however, diametrically opposes the goals of the reform of church law, which was initiated by John XXIII during the Second Vatican Council. This reform ought to have taken into account the "changed challenges of the modern world" and the "needs of God's people."[17] However, the concept of church as "God's people," newly taken up by the Council, which stresses the idea of equality of all members of the church, has not become decisive for the Code of Canon Law of 1983. Rather, the church book of law adheres to the established organized structure of the church which was already characteristic of the Code of Canon Law of 1917 (cf. cc. 207 § 1; 212 § 1 *CIC*/1983). According to this, women belong only to the laity which is subordinate to church officials and has the duty to obey them. As a result of women's exclusion from ordination and its related consecrated offices (c. 1024), their right for a free choice of vocation is severely restricted, even though it was declared an inviolable human right in the Encyclical *Pacem in terris* (1963) by John XXIII, and even though it belongs to the fundamental rights of the church (cf. c. 219). The contradiction between this fundamental right in connection with c. 208, which stresses the equality of all faithful because of their "rebirth in Christ," and the rule of c. 1024 is obvious![18]

A large degree of equality of women and men in the "new" church law has only been achieved in the laity. However, as soon as duties in the cultic-liturgical field are concerned, it becomes obvious that women will remain second-class lay persons as long as they are excluded from the priesthood, because according to c. 230 § 1, the duties of a lector and acolyte, conferred permanently through a liturgical rite, continue to be reserved for men only. Women can only carry out some of the duties that are connected with these positions for a limited period of time, e.g., the role of lector, assisting the distribution of the Holy Communion, as well as altar service and altar duties. After the Council, the lengthy arguments about the admission of female altar servers were finally settled through an official interpretation of c. 230 § 2 by the responsible Vatican authority, which decided that the liturgical "service at the altar" can also be carried out by women, but not without restrictions.[19] This means that the explicit ban for women to enter the altar area has been cancelled.[20] In addition, there are several other positive developments, which partly result from the pastoral emergency situation: lay persons, including women, can carry out pastoral duties in parishes without a priest, of course under the supervision of a priest or pastor assigned by the responsible bishop (cf. *CIC*, c. 517 § 2). Furthermore, laymen of both genders can participate as judges in an ecclesiastical tribunal (*CIC*, cc. 1421 § 2, 1435); they are also permitted as financial administrators (*CIC*, cc. 494 § 1, 537, 1282). These examples show that the societal change has not "completely passed by church law"—however, the real, urgently needed "major breakthrough is still to come."[21]

Lasting Relevance of the Issue in the Present

It is evident in light of this background that a reprint of the dissertation is still relevant (unfortunately, I might add), because it includes a critical analysis of the numerous sources (legal, patristic and biblical) that form the basis and structural grounds for the continuing exclusion of women from ordination and priesthood. To round off this work, several articles by the author have been added (in an appendix). Arising from particular situations, they discuss, among other things, the stereotypical arguments against the ordination of women which are expressed, for example, in the declaration *Inter insigniores* (1976) and the Apostolic Letter *Ordinatio Sacerdotalis* (1994). Another article is devoted to the emergence and development of the (by now worldwide) movement for the ordination of women in European countries up until the present. In addition, there is an updated bibliography that documents the publications about this issue since the first printing of this dissertation.

Continuation of the Discrimination against Women in the Roman Catholic Church

The knowledge of the long history of discrimination against women because of their gender, one important period of which is described in this work, can help us increase our awareness of the continuing inferior valuation of women. Despite all reassurances of the equality of women (e.g., in *Mulieris Dignitatem*), and despite the praise of the "genius of woman,"[22] the history of discrimination against women in the Roman Catholic Church continues. It will continue as long as men in the highest positions of the church have power over the spirit and souls of women by defining the nature and "dignity" of women through their difference from that of men, creating legal consequences and arbitrarily setting limits to their work in the church. It will continue as long as men of the church deny women a calling to the priesthood—ignoring the free working of the Holy Spirit which is "allotted to each one individually just as the Spirit chooses" (cf. 1 Cor. 12:11). In assuming control, men of the church thereby place themselves between God and women, disregarding the inviolability of the person of woman, her immediacy with God, her freedom to decide for herself as a person in religious matters.

The definitive exclusion of women from ordination and related consecrated offices because of their gender, imposed by the men of the church, reveals the continuing and sinful disruption of gender relations in the church, which are determined by power and control. As long as this deplorable state of affairs continues, the central Christian message cannot be fulfilled: "For as many of you as have been baptised into Christ have put on Christ . . . there is neither male nor female: for ye are all one in Christ Jesus." (Gal. 3:27f.).

The Calling of Women to the Priesthood—God's Grace for a Renewal of the Church

By adhering to the dominance of man over woman, the Vatican shuts itself off from the new things (Rev. 21:5) that have emerged through the beginning of the Kingdom of God in Jesus. It also shuts itself off from the working of the spirit of Jesus in the church of our times. God continually gives the church new graces. To these belong the charisms that qualify one for the priesthood (cf. Eph. 4:8, 10-12). God gives them to women as well as men. A representative example for the free working of the Holy Spirit that allots to every one as she wills (cf. 1 Cor. 12:11)—and not how it is ruled by the church hierarchy—is the testimony of St. Theres of Lisieux (declared a Doctor of the Church in 1997): "I feel called to priesthood!" She is seen as the patron of those women who rise in many countries today and publicly affirm their calling and being called by God to the priesthood.[23] The diverse graces, which are given to both women and men, are meant to bring about continuous renewal and rejuvenation of the church and its offices. The responsible authorities therefore do not have the right to reject these graces and callings—just because they were given to women (cf. 1 Cor. 12:12-25; 1 Tim. 5:19). The continuing resistance of the church leadership against the acceptance of women's callings to priesthood, as well as the legal obstacles that it sets against their unfolding, lead to a one-sided, patriarchal character of the office, which also leads to the stagnation and impoverishment that we are experiencing in the contemporary church. This is why the church leadership's attitude towards the question of women and ordination of women will decide the future fate of the Roman Catholic Church.

All men and women in the church are therefore called upon to make an effort for the creation of a relationship between genders, which is marked by justice, truthfulness and mutual respect. Too many men, clerics and laymen, overlook without sensitivity the situation of their sisters in faith and leave them to their fate—but also too many women still remain in the position of a spectator, not affected by their own situation in the church, not willing to burden themselves with the exhausting fight for a dignified position in the church. For the sake of the credibility and renewal of the church, however, all members of the church share the responsibility for the full acceptance of the diverse charisma—regardless of person and gender.

Sent and Authorized " . . . to preach deliverance to the captives" (cf. Lk. 4:18f.)

However, the highest ecclesiastical authorities of the church carry the main responsibility for this. If they justify the rejection of the ordination of women by saying "that the Church has no authority whatsoever to confer priestly ordination on women" (*Ordinatio Sacerdotalis*, no. 4), this argument is not convincing. It seems to be a mere pretext to conceal the patriarchal unwillingness. It is conspicuous that in the case of the exclusion of women from ordination and priesthood, the leading ecclesiastical authorities were able to use their (alleged) authority without hesitation and scruples, even though this exclusion cannot be justified theologically and prevents the unfolding of charism to the detriment of the church. In this case, the question about the limits of their legitimate authority would have been indeed necessary because this action was undoubtedly an abuse of power!

It is now time to end this detriment to the church, to free women in the church from the chains of patriarchal power and to let them finally experience the freedom of God's children. The responsible ecclesiastical authorities *do indeed have the legitimate authority* for such an act of liberation. Christ Himself, the head of the church, gives it to them, because through the baptism in His name, any social distinction between men and women has been lifted (cf. Gal. 3:27f.).

Ida Raming
Summer 2001

Notes

1. Conference reports, papers and the wording of the resolutions can be found on the web site: www.wow2001.org.

2. The declaration of the Congregation for the Doctrine of the Faith on the admission of women to the priesthood, *Inter Insignores* is in *Acta Apostolica Sedis*, 69 (1977): 98-116. The English translation of *Inter Insignores* appeared in *Origins*, 6 (1977): 517-524 with commentary on pp. 524-531. The commentary has also been included as an appendix in Leonard Swidler and Arlene Swidler, eds., *Women Priests. A Catholic Commentary on the Vatican Declaration*, (New York: Paulist Press, 1977), 319-337.

3. Walter Groß, "Bericht der Päpstlichen Bibelkommission, 1976," in Walter Groß, *Frauenordination. Stand der Diskussion in der katholischen Kirche*, (Münich: E. Wewel Verlag, 1996), 25-31, esp. 25f.

4. Cf. Karl Rahner, "Priestertum der Frau?" *Stimmen der Zeit* 195 (1977): 291-301, esp. 292f.

5. Peter Hünermann, "Roma locuta-causa finita?" *Herder Korrespondenz* 31 (1977): 206-209, esp. 209.

6. See also Ida Raming, *Frauenbewegung und Kirche. Bilanz eines 25jährigen Kampfes für Gleichberechtigung und Befreiung der Frau seit dem 2. Vatikanischen Konzil*, 2nd ed. (Weinheim: Dt. Studien Verlag, 1991) 65, 127.

7. *Acta Apostolica Sedis* 80 (1988), 1653-1729. English translation *On the Dignity and Vocation of Women (Mulieris Dignitatem)*, (Washington, D.C.: United States Catholic Conference, 1988).

8. See Elisabeth Gössmann, "Kommentar zu *Mulieris Dignitatem*," in *Die Zeit der Frau. Apostolisches Schreiben "Mulieris Dignitatem" Papst Johannes Pauls II.*, (Freiburg-Basel—Wien: Herder, 1988) 121-150, esp. 146.

9. *Acta Apostolica Sedis*, 86 (1994): 546-549 with commentary in the English edition of *Osservatore Romano*, 22/1343 (1994): 1-2 and in *Origins*, 24 (1994): 49-52 with commentary on pp. 52-53 and comments by U.S. bishops on pp. 53-58.

10. Ulrich Ruh, "Lehramt im Abseits?" *Herder-Korrespondenz* 48 (1994): 327.

11. See for example Peter Hünermann, "Schwerwiegende Bedenken. Eine Analyse des Apostolischen Schreibens 'Ordinatio Sacerdotalis,'" *Herder-Korrespondenz* 48 (1994): 406-410 and Ida Raming, "Endgültiges Nein zum Priestertum der Frau? Zum Apostolischen Schreiben Papst Johannes Pauls II. 'Ordinatio Sacerdotalis'" *Orientierung* 58 (1994) 190-193 (republished here on pp. 255-264.

12. "This teaching requires definitive assent, since, founded on the written Word of God, and from the beginning constantly preserved and applied in the Tradition of the Church, it has been set forth infallibly by the ordinary and universal Magisterium." Criticisms of this text are given by P. Hünermann "Dogmatische Reflexionen anläßlich der Antwort der Glaubenskongregation vom 28. Oktober 1995," Groß, *Frauenordination,* 129-146.

13. So Ladislas Örsy, "Von der Autorität kirchlicher Dokumente. Eine Fallstudie zum Apostolischen Schreiben *Ad tuendam fidem,*" *Stimmen der Zeit* 123 (1998): 735-740, esp. 737; see also Örsy, "Antwort an Kardinal Ratzinger," *Stimmen der Zeit* 124 (1999): 305-316.

14. See note 16.

15. According to Wolfgang Beinert, "Dogmatische Überlegungen zum Thema Priestertum der Frau," in: Groß, *Frauenordination*, 64-82, esp. 64f.

16. John Paul II., Apostolic Letter *Motu Proprio Ad tuendam fidem,* May 18 1998, *Acta Apostolica Sedis* no. 90 (1998): 457-461. For a critical analysis, see note 13. English edition in *Origens* 28/8 (1998): 113, 115-16; commentary by Cardinal Ratzinger, 116-119.

17. Address by Paul VI on November 20, 1965; see the introduction to *CIC*, XXXIX. See also Richard Puza, "Strömungen und Tendenzen im neuen Kirchenrecht," *Theologische Quartalschrift* 163 (1983):163-178, esp. 163.

18. For criticism of this as well on the mitigated formulation of c. 219 in comparison to the text in *Pacem in terris*, see Ida Raming, "Ungenutzte Chancen für Frauen im Kirchenrecht. Widersprüche im CIC/1983 und ihre Konsequenzen," *Orientierung* 58 (1994): 68-70.

19. Papal confirmation on the interpretation of legal texts, July 11, 1992, Certification of feminine ministrants, *Acta apostolica sedis*, 86 (1994) 541f; the English version of this text can be found on the website: http://www.ewtn.com/library/curia/cdwcomm.htm. The letter of the prefect of the Congregation for Divine Worship of March 15, 1994 acquiescing to this decision narrowed the admittance of altar girls to ministry, among other things, stated that "the permission given in this regard by some Bishops can in no way be considered as

binding on other Bishops." That is, an individual bishop decides whether altar girls could be permitted in his diocese or not.

20. This law was included in the 1917 code of canon law, *Codex Juris Canonici Pii X pontificis maximi iussu digestus.* (Vatican City: Typis Polyglottis Vaticanis, 1948) c. 813 § 2. For further examples as well as more detailed explanations on this subject, see Ida Raming, "Die Frauen in der Kirche," *Stimmen der Zeit* 115 (1990): 415-426, esp. 419f.

21. Richard Puza, "Zur Stellung der Frau im alten und neuen Kirchenrecht," *Theologische Quartalschrift* 163 (1983): 109-122, esp. 110.

22. Pope John Paul II, *Letter to Women*, 1995 *Acta apostolica sedis* 87 (1995): 803-812, par. 9. English edition in *Origins*, 25/19 (1995) 137, 139-143.

23. For documentation see *Zur Priesterin berufen. Gott sieht nicht auf das Geschlecht. Zeugnise römisch-katholischer Frauen*, edited by Ida Raming, Gertrud Jansen, Iris Müller and Mechtilde Neuendorff (München: Schnell & Steiner, 1998).

Preface to the First Edition

Leonard and Arlene Swidler

The study of canon law is something anyone interested in the renewal of the Catholic Church cannot afford to neglect. All institutions of any longevity naturally develop a body of law, though with varying degrees of formality. Since the Roman Catholic Church has the great legal traditions of both Judaism and the Roman Empire as part of its heritage, the place of law in its life should be expected to be substantial. As in all human affairs, this is not something in itself to be regretted. In modern civil society we express the desire to be governed not by people but by law, hopefully choosing thereby order rather than caprice. Law is seen as an essential instrument, an indispensable means, to a successful society. To be effective, however, the law must always remain alive, growing, responsive to the needs of the people it governs and thereby serves. But to be made responsive, the law must first be studied and understood. This is also true when the question addressed is how women, one half the People of God, can exercise their full talents in and through the Church, including all its clerical offices. It is to an essential part of this task of research and understanding that Dr. Ida Raming has devoted herself in this book.

Dr. Raming's research uncovers the disturbing fact that the ecclesiastical law which restricts Holy Orders to baptized males (canon 968, § 1) is largely based on forgeries, mistaken identities, and suppressions. The patriarch of canon law, Gratian, laid the foundation of the science of canon law with his massive work of codification, the *Decretum*, in the 12th century (1140). In this work, Gratian formulated a number of laws restrictive to women on the assumption that women as such were inferior human beings. Among the legal sources for these laws and this assumption, he cited as authoritative the Pseudo-Isidorian Decretals, which he did not know were largely forgeries. Another "authoritative" source used against women by Gratian were the decrees of the Council of Carthage (A.D. 389) as he found them in the *Statuta Ecclesiae Antiqua.* We now know that the *Statuta* were composed by Gennadius of Marseille between 476 and 485, and the quotations Gratian used are not at all from a (nonexistent) Council of Carthage in A.D. 389, or any other Council—the legal basis of Gratian's restrictive law (and of course all subsequent canon law on this matter) is thus undermined.

Gratian also based some of his restrictive laws against women on laws of the Roman Empire. His references are authentic enough, but what is depressing is his habit of choosing only those Roman laws which supported the subordination of women and ignoring those which supported the equality of women. He tended, moreover, to pick out the earlier Roman laws, more restrictive of women, rather than the later ones, which tended to liberate women. A similar predisposition was also exhibited in Gratian's use of the decree from the Ecumenical Council of Chalcedon (A.D. 451). This authentic decree stated, "Deaconesses may not be ordained (*ordinari*) before forty years of age" and went on to speak about their remaining celibate after ordination. Gratian did record the decree, but only as evidence that "those who take the vow of celibacy may not marry."

The fact of the *ordination* of women as deaconesses was ignored by him here, and downgraded to a nonclerical vow elsewhere, even though the original Greek of the Council decree used the proper technical term, *cheirontonia*, for ordaining deaconesses.

Indeed, in the ancient Byzantine liturgy the ordination of the deaconess, which took place between that of the deacon and the subdeacon, exactly paralleled the deacon's: "The archbishop likewise having *placed his hands on the head of the (woman) to be ordained* prayed thus (homoiōs ho archiepiskopos tēn *cheira epi tēn kephalēn cheirotonoumenēs* epeuchetai koutōs): Lord and Ruler . . . grant the grace of your Holy Spirit to your handmaid . . . and fill (her) with the grace of the diaconate (kai tēn *tēs diakonias* apoplērōsai charin)—as you gave the grace of the diaconate to your Phoebe—whom *you called to the work of this public divine service* (hēn ekalesas eis to *ergon tēs leitourgias*)." The deaconess was then invested with the stole (*stolam diaconicam* in the

Latin translation), received the holy chalice (to hagion potērion) and placed it on the "holy table" altar (apotithetai en tē hagia trapedzē).

But all this clear documentation of the full ordination of women as deaconesses is overlooked by Gratian and most of his Latin successors. Perhaps the single most important exception is to be found in the writing of Joannes Teutonicus, whose work early in the 13th century became the *Glossa Ordinaria* commentary on Gratian's *Decretum*. There Joannes Teutonicus records the opinion of canonists who disagree with him and insist that women can be ordained because anyone who has been baptized can be ordained (*post baptismum quilibet potest ordinari*). Again it is depressing to learn from Dr. Raming's research that the collection of canon law, *Corpus Juris Canonici*, which served as a source book for the 1917 Code of Canon Law now in force, records only the anti-woman opinion of Joannes Teutonicus and neglects entirely any reference to this opposite opinion recorded by him.

Ultimately, Dr. Raming finds, *all* the arguments against the ordination of women are founded on the assumption that women are inferior to men and that consequently they ought to—and in fact do—live in a state of subjection (*in statu subjectionis*) to men. This assumption surfaces again and again in the writings of canonists, theologians, Fathers of the Church, and even biblical writers. Even to a late 20th-century thinker such an assumption would not seem strange. But what might be surprising to her or him is the fact that these earlier Christian writers expressed that assumption with absolutely no embarrassment. To them it was as perfectly clear that women were inferior to men as, say, that the sun rose in the East and set in the West. With extremely rare exceptions, it is only after the Enlightenment and the subsequent feminist movement in the 19th century that some Christian, as well as other writers began to be discomfited and attempted to argue that far from treating women in an inferior manner, Christianity had in fact raised the status of women.

To develop this argument, Christian scholars usually described the status of women in the Greco-Roman world into which Christianity was born as extremely low and depraved. This was a difficult feat to accomplish for it was clear from an abundance of documents that many women in the Hellenistic and Imperial Roman world were quite unrestricted in many facets of private, social, economic and religious life: they could marry or divorce as they decided, mix freely in society, own and inherit property as a man did, take leading, indeed, *priestly*, roles in religion. But this difficulty was usually overcome by modern Christian scholars with a double attack: On the one hand the Greco-Roman freedom for women was depicted not as something good, or even as a mixed value, but as an essentially evil kind of licentiousness that was leading women, and men and the world, to perdition. For such a view the writings of the Fathers of the Church (is it strange that there are no Mothers of the Church? In parallel fashion, one reads almost solely of the Desert Fathers, although there were already 20,000 Desert Mothers when St. Pachomius first began to gather his male followers) provided a storehouse of railliery against both the immoral license of pagan Roman society and woman's central role in it.

On the other hand, these modern Christian scholars, almost inevitably and paradoxically, also brought forth documentation to show how restricted and unfree a status women had in the Greco-Roman world. Unfortunately, for their argument, all of this documentation concerns the Rome of two or three hundred years before Christ and the Greece of four or five hundred years B.C. The historical facts are that an ever-growing women's liberation movement in the Greek world from around three hundred B.C. onward continued to deepen and broaden almost until the demise of the Roman empire in the West—that is, until the public triumph of Christianity. The status of women went into severe decline thereafter. Thus, in reality, Christianity (but not Jesus) heralded not a raising but a lowering of the status of women, and in many ways significantly contributed to that decline.

A modern Christian of course can, without too much difficulty, admit that there have been errors committed in the name of Christianity and the Church, even horrors such as conversions by the sword, and the Inquisition. The difficulty becomes more acute, however, when the problem is moved back into the New Testament. What does the believing Christian do with St. Paul's statement: "The women should keep silence in the churches" (1 Cor. 14:34)? Or, "A man . . . is the image of God and reflects God's glory; but woman is the reflection of man's glory" (1 Cor. 11:7—a reference to Gen. 1:27, "God created man in his own image")? Especially when the same St. Paul, speaking of how men and women should conduct themselves at services, refers to a "woman who prays or prophesies with her head unveiled" (1 Cor. 11:5), clearly assuming women do rightfully pray or prophesy aloud in church. Or again, "there is neither Jew nor Greek, there is neither slave nor free, there is neither male nor female; for you are all one in Christ Jesus" (Gal. 3:28).

Dr. Raming carefully analyzes these and other pertinent passages, applying two basic accepted modern exegetical principles. First, a careful distinction has to be made between the central religious message of a passage and the contingent cultural vehicle, including scientific, social and moral assumptions of the New Testament author's time and place—thus Paul's silencing of women is seen not as part of the Gospel, but of Paul's contingent moral values, like his acceptance of slavery. Second, if an earlier Scripture statement or story is used by a later Scripture author, the original passage still must properly be understood within the context of its own time—thus modern exegesis understands that Gen. 1:27 was originally an egalitarian statement ("God created *humanity* (*ha adam*) in his own image . . . male and female he created them") and Paul's use of it in 1 Cor. 11:7 in a superior/inferior fashion is a reflection of the contingent use of Scripture of his time and culture, namely that of a Pharisaic Jew living in an "apocalyptic" era.

Dr. Raming finds, again rather depressingly, that Catholic exegetes, even with the approval of Vatican documents, have long been able and willing to make the distinction called for by the first principle in such areas as slavery, but not in the question of the status of women. The metaphorical rather than the literal understanding of Genesis, demanded by the second principle, has become acceptable in many areas, to Catholic scholars, and even to the Roman Biblical Commission, but in considering the creation of woman and man there is still among them a clinging to the assumption of a historical, literal understanding of the story of Adam and Eve, with the implication of man's superiority over woman. Again, as so often throughout history, a sort of second standard is applied to women.

The Christian subordination of women on a biblical, especially New Testament, basis is particularly puzzling in light of Jesus' attitude toward women. In a religious and social culture that forbade men to speak to women, even wives, in public, in effect prohibited women from studying Scripture, refused to allow any legal standing to the testimony of women, made women ritually unclean and untouchable during their menses, and encouraged men to pray daily, "Praised be God for not having made me a woman," Jesus never said or did anything that indicated he thought of women as inferior to men. Instead he often went out of his way to breach the misogynist customs of his time. Jesus frequently spoke to women in public (cf. John 4: lff.), permitted women of ill-repute to touch him (Luke 7:36-50), had women disciples (Luke 8:1-3), rejected the blood taboo (Mark 5:24-34; Matthew 9:18-26; Luke 8:40-56), insisted women had a vocation to the intellectual life as a rabbinical disciple (Luke 10:38-42), first revealed himself to women as the Messiah (Luke 1:40-42) and as the Resurrection (John 11:25), appeared as the Risen One first to women (Matthew 28:9), and sent women to give testimony, to be "evangelists," of the most important event of his life, his resurrection (Matthew 28:10; John 20:17).

In comparing Jesus' attitude toward women with that found in the Pauline writings, and the first epistle attributed to Peter, one finds a dramatic contrast. Jesus' attitude is totally positive, even aggressively so, whereas the attitude expressed in the Pauline and Petrine epistles is ambivalent, and at times clearly subordinationist, apparently flowing for the most part from Paul's rabbinic Jewish background. What is puzzling here is that, although a strong anti-Jewish and pro-Greek trend quickly developed in Christianity as it spread throughout the gentile world, unfortunately leading to a rejection of much of Jesus' and Christianity's Jewish heritage, on the subject of women it was the Hellenic stance which was rejected. Why, with such a clear difference in attitude expressed by Jesus and by some of the Pauline writings, did Christianity's choice go not to Jesus but to the Pauline writings? Apparently the rigid patriarchal system, which Jesus did his best to dismantle (cf. Matthew 10:37f.; Luke 14:26), was so pervasive in the lives of the majority of Christians that they were blind to this choice; they automatically gravitated toward the most restrictive, subordinationist passages of the New Testament.

Perhaps the most depressing revelation of Dr. Raming's book is that this restrictive attitude did not simply overcome the liberationist thrust of Jesus' life and "Good News" and then stabilize itself on a sort of plateau. Rather, the restrictiveness grew. For Jesus, Mary Magdalene was an apostle to the apostles ("Go to the brethren and tell them . . . ." John 20:17; Matthew 28:9). For Paul, Phoebe was a woman deacon, not a deaconess (*diakonon*, not *diakonissa*, Rom. 16:2) and a ruler (*prostatis*—nowhere in Greek literature does this word mean anything like "helper," as it usually is translated here) over many, and even Paul himself (Rom. 16:2; see the Greek rather than translations). After the third century women could be deaconesses (*diakonissa*), a Holy Order lesser in status than that of the male deacon.

By the early middle ages even this Holy Order was lost to women in the West. In the 12th century Gratian, as we have seen, codified and "legalized" the restrictive views prevalent up to then. The Decretals of Pope Gregory IX (1234) took from abbesses their right of public preaching and reading of the Gospel and of hearing the confessions of their nuns. Slowly through the rest of the late middle ages the significant quasi-episcopal jurisdiction of abbesses (consult Joan Morris, *The Lady Was a Bishop*, Cambridge: Cambridge University Press, 1978) was eroded, specially by the Council of Trent, which in several ways forced most convents under the jurisdiction of bishops. The few exceptional cases where the decrees of Trent did not bind were wiped out by the French Revolution and its aftermath, except for the convent of Las Huelgas of Burgos, Spain, and its twelve dependent abbeys. Then in 1873 Pope Pius IX suppressed this last vestige of quasi-episcopal jurisdiction of an abbess; the irony was that Pius IX, as persistent and violent an opponent of democracy as the papacy has ever seen, gave as his reason for the suppression that with the change in contemporary society it was inopportune, even harmful, for such a power to be wielded by an abbess.

Thus it can be argued that today women stand at the lowest point legally in the Church that they have ever occupied in the history of Christianity.

Canon 968, § 1, which decrees that only a male is proper subject for ordination, is merely one of a substantial number of canons which distinguish between men and women to the detriment of the latter. It is, of course, the most important, for even in these days when papal statements encourage women to contribute creatively to the world's culture, all canon law, including that relating solely to women, is formulated by male clerics. When women are consulted, it is solely on matters which are considered of special interest to them, with the rest of ecclesiastical reality remaining a clerical, male preserve. The Commission that has been re-writing canon law these past few years is entirely male. Clearly women cannot expect to have their ideas represented in ecclesiastical legislation until some of their sex are ordained to the priesthood and episcopacy.

At the same time the admission of women to Holy Orders—or even the admission that there are no impediments besides social attitudes within the Church—would be such a dramatic statement of women's equality that all lesser restrictions would soon disappear. Here is the dual reason for the focus on the priesthood question: the exclusion of women is both symbol and cause of their state of subjection within the Church.

A look at the legal context within which Canon 968 appears is worthwhile. Even those canons which have traditionally been interpreted as favoring women take on new color in the light of contemporary feminist thought. Canon 1067, § 1, which permits a "man" to marry at 16 and a "woman" at 14, does indeed recognize that women mature earlier, but the maturity is strictly physical. At the same time the canon adds its support to the common assumption that a wife ought to be younger—and hence more inexperienced and less educated—than her husband, and thus dependent upon him and his judgment. It also assumes a woman has little need to prepare herself for a productive adulthood.

Again, Canon 98, § 4, which makes it a simple matter for a married woman to change to the rite of her husband at marriage and then back to her original rite at the death of her husband, all without having to get specific permission—though the husband had no parallel freedom—is no longer seen as a kindness to the woman. It merely assumes that the rite of the husband is more important, and thus suggests that a woman's membership in her parish is subordinate to that of her husband. The stipulation in Canon 756, § 2 that when the parents are of two different rites the child takes the rite of the father, confirms the inferiority of the wife.

Even canons which have been seen as fairly trivial in the past play important roles in forming the image and self-image of women. The fact that women may not initiate a cause for canonization of saints (Canon 2004, § 1), for example, means that all the ecclesiastical role models for women are installed by males according to standards set up by males for what they would like their women to be. The limitation of membership on seminary boards of governors to clerics (Canon 1359, § 2) means that women are denied that voice in determining the education of the men who will later lead and teach them and their daughters.

From the above it can be seen that the canons discriminating against women are varied. Some are specifically directed against women, some merely against the laity (juridically all women, including sisters, are laity). Some deal with participation in church and liturgy, some with marriage; a goodly number deal with restrictions placed on religious women. The following are typical. (Translations of the canons are taken from John A. Abbo and Jerome D. Hannan, *The Sacred Canons* [St. Louis: B. Herder, 1957]).

Canon 506, § 2 and § 4. "In monasteries of nuns, assemblies convoked for the election of the superiores shall be held under the presidency, without his entering the cloister, of the local ordinary or his delegate, with two priests as tellers, if the nuns are subject to the local ordinary; if not subject to him, under the presidency of the regular superior; but even in this case the local ordinary shall be duly informed of the day and the hour of the election, that he may assist at it, either personally or through a delegate, along with the regular superior, and by assisting preside over it."

"In congregations of women, the election of the mother general shall be held under the presidency, either in person or by delegate, of the ordinary of the place in which the election is held; and in the case of a congregation of diocesan approval, the local ordinary has the right to confirm or rescind the election as his conscience may dictate."

Canon 607. "Superioresses and local ordinaries shall be vigilant to prevent religious women from going out alone without necessity."

Canon 742, § 2. "(Non-solemn baptism can be administered by anyone. . . .)" "But if a priest is present, he should be preferred to a deacon; a deacon, to a subdeacon; a cleric to a layman; and a man to a woman, unless in the interest of modesty it is more becoming that a woman rather than a man should baptize or unless a woman is better acquainted with the form and the method required in baptizing."

Canon 813, § 2. "The Mass server shall not be a woman unless a sound reason justifies it when a man is not available, and in that case the woman must recite the responses from a distance and she must not for any reason approach the altar."

Canon 1264, § 2. "Women religious may sing in their own church or oratory, if they are permitted to do so by their constitutions and by the laws of the liturgy and if they have the permission of the local ordinary, but they must do so in a place in which they cannot be seen by the people."

Canon 1312, § 1. "One who legitimately exercises dominative power over the will of the person who made a vow may validly and also, for a justifying reason, lawfully annul it in such a way that its obligation never subsequently revives."

Commenting on this last law, the 1957 edition of Abbo-Hannan, perhaps the most distinguished canon law textbook in the United States, says "There is a sharp division of opinion in regard to the authority of a husband to act directly on a vow of his wife; his right to do so is supported by no convincing arguments, but authors of high repute affirm that he possesses it, and their contention enjoys the tacit approbation of the Church."

* * *

As this book was in press, a good deal of attention was focusing on the Ordination Conference, "Women in Future Priesthood Now," held in

Detroit, November 28-30, 1975. Over 1200 people attended to share experiences and hear major talks by S. Elizabeth Carroll, a former college president and former president of the Leadership Conference of Women Religious (LCWR); S. Anne Carr, assistant dean of the University of Chicago Divinity School; S. Margaret Farley, associate professor of ethics at Yale Divinity School; S. Marie Augusta Neal, professor of sociology at Emmanuel College; S. Mary Daniel Turner, executive director of the LCWR; and S. Marjorie Tuite of the Jesuit School of Theology in Chicago. The official respondents included such lay people as Rosemary Ruether, Elisabeth Fiorenza, Arlene Swidler and Leonard Swidler, and such priests as George Tavard and William Callahan. (Callahan is the founder and executive secretary of "Priests for Equality," a group supporting the ordination of women; started in July 1975, it had grown to 660 members at the time of the Conference.)

The success of the Conference, first as a convening of women either hoping for ordination themselves or sympathetic to the cause, and secondly as a model and impetus of further action around the country, is occasionally cited as an indication that the emphasis on the question of ordination for women is somehow a peculiarly American phenomenon. The earlier excitement over the illegal ordinations of women within the American Episcopal Church simply confirmed this attitude in some minds.

This book, of course, is one piece of evidence to the contrary, but there are many more.

The earliest positive analyses of this ordination question are apparently two works by Jesuit priests—Dutch Father Haye van der Meer's doctoral thesis written under Karl Rahner in Innsbruck in 1962 (now available in English as *Women Priests in the Catholic Church?* trans. by Arlene and Leonard Swidler, Philadelphia: Temple University Press, 1973), and Peruvian Father Jose Idigoras' booklet *La Mujer dentro del Orden Sagrado* (Lima, 1963), the following year. The subject first came to broad public attention with the petition to the Second Vatican Council of a Swiss attorney, Gertrud Heinzelmann. St. Joan's International Alliance, a group with a largely European membership, then presented the first of what were to be annual petitions to the Vatican in 1963:

> St. Joan's International Alliance re-affirms its loyalty and filial devotion and expresses its conviction that should the Church in her wisdom and in her good time decide to extend to women the dignity of the priesthood, women would be willing and eager to respond.

Thus, American contribution to the movement for women priests in the Catholic Church has been relatively recent. However, it has now clearly attained considerable momentum in America, both in the spheres of research and activism. The publication and translation into English of Dr. Raming's fundamental research in the juridical area of this question could not, therefore, have come at a more opportune time; it is certain to significantly accelerate that momentum. Hence, profound thanks are due to Dr. Raming, and also to Prof. Norman Adams for his painstakingly precise and timely translation, as well as the Scarecrow Press for making publication possible.

Introduction

Among the questions and challenges which spontaneously arose during Vatican II were those that concerned the contemporary place of women in the Church. For the first time, the complete absence of women in the Council, which had been originally constituted as an assembly of men only, created an unfavorable impression and was considered a defect. In addition, several Council speeches and interventions dealt with the need for the reform of women's place in society and in the Church, and offered guidelines and suggestions for improvement.[1] Also, outside the Council meetings the value and position of women in the church were critically investigated and recommendations for changes were brought forward in various Council petitions and pronouncements.[2] Following the Council, the quest for reform of the situation of women in the church has by no means subsided: on the contrary, it is increasing in importance and relevance.[3] Various factors have brought about this critical questioning. On the basis of the political rights of women already achieved in many state constitutions, which have given women an independent vocational existence in the secular realm and which have made possible the development of their personalities, the discrepancy between the ecclesiastical and the secular orders of society has become obvious to many women who have come of age in the modern world. They have been increasingly offended by the fact that in the church they are not regarded as equal to men.

Nevertheless, the demand women make for a position appropriate to the times in which we live—expressed concretely in the demand for ecclesiastical office[4]—does not arise simply out of a comparison between the secular and ecclesiastical structures of society or from the contrast between legal rights in the Catholic Church and in the Protestant Church, in many branches of which women already have a share of official positions.[5] More deeply understood, the issue is a religious one, since in it the wish is expressed for women to obey their call to the priestly vocation. Of course it is true that this struggle is against an almost two thousand year tradition of church teaching and canonical practice, which has kept women, just because they are women, from becoming priests, and which allegedly rests on divine law,[6] according to widespread theological opinion, and therefore cannot be changed. This tradition, however, as well as the ecclesiastical regulations based on it, severely limits the religious freedom of human beings because it denies women in principle, yet solely on the basis of sex, the practice of a priestly vocation, which is obviously so important to the redemptive activity of the church. Obviously such a tradition ought to be theologically incontestable and able to defend itself against any cross questioning if it is to uphold the claim to have divine origin and therefore be unchangeable.[7] Nevertheless, this very presupposition is not established by the arguments so long advanced by Catholic theology. It can be shown by several lines of theological investigation that the traditional exegetical and dogmatic arguments for the exclusion of women from priestly office are not valid[8] and therefore cannot justify this exclusion.

It is hoped that the present work, which is developed from the standpoint of the history of canon law, will help to clarify the problem. The basis for the regulation in the official ecclesiastical law book (canon 968, § 1, Code), according to which only the (baptized) male can be validly ordained—implying that women are incapable of ordination—will be carefully investigated.[9] The major emphasis will be a consideration and critical analysis of the supporting evidence for the above canon in the *Corpus Iuris Canonici*, which is the most important of the sources for the ecclesiastical law book presently in force. These sources will be investigated not only from the aspect of their relationship to canon 968, § 1, and other canons closely related to it, but also according to the conception of women which lies at their basis. Actually, an examination of these components is necessary if we are to form an objective opinion about prohibitions and legal limitations relating to women. We shall also make an investigation of the works of the canonists of the Middle Ages, where they are available. These are informative in the interpretation and evaluation of sources contained in the *Corpus Iuris Canonici* and therefore important in the development of church law.

In an exegetical excursus adjoined to the historical part of the present work, the validity of patristic scriptural evidence used in the *Corpus Iuris Canonici,* and especially in Gratian's *Decretum*, to support the position of female subordination will be examined by the use of historical-critical-exegesis. The reason for this study is that patristic interpretations of particular biblical passages (Gen. 2:18-24; 3; 1 Cor. 11:3-9, 14:34f.; Eph. 5:22-33, and others) comprise an essential support for the inferior position of women in church law.

In the dogmatic part of the book, a critical analysis of the traditional understanding of office and representation is intended as a supplement to the exegetical-dogmatical investigations already undertaken.[10] Arguments are made on the basis of this traditional understanding against permitting women to be ordained, and it does not seem to me that enough is being written in current literature concerning such argumentation.

Finally, drawing our conclusions together it will be indicated that in excluding women from ordination and thus from ecclesiastical office because of their sex, a limitation of freedom results that means an injury to the personal dignity of women and a rejection of responsibility to God. The removal of such limitation is demanded in the name of justice, in order that the gifts with which women are endowed may develop without hindrance in the church.

Notes

1. Cf. W. Seibel and L. A. Dorn, *Tagebuch des Konzils. Die Arbeit der zweiten Session* (Nuremberg: Sailer, 1964), 92f., 104; L. A. Dorn and G. Denzler, *Tagebuch des Konzils. Die Arbeit der dritten Session* (Nüremberg: Sailer, 1965), 256f., 262, 278; G. Heinzelmann, *Die getrennten Schwestern. Frauen nach dem Konzil* (hereafter cited as *Schwestern*) (Zürich Interfeminas-Verl., 1967), 71-82.

2. Most of the contributions were collected in the brochure edited by G. Heinzelmann titled *Wir schweigen nicht länger! Frauen äussern sich zum II. Vatikanischen Konzil* (Zürich Interfeminas-Verl., 1964).

3. This fact is obvious not only from the increasing number of publications concerning this theme (see n. 8, below; also chapter 7, n. 1), but also from the fact that various synods since Vatican II have taken up the question of woman's place in the church. In the fifth session of the Dutch Pastoral Council, the majority supported the integration of women into all forms of ecclesiastical service, including that of the priesthood. (See *Herder Correspondence*, vol. 7, no. 3 (March, 1970): 83f. and vol. 7, no. 5:137ff.) The themes of the General Synod of dioceses of West Germany include a consideration of the question. (*Kirchliches*

Amtsblatt für die Diözese Münster 102 1969, 126.) The need for reform of the position of women in the church was also the subject of several interventions in the second regular Bishops' Synod in Rome in the fall of 1971: Cardinal Flahiff (Winnipeg) proposed for the first time the admission of women to the priestly office as well as to church office in general. In the name of the Canadian Bishops' Conference he recommended the creation of a mixed commission, which would thoroughly examine the question. (Cf. *L'Osservatore Romano*, weekly ed. in English [October 28, 1971]: 5.) Archbishop Carter (Kingston, Jamaica) supported his intervention noting that earlier "cultural, not theological grounds against the ordination of women as priests are no longer valid" (op. cit., German ed., no. 5.11.1971, p. 4). Cf. also chapter 8, n. 24.

4. Cf. n. 3, above, and chapter 8, n. 24.

5. See the documentation: "Women's Place in the Ministry of Non-Catholic Christian Churches," in *Concilium*, vol. 34 (Maryknoll, N.Y.: Orbis Books 1968), 163-177.

6. Among other references see E. Krebs, *Katholische Lebenswerte*, 5/2/1-2, (Paderborn Bonifacius-Dr., 1925), 478-F; J. Pohre and M. Gierens, *Lehrbuch der Dogmatik*, 3/9 (Paderborn: Schöningh, 1937), 581; F. Diekamp and K. Jüssen, *Katholische Dogmatik*, 3/11-12 (Münster: Aschendorff; 1954), 372f.; M. Premm, *Katholische Glaubenskunde*, 3/2 (Vienna: Herder; 1955), 240; L. Ott, *Grundriss der katholischen Dogmatik*, 5th ed. (Freiburg: Herder, 1961), 548. Cf. also chapter 7, the latter containing a listing of other authors who represent this position.

7. H. van der Meer, *Priestertum der Frau? Eine theologie-geschichtliche Untersuchung*, (Freiburg: Herder, 1969) cited here and hereafter from English translation by Arlene and Leonard Swidler, *Women Priests in the Catholic Church?* (Philadelphia: Temple University Press 1973), 10f. rightly points out that the burden of proof for the contention that women are on principle and permanently excluded from the priesthood rests upon those who defend this contention.

8. Besides the study by H. van der Meer noted in n. 7, the following literature should be especially mentioned: V. E. Hannon, *The Question of Women and the Priesthood; Can Women Be Admitted to Holy Orders?* (London G. Chapman, 1967) R. J. A. van Eyden, "Die Frau im Kirchenamt," in *Wort und Wahrheit* 22 (1967): 350-362; M. Daly, *The Church and the Second Sex* (New York: Harper & Row 1968); see also chapter 7, n. 1, where there is a further listing of literature.

9. A thorough treatment of the problem from the viewpoint of legal history has not yet appeared; the following studies offer either a simple summary survey of the historical development of the position of women in the church, or they deal with a very limited period of time. R. Metz, "Recherches sur le statut de la femme en droit canonique: bilan historique et perspectives d'avenir," in *L'Année canonique*, 12 (1968), 85-113; also by R. Metz, "Le statut de la femme en droit canonique médiéval," in *Recueils de la Société Jean Bodin*, 12/2 (Brussels:Librairie Encyclopédique, 1962) (hereafter cited as " *Statut*"); and his "Recherches sur la condition de la femme selon Gratien," in *Studia Gratiana*, 12 (1967), 377-396; F. Gillman, "Weibliche Kleriker nach dem Urteil der Frühscholastik," *Archiv für katholisches Kirchenrecht*, 93 (1913), 239-253.

10. Cf. the literature given in n. 8, above.

Part I

Canon Law Background

Foundation of the Code of Canon Law 968,5 § 1 in the *Corpus Iuris Canonici*

The current Code of Canon Law preserves to a great extent the connection with the traditional church law largely set forth in the *Corpus Iuris Canonici*.[1] The Code appropriated the massive legal materials in the *Corpus*, in so far as they belonged to "*vigens ecclesiae disciplina* (active law of the church)" at the time it was drawn up, and reduced them to a succinct form.[2] Thus the normal "agreement" of previous law with that of the Code[3] holds also for canon 968, § 1 (Code),[4] according to which only the baptized man can be validly ordained, and a woman, including one baptized, is thereby excluded from the reception of ordination. It is true that in the quotations from the *Corpus luris Canonici* cited by Cardinal Gasparri[5] for this regulation it is not obvious that the male requirement for ordination has its basis in the old law, since the reference here is exclusively related to the baptismal requirement for valid ordination.[6] It is quite possible that this lack of reference to sex may be due to the fact that the further requirement of masculinity was simply taken for granted, so that Gasparri felt that a quotation to this effect would be superfluous. In any case, we cannot draw the conclusion that the masculine requirement has no support in classical canon law, even though, we should note, it does not appeal to a "divine law" (*ius divinum*).[7] Actually, we discover just the opposite if we look through the *Corpus Iuris Canonici* for relevant evidence: Numerous stipulations in the *Corpus Iuris* concerning the ecclesiastical position of women—statements which become, at least in part, the basis for other canons of the Code consistent with canon 968, § 1, and which are in fact based upon it—make clear that this canonical requirement (only a baptized male validly receives sacred orders) goes back to classic canon law—not, to be sure, in form but certainly in direction and content. In this respect the Code clearly upholds the legal tradition.

Beyond this, the relevant sources of the *Corpus Iuris Canonici* (and the texts used to explain them) provide an insight into the evaluation of women[8] that is basic to these sources and do so more clearly than the succinctly formulated canons of the Code, which to a certain extent only present an extract of the sources. This insight is indispensable for the interpretation and critique of the legal sources as well as of canon 968, § 1 of the Code that derives from them. Only when the evaluation of women is understood can the reasons for the regulations concerning women be uncovered and explained.

Chapter 1

Gratian's *Decretum* as Source for Sex Discrimination in the Priesthood

Gratian's Sources

Gratian's *Decretum,*[9] the *Concordia Discordantium Canonum*, contains important source material for our question.[10] In large part taken from older collections and systematically reworked,[11] a great mass of source materials is to be found in this textbook of church law, which was composed in scholastic form about the middle of the 12th century (perhaps around 1140)[12] by the Camaldolese monk and teacher, Gratian of Bologna. In the course of time, already toward the end of the 12th century, people forgot the private "character of the Decree and considered it to be *Corpus Iuris Canonici* from ancient times to Gratian's day."[13]

The following references in this collection are relevant to our inquiry: (1) c. 25 of *distinctio* 23, containing the prohibition of women from carrying out certain ceremonial functions, namely touching the consecrated vessels and cloths and incensing the altar; (2) cc. 41 and 42 of *distinctio* 1, *de consecratione*, which reserve to ordained men any handling of these objects, and thus, indirectly if not specifically, exclude women from such action; (3) the explicit prohibition in c. 29 of *distinctio* 2, *de consecratione* which forbids women to take communion to the sick; (4) the prohibition against teaching by women, contained in c. 29 of *distinctio* 23 and in c. 20 of *distinctio* 4, *de consecratione*, in the latter case mixed with a baptism prohibition; and (5) finally, regulation *distinctio* 32 c. 19, according to which no so-called *presbytera* (female priest) may be established in the church. (6) Besides these chapters, which contain exclusively prohibitions of liturgical and cultic activity of women, we must take account of other sources which mention deaconesses, especially c. 23 in *questio* 1 of *causa* 27, then also cc. 38, *causa* 11, q. 1 and 30, *causa* 27, q. 1.

The first passage to be discussed here, *distinctio* 23 c. 25, is arranged in a context that is noteworthy in regard to our question and therefore deserves our attention. In accordance with the introductory paragraph,[14] *distinctio* 23 describes the ordination of various clerics from the highest level to the lowest. The ordination regulations for each clerical grade, including those of the so-called minor orders, presuppose only male ordinands. This fact is a clear indication that canon law in the time of Gratian is aware of an exclusively male priesthood; the deaconess is nowhere mentioned.[15] Except for the regulation of c. 24, which concerns the dress of a nun (*sanctimonialis virgo*) at the time of her consecration, *distinctio* 23 contains nothing but prohibition for a woman. It is clear from the structure of this *distinctio*[16] that it has to do with legal prescriptions binding in the time of Gratian. Gratian's *paragraphus* to c. 25 presents additional support for this conclusion: "Women who are consecrated to God are forbidden (*prohibentur*) to touch the sacred vessels and altar cloths and to carry incense around the altar"[17] Gratian's words, according to the rubric to c. 25,[18] are based on an excerpt from a letter written by Pope Soter to the Italian bishops, which reads as follows:

> It has been brought to the attention of the apostolic see that women consecrated to God, or nuns, touch the sacred vessels or blessed palls, that is in the presence of your company, and carry incense around the altar. That all this is blameworthy conduct to be fully censured can be rightly doubted by no wise person. Because of this, by the authority of this Holy See, lest this disease spread more widely, we order all provinces to most swiftly drive it out.[19]

Actually this quotation, which Gratian cites as papal authority, is a part of the (second) Pseudo-Isidorian *epistola decretalis* of Soter[20] and thus a forgery. It was, however, like the whole Pseudo-Isidorian collection, considered genuine by Gratian in agreement with the dominant opinion of the Middle Ages.[21] Haye van der Meer[22] has already pointed out the fact of forgery in this text and in other decretals similar in content although not included in the *Corpus Iuris Canonici*, and he has rightly objected to the uncritical use of such materials as traditional proofs for the exclusion of women from the priesthood.[23]

Yet aside from the unquestionably spurious nature of this so-called *epistola Soter*, there still remains the question of its historical worth. As a source for this excerpt from the decretal, which Gratian numbers c. 25 in *distinctio* 23, Hinschius,[24] followed by Friedberg,[25] points to c. 2 in the *Life of Pope Soter* of the *Liber Pontificalis*, according to which Soter decrees that no monk (*nullus monachus*) may touch the sacred altar clothes or incense the church.[26] Duchesne has suggested why this chapter could serve as the source for the decretal excerpt, despite the *nullus monachus* instead of the expected *nulla monacha* (no nun):

> This decree reappears in the notice of Boniface I[27] but applied to nuns. Here the very words 'no monk' (*nullus monachus*) have been changed in many manuscripts to 'no nun' (*nulla monacha*). . . . The author of the *Liber Pontificalis* is a cleric, so also the copiers; their principle is always, monks for prayer, clerics for serving at the altar.[28]

Thus in many manuscripts *nullus monachus* (no monk) has been changed to *nulla monacha* (no nun), doubtless because of a contempt for women widespread at that time, especially in clerical circles. Besides, as Duchesne points out, the *Liber Pontificalis*, product of a (Roman) cleric, is itself not free from a biased presentation, which, of course, damages its historical validity. Its first part, entries up to the year 496, is considered to be generally unreliable—not, to be sure, for all items but probably for those concerning discipline and liturgy—and therefore must be used carefully.[29]

In conclusion, it is clear that the excerpt from the Pseudo-Isidorian decretal of Soter, which Gratian in *distinctio* 23, c. 25 takes as an authority, has no convincing historical basis and therefore cannot be used uncritically, i.e., without considering this fact as a traditional proof for the exclusion of women from liturgical functions. Furthermore, it is clear from the contents and style of the *epistola* that a derogatory conception of women is the basis for the prohibition. Although in earlier times and in various churches deaconesses were permitted to enter the chancel and to incense for the mass—it was even possible to go beyond what was forbidden in the decretal, for instance to distribute Holy Communion[30]—all this is now sharply condemned as censurable behavior (That all this is blameworthy conduct to be fully censured can be rightly doubted by no wise person.) The bishops who receive the letter must put a complete end to such repulsive pestilence as quickly as possible.[31] This ruthless action against the service of women in the chancel is explained—in the context of the decretal immediately following the passage cited above, although omitted by Gratian—as follows:

> the Apostle says:[32] "I have betrothed you to one man, in order to present you as pure virgin to Christ." That is to say, the virgin is virgin Church, bride of the one man Christ, a bride who will not permit herself to be besmirched by any kind of error or dishonorable fault, so that she might be for us the single purity of the one pure communion throughout the whole world.[33]

The basis of such an argument is obviously the concept that the chastity and purity of the virgin Church would suffer great injury from a cultic-liturgical activity of women, a concept which can only be explained by saying that women are impure creatures—in the sense of the Old Testament laws about impurity (cf. Lev. 12:1ff.; 15:19ff.)[34]—or by devaluing them as temptation for men.

The same situation is apparent in cc. 41 and 42 of *distinctio* 1, *de consecratione*[35] in the third section of the *Decretum*. Here too are excerpts from the Pseudo-Isidorian decretals, thus forgeries. Like c. 25 of *distinctio* 23, they contain regulations, although only by implication, prohibiting women from touching consecrated vessels and altar linens. According to the *summaria* (brief headlines) of the chapters,[36] it would seem that the only ground for the prohibition is the the unordained status (*insacratum esse*), but the content (and context) of c. 41 makes it clear that ordination is simply an additional requirement for the cultic function, while the basic presupposition is that the functioner be a male. The text of c. 41 is as follows:

> At the Holy See it has been decreed that the consecrated vessels may be handled by no one other than the aforesaid men [*hominibus*] consecrated to the Lord. Lest through such presumption, the Lord's anger may not strike a blow against His people, and those who have not sinned may also perish, since the just most often perish on behalf of the unjust.[37]

Gratian omits the passage in the Pseudo-Isidorian decretal which immediately follows the word *hominibus*, although it appears in the so-called *Editio Romana*[38] of Gratian's *Decretum*. What it says is: "For it is highly improper that any holy vessels of the Lord, whichever they might be, should serve human purposes or be touched by other than the serants of the Lord and by the aforesaid men [*viris*]."[39] There can be no doubt that the word *homines*, according to usage at that time,[40] refers to the male sex. In a similar regulation of c. 42, which permits only the *sacrati homines* (consecrated men) to touch the sacred altar linen,[41] *homines* is also clearly limited to the male gender.

Even if these texts may not be valued as authentic evidences of tradition—we are dealing here as above with forgeries—they are nevertheless, if considered in the context of c. 25 of *distinctio* 23, very instructive concerning the evaluation of women in the ecclesiastical realm. For while in the case of men some form of consecration (*consecratio*)[42] is everywhere recognized as sufficient qualification for the cultic functions we have been considering—it is of course characteristic of the thinking of that age that baptism as such is not sufficient although in conjunction with faith it lays the basis for Christian existence[43]—the case is not the same for women. A "woman consecrated to God" (*sacrata Deo femina*, cf. p. 6) stands on the same level with "non-consecrated men" (*viri insacrati*): For her as well as for them admission to the chancel and touching of consecrated objects is forbidden. From this it follows that the basic requirement for cultic practice is not the religious quality of being dedicated to God, but rather just being a male, which is actually in itself a religiously irrelevant fact. Contrary to a man, a woman is considered to be burdened with such a grave defect that no kind of religious act of consecration can eradicate it. This conception is essentially conditioned by the continuing influence of Old Testament prescriptions for ceremonial purity, which hold the Christian service of worship in captivity to Old Testament laws and which together with other causes have deprived women of admittance to cultic function.[44]

Although the two texts we have discussed—c. 25 of *distinctio* 23 and cc. 41 and 42 of *distinctio* 1, *de consecatione*—are a clear expression of devaluation of women and in addition are forgeries, they have nevertheless been used as sources for the law of the Code.[45]

If according to the texts we have so far discussed, women are considered unworthy to handle holy cloths and vessels, it is quite certain, as we discover from c. 29 of *distinctio* 2, *de consecratione* that they are not entrusted with the Body of the Lord, even if only to take it to the sick. The strongly binding character of the prohibition is emphasized by the severity of its restrictions:

> It has come to our attention that certain priests, hold the the divine mysteries in such low esteeem that they hand over the holy Body of the Lord to laity or women for distribution to the sick, and to those to whom it is forbidden lest they enter into the sanctuary or approach the

> altar, to these the holy of holies is entrusted. The prudence of all religious people understands how horrible and destestible this would be. Therefore the synod forbids it in every respect, lest such imprudent audacity continue to be done; rather the priest himself ought to communicate the sick in every case. If anyone would do otherwise, his rank would be subject to legal action.[46]

According to the rubric, this chapter concerns canon 2 of a synod at Reims. (This may be the synod which Hefele-Leclerq places between the years 624 and 625.)[47] It is true that one does not find the above cited regulation among the 25 canons of this synod that are listed in the history of the councils. However, according to Hefele-Leclercq[48] other canons were attributed to the Synod of Reims by Burchard of Worms and Ivo of Chartres. upon whose collections of source materials Gratian depends,[49] and the above canon belongs to these.[50] Admittedly Friedberg gives no indication of the source of the canon, but he does refer to a resolution of the Synod of Rouen A.D. 650,[51] which has a similar content: Women and laity shall by no means be given the holy Eucharist in the hand, but only in the mouth. Violation of this prohibition will be considered as contempt for God and appropriately punished.[52] Likewise, *distintio* 2, *de consecratione* c. 29 declares that it is rude disrespect of the divine mysteries for (male) laity and women to be given the Body of the Lord in order to take it to the sick. As those who are forbidden to approach the altar,[53] they are not considered worthy to hold the *sancta sanctorum* in their hands. Now of course we must not overlook the fact that the prohibition applies to the laity as to women. But when besides the laity, women are specifically named, we see in the unnecessary differentiation, which also appears in other texts,[54] a conscious formulation which intends to express the fact that the (male) layperson *qua laicus* (as laity) may not take communion to the sick because of his low position in the church, as any layperson was considered to be in a low position at that time, but that women may not take communion to the sick not because they are laity but *qua femina* (as a female) because, that is to say, of their disrespected sex.[55] The *Glossa Ordinaria* at this place proves that this interpretation is not misguided, as may be mentioned here, somewhat in anticipation: for the case in which the priest is prevented from taking communion to the sick, which he himself is stringently required to do, the gloss provides for the following solution, that besides a deacon a catholic layperson (*laicus catholicus*) may represent the priest.[56] Without doubt this means only a *male* layperson for according to the understanding of some decretists even a *puer catholicus*, a boy, could take over the task of the hindered priest.[57] A woman, however, even one consecrated to God, is not considered worthy to perform this service, even in an emergency.[58] It is thus clear that church discipline in the Middle Ages did not actually and exclusively classify woman under the rubric of laity, but rather because of her sex she was given a special and prejudicial treatment. She was assigned a status below the level of the male laity. Here is the reason for the fact that the higher evaluation of the laity, which took place in the course of time, was mainly limited to the male laity (for instance, admission to sacristan and lector positions).

The rule in c. 29 of *distinctio* 2, *de consecratione* creates the basis for canon 845 of the Code, according to which the administration of Holy Communion by laypersons is forbidden.[59] Some easing of the prohibition took place in the post Vatican II period, but, characteristically, this applied first only to male laity or in special cases to nuns,[60] and only later to female laity.[61]

Two more prohibitions, found in c. 29 of *distinctio* 23 and in c. 20 of *distinctio* 4, *de consecratione* have the same goal as the regulations we have already noticed, to exclude women from any official religious activity, including any liturgical function. (Since one of the prohibitions, that concerning teaching, is common to both chapters, it seems best to treat the texts together.) The wording is as follows: "A woman, however learned and holy, ought not to presume to teach men in an assembly. A lay person ought not dare to teach in the presence of clerics (except in petitioning)."[62] "A woman, however learned and holy, ought not to presume to baptize others or to teach men in an assembly."[63] According to the respective rubrics both chapters are decrees of a council of Carthage.[64] But actually what we have in each case is a composite of two canons of the *Statuta Ecclesiae Antiqua*,[65] a collection of 102 chapters on church discipline, which are given in the *Collectio Hispana (Isidoriana)*[66]—which was for a long time the only source of our knowledge of the *Statuta*—under the title of a council of Carthage (the fourth) in the year 389.[67] As canons of this council the two prohibitions next became parts of the Pseudo-Isidorian collection[68]—by way of the *Hispana Gallica Augustodunensis*—which in turn served as source for medieval canon law collections, especially Gratian's *Decretum*, including the canons we are now considering.[69] In this way the *Statuta* became widely known and, what is more decisive, were for a long time considered to be regulations of the fourth Council of Carthage.[70] The *Editio Romana* (1582) of Gratian's *Decretum* also assigns the canons of the *Statuta* accepted by Gratian to this Council.[71] However the results of research long ago[72] proved that the

Statuta cannot be attributed to the fourth Council of Carthage—supposedly held in A.D. 398, although there is no evidence that it ever took place[73]—nor to a later (A.D. 418) Council of Carthage.[74] The source of the *Statuta* has really nothing to do with any council. They are rather the work of an anonymous author, or compiler, and in fact, as Munier has been able to show, he is the presbyter Gennadius of Marseille.[75] The collection was brought together between 476 and 485.[76]

We are here mainly interested in the kind of materials and sources Gennadius may have utilized for his compilation. Munier's investigations give us information about this too.[77] They show that the *Statuta* in the composition of its different parts is derived from many source materials. The *Statuta's* regulations about discipline, to which the chapters from Gratian's *Decretum* which we have been discussing belong, are mainly dependent upon the so-called *Apostolic Constitutions*,[78] the most important of the pseudo-apostolic collections containing church law and liturgy from the fourth century.[79] The connection between the *Statuta* and the *Constitutions*, in the case of cc. 37 and 41 concerning women, which Gratian has taken from the *Statuta*, is quite obvious.[80] The prohibition against teaching is based on the corresponding detailed regulation of the Apostolic *Constitutions* (III, 6) and reduces it to a concise formula. It is true that the special tendency of the prohibition, that women must not presume to teach men in an assembly, does not derive directly from the *Constitutions* nor from the Syriac *Didascalia*, which lies behind the *Constitutions*. (The *Didascalia* is itself a pseudo-apostolic writing from the first decades of the third century).[81] It is possible that such a precise prohibition is intended to serve as a protection of the celibacy of the clergy (or monks), especially since further chapters of the *Statuta* support this objective.[82]

Concerning the question we are discussing, we may draw the conclusion that the prohibition against women's religious-cultic activity is closely connected to measures taken to protect celibacy, as will often become clear in the course of our continuing investigation. We should more probably assume, however, that the prohibition against the practice of public teaching by women in a congregational gathering[83] consisting mostly of men is intended to circumvent the suspected desire of women to rule over men, a contradiction of the "order of creation."[84] At any rate this aspect of the question is clearly the intent of the text of c. 37 of the *Statuta* taken over by Gratian, the prohibition in the Apostolic *Constitutions* against teaching, which reads as follows:

> We do not permit women to practice the office of teaching in the church; instead they should pray and listen to teachers. For our Teacher

> and Lord, Jesus himself, sent only us Twelve to instruct the people [Israel] and the heathen, but he never sent women, although women were not lacking: with us was the mother of the Lord and her sisters, and also Mary Magdalene and Mary, the mother of James, and Martha and Mary, the sisters of Lazarus, Salome and some others. Thus if it had been suitable for women to proclaim the teachings of Jesus, he would himself have called them from the beginning to undertake with us the instruction of the people. For if the man is the head of the woman, it is not proper that the rest of the body should rule the head. So the widow should always remember that she is the "sarificial altar"[85] of God, and she should remain at home and under no pretext enter the homes of believers, in order to get something, for the altar of God does not wander about but rather remains fixed in a definite place.[86]

The sentence of the *Constitutions*, "For if the man is the head of the woman . . . " paraphrases the so-called order of creation. The author clearly relies on 1 Cor. 11:3 and Eph. 5:23, 28f.[87] The other reference used as justification for the prohibition of teaching—which some are still fond of today[88]—that Jesus commissioned no women to proclaim the Gospel, is refuted by the *Didascalia* itself, the forerunner of the *Constitutions*. For, immediately before the teaching prohibition, *Didascalia* 3, 5, we read:

> [the widow] should send those who want to be instructed to the heads of the community. . . . But no widow or layman is obliged to speak about the destruction of idols, about the fact that God is one, about the kingdom of the name of Christ and about his leadership. For in so far as they speak *without knowledge* of the teaching, they bring contempt upon the Word. For if educated heathen hear the Word of God but it is not proclaimed to them in an orderly and suitable fashion for the production of eternal life, especially *because it is a woman who is telling them* how the Lord assumed a body and how he suffered, they will laugh and mock instead of praising the teachings. In such fashion a woman brings guilt upon herself in the great Day of Judgment.[89]

Here we find expressed, though doubtless unintentionally, such a strongly pronounced bias of society against women in the early third century, when the *Didascalia* appeared, that women clearly had no opportunity at all to be teachers in public life. Because of their despised sex and also because of their lack of culture, their word was from the first not accepted and taken seriously. Since the Syriac *Didascalia* is considered a valuable historical source,[90] as far as its description of congregational relationships is concerned, it may be assumed that the social evaluation and the position of women set forth in *Didascalia* 3, 5, correctly characterizes the circumstances of that time. Now we are also well-informed about the situation of women in the time of Jesus,[91] and it is in no way more favorable. Jesus did what could be done for women in his time: his example and his teaching give impressive witness to that fact.[92] In his recognition of women as directly called and blessed by God, he created the internal impulse for and the basis of her emancipation from the position of inferiority to men, a fact which was, to be sure, overlooked by the early church, imprisoned by rabbinic ways of thinking.[93] Still, Jesus could not send women out as apostles, that is, as official witnesses of the Gospel, since that was forbidden by the conditions of the time. This is also, rightly, the opinion of René Metz: "If he had wished, Christ could not really have acted in any other manner. It would have been asking too much of his companions whose feelings about this he could not offend: a female apostle was inconceivable in the Jewish milieu at that time."[94] But out of this silence of Jesus—clearly understandable from the situation—the *Didascalia*, and following it the *Apostolic Constitutions*, construct a prohibition. (This is a methodology used even today.)[95]

The prohibition against teaching in the *Didascalia* and the *Apostolic Constitutions*, which served as model for that in the *Statuta* takes up a tradition based on the statements of 1 Cor. 14-34f. and 1 Tim. 2:llf., themselves in turn influenced by rabbinical regulations and conceptions.[96] (The partial word-by-word dependence on these texts cannot be overlooked.)[97] Thus we trace back to its origin, through its developmental stages in the *Apostolic Constitutions* and the *Didascalia*, the teaching prohibition of the *Statuta* which Gratian considered binding. We get back to the basic understanding of women as essentially and ethically inferior, clearly evident in the motivation of the teaching prohibition of 1 Tim. 2: "I do not permit a woman to teach. . . . For Adam was created first and then Eve. And Adam was not deceived but the woman allowed herself to be deceived and became a transgressor" (1 Tim. 2:12-14).

The textual source of the *Statuta*'s prohibition of baptizing (*Mulier baptizare non praesumat*, c. 41), which Gratian places with the prohibition of teaching in c. 20 in *distinctio* 4, *de consecratione* (see p. 11) is to be found, according to Munier,[98] in the *Apostolic Constitutions* 3, 9. Both prohibitions are universal, and in the *Constitutions* the intention is so basically a matter of principle that the regulation can hardly be interpreted in the sense that it forbids women to baptize officially in public worship but does not forbid them to do so in cases of emergency.[99] Besides, an exception in such cases was apparently made first by Pope Urban II (1088-1099).[100] The baptizing prohibition of the *Constitutions* is quite informative, especially in the reasons given, in the matter of evaluation of women. The following text can be seen as the context and background of the concise formulation of c. 41 of the *Statuta*:

> About baptizing by women we want you to know that those who presume to baptize bring themselves into no small danger. So we do not advise it, for it is dangerous, yes, even forbidden and godless. That is to say, if man is the head of woman and he is promoted to the priesthood, it militates against divine justice to disturb the arrangement of the Creator by degrading man from the preeminence granted to him to the lowest place. For woman is the body of man, has come from his rib and is placed in subjection to him, for which reason also she has been chosen to bear children. The Lord says, 'He will rule over her.' Man has lordship over the woman, since he is also her head. But if we have already forbidden women to preach how would anyone want to permit them to enter the priesthood? It would be unnatural. For women to be priests is an error of heathen godlessness but not of Christ's way. But if women are permitted to baptize, then Christ would surely have been baptized by his mother and not by John and he would have sent women with us to baptize also, when he sent us out to baptize. But now the Lord never made any such arrangements nor left us with any such scriptural admonition, since he as creator of nature and founder of its order knew the gradations of nature and what is proper.[101]

The evidence in this text is undeniable that the baptizing prohibition and the exclusion of women from priestly office connected with it rests on a pronounced contempt for woman ("the lowest member [τὸ ἔσχατον σῶμα] . . . of the body of man, . . . from his rib and subject to him") and on her classification as biological and sexual: "chosen to bear children." The author of the *Constitutions* sees in woman's participation in the priestly office a disturbance of "the order of the creator." He is very zealous to maintain this order, but surely his questionable motive is clear: This order assures to man the position of superiority and authority over woman. As support for his argument he interprets, and misinterprets, a similar scriptural passage, Genesis 3:16 ("but he will rule over her") as divine sanction for the predominance of man.[102] Because of his manner of thinking, characterized by a thoroughly patriarchal environment, the author of the *Constitutions* cannot imagine a community of men and women together in the priestly office and service. The clear-cut desire to "rule," which betrays itself in the repeated use of this word and which completely misunderstands the teaching office (cf. the teaching prohibition, p. 12-13) and the priestly office as a form of ruling and exercise of power, completely excludes the possibility of such a community of men and women. The additional argument taken up by the *Constitutions* from the *Didascalia* that Jesus was not baptized by Mary but by John witnesses to an immature theological mentality conditioned by its time and therefore equally untenable. On the contrary, it should be noted that John was the one at that time called by God to baptize for repentance, and he was the one by whom Jesus wished to be baptized in solidarity with sinful humanity, whose guilt he vicariously took upon himself. Baptism by Mary would have had no meaning or relationship to salvation history.[103]

The baptizing prohibition as well as the teaching prohibition is specifically directed against the church widow. Apparently she had previously baptized on the basis of charismatic qualifications.[104] In any case the prohibition itself suggests that she had carried out this function.[105] According to Achelis-Flemming, the erosion of the widow's eccelesiastical rights and activities has its origin in the movement to strengthen the monarchical episcopate, which the author of the *Didascalia* strongly advocates.[106] In place of the charismatic institution of churchly widows which is henceforth limited to quiet prayer and at most also the care of the sick,[107] the *Didascalia* substitutes the female office of the diaconate as a pliable organ in the hand of the bishop with a firm place in ecclesiastical hierarchy.[108] Some functions that the widow had carried out are now taken over by the deaconess.[109] But of the former baptismal functions of the widow there remain for the deaconess only certain acts of assistance in the baptism of women by immersion, such as anointing the body—which seems proper for women to do—while the anointing of the head and the baptismal act itself are reserved for the bishop, then in his place the presbyter and the deacon—exclusively male clergy.[110] The development initiated in the Syriac *Didascalia* concerning the position of widows and the office of deaconesses reached its conclusion in the *Apostolic Constitutions* about one hundred years later.[111]

Concerning the prohibition of baptizing in the *Statuta*, it seems to be directed toward the churchly widow and the nun, especially since according to c. 100 of the *Statuta*[112] the preparation of women catechumens for baptism and their instruction in the basics of Christian living are given over to them. It is clear that the reference is not to the deaconess because the *Statuta* never even mentions this office, which is not surprising since the office of the female diaconate had nearly disappeared in Gaul in the second half of the 5th century, when the *Statuta* was composed.[113] But also the church widow, though still in existence, is no longer included in the ecclesiastical hierarchy according to the *Statuta*.[114]

The *Apostolic Constitutions* had already decreed that the widow, in contrast to the deaconess should receive no ordination with laying on of hands. She was to be installed in her position only through taking the vow—like the *virgo sacrata*.[115] The conclusion of this development is found in the *Statuta*: here too we find the common treatment of widows and nuns (cf. c. 100) as in the *Constitutions*, the direction of the widow to prayer (cf. c. 102)[116] her exclusion from the official teaching function (c. 37) and from baptizing (c. 41).

Gratian weakens the prohibition of baptizing in the *Statuta* insofar as he does not consider it to be binding in cases of emergency.[117] He refers in this to the already mentioned (p. 14) decretal of Urban II, *Super Quibus* (*causa* 30, q. 3, c. 4), according to which emergency baptisms may be performed by women and their validity recognized.

Both regulations the prohibitions of teaching and baptism in the *Decretum*, influenced the presently operative law of the church: c. 1342, § 2 of the Code, forbids all lay persons, including the religious, to preach in the church;[118] among other legal sources, *distinctio* 4, *de consecratione*, c. 20, is cited.[119] It is true that the canon concerns laity in general, but it especially has practical consequences for women. Thus although the regulation was limited by article 35, number 4, of the *Constitution on the Sacred Liturgy*[120] of Vatican II—so that leadership of a "service of the word," which should at the most include a talk,[121] may be turned over by the bishop to a commissioned layperson—this possibility is not as yet granted to women, except in actual distressed areas of the church, for instance in Latin America.[122] Furthermore, several male laypersons were permitted to lecture in the Council lecture hall but not a single woman.[123] Even the office of lector was at first sternly denied to women in the post conciliar period;[124] it was finally permitted, but only hesitantly and with limitations on the basis of new decrees.[125]

It is true that the baptismal prohibition (in c. 20, *distinctio* 4, *de consecratione*) does not appear among the *fontes* of the Code's regulations about baptizers, but it certainly influenced the content of the Code, canon 742, § 2. Although § 1 had said that anyone can baptize in case of emergency, preference is given in § 2 to a cleric if present, but if he is not present, preference is given among laypersons to a man rather than a woman.[126] Among other sources for this relegation of women to the last place in the "hierarchy" of possible baptizers, Hinschius[127] sees a dependence on the *Apostolic Constitutions* c. 9, and c. 41 of the *Statuta*, in other words a dependence on the baptizing prohibitions discussed above. Moreover, the gradations of canon 742, § 2 of the Code remind us clearly of 1 Cor. 11:3, where the woman is to receive less honor than the man and an immediate subordination to Christ is denied her. (On this cf. chapter 6, Exegetical Excursus.)

The so-called *presbytera* is the subject of a prohibition presented in c. 9 of *distinctio* 32. It has to do with canon 11 of the Synod of Laodicea.[128] The canon appears in Gratian according to the version of the *Hispana*,[129] which differs somewhat from the Greek original,[130] and reads as follows: "'Those women who are called *presbytides* [*presbyterae*] by the Greeks but by us are called widows, senior women, *univirae* and *matricuriae*, may not be installed in the church as ordained persons.'"[131] Gratian's introductory paragraph ("Truly we ought to understand *presbitera* as the Council of Laodicea expresses it, saying . . . ") as well as the *summarium* to the chapter ("Widows or older women are called *presbyterae*),[132] inform us that the chapter in the context of the *distinctio* has only the function of more carefully explaining and defining the concept *presbitera*, which has appeared in the immediately preceding chapter (18), where it means the wife of a presbyter. But this use of *auctoritas* by Gratian does not remove the prohibition. For the basic principle remains that each item of source material in the *Decretum* has that applicability and authority "which belongs to it itself, quite apart from its acceptance in the *Decretum*."[133] So the question is what the canon actually forbids. As Hefele shows,[134] the decree has experienced various interpretations, which came about because the meaning of πρεσβύτιδεσ (*presbytides*) and προκαθημέναι (female directors) on the one hand, and of ἑν Ἐκκλησία καθίτασθαι (being installed in the church) on the other hand, is not clear and simple. On the basis of the treatise by Epiphanius against the Collyridian women,[135] Hefele comes to the conclusion that the *presbytides* were the oldest of the deaconesses,[136] possibly the directors (προκαθημέναι) of the other deaconesses. According to this, the canon may be understood to mean that in the future no more such "archdeaconesses" or *presbytides* should be installed.[137]

Another explanation[138] has it that the πρεσβύτιδεσ were the ordinary deaconnesses; their characterization as directors refers to their oversight over the women in the Christian community, whereas the characterization *presbytides* comes from the repeated directive to accept only older women into the diaconate. The phrase μὴ δεῖν . . . ἐν τῆ Ἐκκλησία καθίστασθαι would mean that no more deaconesses were to be ceremonially ordained in the church. But against this Hefele points out that while it is true that some later Synods[139] did stop the older practice of ordaining deaconesses, ordination—a χειροτονείσθαι of deaconesses—was still taking place in the Greek church at least at the time of the Trullian Synod (A.D. 692; see canon 14). Besides, he notes, the canon says nothing about ceremonial consecration nor anything at all about ordination, but only about a καθίστασθαι.

A third and final explanation[140] is that the *presbytides* are not "archdeaconesses" but older women from the people who had been given oversight of the women in the church. This arrangement was then, according to this theory, set aside by the Synod of Laodicea. The *Correctores Romani*[141] allied themselves to this interpretation of the canon.[142] The version of the canon which Gratian accepted (cf. p. 18) seems to point to another, peculiar manner of understanding: It substitutes a long list of (Latin) designations (*viduae*, *seniores*, *univirae* and *matricuriae*) for the concept of the Greek version. (From this we may conclude that the office of πρεσβύτιδεσ was not known in the Latin church or that it had a different definition.) Gratian's version also understands καθίστασθαι in the sense of ordination ("they ought not to be installed in a church as if ordained to it [*ordinatas*]").[143]

Although the exact meaning of the canon can hardly be determined, as the various interpretations may have shown, it is nevertheless certain that by the regulation a specific and still extant functional area—an office, so to speak—was closed to women. We still cannot say why it happened. However since the Synod of Laodicea in its regulations about discipline exhibit a strong ascetic orientation in regard to sexual relations,[144] and since it shows itself concerned about "more strictness with regard to the hierarchical order,"[145] we can rightly assume that here, and especially in the first factor named, lies the basis for the elimination of women's ecclesiastical office by means of canon 11. So motivated, this in effect antifeminist action also shows itself especially clearly in canon 44 of the same Synod, since this canon for the first time presents a general exclusion of women from the chancel area,[146] and in so doing created a situation, operative through the centuries until today, in which discrimination against women in the church is a most obvious fact.

The regulations we have been discussing, which effectively excluded women from any official function in the church and which, as we have shown, have continued to influence operative church law as a result of its strong ties to classic canonical law, brought to an end a development that tended toward the active participation of women in ecclesiastical affairs. Besides two unimportant texts, there is in Gratian a regulation about deaconesses that is a direct reference to an earlier more favorable position of women in the church, a position we can only infer from the above prohibitions. The way in which Gratian utilizes this source, by the way, shows that in contrast to the prohibitions we have discussed, it no longer had anything to do with a determination of the law operative at that time. This is no doubt the reason why it did not have any influence on the present Code of Canon Law.

This regulation about deaconesses, a resolution of the Council of Chalcedon in 451, is placed by Gratian in c. 23 of *causa* 27, *questio* 1—i.e., in the section of his collection of sources given over to marital law—and reads as follows:

> No woman shall be consecrated as deaconess before she is forty years old, and then only after careful examination. But if, after receiving this consecration and fulfilling her office for a period of time, she should marry, thus disdaining the grace of God, let her be anathema along with him who entered marriage with her.[147]

The canon is used as evidence for the paragraph which introduces *questio* 1: "That truly those taking vows are not able to contract a marriage"[148] This shows that although the first part of the canon, the regulation about the age limit of forty years for admission of women to the diaconate consecration,[149] is in itself important, it was thought by Gratian to be quite unimportant. He considered that only the second part, concerning the celibacy obligation of deaconesses, justified acceptance of the canon, which would also explain the fact that the regulation does not appear in *distinctio* 23, in which the requirements for all ecclesiastical offices are found.[150] While Gratian in accordance with the introductory paragraph seems to consider the deaconess' *ordinatio* regulated by the canon as a vow, comparable to or identical with that of the widow or the God-consecrated virgin,[151] it is in actuality a matter of clerical ordination. The original form of the canon used here the technical term κειροθεσία or κειροτονία.[152] The consecration formulation[153] which has come down to us proves that the consecration of the deaconess in Byzantine Asia Minor was conducted in a form parallel to that of the deacon: The deaconess like the deacon was ordained by the laying on of hands by the bishop. The first part of the consecration prayer goes back to the one recorded in the *Apostolic Constitutions* (8, 20),[154] where it forms, along with the κειροτονία of the bishop, the consecration rite of the deaconess, which is placed between that of the deacon and that of the sub-deacon.[155] In the text of the prayer of the Byzantine consecration formula, which goes beyond its models in the *Constituitions*, it is said that the deaconess is accepted in the *ordo ministrorum* (order of ministers) by the grace of God.

God is implored to grant the ordinand the spiritual gifts of the diaconate, which he has also granted to the deaconess Phoebe (cf. Rom. 16:1).[156] The consecration takes place in conjunction with the liturgy of the Mass. At the conclusion of the consecration the deaconess was invested with the stole and presented the chalice, which she herself then returned to the altar.

After observing such a well-developed rite of consecration—there is good evidence that it was by no means limited to the Byzantine deaconess but was used in similar form for this office in other lands[157]—some authors have declared that the clerical character of the deaconess consecration cannot be denied; some place it among the lower clerical rites[158] while others count it among the higher.[159] It is of course true that there are some who represent the opposite opinion, considering the deaconess ordination as simply a benediction.[160] In part they base this opinion on the smaller authority granted to the deaconess in comparison to the powers of the deacon.[161] Although there is not in every respect an equalization of the deaconess with the deacon,[162] this is doubtless due to the fact that women as such were considered inferior, and not to any lesser quality of her consecration. Discrimination against women is surely the reason why the office was not uncontested even during the time of its existence and why finally it was condemned to perish.[163] In my opinion it is because of a lack of knowledge or consideration of these interrelations that some have much too hastily concluded that the consecration of the deaconess is not really a clerical consecration. The strict celibacy obligation in the above canon (*causa* 27, *questio* 1, c. 23), which results from ordination for the deaconess as well as for the clergy,[164] implies the clerical character of the consecration. Any disloyalty to this law of celibacy is, according to the chapter, an affront to the grace of God; this could indirectly constitute additional evidence of clerical consecration as means of grace.

As this canon further tells us, the deaconess was given an ecclesiastical office (*ministerium*; the original text uses λιτουργία). In Byzantine Asia Minor this consisted more than anything else in assistance at baptism.[165] There is evidence of this deaconess function, as well as of that of instructing baptized women in Christian living, in other areas of the East, and in many places there was in addition the distribution of the Holy Communion to women and children, as well as non-liturgical activity such as caring for the sick.[166] According to the report of Theodor Balsamon, the famous canonist of the Orthodox Church of the 12th century[167] (who used a vivid imagination, though marked by tradition, in his account of the deaconess in Byzantium), deaconesses as well as deacons shared in altar functions. When asked about the office of deaconesses, he gives the following instructive answer—which also contains information about the cause of the dissolution of the office:

> Formerly the order of deaconesses was recognized as in accordance with ecclesiastical law. They themselves had access to the altar. But because of their monthly defilement their office was removed from the cultic sphere and from the holy altar. It is true that deaconesses are [still] being chosen in the venerable church at Constantinople, although they are no [longer] admitted to altar [duties]. In several places they have convents and direct there a community of women according to church regulation.[168]

Thus in the 12th century there was nothing left of the former *ministerium liturgicum* (liturgical ministry). By that time deaconesses had only the direction of communities of women, a task they earlier had in part, in addition to ecclesiastical service.[169] So the deaconess was restricted to convent life and in this way excluded from the service of the congregation. This happened not only in the Byzantine area but also elsewhere in the Orient as in the West, and it is traceable to the victorious advance of monasticism.[170] Also Balsamon's commentary on the Chalce donian canon 15 about the deaconess, which appears in Gratian, shows that the regulation was effect in his (Balsamon's) day, because an antithetical canon debarred women from the altar.[171]

Two further sources used by Gratian that mention the deaconess are taken from imperial laws. They characterize the deaconess as an ecclesiastical official who enjoys the special privileges recognized by public law and receives official protection. In a letter of Pope Gregory the Great to a certain *Defensor Johannes*—the first part of which is found in Gratian, c. 38, in *causa* 11, *questio* 1—the *Prooemium* of c. 21 of *Novel* 123[172] is quoted word for word: It grants to the deaconess, along with other ecclesiastical persons, the *privilegium fori* and says that she is under the authority of the bishop.[173] According to *causa* 27, *questio* 1, c. 30, taken from Julian's *Epitome Novellarum*, *Const.* 115, c. 67,[174] the deaconess, and also the female ascetic[175] and the nun, are protected by imperial law against robbery, abduction and rape.

Now it is true that these final *capitula* from Gratian do not say much for the membership of the deaconess in the clergy, since the nun is also granted the same privileges. But other texts, not used by Gratian, from the imperial legislation of the eastern Roman Empire provide evidence for the ordination as well as for the clerical position of the deaconess.[176]

Gratian's Opinion

Because Gratian's *Decretum* is of interest to us not only as a collection of sources, but also as a textbook,[177] the question arises what Magister Gratian himself thought of the possibility of ordination of women.[178] As a matter of fact, the sources which he collected (treated in the preceding section of this book) point in a definite direction. For the choice of these legal texts and the manner of their arrangement in the *Decretum* are doubtless conditioned by his opinion about this question. So his one utterance on the subject does not at all surprise us: "a woman cannot be promoted either to the priesthood or even to the diaconate . . . ,"[179] (*causa* 15, *questio* 3, *princ.*). It is not clear, to be sure, whether Gratian understands the "cannot be promoted" (*non posse provehi*), the fact that women cannot be admitted to the diaconate and the priesthood, as being the result of ecclesiastical law alone—in which case it is difficult to understand why he did not deal with all clerical levels—or whether he understands it as being the result of a divine and therefore unchangeable apostolic decree. Several observations in the larger context of the treatment seem to point to the second explanation.[180]

Since Gratian knows and uses legal sources that refer to the female office of the diaconate, especially canon 15 of the Council of Chalcedon, it is astonishing that he as decisively denies the possibility of the admission of women to the diaconate as to the presbyterate. This contradiction may be explained, on the one hand, by the fact that in the time of Gratian (12th century) there were no more deaconesses in the Western Church. It is true that several 11th century decretals,[181] as well as the *Ordines Romani*,[182] refer to a consecration of the deaconess reserved to the bishop, which took place by a laying on of hands and which was considered to be a part of the consecration of the higher clergy.[183] But these regulations were limited to the city of Rome.[184] In other areas of the Western Church the female office of the diaconate disappeared more quickly. Several synods in Gaul from the 4th to the 6th centuries expressly forbade the ordination of deaconesses.[185] In the Western Church[186] there is no evidence for such wide extent and such relative permanence of the office of deaconesses as in the Eastern Church, where, for instance in Byzantium, it is still traceable in the 11th century.[187] According to an extant 10th century Western source, only unclear conceptions of the female diaconate prevailed at that time.[188] The sporadically early disappearance of the office in the Latin church as well as its relatively weak beginnings there and perhaps also its different complexion there,[189] could be the source of

Gratian's denial of ordination of women to the diaconate. Some decretists also find similar reasons for Gratian's statement: They suggest that Gratian specifically mentions the diaconate because entrance of women to this order seemed possible, since there were deaconesses earlier, whereas in his time this office no longer existed in the church.[190]

On the other hand, the statement of Gratian may have another source: The Magister may have doubted that the early Christian female diaconate was a true diaconate order in the strictest sense of the word.[191] At any rate this is the position of several decretists who had themselves no knowledge of the historical source materials concerning the consecration of deaconesses and the office joined to it.[192] They support their position by reference to a text of Ambrosiaster falsely attributed to Ambrose, according to which the ordination of deaconesses is described as contrary to the authoritative (apostolic) decree and therefore inadmissible.[193] It must be assumed that Gratian was familiar with this patristic authority directed against the deaconess, especially since he had a high opinion of the teachings of the fathers and on many issues finds a place for them in his collection of sources.

Source of Discrimination: Denigration of Women

An objective evaluation of the sources we have studied, as well as of Gratian's own opinion about the exclusion of women from office in the church, necessarily requires a more exhaustive investigation of the question, What conception of women is implied or presupposed?[194] Clear understanding about the justification or lack of justification of legal regulations will result from a knowledge of how and in what manner women are esteemed. It might already be concluded that the evaluation of women as inferior underlies their exclusion from cultic-liturgical activity. Such evaluation of inferiority is shown with full clarity by other texts in Gratian's *Decretum*, texts which in part go beyond our special interests here. Statements of condescension directed toward women are found in great numbers in the *Decretum* and they stand in causal relationship to the legal limitations and prohibitions which women suffer and which also concern other areas of life.

Depending upon a long tradition, the author of the *Decretum* is guided and influenced[195] in his presentation of the legal status of women by a very low evaluation of women. This evaluation is explicit at various places in the book, as it is also in the dictum[196]—which introduces the third *questio* in *causa* 15 (i.e., in the context of the statement of Gratian already mentioned)—that women should have access neither to the priesthood nor to the diaconate. Gratian is here dealing with the question, whether a woman may go to court as plaintiff against a priest. Gratian observes that according to canon law, this would seem to be completely excluded, for there is a general decree in a decretal of Pope Fabian (*causa* 21, *questio* 7, c. 6)[197] that neither complaint nor testimony may be raised against the priests of the Lord by those who "are not of his order, nor are capable of being so," that is, those who do not have (or cannot have) an equal status with them. Gratian applies this generalized regulation to women, as follows: "A woman cannot be promoted either to the priesthood or even to the diaconate and for this reason they may not raise a complaint or give testimony against priests in court."[198] To sustain his argument Gratian appeals, however, not only to canonical law but also to Roman law.[199] In Roman law, too, Gratian says, a woman is forbidden to bring a complaint before a court, and the reason is the necessity for feminine modesty, unless she wishes to prosecute an injustice done to her or to a member of her family.[200] From this it might be concluded, Gratian continues, that a woman for whom the exception is not applicable may not be permitted to register a judicial complaint against a priest.

But Gratian, in a kind of dialectical procedure, raises an objection to this preliminary conclusion, supported as it is by ecclesiastical and secular law. First, he points out that anyone who can be a judge may not be prevented from becoming a plaintiff in court. But women became judges in the Old Covenant, as the Book of Judges clearly shows. (Here obviously reference is made to Deborah, a judge with prophetic talents, as the fourth chapter of the Book of Judges relates.) So it may be said that those cannot be excluded from the role of plaintiff who have often fulfilled the role of judge and who are not forbidden by any word of Scripture to act as plaintiff. The solution of this problem, which doesn't seem to be a difficult one for Gratian, shows clearly that he is limited by the bias of an ideology that is marked by rabbinical, Pauline concepts and that suppresses the freedom of women. Thus he argues as follows:[201]

> In the Old Covenant much was permitted which today [i.e., in the New Covenant] is abolished, through the perfection of grace. So if [in the Old Covenant] women were permitted to judge the people, today because of sin, which woman brought into the world, women are admonished by the Apostle to be careful to practice a modest restraint, to be subject to men and to veil themselves as a sign of subjugation. . . .

Thus Gratian perceived the Old Covenant practice of allowing women to be judges to be basically an unauthorized concession, an imperfection that was overcome by means of the New Covenant, whose perfection in grace manifests itself, in the case of women, in her punishment because of original sin, for the entrance of which into human history she and she alone is responsible. The punishment takes the form of her both losing the freedom of an independent human being and her status of subjection to man.

The conception of woman as being continuously subordinated by the stain of quit and punishment, was for the most part, adopted by Gratian presumably by way of patristic texts,[202] from 1 Tim. 2:12-14, ascribed to the Apostle Paul, a passage manifestly exhibiting rabbinic ways of thinking.[203] Beyond this he was able to support his position about the subordination required of women by reference to Eph. 5:22, 24; Col. 3:18; 1 Cor. 11:7-10 and 14:34f. Women's status of subordination justified further legal limitations according to Gratian: their exclusion from being judges and from the right of complaint in a court room (likewise established in Roman law), as follows from *dictum causa* 15, *questio* 3 *princ.* The exclusion of women, mentioned in the same context, from the diaconate and the presbyterate, is doubtless no exception, since it is likewise based on the situation of subordination inflicted on women.

The conviction of Gratian about the ethical inferiority of women, which led him in *dictum causa* 15, *questio* 3 *princ.* to depict woman as the author of sin, is expressed very clearly in another connection and nuance, in the *dictum* added to c. 18 in *causa* 32, *questio* 7. Here Gratian is critical of the comments on 1 Cor. 7:10f., which appear in the commentary of the so-called Ambrosiaster[204] (mistakenly attributed to Ambrose) and which Gratian uses in c. 17. Discussing the Corinthian passage, Ambrosiaster says that a woman who has separated from an adulterous husband must either remain unmarried or become reconciled to her husband, whereas a husband is permitted in the case of an adulterous wife to remarry.[205] The Magister does not doubt that this conception, giving such freedom to a husband during the lifetime of his wife, is contrary to the official church teaching and tradition. Yet he refers to a contemporary interpretation, which in order not to question the authority of Ambrose tries to bring his meaning into line with church teaching by insisting that the statement is limited to a very particular case, that of adultery with blood relations. This interpretation is taken over by Gratian and corrected by him to conform with church teachings.[206] In this way, it is true, a certain assimilation of patristic doctrine to the ecclesiastical viewpoint on marriage was achieved, but meanwhile the possibility existed that a man might protest that he is not being allowed more freedom in marital legality than a woman in a similar situation. Gratian anticipates such a possible protest by a man, and does so in a way quite characteristic of his concept of women: The man should realize that the designation *vir* (male) is, according to Ambrose, not derived from the sex but rather from *virtus animi,* (strength of soul) that is, moral strength, perfection, and that the designation *mulier* (woman) on the contrary derives from *mollities mentis* (softness of mind) that is, from weakness and softness of character.[207] The feeling of superiority and higher value because of being male asserts itself here in crass form, exhibiting at the same time a contemptuous condescension toward the "weak sex," whose characteristic is, according to Gratian, the *mollities mentis* and for whom the opposite of *mollities*,[208] the *virtus animi* of the man, is hardly attainable. For Gratian, who doubtless adopts for himself the prevailing viewpoint of his time, the concept *mulier* is so closely associated with low morality that *mulier* can be used as appropriate designation for lack of chastity and for adultery in the case of both sexes because of their wicked depravity: "[prostitute or fornicator], each of whom . . . is called a woman by reason of the corruption of lust."[209] Thus, far from being a value-neutral concept, *mulier* (or, *femina*), according to a centuries-old understanding that Gratian takes up and mediates to the future, implies a serious stain and inferiority, while *vir* indicates according to the same traditional way of thinking a human being in ideal form, and is thus likewise an ethically qualified term.[210]

Of course Gratian agreed with the church tradition of monogamy and unbroken marriage[211] On the one hand this limited the greater sexual freedom man had come to demand as his natural right, since he was obligated to be faithful in sexual matters to the same degree that had always been expected from the woman. On the other hand, the man was granted, as a kind of recompense for his "sacrifices," unlimited dominion over the woman.[212] Here too Gratian was not breaking with tradition, as we may see from his remarks added to c. 11 and 20 in *causa* 33, *questio* 5. According to the *dictum p.c.* 11[213] which is supported by various authorities, the dominion of man over woman is limited only in the area of intimate relationship, where husband and wife seem to be given equal rights ("A women has power equal to that of a man in conjugal obligations, as does a man to a woman"). So for instance one partner may not take a vow of sexual abstention without the agreement of the other. But in all other areas of life, as Gratian emphasizes, the relationship of superiority and inferiority obtains between man and wife. "Because truly in other matters the man is the head of the woman and the woman the body of the man." (It is however obvious that this duty of subordination on the part of the wife could only reflect negatively on her rights involving intimate relationship, where her equality was recognized. . . .)[214]

The rulership of the man is implied, Gratian thinks, by the idea that man is the "head," a conception taken from Paul (especially from Eph. 5.22f. and 1 Cor. 11:3) and from patristic texts.[215] The idea that woman is the "body," on the other hand, implies her subordination to man. The characterization of woman as "body of man" is likewise borrowed by Gratian from Pauline terminology. It appears in similar form in Eph. 5:28f., in a somewhat different context, however, since it serves there in the first place as a description of the harmony of husband and wife.[216] Paul's usage, followed by Gratian, of the concepts "head" and "body" for husband and wife in their relationship to each other derives in the final analysis from a literal rabbinic understanding of the Yahwistic creation narrative according to which woman was formed from the body of man.[217] Such a usage of "head" and "body" results from the concept of the inferiority of woman from the very creation. The obvious consequence of this type of thinking, as well as of the abovementioned concept of the ethical inferiority of woman, is her status of subjection and the concrete legal limitations which accompany such a status. These limitations, according to the *dictum p.c.* 11, include the prohibition without the approval of her husband to take a vow of self-denial (fasting, etc.) for religious reasons. (This so-called *votum abstinentiae* is clearly separated by Gratian from the *votum continentiae*, which aims at sexual abstinence.) In this way, Gratian makes the wife so subject to the dominion of her husband that she cannot fulfill a vow made with his approval if he afterwards retracts his consent. "And this is, as we have said, because of the situation of submission by which she ought to be subject to the male in all things."[218] Gratian has no difficulty finding support, incontestable in those days, for the "condition of servitude" assigned to women. He quotes ten passages (genuine and spurious) from church fathers, which deduce woman's subject status from her ostensible inferiority, both creaturely and morally.[219] On the basis of this authority he formulates the following (*p.c.* 20) as conclusive result, which harmonizes with the previous *dictum* (*p.c.* 11):

> And so it is most clearly evident that a man is so much the head of a woman that she is allowed to offer herself to God by no vow of abstinence or by conversion to the religious life without his permission; even if she should bind herself with his permission, it would not be

allowed for her to fulfill her vow, if the man would change and revoke his permission.[220]

The degradation and insult of such "order" lies not least in the fact that it takes from woman control over even the most personal affairs of her life and thus she is denied the independent activity of an unmediated relationship with God. Her relation to God is regulated by and through the husband so that she herself is demoted to an inferior being like a minor. The Old Testament has the same regulation.[221] It is therefore clear that Gratian has to a large degree preserved the Old Covenant order of law which resulted from extreme patriarchal thinking. According to this legal order the wife is the property and possession of the husband,[222] and this was true despite the fact that the New Covenant had been in existence for hundreds of years. If we presume that today no one would seriously question the immediacy of a woman's relationship to God, the Old Testament legality is still not overcome, insofar as women still find themselves dependent upon men in their relationship to God. The reason is that only men are the official preachers of the Word of God and administrators of the Eucharist and of Penance, sacraments definitive of Christian existence.[223]

All legal limitations and every kind of legal deprivation of women may be traced back to the subject status laid upon women because of their alleged inferiority, as René Metz rightly emphasizes: "All the juridical incapacities of which she may be the object are explained by her status of subjection: 'Because of the condition of servitude, which [the woman] owes to man in all things, she submits.'"[224] Herein is also the cause of the exclusion of women from ordination.[225]

Gratian's judgment of women, which is not only personal but reflects also the thinking of his age,[226] is decisively marked by several factors: Besides those Pauline statements about women we have already discussed there is, first, the viewpoint of the Church Fathers and, secondly, the viewpoint of Roman law. These two bases of Gratian's thinking are extensively treated in the *Decretum* and therefore deserve special consideration.

Influence of the Church Fathers

The authority of the Church Fathers was held in high esteem during the Middle Ages. Their statements were considered as genuine legal evidence[227] and as such had the same standing as decisions of councils and papal dispensations.[228] But it was particularly in the area of scriptural interpretation that the Fathers had unrivaled primacy. Thought to be inspired by the Holy Spirit, they were considered as authoritative commentators and exegetes.[229] Gratian makes use of their scriptural exegesis in his *questio* 5 of *causa* 33—which is especially interesting at this point—in order to establish and legitimize the assigned place of women as "condition of servitude, since she must be subject to her husband in everything." (*dictum p.c.* 11). The passages from the Fathers that Gratian uses fulfill this objective in a manner which could hardly be more literal or uncritical in its interpretation of the Bible.[230] There are statements in various texts concerning a female inferiority already set forth in the creation and the consequence is that the *imago dei* (image of God) is expressly denied to women. Here the extent of derogation is especially visible, as in Gratian's c. 13—taken from *Questions on the Old and New Testament*—attributed to Augustine,

> This image of God exists in the male that he might be made the one from whom all others originate having the dominion of God; in some sense as His representative as he has the image of the one God. And therefore woman is not created in the image of God. For indeed it is said,: "And God made man; in God's image he made him." Here also the Apostle: "A male," he said, "ought not to cover his head, because he is the image and glory of God, for that reason a woman covers her head because she is not the glory or the image of God." [231]

That woman is not the image of God is likewise asserted in the passage of c. 19 attributed to Ambrose in explanation of 1 Cor. 11:3ff.: "A woman must cover her head because she is not the likeness of God; in order that she may appear submissive . . . she must wear this sign. . . ."[232] It is true that the texts do not come from Augustine and Ambrose, as Gratian supposes, but rather from Pseudo-Augustine and Pseudo-Ambrose;[233] their attribution by Gratian to the great Church Fathers agreed with prevailing opinion in the Middle Ages.[234] Today it can be taken as certain that the commentary to the thirteen Pauline letters, from which the text of c. 19 is taken, and the questionable *Questions*, are products of the same author, in other words a Pseudo-Augustine and Pseudo-Ambrose are the same person.[235] The identity of the author, so-called Ambrosiaster, is not yet clear.[236] From his writings we conclude that he was schooled in Roman law.[237]

The scriptural proof for the contention of Ambrosiaster that woman is not in the image of God is derived in c. 13 from the Yahwistic creation narrative (Gen. 2), then from Gen. 1:27 (taken over almost word for word), and from 1 Cor. 11:6f. (with an addition not found in Paul[238]). From this last passage is also derived in c. 19 the not-in-God's-image status of women. The genuine Ambrose in his *Book of Paradise* also derives the pre-eminence and primacy of the male and the secondary position of the female from the Yahwistic creation narrative. The relevant passage is placed by Gratian in *causa* 33, *questio* 5, c. 20:

> Nor is it insignificant that woman was made not from the same earth from which Adam was formed, but from a rib of Adam himself . . . Therefore two, male and female, were not made from the beginning, nor were two males, nor two females, but first male and then female from him. . . .[239]

Jerome in his Titus commentary (Tit. 2:5) refers to 1 Cor. 11:3 (likewise derived from Gen. 2[240]), the passage about the man being "head" of the woman, in order to give a religious basis to the requirement that women be subordinate to men—thus giving this requirement the needed emphasis. The text appears in Gratian as *causa* 33, *questio* 5, c. 15: "Since the male is the head of the female, as Christ is the head of the male, any wife who is not subject in every thing to her husband, that is her head, is accused of the same thing as a man who does is not subject to his head. . . ."[241]

In connection with the so-called order of creation Jerome also introduces natural law in support of an inferior position for women.[242] Augustine likewise makes use of this category in his commentary on Genesis (*questio* 153; *causa* 33, *questio* 5, c. 12 in Gratian) in order to legitimate the servile relationship of women to men: It corresponds to nature's just ways that the lesser should serve the higher.[243] René Metz has rightly noted that the concept of "natural order" as used by Augustine simply characterizes the actual situation—understood of course as unchangeable and determined by nature—in which women were placed, in state and in church, at that time: "From a factual situation St. Augustine deduces a condition of right; he infers from it the inferiority of woman vis-a-vis man."[244] From Augustine's standpoint the Old Testament regulations about the subordination of women contain nothing foreign or offensive. The Church Father sees in them only a manifestation of the order of nature, as well as a recognition of divine law. An illustration is the stipulation of Num. 30:7ff, according to which a wife is completely dependent upon the will of her husband in taking a vow. (Gratian gives this Augustinian commentary as cc.11 and 16 in *causa* 33, *questio* 5.) Another illustration is the regulation of Dt. 22:13-21, where a wife—accused by her husband of unchastity before their marriage—was to be stoned if the evidence of the husband proved to be true. However the same punishment of stoning did not apply to a false witness, although in other cases in Israel the basic *ius talionis* was in effect—that is, the false witness was punished in the same fashion as the accused person in the case of truthful evidence. (The Augustinian commentary on this passage appears in Gratian as *causa* 33, *questio* 5, c. 14.) This Augustinian type of reasoning, to deduce norms of natural law from the factual, is by no means unique in the history of natural law. Similarly, for instance, the actual existence of slavery was rationalized as natural necessity, which in turn led to the fundamental permission to hold slaves:[245] they were considered as "by nature not free" and so by nature "intended for servitude."[246] This unhistorical, superficial and shortsighted type of judging, in which the actual subordination of women is understood as determined by natural law—went further in the case of Augustine. It led him to understand the lack of development of the character of women (their ignorance and lack of education), hindered as it was by profound injustice, as if it was a psychic weakness and inferiority determined by nature. For it is said, in the Augustinian text mentioned above (p. 31) and given by Gratian (*causa* 33, *questio* 5, c. 12), "that the lesser should serve the greater," or more clearly in the original text, "the weaker reason serves the stronger" Likewise the next sentence (not used by Gratian) reads as follows: "This is justice that the weaker rule serves the stronger. This clear justice is accordingly found in rulers and in servants that those who excel in reason, excel in ruling."[247] Pseudo-Augustine (Ambrosiaster) even goes so far as to derive women's not-in-the-image-of-God status from the fact that women exercise no public, legal functions. He holds it absurd to think that women as well as men are distinguished by the image of God and thus intended for dominion. He rejects applicability of the image of God to women by pointing to their immaturity and lack of business skills in public affairs. He asks, "Truly how is anyone able to explain how a woman, if she is in the image of God, remains subject to the rule of males and has no authority? For she is not able to teach or to be a witness nor to make loans nor to judge, much less to rule!" (like a man!)[248] Gratian uses the text in somewhat shorter form[249] and attributes it to Ambrose.

The legal situation of women exhibited in c. 12 is clearly recognizable as one imposed on women by Roman law. In the latter they may not serve as witnesses,[250] they may not be active as citizen and judge, they are completely excluded from all public office.[251] But Ambrosiaster is in no way critical, from his Christian point of view, of this severe oppression of women by secular law. On the contrary he tries to show the agreement of Roman law, well-known to him and also highly valued by him,[252] with the "order of creation." He tries to derive the inferiority of women as created and her not-in-the-image-of-God status from Roman legal regulations—that is, to confirm the former by the latter.[253] Since women, because of their exclusion from all official church functions, are no better off by ecclesiastical law than by Roman law, Ambrosiaster certainly did not need to feel his opinion about women was any contradiction of ecclesiastical understanding.

The statements of Augustine and of Ambrosiaster have not lost relevance even to the present day. Their prejudicial and hasty manner of judging women is by no means overcome today: Because women hold practically no church office, because of the canon law which forbids it, it is concluded that they are not capable of holding such office. It is today forgotten but not therefore less true that women were, as long as the law permitted, considered incapable of profiting from any education and there were no available means for education,[254] until finally experience disposed of this prejudice. Furthermore, from women's present situation and behavior, one infers forthwith an unchangeable, inferior feminine nature, without at all taking account of the fact that the long-existing suppression of women did not fail to make an impression on them, that their personalities were not a little stunted and undeveloped, which often in fact makes them seem inferior and worthy of contempt. It was precisely the failure to take account of these components of historical development which determined the mistaken judgment, namely the depreciation of women (for instance, in Ambrosiaster).[255] This devaluation, although seldom pronounced openly today, nevertheless expresses itself clearly in the present situation of women.

Besides the secondary creation of women (after and out of Adam), from which their not-in-the-image-of-God status is concluded, and besides the "order of nature" argument, the Fathers bring up the question of original sin, for which women are said to bear the principal guilt or even the only guilt. This contention becomes another way to establish and sanction their subject status, and it determines the line of thought in Gratian's chapters 18 and 19. According to c. 18, which is taken from the *Hexaemeron* of Ambrose but which also depends on 1 Tim. 2:14, Eve—and with her, womankind—receives the blame for man's being seduced into sin. Man, the victim of her seduction, should to a certain extent act in the place of God to see to her punishment by bringing her under his dominion. It is implied that an attitude of constant mistrust toward women seems advisable.[256] Similarly c. 19,[257] which is taken from the Ambrosiaster commentary,[258] shifts original guilt and the punishment of mankind onto women alone, and as the text makes clear, not without a certain psychological intent: In this way women are induced to keep their essential and ethical inferiority in mind. Thus intimidated and submissive, they will adapt themselves as meekly as possible to a strictly hierarchical and patriarchically structured system:

> A woman ought to cover her head because she is not an image of God. But as she is shown to be subservient and because the transgression began through her, she ought to have this sign in church out of reverence for the bishop; she should not have her head free, but covered by a veil; she does not have the power of speaking because the bishop holds the person of Christ. Therefore, as though before Christ the judge, she is thus before the bishop because he is the vicar of the Lord; she ought to be seen to be subservient because of original sin.[259]

Gratian's Use of Roman Law

Besides the writings of the Fathers (which in turn rely on Genesis and the Pauline letters), Gratian makes use of the regulations of Roman law, in order to support his opinion of the worth and place of women in the affairs of the church. Since Gratian was a teacher in Bologna, it was easy for him to utilize Roman law, the scholarly study of which reached a time of flowering in the famous Bologna law school of the 11th and 12th centuries and won for Roman law the rank of world law.[260] But for the monk Gratian, the more decisive reason for utilizing Roman law was probably the fact that the church had always such a high esteem for the *lex romana*. "The church lives under the Roman law"[261] was an uncontested axiom in the lands of the Western Church. The church constitution as well as the canonical discipline were to a large extent influenced by Roman institutions and Roman principles.[262]

Roman law was already accepted in the collections of law made before the time of Gratian. But Gratian's *Decretum* contains, besides the texts that appear in these collections, further Roman legal sources, which imply a direct knowledge and usage of the Justinian compilations.[263] Gratian discusses the relation between secular and ecclesiastic law in *distinctio* 10 of the first section of his *Concordia*. To a certain extent he postulates here the theory that is basic to his usage of secular law in his collection. He begins by explaining (*distinctio* 10 *princ.*) that legal regulations of secular rulers do not take precedence over ecclesiastical laws but rather are subordinate to them.[264] He supports this principle by reference to various papal dispensations (cc. l-6) and them completes it with a further principle, at the beginning of the second section of the *distinctio* (*dictum ante causa* 7, *sententia* 2): "Where they are not contrary to gospel and canonical regulations they deserve full respect in deference."[265] Next Gratian cites various authorities as proof, specifically emphasizing the duty to recognize Roman law and to obey it.[266] Thus Roman law, when it agrees with church law, always has a subsidiary function in relation to it. It serves as a supplementary source of law[267] and is as such dignified with every recognition and deference. Undoubtedly this principle of the relation existing between ecclesiastical and Roman law is important for the question at issue: Since Roman law was prejudicial to women in the same way as church law,[268] it was used by Gratian exclusively as subsidiary authority. As a result, it gave considerable emphasis to the Pauline and patristic statements about the inferiority and subject status of women, which we have already discussed. The regulations from Roman law that Gratian accepted should be understood as part of the larger pattern presented in the following section, summarizing the situation of women according to Roman law, and which became one of the factors determining the legal status of women in the church.

Survey of the Position of Women According to Roman Law

Roman Family Law

In old Roman (patrician) times Roman family law is decisively marked by the *patria potestas*, the paternal authority over the agnate family, i.e., the association naturally formed by blood relationship on the father's side (*per virilem sexum*) or artificially formed on the strength of legal transactions (by adoption or *in manum conventio*). So this association, by blood and law or else by law alone, stands under a common *pater familias*.[269] The "Roman-patrician agnate principle," or the institution of *patria potestas*, is based on the theory of male procreation, according to which the male is exclusively the procreator of posterity and is, so to speak, its "most logical continuation."[270] The contribution of women to the production of new life (partnership in procreation, giving birth) is so thoroughly ignored in the old Roman agnate family and the so-called *manus* marriage that the wife has a sort of child relationship to her husband and consequently a sort of sister relationship to her own children. Together with her children she is subject to the household authority (*patria potestas*).[271] It is clear from the formation of the old Roman *manus* marriage (*coemptio, confarreatio, usus*—that is, possession of *manus*),[272] and especially from the general rights of husbands over wives—rights which are connected with the *manus* authority over wives and which are identical with those which come from the *patria potestas*[273]—that a wife is the possession of her husband and is completely subject to his control. In regard to her he has the authority of life and death (*ius vitae ac necis*), and he is permitted any kind of punishment of her.[274] A wife caught in such a degree of arbitrary power and violence had recourse for some protection only to the court set up for difficult family problems.[275] A wife in *manu* also remains on the level of a child in matters of property law. She has no rights of possession: Everything which she and her children acquire belongs to the master of the house, including the inheritance which the wife brings to the marriage.[276]

In the course of time, however, the *manus* marriage with its strict patriarchalism could not last; by the end of the Republic it is more and more superseded by the so-called free marriage.[277] Already the law of the Twelve Tables (450 B.C.) knows both forms.[278] Nevertheless the *manus* marriage did not fully disappear until the Empire. In the legislation of Justinian, free marriage, which takes place by mutual agreement, is the only form recognized.[279] It is true that in free marriage the wife no longer stands under the *patria potestas* of her husband—both father and mother are legally head of the family—but still the husband has the legal authority (although it is less strict than the *patria potestas*) "to be the final arbiter in all questions of married life."[280] He decides the place of residence, which the wife has to share with him, he determines what is to be the education of the children, to him alone is formally granted the right to live together with his wife,[281] from which follows that violation of marital fidelity by him remains largely unpunished.[282] While adultery by a wife is legitimate grounds for divorce in every stage of development of Roman law, it is only in the late empire that adultery of the husband is recognized—through the influence of Christianity—as grounds for divorce.[283] On the other hand, in free marriage the wife gains a basic independence and considerable equality with the husband in regard to the laws of property, because separation of property laws are then in force.[284]

General Civil Law

Corresponding to her subordinate position in the Roman family, a Roman woman as a female is also disadvantaged as *civis Romanus*,[285] that is to say, in the area of general civil law. This is true in regard to her legal competence as well as her commercial rights (*Dig.*, 1, 5, 9: "In many parts of our laws, the condition of women is worse than that of men").[286] The limitation of her legal rights is clear from her exclusion from all public office and legal proceedings.[287] Absolute impediments to eligibility for office are: female sex and physical or mental illness.[288] Besides passive franchise, active franchise is also denied her.[289] In civil cases she has no rights *pro aliis*, that is, to go to court for another person,[290] or to be a juror.[291] In criminal cases also she only very exceptionally has the right of plaintiff—actually only "as plaintiff in an offense against her or against her family."[292] Further, a woman is denied the right to be a guardian (*Dig.* 26, 1, 16 and 18: "A guardian is a male office");[293] only in Justinian's law have mother and grandmother the right of guardianship over child and grandchild provided they do not marry again.[294] In drawing up a will, a woman cannot function as witness (*Institutiones Justiniana* 2, 10, 6),[295] and she has no legal competence for "sollenity" testimony, i.e., "the use of witnesses in legal affairs."[296] The denigration of women in Roman law[297] is also obvious from the fact of their being listed along with minors, slaves, deaf mutes and men deprived of civil rights, as legal incompetents.[298]

Besides age and health, sex is one of the factors in Roman law which influence commercial rights: The limitations of women in this area prevent their undertaking certain acts of civil law without a guardian (*tutor*).[299] Even under classical law an adult woman, if she is not under the authority of her father (*in patria potestate*) nor that of her husband (*in manu mariti*), she comes under legal guardianship (*tutela legitima*) of the closest agnate (i.e., the closest male relative of her father or her deceased husband). Only the Vestals were free from this guardianship. The reason for the requirement of guardianship is again very characteristic of the estimation of women: They need a guardian because of the weakness of their sex and because of their ignorance of public affairs.[300] By means of the *Lex Julia* (A.D. 4) and *Papia* (A.D. 9) women were excused from the agnate *tutela* if they had the law of the free (*ius liberorum*) (in the case of three children of a free-born woman or four of an emancipated). Childless women were also granted the privilege of *ius liberorum*.[301] Claudius rescinded the *tutela legitima* of the agnate and thus its practical significance was lost,[302] but the *tutela mulieris* disappeared altogether only in the 5th century.[303]

The privileges granted to women by Roman law because of their sex (*privilegia favorabilia*) hardly improved their disadvantaged legal situation, especially in the old Roman and early classic period. These privileges are rather the result of that disadvantaged situation, and express the fact that women are not accepted as of age, as responsible persons. An illustration is regulation *Dig*. 22, 6, 9 *pr*., to the effect that women are to be forgiven legal errors "because of the weakness of their sex." This privilege holds for minors, soldiers and others who are ignorant of business.[304]

Although it is true that because of the influence of humanitarian ideas on Roman law, the situation of women began to improve—they became more independent legally and in business[305]—still "the Roman basic principle" remained that women "belong in the home," despite the "humanitarian demands of legal equality for the sexes." The regulation, which resulted from this basic principle—"Women are excluded from all political or public office . . . " (*Dig*. 50, 17, 2)—continued to be binding for the whole Roman law and thus for the legal standard characterizing the evaluation and the status of women.[306]

Influence on Gratian

In the legal aspects of marriage and in the matter of lawsuits, we see in Gratian the negative influence of Roman law on the place of women in classic canon law. It should be noted that the more favorable situation of women in late Roman marital law was ignored by Gratian.

In discussing the question (*causa* 32, *questio* 1) whether a man may marry a prostitute in which term Gratian includes an adulteress, Gratian rests his case on a Roman legal decree which requires a man to prosecute and separate from his adulterous wife.[307] If he does not do so, he is a "protector of immorality" and is guilty of pandering (*dictum p.c.* 10). Gratian expressly says that, on the other hand, a wife does not have the same responsibility in the case of an adulterous husband. She is in fact not permitted to accuse her husband of adultery, as Gratian proves by reference to a Roman law.[308] Gratian has not one word of disapproval for this crass "double standard" of Roman law, involving as it does a "double morality," strictly requiring wives to remain true but allowing husbands to go unpunished for unfaithfulness to the extent of adultery.[309] It is true that at the end of the *dictum* Gratian insists: "Fidelity and the symbol of union (*sacramentum*) ought to be observed between spouses, for when they are lacking, they ought to be called not spouses, but adulterers."[310] This statement implies the obligation of husbands to marriage fidelity, but, on the other hand, the one-sided faithfulness of wives is so strongly emphasized by means of ecclesiastical and Roman legal authorities that the above quotation from Gratian does not restore the balance, and thus the message of Christ concerning the complete equality of marriage partners (cf. Mt. 19:3-9) does not become productive.[311] Since Gratian in granting a husband (specifically a cleric) the right to punish his unfaithful wife appeals to a council decree[312] that was influenced by Roman law, it is clear how little church law was able to distance itself from the conceptions of old Roman law, according to which women were the possession of men and therefore subject to their disposal. In only one respect does Gratian (in dependence on cc. 5-9 in *causa* 33, *questio* 2) deviate from Roman law: He rejects the death penalty for wives. He goes no farther in opposing the objection of Christian conscience to the inhumanity of secular law: "If their wives sin, it is furthermore allowed for clerics to hold them in custody without the severity of death and to force them to fast, not however to weaken them to death."[313] Gratian never speaks of such punishment for an unfaithful husband.

The negative evaluation of the female sex that is characteristic of Roman law, considerably limiting the legal and commercial capability of this sex, has influenced not only marital law but also the decrees of classical canon law concerning litigation.[314] Simply because of her sex a woman is forbidden by canon law to accuse someone in court—there are a few exceptions (cf. *causa* 15, *questio* 3)[315]—to be a witness in cases involving punishment and in matters relating to wills (*causa* 4, *questio* 2/3 c. 1[316] and c. 3, § 22),[317] to postulate for someone (*causa* 3, *questio* 7 c. 2, § 2 and *causa* 15, *questio* 3 *princ.*). Likewise, she is excluded from the office of judge and from all functions connected with judgeship[318] (such as *procurare, advocare, postulate*). (Cf. *causa* 3, *questio* 7, *dict. p.c.* 2, § 2.) The determining factor in the possession or nonpossession of these important rights and functions and in the admission or nonadmission of persons to them both in Roman law and in canon law, is *before anything else the sex* of the persons in consideration. Only in the second place is their spiritual and ethical condition of importance, as it is unmistakably clear in the decree about witnesses in wills,[319] which Gratian took over from Roman law, according to which a hermaphrodite's legal capability is determined only by which sex predominates. The ecclesiastical use of this kind of irrelevant principle—to make one's sex the standardizing criterion—determined together with the Pauline and patristic statements we have noted, the inferior legal status of women in the church and certified its tenacity. Thus even today we witness the continuing exclusion of women from public liturgical-cultic functions, especially those of the diaconate and the presbyterate.[320]

Notes

1. *Der Geist des Codex juris canonici. Kirchenrechtliche Abhandlungen*, U. Sturz, ed., no. 92/93 (Stuttgart: Enke, 1918), 51f., 163f., 177; J. B. Sägmüller, *Lehrbuch des katholischen Kirchenrechts*, vol. 1, 4th ed (Freiburg: Herder, 1925), 267; see also the Code of Canon Law, canon 6, which governs the relationship of current law to old law and in ns. 2, 3 and 4 prescribes that the canons of the Code should be interpreted in the sense of the old law according to specified presuppositions. *Codex Juris Canonici Pii X Pontificis Maximi iussu digestus. Benedicti Papae XV auctoritate promulgatus, praefatione, fontium annotatione et indice analytico-alphabetico ab Emmo. Petro Card. Gaparri auctus* (Vatican City: Typis Polyglottis Vaticanis, 1948), hereafter cited as Code.

2. Cf. Stutz, *Der Geist*, 161, 164.

3. Ibid. 163.

4. "Only a baptized male validly receives sacred orders" in the language of the Code, the expressions "to ordain," "an order," "ordination" and "sacred ordination" are used for all stages of consecration, including those for the bishop and for the first tonsure, except where in the nature of the case or from the context it is obvious that another usage is intended. Cf. the Code, canon 950.

5. As leader of the work of the so-called commission of codification, Gasparri played a normative role in the genesis of the Code. On this see Stutz, *Der Geist*, 10f.; K. Mörsdorf, *Lehrbuch des Kirchenrechts auf Grund des Codex Juris Canonici*, 11th ed., vol. 1, (Munich-Paderborn-Vienna: Schöningh, 1964), 30.

6. As *fontes* from the Corpus the following are given: causa 1, q. 1, cc. 52, 60; *Extra* 3, 43, cc. 1, 3 (Code, 322, n. 4). Further evidence, not taken from the *Corpus Iuris Canonici*, has to do with the characteristics of ordinands which are required for the permitted ordinations.

7. The canon says nothing about the question whether the exclusion of women from ordination is based, according to the lawgiver, on divine or on human law (*ius mere ecclesiasticum*). But if we consider the fact that the theologians had for a long time assumed in general a divine law (*ius divinum*) in this question (cf. Van der Meer, *Women Priests* 5f., 9 and that the Code itself repeatedly uses this concept (cf. J. A. Fassbender, *Das göttliche Recht im Codex*

Iuris Canonici, unpublished dissertation, Catholic Theological Faculty [Bonn, 1947] 232) it is noteworthy that no declaration of divine law is made in this canon. To be sure, according to Fassbender, 118, there are in the Code many legal statements, which, in the view of the lawgiver, must be ascribed to natural law or to revelation, but which nevertheless contain no formal references to these. But in the case we are considering, the lack of formal reference to divine law could, in my opinion, be traced back to the fact that we have no record of a definitive position taken by the extraordinary magisterium on the question at issue.

8. Unfortunately the otherwise very noteworthy study by F. Gillmann, "Weiblicher Kleriker nach dem Urteil der Frühscholastiker," *Archiv für katholisches Kirchenrecht* (hereafter cited as *AkKR*) 93 (1913) 239-253, does not deal with this aspect of legal evidence. A complete survey of the question requires consideration of the evaluation of women which lies at the basis of the texts.

9. F. Heyer, in *Staatslexikon, im auftrag der Görres-gesellschaft unter mitwirkung zahlreicher fachleute*, Hermann Sacher ed., 5th ed., (Freiburg im Breisgau: Herder, 1926-1932) 1:1545 prefers the term "*Decretum*."

10. Evidence for this title exists in the majority of handwritten manuscripts of the *Decretum* and in the early decretists, and probably comes from Gratian himself. See on this question F. Heyer, "Der Titel der Kanonensammlung Gratians," in *Zeitschrift der Savigny-Stiftung für Rechtsgeschichte* (hereafter cited as *ZRG*), Kanonistische Abteilung 2 (Vienna; Cologne; Weimar: Böhlau, 1912): 336-342; also by F. Heyer, "Namen und Titel des gratianischen Dekretes," in *AkKR* 94 (1914): 501-517. The title refers to the purpose of the work, "to resolve the many inconsistencies found in the earlier collections" (J. F. v. Schulte, *Die Geschichte der Quellen und Literatur des canonischen Rechts von Gratian bis auf die Gegenwart*, vol. 1 (Stuttgart: Enke, 1875) 60 and in doing so "to bring uniformity to ecclesiastical law" (Sägmüller, *Lehrbuch* 235).

11. A. M. Stickler, *Historia iuris canonici latini institutiones academicae* (Turin: Libraria Pontif. Athenaei Salesiani, 1950) 1:201ff.; Sägmüller, *Lehrbuch*, 1:233ff.

12. Stickler, *Historia iuris canonici*, 1:204; H. E. Feine, *Kirchliche Rechtsgeschichte: die Katholische Kirche* (Cologne: Böhlau, 1964), 4th ed., 276.

13. Schulte, *Die Geschichte der Quellen*, 1:67.

14. "Now beginning with the highest grade and descending to the lowest grade, we will show how each of them ought to be ordained according to holy authorities." *Corpus Iuris Canonici*, Emil Friedberg, ed., 2 vols. (Graz: Akade mische Druck- u. Verlagsanstalt, 1959) (hereafter Friedberg) 1:76.

15. The chapters treated more fully on pp. 19 ff., which are concerned with the deaconess, contain no law in force during Gratian's time.

16. The *distinctio* makes no use of the scholastic method otherwise so normal with Gratian, according to which contradictory authorities are placed over against each other in dialectical fashion, with a final harmonization which Gratian seeks to base on specific principles. Cf. Schulte, *Die Geschichte der Quellen*, 1:60f. and Stickler, *Historia iuris canonici*, 1:208-210.

17. "Women dedicated to God are prohibited from touching the sacred vessels and vestments of the altar and from carrying the incense around the altar." *Corpus*, ed. Friedberg, 1:85f.

18. "Thus Pope Sother to the bishops of Italy," *Corpus*, (Friedberg, 1:86).

19. *Corpus*, (Friedberg, 1:86).

20. *Corpus*, (Friedberg, 1:86, n. 324) with reference to *Decretales Pseudo-Isidoriana*, Paul Hinschius, ed., (Leipzig: B. Tauchnitz, 1863; reprinted Aalen: Scientia Verlag, 1963) 124 (hereafter cited as *Decretales*).

21. Cf. Sägmuller, 1:225. (He writes that "for many centuries the collection, thought to be genuine, was attributed to Isidore of Seville, and materials were taken from it without hesitation, as Gratian also did.") See also Feine, *Kirchliche Rechtsgeschichte*, 276f. Concerning Isidore of Seville (560-636) see K. Baus, "Isidor," in *Lexicon für Theologie und Kirche*, Michael Buchberger, ed., 10 vols. and indexes and supplements, (Freiburg: Herder, 1957-1968) (hereafter cited as *LThK*) 5:786f.

22. Van der Meer, *Women Priests*, 91ff.

23. Van der Meer's critique (91ff., 100) is directed against the study by Santiago Giner Sempere, "La mujer y la potestad de orden; incapacidad de la mujer," in *Revista Española de derecho canónico* 9 (1954) 841-869, in which forgeries are not distinguished from authentic sources, according to Van der Meer; as a result the impression is given that there is an abundance of traditional evidence against admitting women to holy orders.

24. *Decretales*, 124.

25. *Corpus*, ed. Friedberg, 1:86, n. 324.

26. *Le Liber pontificalis*, L. Duchesne, ed. (Paris: E. Thorin, 1886-1957) 3 vols. (hereafter cited as *Lib. pont.*) 1:135.

27. *Lib. pont.* 1:227: "Here Boniface ordered that no woman or nun touch or wash the sacred pallam or place incense in the church except the minister (one section of the manuscript has, correctly, ". . . might touch or might wash" etc.); on this see p. 229, n. 11: "On sait que les femmes, même les diaconesses, étaient rigoureusement exclues du ministère de l'autel (Gélase, *epistola ad episcopos Lucaniae*, c. 26); quant aux fonctions dont il est ici question, ce sont celles des bas cleres, des ostiaires on des sacristains. La seconde épître apocryphes de Clément à Jacques (*Patrologiae cursus completus: series graeca*, J. P. Migne, ed. (Paris: J. P. Migne, 1857-1866) 161 vols. (hereafter cited as *PG*) 1:483) les décrit longuement, supposant toujours qu'elles sont remplies par des clercs."

28. *Lib. pont.*, 1:135, n. 3.

29. Cf. A. Stuiber, "Liber pontificalis," in *LThK* 6:1016f.; G. Chr. Hansen, "Liber pontificalis," in *Die Religion in Geschichte und Gegenwart; Handwörterbuch für Theologie und Religionswissenschaft*, 3rd ed., Kurt Galling, ed. (Tübingen: Mohr, 1957-1965) 7 vols. (hereafter cited as *RGG*) 4:343f.

30. Concerning this and other functions of the widow and the deaconess in the early church, see Adolf Kalsbach, *Die altkirchliche Einrichtung der Diakonissen bis zu ihrem Erlöschen* (Freiberg: Herder, 1926) 45, 57f., 65; J. Funk, "Kerikale Frauen?" in *Österreichisches Archiv für Kirchenrecht*, 14 (1963):

274ff.; K. H. Schäfer, *Die Kanonissenstifter im deutschen Mittelalter: ihre Entwicklung und innere Einrichtung im Zusammenhang mit dem altchristlichen Sanktimonialentum*, (Amsterdam: P. Schippers, 1965) 32, 58f.; L. Zscharnack, *Der Dienst der Frau in den ersten Jahrhunderten der christlichen Kirche* (Göttingen: Vandenhoeck & Ruprecht, 1902) 130ff.

31. Of course one finds a similar, blunt rejection of feminine participation in liturgy in authentic texts, as for instance in a decretal of Pope Gelasius I to the bishops of Lucania in A.D. 494, which reads as follows: "No less impatiently we have heard, suggesting such a disrespect for divine things, that women are allowed to minister at the holy altar and a sex which is not competent to display all those things that are not assigned except to the service of males." J. D. Mansi, *Sacrorum consiliorum nova et amplissima collectio*, (Paris: H. Welter, 1901-1927) 54 vols., 8:44, cap. 6. Accordingly the liturgical ministry of women is considered to be disrespectful of divine, holy "things."

32. 2 Cor. 11:2b.

33. Hinschius, *Decretales*, 124.

34. Cf. on this P. Browe, *Beiträge zur Sexualethik des Mittelalters* (Breslau: Müller & Seiffert, 1932) 1-35; R. Kottje, *Studien zum Einfluss des Alten Testamentes auf Recht und Liturgie des frühen Mittelalters* (Bonn: L. Röhrscheid, 1964) 69-83.

35. Chapter 41 is taken from the second epistle of Sixtus I; the first part of the excerpt from the letter comes from the *Vita Sixti I*, c. 2 (*Lib. pont.*, 1:128). Cf. *Corpus*, ed. Friedberg, 1:1304, n. 451 with reference to Hinschius, *Decretales*, 108. Chapter 42 is an excerpt from the first epistle of Stephan I and has its source in the *Vita Stephani I*, c. 3 (*Lib. pont.*, 1:154). Cf. *Corpus*, ed. Friedberg, 1:1305, n. 465 with reference to Hinschius, *Decretales*, 183.

36. "Blessed vessels are not to be handled except by blessed men (*sacratis hominibus*)." c. 41; *Corpus*, ed. Friedberg, 1:1304. "Blessed vestments are not to be worn except by blessed men (*sacratis hominibus*)." on c. 42; *Corpus*, ed. Friedberg, 1:1305.

37. *Corpus*, ed. Friedberg, 1:1304f.

38. This critical edition of the *Decretum* was produced by the so-called *Correctores Romani* commission, established by Pius V in 1566 and consisting of many doctors and cardinals. It appeared in 1582 and was declared to be authentic and the only official edition by the constitution of Gregory XIII, "*Cum pro munere*" (from 1580). Cf. Schulte, *Die Geschichte der Quellen*, 1:72f.; Sägmüller, *Lehrbuch*, 1:238f.

39. *Corpus*, ed. Friedberg, 1:1304, note to c. 41.

40. Cf. *Mittellateinisches Glossar*, E. Habel, ed., 2nd ed. (Paderborn: F. Schöningh, 1959), col. 178; *Glossarium mediae et infirmae latinitatis*, C. Ducange, ed., (Graz: Abakdemische Druck-U. Verlagsanstalt, 1954; reprint of the Paris, 1883-1887 edition), 4:224- 226.

41. "Church vestments . . . ought not to be touched by or handed over to anyone except consecrated men (*sacratis hominibus*)." *Corpus*, ed. Friedberg, 1:1305.

42. It is not clear from the relevant chapters what kind of consecration is required, but presumably a clerical, though not necessarily a priestly. For according to *distinctio* 23, cc. 31 and 32, for instance, the acolyte status and the subdiaconate are prerequisite to the liturgical functions mentioned.

43. The overemphasis on ordination to the detriment of the sacrament of baptism is probably based on an excessive sacralization of the cult, which is characteristic of these chapters, and on the taboo of consecrated objects. This overemphasis has today considerable influence in the liturgical area: cf. the critical comment on the Third Instruction concerning the orderly carrying out of the Constitution on the Liturgy (from November 5, 1970): "Ist die Liturgiereform für Rom beendet?" in *Herder-Korrespondenz* 24 (1970) 557-559; see also n. 45, below.

44. On the basis of source materials, Browe, *Beiträge zur Sexualethik*, 3, remarks: "From this point of view one realizes not only that women are kept from touching holy objects like chalice, altar, etc.,—since this prohibition applied though not so insistently also to lay people in general —but also that the reason given was sometimes women's weakness and uncleanness" (see also pp. 64 f.). One can see how strong were the influences of Old Testament regulations, among other things, on synodal resolutions, if one reads, for instance, the following canons of the diocesan synod of Auxerre, France, in 585 or 578: c. 36 ("No woman may receive the holy Eucharist with bare hands"); c. 37 ("Also she may not touch the pall"); c. 42 ("Every woman must have her *dominicale* at communion"). C. J. von Hefele, *Conciliengeschichte*, 2nd ed. (Freiburg im Breisgau: Herder, 1855-1890), 9 vols., 3:45f. (According to Duchesne, *Christian Worship, Its Origin and Evolution*, 5th ed. [London Society for Promoting Christian Knowledge, 1956] 224, the so-called *dominicale* is a linen cloth with which the hand is to be covered.) The influences of Old Testament cleanliness regulations in Gratian's *Decretum* are apparent in the following declarations, although it is true that they do not deal with the question we are considering at the moment: *distinctio* 2, *de consecratione*, cc. 21, 23, § 2; *distinctio* 23, c. 33; *causa* 33, q. 4, cc. 2-11. Gratian separates himself from these viewpoints to the extent of agreeing with many authorities (*distinctio* 5, pr. § 2; *Corpus*, ed. Friedberg, 1:7) that menstruating women may not be denied the right to go to church and to receive the holy communion. Also after the birth of a child a woman may not be forbidden to enter a church, although nothing is said in this connection about receiving the sacrament at this time. Yet regulation *distinctio* 5, c. 4, which is considered binding by Gratian, still presupposes the rite of purification, as the summary of c. 4 shows: "Before a child is weaned or a mother is purified, a male should not undertake sexual intercourse." *Corpus*, ed. Friedberg, 1:8. See also J. Freisen, *Geschichte des canonischen Eherechts bis zum Verfall der Glossenliteratur*, 2nd ed. (Paderborn: F. Schöningh, 1893) 849ff.

45. These chapters support the Code, canon 1306, § 1, which requires that chalices and patens, as well as purificators, palls and corporals, may be touched before their washing only by clerics or by those who are responsible for them. See the Code, p. 445, n. 1. According to canon 1306, § 2, which should also be

mentioned in this connection, the first washing of purificators, etc., may be done only by clergy in higher orders. However the *Motu proprio, Pastorale munus* of Pope Paul VI, November 30, 1963, takes account of the prescriptive law which has been in effect for a long time, when in its n. 28 it gives local bishops the right to permit clergy of lower rank, (male) lay persons and also devout women, to perform the first washing of palls, corporals and purificators. *Acta Apostolicae Sedis, Commentarium officiale*, (hereafter cited *AAS*) 56 [1964] 10). It is instructive to notice in this regulation the special mention of women—in itself superfluous—along with laity.

46. *Corpus*, ed. Friedberg, 1:1323f.

47. See C. J. von Hefele and H. Leclercq, *Histoire des conciles d'après les documents originaux* (Paris: Letouzey et Ané, 1907-1952) (hereafter cited as Hefele-Leclercq), 3/1:261.

48. Hefele-Leclercq, 3/1:264.

49. *Corpus*, ed. Friedberg, 1:XLVff., LIVff.

50. *Corpus*, ed. Friedberg, 1:1323, n. 369.

51. *Ibid.*

52. The relevant canon of the Synod of Rouen reads: "We have been told that, mass having been celebrated, certain priests declining themselves to take the divine mysteries which they have consecrated, hand the chalice of the Lord to mere women (*mulierculis*) who offer it at masses or to certain laity who do not know how to discern the Body of the Lord, . . . the piety of the faithful know how contrary this would be to all ecclesiastical reverence. Whence we forbid all priests lest anyone presume to do this in the future, but the priest himself should consume with all reverence and hand to the deacon or subdeacon who together comprise the ministers of the altar . . . furthermore he should place the Eucharist in the hand of no laity or women, but only in his or her mouth. . . . If anyone has transgressed in this way, since he has defied almighty God, and has dishonored that which is in him, he should be removed from the altar." H. Th. Bruns, ed. *Canones Apostolorum et Conciliorum saeculorum* (Berlin: G. Reimeri, 1839, reprinted Torino: Bottego d'Erasmo, 1959) 2:268f.

53. This prohibition—in its application to women—was first promulgated by the Synod of Laodicea (between A.D. 347 and 381) in canon 44: "Women are not permitted to enter the sanctuary" (cf. Hefele-Leclercq, 1/2:1020). The canon was repeated by many later synods. Cf. Van der Meer, *Women Priests*, 94.

54. So for instance in *distinctio* 23, c. 29, "A woman, however learned and holy, ought not to presume to teach men in an assembly. A lay person ought not dare to teach in the presence of clerics (except in petitioning)." *Corpus*, ed. Friedberg, 1:86 (also see n. 52 above). We should note further the capitulary of Bishop Theodulf of Orleans (750 or 760 to 821), in chapter 6 of which it is stated: "Women should never approach the altar while the priest is celebrating mass, but stand in their place and from here the priest will accept their offerings to be offered to God. Indeed women ought to be mindful of their infirmity and feebleness of their sex and for that reason they ought to greatly fear to touch any holy thing in the ministry of the church. Even lay men ought to greatly fear these

things lest they undergo the punishment of Oza who died by the Lord striking him when he wished to touch the arc of the Lord inappropriately (2 Sam. 6:3-8)."

55. See the documents cited above, n. 44 and n. 54.

56. On this see p. 94.

57. Cf. pp. 83, 84.

58. Such an unfavorable and lowly position for women did not always exist in this respect: according to the *Testamentum Domini*, the older sections of which may go back to the second or third century, deaconesses are duty bound to take the Holy Communion to sick women. There is evidence that Monophysite deaconesses likewise had the right to distribute Communion. In the West it seems that deaconesses, specifically *sanctimonialia* (holy women), as late as the 9th century, carried out this duty, but the official church objected strongly. See Schäfer, *Kanonissenstifter*, 32, 59f. Kalsbach, *Die altkirchliche Einrichtung*, 45, 57.

59. Cf. *Codex Juris Canonici Pii X pontificus maximi iussu digestus*. Rome: Typis Polyglottis Vaticanis, 1948 (hereafter the Code) 283, n. 4. The canon reads as follows: "The ordinary minister of holy communion is the priest alone (§ 1). The extraordinary [minister] is the deacon given the permission of the ordinary or the pastor; this granted to him for serious cause which is presumed in a legitimate case of necessity." (§ 2). Concerning the inhuman consequences which the regulation entailed for women, see Heinzelmann, *Schwestern*, 67f.

60. On the basis of rescripts from the Congregation of Sacraments (from November 28, 1967 and from February 14, 1968) the Conference of Bishops in Germany received a three-year authorization to permit (male) laypersons (*viri probati*) to distribute the Holy Communion (Similar authorization was granted for other areas). The permission, according to this (temporary) ruling, could be extended to Mothers Superior of convents, if the local church official should be absent for several days. See Kirchliches *Amtsblatt für die Diözese Münster*, 102 (1968). 7f.

61. On the basis of a general Instruction (*Fidei custos*) released by the Congregation of Sacraments on April 30, 1969, which concerns extraordinary distribution of Communion, lay women as well as nuns may be in principle empowered to distribute Communion, under certain conditions. (Texts of the Liturgical Commission of the German Conference of Bishops, for the plenary meeting of the Conference of Bishops, February, 1970, pp. 44-47.) But according to the order of succession prescribed in No. 3 of the Instruction, by which the choice is made for extraordinary distributors, laywomen are listed in last place. According to No. 5 of the instruction, they are to be used only in emergencies, when a more suitable person cannot be found—which can only mean a man or at least a nun! ("A woman of proven piety may be chosen in case of necessity, only of course when another suitable person cannot be found." *Ibid.*, 46.) By rescript from the Congregation of Sacraments dated November 13, 1969, the request of the German Bishops' Conference was granted for a three-year period, whereby the general rule (*Fidei custos*) would apply in their area (cf. *Kirchliches Amtsblatt für die Diözese Münster*, 103 [1970]: 51f.) Women are put in a somewhat inferior position over against men, since the regulations of the Bishops' Confer-

ence—actually more positive in comparison to the Roman Instruction—directs male laypersons to wear a cassock and surplice or an alb during the distribution of the sacrament, but women should wear "decent, civilian clothing as unshowy as possible" (*Ibid.*, 51). From this rule one will draw the conclusion that women's work in the church, if permitted at all, must retain an unofficial character.

62. *Corpus*, ed. Friedberg, 1:86.

63. *Corpus*, ed. Friedberg, 1:1367.

64. Gratian assigns *distinctio* 23, c. 29, to the fourth Council of Carthage; *distinctio* 4, *de consecratione*, c. 20, to the fifth.

65. *Distinctio* 23, c. 29 is put together from cc. 36 and 37 of the collection; *distinctio* 4, *de consecratione*, c. 20 from cc. 37 and 41. *Corpus*, ed. Friedberg, 1:86, n. 344 and 1:1367, n. 242.

66. The *Hispana*, traditional material from the old Spanish church, contains canons of councils and papal decretals. It belongs to the most important legal collections of the first Christian millennium and was erroneously attributed to Isidore of Seville since the 9th century. See A. M. Stickler, "Hispana collectio," *LTHK*, 5:390; Sägmüller, 1:212.

67. Cf. F. Maassen, *Geschichte der Quellen und der Literatur des canonischen Rechts im Abendlande* (Graz: Akademische Druck- und Verlag-sanstalt, 1956) 1:382f; Hefele-Leclercq, 2/2:102ff . The critical edition of the *Statuta*, upon which I base the following discussion, was prepared by Charles Munier, *Les Statuta Ecclesiae Antiqua. Les Statuta Ecclesiae Antiqua, Edition etudes critiques*, Bibliotheque de l'institut de droit canonique de l'université de Strasbourg, 5 (Paris: Presses universitaires de France, 1960).

68. Cf. Sägmüller, 1:224; Duchesne, *Christian Worship*, 350, n. 2.

69. See Munier, *Statuta*, 70. Gratian took a rather large number of canons from the *Statuta*. Cf. *Corpus*, ed. Friedberg 1:xxi.

70. Cf. Munier, *Statuta*, 70, 101; Duchesne, *Christian Worship*, 350, n. 2.: "It [the *Statuta*] is still quoted by many under the latter title [Fourth Council of Carthage], and what is more serious, pronounced as an authority for African ecclesiastical usages in the 4th century."

71. Cf. *Corpus*, ed. Friedberg 1:1367, n. a on *distinctio* 4, *de consecratione*, c. 20.

72. The brothers Ballerini, who were famous for their critical-historical and canonical research, were the first to reject, about the middle of the 18th century, the assigning of the *Statuta* to a council of Carthage, and instead recognized its origin in southern Gaul. Munier, *Statuta*, 24f., 101.

73. Cf. Hefele-Leclercq, 2/1:102ff.

74. Cf. Maassen, *Geschichte der Quellen*. 1:387ff. and Munier, *Statuta*, 24, 101, 209.

75. Munier, *Statuta*, 209ff., H. Lentze, *Österreichisches Archiv für Kirchenrecht*, 12 (1961) 174 and G. May, "*ZRG*, Kan. Abt." 48 (1962) 38lff., find Munier's conclusions about authorship convincing. The anonymity of the author is the result of a desire to give the collection the authority of tradition, since it was

intended for the purpose of reform; cf. Munier, *Statuta*, 242. Concerning the person of the author, see also Th. Payr, "Gennadius" in *LTHK*, 4:677f.

76. Munier, *Statuta*, 242.

77. Especially the chapter, "Les sources des *Statuta Ecclesiae Antiqua*," in Munier, *Statuta*, 105-185.

78. Cf. Munier, *Statuta*, 127f.

79. Cf. H. Rahner, "Apostolische Konstitutionen," *LTHK*, 1:759; J. Quasten, "Kirchenordnungen," *LTHK*, 6:239.

80. Munier, *Statuta*, 137f.

81. See J. A. Jungmann, "Didaskalia," *LTHK*, 3:371f. Rahner, "Apostolische Konstitutionen," *LTHK*, 1:759; "the first six books [of the *Apostolic Constitutions*] are an extension of the Syriac *Didascalia* [about the year 250] to conform to conditions of the later period."

82. For instance cc. 27 and 68, Munier, *Statuta*, 84, 91. According to Munier, *Statuta*, 202f., 238, Gennadius felt an obligation to the ascetic ideals of a monasticism characterized by Oriental ways of thinking.

83. A. Sleumer, *Kirchenlateinisches Wörterbuch*, 2nd ed. (Limburg: a.d. Lahn, Gebrüder Steffen, 1926) 241, says that the word *conventus* can have the general meaning of congregational assembly as well as the specific meaning of monastic community.

84. Even in our times this concept is used in order to give divine sanction to the disorder brought about in sex relationships by power-seeking actions, e.g., G. Concetti, "La donna e il sacerdozio," in *L'Osservatore Romano*, Nov. 1965, quoted by Heinzelmann, *Schwestern*, 89-101, esp. 99. Some male writers readily admit that the assumed superiority of men over women, exactly because it is unjust, is supported by these and similar spurious means. See, for example, B. J. Leclercq, *Familie im Umbruch. Ehe und Familie im Strukturwandel unserer Gesellschaft* (Luecerne, 1965) 61: "Woman was considered capable of doing whatever man wanted her to do, but she was considered incapable of doing whatever man did not want her to do"; 63 "The main virtue of woman in marriage was to be subject to her husband." See also Metz, "Statut," 65, who comments as follows on the attempt to establish and justify the exclusion of women from liturgical functions: "L'imagination de l'homme est féconde, quand la défense de ses intérêts est en jeu."

85. The church widow of early Christian times, to whom this rule against teaching is directed, was called the "altar of God" because she regularly received the gifts of the congregation for her livelihood. See H. Achelis and J. Flemming, *Die syrische Didaskalia* (Leipzig: J.C. Hinrichs, 1904) 274. When C. Bamberg, "Die Aufgabe der Frau in der Liturgie," in *Anima* 19 (1964): 312, uses the designation "altar of God" to describe the "true nature of women" and in this way argues against the admission of women to the office of the priesthood, she has made an irresponsible use of this concept, separating it fully from its historical background and "mystifying" it immoderately—just as women's veil (1 Cor. 11:5ff.), in actuality a sign of her inferiority is glorified and mystified into a symbol of the *sponsa Christi*.

86. *Apostolic Constitutions*, Bk. 3. 6 (*The Ante-Nicene fathers, Translations of the Writings of the Fathers Down to A.D 325*, Alexander Roberts, D. D., and James Donaldson, eds. [New York, Scribner, 1925] 7:427f.). The prohibition against teaching in the *Didascalia* is very little different from that of the *Constitutions*. See on this *Didascalia et Constitutiones Apostolorum*, Franz Xaver von. Funk, ed. (Paderborn: Ferdinandi Schoeningh, 1905) 1:190.

87. Concerning the dependence of these Pauline passages on rabbinical ways of thinking and methods of scriptural exegesis, see chapter 6, pp. 177ff., 180ff.

88. Cf., for instance, Concetti, "La donna" F. X. Remberger, "Priestertum der Frau?" in *Theologie der Gegenwart* 9 (1966): 133; also by Remberger, writing against the viewpoint of Van der Meer, "Priestertum der Frau? Zuciner neuen Untersuchung," in *Theologie der Gegenwart* 13 (1970): 93f., 98f.

89. Achelis and Flemming, *Die syrische Didaskalia*, 76f. (emphasis added). The author of the *Apostolic Constitutions* expresses himself similarly if somewhat more cautiously: "When she [the widow] is asked anything by anyone, let her not easily answer, excepting questions concerning the faith . . . remitting those that desire to be instructed in the doctrines of godliness to the governors. Let her only answer so as may tend to the subversion of the error of polytheism, and let her demonstrate the assertion concerning the monarchy of God. But of the remaining doctrines let her not answer anything rashly, lest by saying anything unlearnedly she should make the word to be blasphemed. . . . For unbelievers, when they hear the doctrine concerning Christ not explained as it ought to be, but defectively, and especially that concerning his incarnation or his passion, will rather reject it with scorn, and laugh at it as false, than praise God for it" *Ante-Nicene Fathers*, 7:427.

90. Cf. Achelis and Flemming, *Die syrische Didaskalia*, 266f.

91. On this see J. Jeremias, *Jerusalem zur Zeit Jesu*, 3rd ed. (Göttingen: Vandenhoeck & Ruprecht, 1962), 395-413; J. Leipoldt and W. Grundmann, eds., *Umwelt des Urchristentums* (Berlin: Evangelische Verlagsanstalt, 1965-1967), 3 vols., 1:173-178.

92. See Jeremias, *Jerusalem zur Zeit Jesu*, 413; J. Leipoldt, *Die Frau in der antiken Welt und im Urchristentum* (Leipzig: Koehlert & Amelang, 1954), 117-145.

93. Cf. Metz, "Statut," 63ff; Van der Meer, "Priestertum der Frau?" 39ff.

94. Metz, "Statut," 62f.; Van der Meer, "Priestertum der Frau?" 10-15. The fact that according to Jewish-rabbinical regulation women were not permitted openly to teach in the synagogue (cf. n. 96 below) creates in itself an essential reason for preventing the sending out of women. The apostles repeatedly report that they themselves actively proclaim the Gospel in the synagogues. Cf. Acts 9:20; 13:14ff.; 14:1; 17:1ff.

95. E.g., by Concetti, "La donna" 89; similarly, Remberger, "Priestertum der Frau?" *Theologie der Gegenwart* 9 (1966), 133f., and in *Theologie der Gegenwart* 13 (1970), 93f., 98.

96. Cf. the proof-texts from the Talmud and Midrash cited by Hermann Strack and Paul Billerbeck, *Kommentar zum Neuen Testament aus Talmud und Midrasch.* (4 vols. Munich: Beck, 1922-1928), 3:467-69, on 1 Cor. 14:34f. For

instance, T. Meg 4:11 [226]: "... A woman must not come to the pulpit to read publically;" Meg 23a Bar: "... Women come in order to hear."

97. Cf. Munier, *Statuta*, p. 137, which points specifically to the dependence of the teaching prohibition of the Constitutions on 1 Cor. 14:34: "Les Constitutions apostoliques citent, â l'appui de cette interdiction . . . 1 Cor. 14:34 —'Mulieribus ut in ecclesia doceant non permittimus.'" On the connection between the *Didascalia*—and also with it the *Constitutions*—and 1 Timothy, see E. Schwartz, "Über die pseudoapostolischen Kirchenordnungen," in *Gesammelte Schriften* (Berlin, 1963), vol. 5, p. 193: "The *Didascalia* is basically nothing but an amplification of 1 Timothy."

98. Munier, *Statuta*, 138.

99. P. Hinschius, *Das Kirchenrecht der Katholiken und Protestanten in Deutschland.* 5 vols. (Berlin: Werdmannsche Bundhandlung, 1869-1893; reprinted Graz: Akademische Druck-u. Verlagsanstalt, 1959) 4, p. 29, n. 4, assumes that the prohibition in the *Statuta* applies also to cases of emergency. Presumably, since it is mentioned in the same connection, this assumption also applies to the *Constitutions*. So also W. Plöchl, *Geschichte des Kirchenrechts*, 2nd ed. 2 vols. (Vienna: Herold, 1960-1962), vol. 1, p. 210.

100. Cf. Zscharnack, *Der Dienst der Frau*, p. 93. The relevant *epistola decretalis* of Pope Urban is given by Gratian in chapter 4 of c. 30, q. 3. "Concerning those things about which your concern consulted us, it seems to us this was answered in the statement that a baptism would take place if in a time of necessity, a woman would baptize a child in the name of the Trinity." *Corpus*, ed. Friedberg, 1:1101.

101. *Apostolic Constitutions*, Bk. 3, 9 (*Ante-Nicene Fathers*, 7, p. 429). Cf. *Didascalia et Constitutiones Apostolorum*, ed. F. X. Funk, pp. 199-201. The *Didascalia* contains the same regulation (*ibid.*,198-200) but in a shorter and milder formulation. Cf. the notes of the editor on *Didascalia.* 3.9.1 and *Constitutiones Apostolorum* 3.9.1.

102. Modern exegesis has rightly emphasized that this biblical passage expresses the disorder which comes into sexual relations as the result of sin, rather than any legitimation of the authority of men over women, cf. chapter 6, p. 175-176f.

103. This certainly does not diminish the value of Mary's vocation in the slightest, which seems to be in fact the meaning of the *Didascalia* and the *Constitutions.*

104 .Cf. Achelis and Flemming, *Die syrische Didaskalia*, 279f.

105. *Ibid.*, 276, 281.

106. *Ibid.*, 276, 280f., 269.

107. *Ibid.*, 280; Kalsbach, *Die altkirchliche Einrichtung*, 29, 25.

108. Achelis and Flemming, *Die syrische Didaskalia*, 281f.

109. Cf. Kalsbach, *Die altkirchliche Einrichtung*, 28: "In the *Didascalia* the work of the ministerium is taken from the widow and given independent status in the office of the deaconess." See also *ibid.*, 29.

110. Cf. *Didascalia* 3.12,2.3, in *Didascalia et Constitutiones Apostolorum*, ed. Funk, 1:208-210; Achelis and Flemming, *Die syrische Didaskalia*, 281, 290. Kalsbach, *Die altkirchliche Einrichtung*, 27, points out that although the characterizations of deacon and deaconess are the same in the *Didascalia*, as far as baptizing is concerned, the deaconess is rated below the deacon.

111. Cf. Kalsbach, *Die altkirchliche Einrichtung*, 28ff. He gives a more exact characterization of the widow and the office of the deaconess in the *Constitutions* in comparison with the *Didascalia*. The baptismal duty of the deaconess in the *Constitutions* corresponds with that of the *Didascalia*, anointment of the female body before baptism.

112. "Widows and holy women, who are chosen for ministry to those to be baptized, ought to be so instructed in the office that they are able to teach with clear and wise discourse ignorant and rustic women, when they are to be baptized, how they should respond to the questioning of those baptizing and how they ought to live once they have accepted baptism." Munier, *Statuta*, 99f.

113. Cf. Munier, *Statuta*, 136. Cf. with this the presentation on p. 23.

114. Munier, *Statuta*, 136.

115. Cf. *Constitutiones Apostolorum* 8.25, 2 (8.24, 2 contains the same arrangement for the virgin concerning the omission of laying on of hands), *Didascalia et Constitutiones Apostolorum*, ed. Funk, 1:529; see on this Kalsbach, *Die altkirchliche Einrichtung*, 28f. The widow of the *Didascalia*, on the contrary, still belongs to the clergy, according to Achelis and Flemming, *Die syrische Didaskalia*, 278, 280f., and possesses an office, to be sure a very modest one. Nevertheless Kalsbach says, p. 22, that her position "in relation to the clergy is just as clearly delimited as to the laity." See also Funk's comments, *Didascalia et Constitutiones Apostolorum*, 1:197, in the notation to *Constitutiones Apostolorum* 3.8, 1. ("The widow in that writing [the *Didascalia*] seems to be the same as a deaconess, in this [the *Constititions*] she is subject to the deaconesses. The *Didascalia* moreover attributes the imposition of hands to the widow something which the author of the *Constititions* does not acknowledge.")

116. Cf. Munier, *Statuta*, 137.

117. Concerning *distinctio*, 4, *de consecratione*, c. 20 (baptismal prohibition) Gratian remarks, "unless forced by a convincing necessity," *Corpus*, ed. Friedberg 1:1367. The limitation of the baptismal prohibition is already evident (according to Plöchl, *Geschichte*, 1:210) in Isidore of Seville.

118. "The laity, however devout, are forbidden to give a public address."

119. The Code, 458, n. 4.

120. "The holy celebration of the Word of God should be cherished . . . especially in a place that lacks a priest in which case the deacon or some one delegated by the bishop should lead the celebration." *AAS* 56 (1964), 109.

121. Cf. the Constitution on the Sacred Liturgy, Walter M. Abbott, *The Documents of Vatican II* (New York: Herder & Herde:, 1966), 137.

122. Cf. M. Daly, *The Church and the Second Sex*, 140; also *Frau und Beruf* 7 (March-April, 1967): 32.

123. On this see Heinzelmann, *Schwestern*, 5: "In this respect the large number of attempts of male auditors" to give women the opportunity to speak, "which had the assistance of several cardinals, was without success." As a sign of the slowly changing attitudes toward women, it is thus important to notice that in the second regular Bishops' Synod, January, 1971, a woman spoke for the first time to the Synod—she was Barbara Ward, professor of political economy and member of the Papal Commission on Justice and Peace. (*Katholische Nachrichten-Agentur*), 45, no. 3 (November, 1971), 3.

124. In 1965 the *Consilium ad exsequendam Constitutionem de Sacra Liturgia* gave a negative answer to the modest question whether an appropriately prepared woman could take over the lector's office in a mass for women alone: the office of lector, it was answered, is a liturgical duty, which is conferred upon men only. For this reason the Epistle is to be read by the celebrant in the case mentioned. *Notitiae*, published by the *Consilium ad exsequendam Constitutionem de Sacra Liturgia*, 1, 1965, pp. 139f., n. 41 and n. 42.

125. The "General Introduction to the Roman Missal" (*Institutio generalis Missalis Romani*), ch. 3, art. 66, which was released in 1969, gives permission to the Bishop's Conference to allow women to read the lessons preceding that of the Gospel, while remaining outside the chancel, in case no man qualified for the duty of lector is present. (*Missale Romanum*, [Vatican City: Typis Polyglottis Vaticanus, 1970], 45) The discrimination against woman contained in this regulation cannot be overlooked: she is admitted to the function of lector only in emergency, and the chancel is taboo for her. (Cf. the critical annotations about this by E. J. Lengeling, "Die neue Ordnung der Eucharistiefeier. Allgemeine Einfahrung in das römische Messbuch . . ." Introduction and Commentary, in *Lebendiger Gottesdienst*, ed. H. Rennings, no. 17/18 (Münster, 1970) 259. Some progress, though not a great deal, was made by the "Third Instruction concerning the Orderly Implementation of the Constitution on the Liturgy," of November 5, 1970: it declares in no. 7a, that the Bishops' Conference may decide where the woman is to stand for the reading. Cf *AAS* 62 (1970): 700.

126. "If however a priest is present, he should be preferred to a deacon, if a deacon [is present, he should be preferred] to a subdeacon if a cleric [is present, he should be preferred] to a layperson, if a male [is present, he should be preferred] to a female, unless because of modesty, it is more suitable for a female to baptize, or unless a female knows the form and method of baptizing better." Canon 742, § 2. An exception to the rule preferring men as the minster of baptism is thus permitted in only two cases: when propriety suggests that a woman baptize, or when the woman is better informed about the form and manner required for proper baptism.

127. *Das Kirchenrecht*, 4:29, with no. 4.

128. The date of the Synod is disputed. Hefele-Leclercq, 1/2:995, put it between 343 (Synod of Sardica) and 381 (Synod of Constantinople) and forego a more exact dating. On this see Franz Xaver von Funk, *Kirchengeschichtliche Abhandlungen und Untersuchungen* (Paderborn: F. Schöningh, 1897-190), 2:369: "As far as one can see from internal evidence, it is more likely to be the end rather

than the beginning of this period of time." Cf. also B. Kötting, "Laodiceia" in *LThK*, 6:794.

129. On this cf. p. 12, with n. 64 above.

130. The wording of which is as follows: "Πεί τοῦ μὴ δεῖν τάσ λεγομένασ πρεβύτιδασ, ἤτοι προκαθημέασ ἐν τῇ Ἐκκλησίᾳ καθίστθαι,"Hefele-Leclercq, 1/2:1003 (translated in Hefele, *Conciliengeschichte* 1:756): "That the so-called *presbytiden* or Mothers Superior should not be appointed in the church."

131. "Women who are called *prebyterae* among the Greeks, but by us, however, they are called elder widows (*viduae seniores*), a once-married women (*unvira*) and little mothers (*matriculariae*) ought not to be installed in a church as if they were appointed (*ordinatas*) to it." *Corpus*, ed. Friedberg 1:122. [Editor's note: On the difficulties involved in translating this passage, see Gary Macy, "The Ordination of Women in the Early Middle Ages," in *A History of Women and Ordination*, vol. 1, *The Ordination of Women in a Medieval Context*, ed. Bernard Cooke and Gary Macy, (Lanham, MD: Scarecrow Press, 2002) 7 and ns. 46, 48 and 49.]

132. *Corpus*, ed. Friedberg 1:122.

133. Schulte, *Die Geschichte der Quellen*, 1:69.

134. Hefele, *Conciliengeschichte* 1:757 (see n. 44 above).

135. *Adversus Haereses* 79, 3.4 (*PG* 42:743ff.).

136. But according to Epiphanius, the *presbytiden* are not, as Hefele interprets, the oldest among the deaconesses but rather the oldest among the widows. ("It should be carefully noted that the office of deaconesses alone was necessary to the ecclesiastical order, and furthermore the widows mentioned by name and among them, those who were the oldest called *presbytidas*, never were made *presbyteridas* (female presbyters) or *sacerdotissas* (female priests)," *PG*, 42,746.) See also Kalsbach, *Die altkirchliche Einrichtung*, 52, on this passage. It is clear from the context that Epiphanius is not speaking of an office of director of *presbytiden* in relation to deaconesses but only of the ministry of deaconesses (or of widows) to women, for instance in baptism. Presumably the widow of the *Testamentum Domini* (see Kalsbach, 41-45) had certain authority as director of the deaconesses.

137. Kalsbach, *Die altkirchliche Einrichtung*, 1:757.

138. Ibid., 1:757f.

139. E.g., according to Hefele, *Conciliengeschichte* 1:758, the first Synod of Orange (A.D. 441) in canon 26 ("Deaconesses are in no way to be ordained; if they already are, they should bow their heads when the people are blessed."); the Synod of Epaon (A.D. 517) in canon 21 ("We completely anull the consecration of widows, which they call deaconessses, in all our territories; imposing the blessing of penance only on those if they strive to change."); the second Synod of Orléans (A.D. 533) in canon 18 ("It has been resolved that henceforth the deaconal blessing is to be trusted to no females on account of their frailty.") Cf. also Kalsbach, *Die altkirchliche Einrichtung*, 1:86f.

140. Hefele, *Conciliengeschichte* 1:758, names Zonaras and Balsamon, famous canonists of the Orthodox Church of the 12th century, as representatives of this conception. Kalsbach, *Die altkirchliche Einrichtung*, 1:53 expressly follows Balsamon in the interpretation of the canon. ("It is hardly likely that the canon directs itself against a simple honoring of age by granting seats of honor in the church. Balsamon read the canon more correctly, when he combined the ἐν Ἐκκλησίᾳ with προκαθημέασ instead of with καθίστθαι—a prohibition against giving elder women disciplinary authority over other women.")

141. On this cf. p. 8, with n. 40 above.

142. Cf. their note on v. *Mulieres*, *Corpus*, ed. Friedberg 1:122.

143. Cf. Hefele, *Conciliengeschichte* 1:759.

144. Cf., e.g., canon 30 (prohibition of community bathing of clerics and male laypersons with women); canon 52 (prohibition of weddings during periods of fast); canon 53 (prohibition of dancing at weddings); canon 54 (prohibition of clerics' watching plays at weddings or at banquets). Cf. Hefele, *Conciliengeschichte* 1:768ff.

145. B. Kötting, "Laodiceia," LThK, 6:794.

146. On this cf. n. 53 above.

147. "We decree that deaconesses ought not be ordained before forty years of age, and this with diligent examination. If a deaconess truly had taken ordination and she had carried out this ministry for whatever length of time, and afterwards handed herself over to marriage, doing injury to the grace of God, she would be anathema along with him who joined her in this marriage." *Corpus*, ed. Friedberg 1:1055.

148. *Corpus*, ed. Friedberg 1:1047.

149. The *Concilium Trullanum* (A.D. 691-692) repeats this regulation in canon 14; cf. Hefele-Leclercq, 3/1:565. The regulation provided for a certain amount of easing of the law of the emperor Theodosius the Great, which was issued in 390, on the basis of 1 Tim. 5:9, and which had set the minimum age for admission of women to the diaconate at 60. See Hefele-Leclercq, 2/2:803; Kalsbach, *Die altkirchliche Einrichtung*, 1:63. Explaining the age determination of forty years in canon 15 of Chalcedon, Balsamon, following Zonaras, gives the following basis for it, which clearly documents a conception of the inferiority of women: "As women are most easily either to be taken in by deception or willingly to give in to her lower nature, by the sanction of this canon, it has been forbidden to choose deaconesses of less than forty years of age," *PG* 137:442f.

150. Cf. p. 6, above.

151. That is to say, he talks about these two in the other chapters of *questio* 1 in *causa* 27, insofar as the chapters refer to women.

152. Bruns, *Canones Apostolorum et Conciliorum saeculorum* 1:29, with n. 14; cf. also canon 14 of the Trullian Synod (Bruns, 1:42), where the concept χειροτονεῖσθαι is used for the consecration of the deaconess as well as for the consecration of the presbyter and that of the deacon.

153. Cf. the Latin form of the formula in Giuseppe Luigi Assemani, *Codex liturgicus ecclesiae universae*, (Rome: Ex typographia Komarek, apud Angelum

Rotilium, 1749-66) 11:115, and an excerpt from it in M. Blastares, *Syntagma alphabeticum* lit. Γ c. 11 (*PG* 144:1173). Both are printed in Kalsbach, *Die altkirchliche Einrichtung*, 69ff.

154. Cf. Kalsbach, *Die altkirchliche Einrichtung*, 71.

155. Cf. *Didascalia et Constitutiones Apostolorum*, 1:522ff.

156. "Stand fast, O Lord; do not reject women, who are themselves consecrated and willing, as it is taught, to minister in your holy house, but receive them into the order of ministers, bestow the grace of your Holy Spirit to this your handmaiden, who wishes to consecrate herself to you, make full the grace of the diaconate and the ministry as you bestowed the grace of your ministry to Phoebe, whom you called to the work of this administration. . . ." *Codex liturgicus* 11:115, quoted from Kalsbach, *Die altkirchliche Einrichtung*, 70f.

157. Cf. Kalsbach, *Die altkirchliche Einrichtung*, 109. ("The χειροονία of the deaconess with its ceremonies is in form parallel to that of the deacon. All consecration formulas, from those of the *Apostolic Constitutions* and the *Testamentum* to those of the Monophysites and the Nestorians and that handed down by Matthaeus Blastares, bear witness to this fact.") See also J. Funk, "Klerikale Frauen?" in *Österreichisches Archiv für Kirchenrecht*, 14 (1963): 278, 280; J. Daniélou, "Le ministère des femmes dans l'Église ancienne," *La Maison-Dieu*, 61 (1960): 95.

158. Thus A. Ludwig, "Weibliche Kleriker in der altchristlichen und frühmittelalterlichen Kirche," in *Theologisch-praktische Monatschrift* 20 (1910): 548-557, 609-617; 21 (1911): 141-149. Long before Ludwig, Joannus Morinus, *Commentarius de sacris ecclesiae ordinationibus* (Antwerp: B. Bellaevallis, 1695) p. 3. ex. 10, f. 143ff. Kalsbach, *Die altkirchliche Einrichtung*, 109. (However in his opinion the widow-deaconess stands between the clergy of lower and those of higher gradation of consecration.) Also Plöchl, *Geschichte*, 1:69; Daniélou, "Le ministère des femmes," 86.

159. E.g., Schäfer, *Kanonissenstifter*, 48-50; and his "Kanonissen und Diakonissen" in Römische Quartalschrift für christliche Altertumskunde und für Kirchengeschichte 24 (1910): 67f.; Funk, "Klerikale Frauen?" 278 (289 in reference to the consecration of the Roman deaconess). The sacramental character of the consecration of deaconesses is not excluded by these authors, and likewise not by Ch. R. Meyer, "Ordained Women in the Early Church," in *The Catholic Citizen* 53 (1967): 118. ("To push the argument against the sacramentality of the ordination of deaconesses too far would be in fact to deny the sacramentality of the ordination of deacons.") Zscharnack, *Der Dienst der Frau*, 113, 117, 149, speaks of the clerical character of the office of deaconess without further differentiation.

160. Thus Pohle and Gierens, *Lehrbuch der Dogmatik*, 3:582. ("Although deaconesses were blessed by ecclesiastical ceremony and among the Greeks even by the laying on of hands [see *Constitutiones Apostolorum*, 8, 19 sq.], this was no consecration . . ." It seems "hasty" to conclude, he thinks, "that the consecration of deaconesses was formerly assigned to the *ordines minores* . . . or even to the *ordines maiores*.") Similarly Premm, *Katholische Glaubenskunde*, 3/2:242;

Thomas Specht, *Lehrbuch der Dogmatik*, 2nd ed. (Regensburg: Manz, 1912), 2 vols., 2:397; Johannes Brinktrine, *Die Lehre von den heiligen Sakramenten der katholischen Kirche,* (Paderborn: F. Schöningh, 1962), 2:196; Emil Friedberg, *Lehrbuch des katholischen und evangelischen Kirchenrecht,* 6th ed: (Leipzig: B. Tauchnitz, 1909), 165, n. 2; Georg Phillips, *Kirchenrecht*, 3rd ed. (Regensberg: Pustet, 1855) 1:449f. Some of the writers mentioned (e.g., Pohle, Specht, Brinktrine, Friedberg, Phillips) derive their contentions from 1 Cor. 14:34f. and 1 Tim. 2:11ff. and in this way their judgment of the sources about the deaconess and her ordination is not free from bias. Others (e.g., Premm) depend on canon 11 of the Council of Nicea, which they interpret to mean that the deaconess received no imposition of hands and consequently she was numbered among the laity. But there is a difference of opinion about the meaning of the canon in question: cf. Kalsbach, *Die altkirchliche Einrichtung*, 46ff.; another meaning is possible, according to Funk, "Klerikale Frauen?" 227, Morinus, *Commentarius de sacris ecclesiae ordinationibus*, f. 148, Daniélou, "Le ministère des femmes," 86 and others. But in any case the laying of hands on the deaconess is specifically provided for by later councils: cf. canon 15 of the Council of Chalcedon and canon 14 of the Trulian Synod. Therefore Morinus, f. 143f., rightly opposes the viewpoint of those theologians who dispute any ordination (capability) of women "If anyone was so strict or harsh he or she sees nothing that looks to the ecclesiatical ordination, and disuputes the ability to concede it to women, he or she is easily refuted by the most ancient traditions of many secular [sources], and is checked by their gravity."

161. Pohle and Gierens, *Lehrbuch der Dogmatik* 3:582; Premm, *Katholische Glaubenskunde*, 3/2:242; Brinktrine, *Die Lehre von den heiligen Sakramenten*, 196. Friedberg, *Lehrbuch des katholischen und evangelischen Kirchenrecht*, 165, n. 2, speaks, but without justification from source materials, only of an activity of the deaconess in the care of the sick and the poor. (In opposition to this, Zscharnack, *Der Dienst der Frau*, 137, says: "The heart of her office has certainly never been and never became the care of the sick.") None of the writers mentioned refers to the authorization to distribute the Holy Communion that the deaconess had in some geographical areas.

162. Concerning the lesser authorization of deaconesses in baptizing, in contrast to that of the deacons, see p. 16, with n. 110 above. A liturgical neglect of the deaconess is likewise found in *Constitutiones Apostolorum*, 28, 4-6 (*Didascalia et Constitutiones Apostolorum*, ed. Funk, 1:530f.). Note also the Nestorian *Ordo chirotoniae mulierum diaconissarum* (in Heinrich Denzinger, *Ritus Orientalium Coptorum Syrorum et Armenorum in administrandis sacramentis* [Würzburg: typis et sumptibus Stahelianis, 1863/64; reprint, Graz: Akademische Druck-u. Verlagsanstalt, 1961] 2:261), to which a marginal note remarks: "A [deaconess] does not accede to the altar, however, since she is a woman" Denzinger, *Ritus Orientalium*, 1:123.

163. On this see the preceding note, 162, and also n. 44 and n. 54 above. Canon 18 of the Synod of Orleans (A.D. 533) decrees: "It has been resolved that

henceforth the deaconal blessing is to be trusted to no females on account of their frailty." Mansi, 8:35.

164. Cf. Kalsbach, *Die altkirchliche Einrichtung*, 66, who in this context (66, n. 5 and 68) points out that the Chalcedonian decree is more strict about the marriage of the deaconess than about that of the God-consecrated virgin, as the Chalcedonian canon 16 shows.

165. Cf. Kalsbach, *Die altkirchliche Einrichtung*, p. 65, concerning the Byzantine deaconess. ("The evidence is overwhelming in its characterization of the deaconess as appointed by the church and of her task, mainly baptismal assistance, as ecclesiastical service; and also in indicating her accountability to ecclesiastical officials.") Cf. also Funk, "Klerikale Frauen?" 276.

166. About this see Kalsbach, *Die altkirchliche Einrichtung*, 29f., 45, 57f.; also his article "Diakonisse," in *Reallexikon für Antike und Christentum*, Theodor Klauser, ed. (Stuttgart: A. Hiersemann, 1950-) (hereafter *RAC*) 3:919ff.; Schäfer, *Kanonissenstifter*, 32, 58f.; Zscharnack, *Der Dienst der Frau*, 137-139. Deaconesses, or widows and sanctimonials—as the case might be—carried out similar functions in particular areas of the Western Church but they soon became an object of strife. Cf. Schäfer, *Kanonissenstifter*, 32, 59f.; Funk, "Klerikale Frauen?" 2791f.; Heinzelmann, *Schwestern*, 55.

167. See E. Herman, "Balsamon," in *Dictionnaire de Droit Canonique* Rajesh K. Naz, ed., (Paris: Librarie Letouzey, 1935-1965) (hereafter *DDC*) 2:76-83.

168. "Once when the orders of canons of deaconesses were recognized, they had their own status at the altar. However, the defilement of the ministry by those menstruating expelled them from the divine and holy altar. In the most holy Church of the See of Constantinople, however deaconesses were appointed, not having the one connection with the altar [with the deacons] nevertheless, having agreement [with them] in a certain sense in many things, and directing womenhood to ecclesiatical unity." *Responsa ad interrogationes Marci* (Interr. 35), *PG* 138:987. Similarly M. Blastares (Greek canonist in the first half of the 14th century), *Syntagma Alphabeticum* Γ c. 11, *PG* 144:1174. ("What the ministry of the deaconesses in the clergy was in those times no one today knows. There are some who say that [deaconesses} ministered to women being baptized. Others say that they were allowed to come to the sacred altar and to exercise the office of the deacons along with them. Clearly the Fathers prohibited this access and their ministry there [at the altar] because of their involuntary menstrual flow.")

169. Cf. Schäfer, *Kanonissenstifter*, 58; Kalsbach, *Die altkirchliche Einrichtung*, 57, 68 ("Balsamon understands the correct relationship, when he sees the lay deaconess as ordinary, the nun deaconess as extraordinary").

170. Cf. Schäfer, *Kanonissenstifter*, 55ff.; Zscharnack, *Der Dienst der Frau*, 153f., 156 ("Early Christianity and the ancient church were both willing to legitimize the service of women and to use them . . . for the upbuilding of the church; then heresy, hierarchy and monasticism became the evil enemies which choked the seed.")

171. "The things which are treated in the present canon have fallen out of use entirely. The deaconess, in fact, today are not ordained, even if certain female ascetic are improperly called deaconesses. There is in fact a canon that decrees that women ought not to enter into the sacred tribunal. How therefore is she who is not able to approach the holy altar, able to exercise the office of a deacon?" in *Canones SS, Apostolorum, Conciliorum commentaria* (in canon 15 Conc. Chalced.), *PG* 137:442.

172. Cf. *Corpus*, ed. Friedberg 1:637 with n. 397; *Corpus Iuris Civilis*, ed. Paulus Krueger, Theodore Mommsen and Rudolfus Schoell (Berlin: Werdmannsche Bundhandlung, 1904-1906) 3:609.

173. Cf. Kalsbach, *Die altkirchliche Einrichtung*, 66 with n. 4.

174. Cf. *Corpus*, ed. Friedberg 1:1057, n. 403; *Juliani epitome latina Novellarum Justiniani*, Gustavus Haenel, ed., (Leipzig: apud Hinrichsium, 1837), 162ff.

175. According to Kalsbach, *Die altkirchliche Einrichtung*, 67, female ascetics (*ascetriae*) are women who live in a more free community form than cloistered nuns.

176. See Kalsbach, *Die altkirchliche Einrichtung* , 65; Funk, "Klerikale Frauen?" 276f.; Heinzelmann, *Schwestern*, 63f.

177. Cf.. Schulte, *Die Geschichte der Quellen*, 1:61f.; Stickler, *Historia iuris canonici*, 1:210.

178. Schulte, *Die Geschichte der Quellen*, 1:70, maintains that while it is true that the *dicta Gratiani* had no legal authority, they did have significant doctrinal authority, insofar as they were not in specific cases disapproved by the schools. He says that Gratian's statements are "a very important witness, even a definitive witness, to the conceptions of his time." Cf. also Stickler, *Historia iuris canonici*, 1:212.

179. "Women however are unable to advance not only to the priesthood but even to the diaconate . . . ," *Corpus*, ed. Friedberg 1:750.

180. See pp. 24ff.

181. According to Funk, "Klerikale Frauen?" 280, these are the decretals of Benedict VIII (1012-1024), *Patrologiae cursus completus*, Latin series, Jacques-Paul Migne, ed. (Paris: Migne, 1878-1890) (hereafter *PL*) 139:1621 or John XIX (1024-1032), *PL* 78:1056; and of Leo IX (1049-1054), *PL* 143:602.

182. See Schäfer, *Kanonissenstifter*, 50 with n. 1.

183. Thus Schäfer, *Kanonissenstifter*, 50 and Funk, "Klerikale Frauen?" 280.

184. Schäfer, *Kanonissenstifter*, 49f.

185. Funk, "Klerikale Frauen?" 279f.; Kalsbach, *Die altkirchliche Einrichtung*, 85ff.; Schäfer, *Kanonissenstifter*, 56ff.; Zscharnack, *Der Dienst der Frau*, 122.

186. Cf. Kalsbach, *Die altkirchliche Einrichtung*, 72, 99; Schäfer, *Kanonissenstifter*, 57, Heinzelmann, *Schwestern*, 55, 65f.

187. Cf. Kalsbach, *Die altkirchliche Einrichtung*, 65, 110; Schäfer, *Kanonissenstifter*, 57, n. 1.

188. Concerning this source—*epistola 8* of Bishop Otto of Vercelli (died A. D. 960)—see Kalsbach, *Die altkirchliche Einrichtung*, 92f.

189. According to Kalsbach, *Die altkirchliche Einrichtung*, 80ff., 110ff, the prevailing form of the feminine diaconate in the West (that is, in Rome, but not in Gaul) was somewhat different from that of the Orient: the Roman (Italian) deaconess was simply "God-consecrated" and not (as the Oriental and the Gaulic deaconess) the holder of an office. See also Kalsbach, "Diakonisse," in *RAC*, 3:926. Here Kalsbach disputes the point of view of Schäfer, *Kanonissenstifter*, 47f., 50, n. 1, according to which the Western deaconess was also holder of office.

190. Cf. the discussion on pp. 83f and 86f.

191. That could also be concluded by the manner in which Gratian arranges and uses canon 15 of the Council of Chalcedon (*causa* 27, *questio* 1, c. 35), which refers to the deaconess. See p. 23 above.

192. As first of the decretists, Rufinus—and then in dependence on him the subsequent decretists—specifically disputes the sacramentality of the deaconess consecration. On this cf. p. 81.

193. See pp. 80f. with n. 76.

194. While as already mentioned (see Part 1, n. 8, above) Gillman ignores this aspect of the question, R. Metz rightly devotes a large section of his study, "Statut," 61-82 (See Introduction, n. 9). Van der Meer, "Priestertum der Frau?" also (99-103) makes a thorough study of this problem and urges (7) an investigation of the time-conditioned prohibitions relating to women.

195. See also Metz, "Statut," 73ff.; and his "Recherches," 379-396 (see Introduction, n. 9 above).

196. *Corpus*, ed. Friedberg 1:750f.

197. According to Friedberg, *Corpus*, ed. Friedberg 1:484, n. 37, this is a section from a Pseudo-Isidorian letter. Cf. Hinschius, *Decretales*, 162.

198. "Women however are unable to advance not only to the priesthood but even to the diaconate, therefore they are intrinsically able neither to accuse priests nor to testify against them." *Corpus*, ed. Friedberg 1:750.

199. Gratian often uses this method; concerning this as well as concerning the significance of Roman law for the evaluation and position of women in the church, see the discussion on pp. 34 and 121ff.

200. *Corpus*, ed. Friedberg 1:750f, n. 3, cites as source from Roman law *Dig.* 50, 17, 2, to which Gratian presumably refers. ("Females are excluded from all civil or public offices and therefore are able to be neither judges nor to conduct nor to seek the office of magistrate nor to intervene for another nor to act as procurators." *Corpus Iuris Civilis*, 1:868.) The cases of exception to the general complainant prohibition for women—which Roman law sets up as exceptions—are given by Gratian as cc. 1-4 in *causa* 15, *questio* 3. It is apparent from his *dictum, p.c.* 4 in *causa* 15, *questio* 3, § 2, that the canonical law follows Roman legal regulations in both normal and exceptional cases.

201. *Corpus*, ed. Friedberg 1:750f

202. The patristic texts which Gratian uses as cc. 11-20 in *causa* 33, *questio* 5, exhibit in part a similar point of view. Cf. p. 33-34.

203. On this cf. chapter 6, p. 178f.

204. See *Corpus*, ed. Friedberg 1:1144, n. 155. Since the early Middle Ages, the oldest Latin commentary on the Pauline letters (called "Ambrosiaster," a characterization also used for the author of the commentary; cf. Wilhelm Mundle, *Die Exegese der paulinischen Briefe im Kommentar des Ambrosiaster*, [Marburg: C. Schaaf, 1919], 8, n. 1) was mistakenly attributed to Ambrose, until proven spurious by Erasmus of Rotterdam. Throughout the Middle Ages the assumption that Ambrose was the author was so dominant that it silenced all evidence to the contrary. Cf. Otto Bardenhewer, *Geschichte der altkirchlichen Literatur.* (Freiberg: Herder, 1902-1932) 3:520. Yet Gratian remarks, probably following Peter Lombard, *Sentences*, book 4, c. 35 (*Magistri Petri Lombardi Sententiae in IV Libris Distinctae,* PP. Collegium S. Bonaventurae, eds., [Editiones Collegii S. Bonaventurae: ad Claras Aquas, 1916], 2:959): "But this (passage) from Ambrose is said to have been inserted by falsifiers." (*dictum p. c.* 18 in *causa* 32, *questio* 7), *Corpus*, ed. Friedberg 1:1145. However, this recognition of the possibility that the Ambrose text is spurious disappears from the following text.

205. The commentary of Ambrosiaster on 1 Cor. 7:10f., which Gratian presents in shortened form as c. 17 (*Corpus*, ed. Friedberg 1:1144), reads in full as follows: "'A wife is not to separate from her husband (*vir*); if she should separate, she is to remain unmarried.' Here the advice of the Apostle is that if she would separate because of wicked intercourse by the husband (*vir*), she now ought to remain unmarried. 'Or she ought to be reconciled to her husband (*vir*).' If she is not able to control herself, he says, because she does not wish to fight against the flesh, she ought to be reconciled to her husband (*vir*); it is not permitted to the women, if she is married, to dismiss her husband (*vir*) for the cause of fornication or apostasy. . . . If however her husband (*vir*) apostatizes, or seeks to alter the custom of his wife, the woman is neither able to marry not to return to him. 'And the husband (*vir*) is not to dismiss his wife.' This should be understood, on the other hand, except for the cause of fornication. And for that reason he is not subservient as is the woman, (the Apostle) saying that if she would be dismissed, she is to remain that way. Since it is allowed for a male to take a wife if he would dismiss a sinning wife because a male is not thus constrained by the law as is a woman, the male is the head of the woman." *PL* 17:230. The manner of argumentation is quite characteristic; the alleged superiority of men is pleaded in order to legitimize, legally, greater marital liberties for men! Othmar Heggelbacher, *Vom romischen zum chistilichen Recht. Juristische Elemente in den Schriften des sog. Ambrosiaster* (Freiberg: Universitätsverlag, 1959), 127f., remarks that the viewpoint of Ambrosiaster has been influenced by Roman law, but he has to admit (127, n. 1) that church discipline, too, in many areas grants men certain privileges in marriage. For example, the penitential discipline of Asia Minor recognized only the unfaithfulness of women as adultery and punished it with fifteen years of penitence, but the same infraction committed by men was punished only by the seven year penitence set up for extramarital sexual relations. Concerning the influence of Ambrosiaster's position on church discipline, see also

B. Kurtscheid, *Die christliche Ehe* in *Religiöse Quellenschriften*, 54, J. Walterscheid, ed., (Düssefdorf: Schwann,1928), 20.

206. "Some truly desiring to preserve the statement of Ambrose judge that when a husband (*vir*) dimisses a wife on account off some fornication and then takes another, the dismissed wife still living, this is not to be understood as any kind of fornication, but only of incestuous fornication." Gratian corrects this interpretation in the following way: "But since it is permitted by no authority that with a wife living, another is added, this [teaching] of Ambrose is to be understood as is the above stated order of fornication; not that he is able to take another [wife] with the dismissed one still living, but after the death of the fornicator (male or female). . . . The one who is innocent of fornication, male or female, is able to be married to others; adulterers on the other hand if they would outlive (their spouse) are in no way able to be married to others." *dictum p.c.* 18 in *causa* 32, *questio* 7, *Corpus*, ed. Friedberg 1:1145. Charles Munier, *Les sources patristiques du droit de l'Eglise du VIII*[e] *au XIII*[e] *siécle* (Mulhouse: Salvator, 1957), 188; points out that this method of changing the meaning of a text in order to save the authority of the author was often used by the compilers of the Middle Ages, which show their great dependence on authority.

207. "Here if he disagrees that no more is allowed to a male than to a woman if a male is cuckolded in some way by another, he ought to know that a male (*virum*) is not called (this) by Ambrose because of his sex, but the strength of his soul (*animi virtute*); he judges a woman (*mulierem*) in some sense literally not by the sex of her body, but the softness of her mind (*mollicie mentis*)." *Corpus*, ed. Friedberg 1:1145.

208. Cf. Karl E. Georges, *Ausführliches lateinisch-deutsches Handwörterbuch* (Basel: B. Schwabe, 1962), 2:201.

209. *Corpus*, ed. Friedberg 1:1145.

210. Patristic statements are the main medium through which Gratian received (cf. p. 29f.) the deprecatory conception of women and the over-rating of men which is already present in the Old Testament (cf., e.g., Ecc. 7:25-28; Ecclesiasticus 19:2; Jer. 49:22; also see chapter 6, pp. 168f.). In the Fathers we often come across the conception of the female sex as essentially base, weak in character and wicked. (Cf. K. Thraede, "Frau," in *RAC*, 8:257ff.) This conception may be traced not only to Jewish sources but also to gnostic-dualistic and neoplatonic sources. (Thraede, 242f.) A result of this manner of thinking is that the Fathers characterize a woman, who, surprisingly enough, exhibits faith and virtue, as "*vir*" (male). Thus Ambrose, *Expositio evangelii secundum Lucam* 10, 161: "Jesus said about this: a women who does not believe is a woman and still is named according to her bodily sex, but one who believes acquires the perfection of a man and no longer has the worldly designation according to her bodily sex." *Corpus scriptorum ecclesiasticorum latinorum* (Vienna: C. Geroldi, 1866-) (hereafter *CSEL*), 32, 4, p. 517; Jerome, *Commentariorum in epistolam ad Ephesios*, book 3, c. 5: "Insofar as a woman serves by bearing children and sons, she has the difference from a male that a body has from a soul. If, however, she should change to serve Christ rather than the world, she will cease to be a woman

and will be called a man." *PL* 26:567; Berengaud, *Expositio in Apocalypsin*, on 12:5: "The feminine sex is weak: a female therefore who having taken on strength of soul, conquers the devil, and strives to please God through good works, not incongruously is called a male, since although in the body she might be female, by virtue of the soul is the equal of good males." *PL* 17:960, *ad opera S. Ambrosii appendix*. Cf. also the primary sources given by Van der Meer, "Priestertum der Frau?" 78ff.

211. See Willibald M. Plöchl, *Das Eherecht des Magisters Gratianus*, (Leipzig: F. Deuticke, 1935) (thereafter cited as *Eherecht*), 37-43.

212. Marianne Weber, *Ehefrau und Mutter in dr Rechsentwicklung* (Tübingen: Mohr, 1907), 181, refers to this fact and to its negative consequences for the personal development of women. Investigating the influence of Christianity on the legal situation of women, she notes that, "Christianity trained men to control their sexual drives, which certainly raised the position of women a great deal, both within and without, and in very definite forms. But on the other hand, the new teaching allowed for the principle of patriarchalism: actual and legal subordination of women as spouse and mother, just as it was found in the Orient, its principles unchanged and even strengthened in many aspects, so that it became a reactionary force in the area of feminine freedom. Because those conceptions of the nature of marriage and the position of women, conditioned as they were by the circumstances of that age, were considered to be the will of God, they hardened into dogma and as such became normative for the whole Christian culture into modern times. Such facts account for the delay of progress in women's rights and the development of their personalities."

213. *Corpus*, ed. Friedberg 1:1254.

214. That is proved, for instance, by the 11th-century wedding ritual of the diocese of Salsbury, which was widely used. Here is the vow made by the bride: "I N., take you, N., to be my wedded husband, to have and to hold from this day forward, in good fortune and in bad fortune, in wealth and in poverty, in sickness and in health, to be modest and obedient in bed and at table, until we are parted by death." (quoted from Joseph Freisen, *Das Eheschliessungsrecht in Spanien, Grossbritannien und Irland und Skandinavien in geschichtlicher Entwicklung mit Abdruck vieler alter Urkunden dargestellt* [Paderborn: Schöningh, 1919], 2:75). Gratian too sees the supremacy of man as preventing an actual equalization in marriage relationship. See this discussion on pp. 38f. Noteworthy also in this connection is the discussion by J. A. Brundage, "The Crusader's Wife: A Canonistic Quandary," in *Studia Gratiana* 12 (1967), 427-441. According to Brundage, it is true that Gratian insisted that a husband was dependent upon his wife's approval, if he wanted to embark on a Crusade. But at the beginning of the 13th century two decretals of Innocent III changed the existing law to allow a man to go on a Crusade without the approval of his wife (434f.). On the contrary, a man was not by any means required to respect a vow of his wife to take part in a Crusade, even if he had already given his permission; although not in itself allowed, he could in fact retract his permission (432, n. 17).

215. Cf. the patristic authorities, which Gratian cites in support of his theory in *causa* 33, *questio* 5, exact explanation of this appears on pp. 29ff.; see also chapter 6, pp. 177ff.

216. Cf. Metz, "Recherches" 381f.; also chapter 6, pp. 180ff. But besides the harmony of the married couple, the obligation of the wife to be subordinate to her husband is also stressed by Paul in Eph. 5. This subordination likewise results from the concept of 'body'—a fact not sufficiently noted, it seems to me, by Metz.

217. See on this chapter 6, pp. 177f., 180.

218. "Because truly in other matters the man is the head of the woman and the woman the body of the man, a woman is able accordingly to promise a vow of abstinence if the man permits; nevertheless, if permission is withdrawn by him, it is not valid or fulfilled; and this is, as we have said, because of the situation of submission by which she ought to be subject to the male in all things, and this is, as we have said, because of the condition of servitude [of the wife], since she must be subject to her husband in everything." *Corpus*, ed. Friedberg 1:1254.

219. There is more on pp. 29ff., about these patristic authorities.

220. *Corpus*, ed. Friedberg 1:1256.

221. Cf. Num. 30:11-15 (especially v. 14: "Any vow and any sworn duty to fast can be validated or invalidated by her husband"). Also see p. 31-32.

222. Cf. Gen. 20:3; Ex. 20:17; 21:22; 2 Sam. 11:26; see also chapter 6, pp. 101f.

223. Especially in regard to the sacrament of penance, the dependence of women on men is very often experienced as basically unacceptable and discriminatory: in no secular area of such a private nature is there such a great dependency. For instance, a woman is free to consult with and be treated by women physicians and psychotherapists. This possibility of choice is generally experienced by women as truly beneficial: not otherwise would she experience and appreciate such a freedom in the sphere of religion. Cf. on this problem Heinzelmann, *Schwestern*, 27f.

224. Metz, "Statut," 74.

225. Cf. Metz, "Recherches," 379 ("Cette condition [d'infériorité] se traduisait par une série d'incapacités auxquelles la femme était soumise, *tout particuliérement dans les fonctions du culte public*"); see also Metz, "Statut," 97ff.,108.

226. The opinion of Schulte, *Die Geschichte der Quellen*, 1:70—"Gratian's statements represent a very important, even definitive witness to the outlook of his age"—applies also in this specific point.

227. Cf. Munier, *Les sources patristiques*, 167.

228. Ibid., 159f.

229. Ibid., 184: "Pour l'interprétation des Ecritures la science des saints docteurs et les lumières de l'Esprit Saint, qui les assiste les recommandent de préférence à tous autres commentateurs, fussent-ils même souverains pontifes." cf. also *distinctio* 20, *princ.* § 1.

230. Patristic scriptural proofs for the subordination, a characteristic biblical understanding not overcome even today, will be investigated more exactly in chapter 6.

231. *Corpus*, ed. Friedberg 1:1254; the *Editio Romana* adds after "that he might be made the one," "somewhat like the Lord" in a note to c. 13.

232. *Corpus*, ed. Friedberg 1:1255.

233. Friedberg, *Corpus*, ed. Friedberg 1:1254, n. 130, remarks on c. 13 only: "they [these texts] are not Augustine's"; a corresponding assertion for c. 19 is lacking.

234. Concerning the mistaken attribution of the Ambrosiaster commentary to Ambrose during the Middle Ages, see n. 204, above; concerning the mistaken attribution of the *Questiones* to Augustine, cf. A. Souter's prolegomena to the edition of the *Questiones* in *CSEL* 50, VII.

235. Alexander Souter, *A Study of Ambrosiaster* (Cambridge: Cambridge University Press, 1905), proved the identity of the author by means of linguistic investigations. Cf. also Mundle, *Die Exegese*, 13f. and Bardenhewer, *Geschichte* 3:524. On the basis of studies in legal history, Heggelbacher, *Vom romischen zum chistilichen Recht*, confirms Souter's conclusions. Cf. the rescension of P. Mikat, *ZRG* Kan. Abt. 48 (1962): 362.

236. See Mundle, *Die Exegese*, 9-13 and H. J. Vogel's prolegomena to the edition of the Ambrosiaster commentary in *Ambrosiastri qui dicitur Commentarius in Epistulas Paulinas*, Henry Joseph Vogels, ed., (Hoelder-Pichler: Vienna, 1966-1969) (*CSEL* 81, pt. 1-3), IX-XVII.

237. Cf. Heggelbacher, *Vom romischen zum chistilichen Recht*, 4; so too Mundle, *Die Exegese*, 14. Concerning Ambrosiaster's origin and manner of thinking, Mundle thinks he was "a Roman of the highest order" (13).

238. While Paul in 1 Cor. 11:7 characterizes woman as the "reflected glory of man," Ambrosiaster draws a sharper conclusion from the words of the apostle: "woman covers her head" (cf. vss. 6 and 10) "because she is not the glory or the image of God."

239. *Corpus*, ed. Friedberg 1:1256.

240. See chapter 6, pp. 177f.

241. *Corpus*, ed. Friedberg 1:1255.

242. "And indeed, the word of the Lord is blasphemed either when the first determination of God is held in contempt and produced for nothing, or when the gospel of Christ is defamed, when against both faith and the law of nature, she who is a Christian and subject to the law of God, sought to rule over a male, when gentile females on the other hand serve their males by the common law of nature." *Corpus*, ed. Friedberg 1:1255.

243. "It is the natural order in humans that females serve males and children parents, since in this is justice that the lesser serve the greater," *Corpus*, ed. Friedberg 1:1255, 125.4.

244. Metz, "Statut," 72; also cf. Metz, "Recherches," 383f.

245. Cf. Felix Flückiger, *Geschichte des Naturrechtes* (Zurich: Evangelischer Verlag,1954), 1:175, 465f.

246. Ibid., 174, 465.

247. *Sancti Aureli Augustini questionum in heptateuchum libri VII*, Joseph Zycha, ed., *CSEL* 28/2, (Vienna: F. Tempsky, 1895), 80. On the question of the deviation of Gratian's text from the original, see the *Notatio correctorum* to c. 12, *Corpus*, ed. Friedberg 1:1253.

248. *Pseudo-Augustini questiones Veteris et Novi Testamenti*, Alexander Souter, ed., *CSEL* 50 (Vienna: F. Tempsky, 1908), 83.

249. As c. 17 in *causa* 33, *questio* 5. (*Corpus*, ed. Friedberg 1:1255; Friedberg, in n. 176, still ascribed the text to Augustine.) The introductory half-sentence ("How truly . . . "), which indicates the causal connection between the subject status of woman and her not-in-the-image-of-God situation, is lacking in Gratian.

250. The prohibition is especially concerned with matters relating to wills. Cf. p. 37. Also in Jewish rabbinical law women were not competent to act as witnesses. Cf. Jeremias, *Jerusalem zur Zeit Jesu*, 412.

251. Cf. the regulation of Roman law cited in n. 200, also see pp. 35f.

252. Cf. Heggelbacher, *Vom romischen zum chistilichen Recht*, 46ff., concerning the positive attitude of Ambrosiaster to Roman law.

253. Cf. Heggelbacher, *Vom romischen zum chistilichen Recht*, 48 with n. 1 and n. 2. Ambrosiaster's crude denigration of women is however minimized rather than criticized by Heggelbacher (32-36). The recension of P. Mikat (*ZRG* Kan. Abt. 48 (1962): 367f.) uncovers this failure of Heggelbacher. He refers to Heggelbacher's sentence, "Since women were obviously full members of the Christian community from the first and since Christianity by preserving the subordination of wife to husband has brought about the equalization of the sexes . . ." (32f.). On the contrary, Mikat says, we see no "equalization" when we look at the position of women in marriage, in the family, in the church and in public life, even after the victory of Christianity in the ancient world, and Heggelbacher's evidence from Ambrosiaster's writings do not in any way justify such a conclusion. In fact Heggelbacher is guilty of a mistaken interpretation when he affirms (35) that according to Ambrosiaster the position of women is *different* from that of men. Actually what Ambrosiaster clearly says (35, n. 3) is that their position is a *lesser* one: "A woman in fact because she is an inferior person, caused by her condition, not by nature, to be subservient to a male, is commanded then to fear him" (*Commentarius in Epistulas Paulinas*, 5:33). A similar minimizing and extenuating interpretation of the statements of Ambrosiaster about women (e.g., that they are not the image of God) is given by L. Voelkl ("Vom römischen zum christlichen Recht," in *Römische Quartalschrift für christliche Altertumskunde und Kirchengeschichte* 60 [1965]: 26): "This negation of women does not imply any denigration of the female sex; it only intends to say that women do not actively participate in God's creative work, and that in their maternal readiness they reply only (!) with a Yes to the call of God. This evaluation of the nature of women coincides with the Roman legal understanding of the position of women, in regard to their legal competence in public affairs."

254. The preconceived opinion of the psychic inferiority of women was supported by "scientific" results, in order to justify in this way the exclusion of women from higher education and especially from study in the university. Theodor Ludwig Wilhelm von Bischoff, *Das Studium und die Ausübung der Medizin durch Frauen* (Munich: Literarisch-artistische Anstalt, T. Riede, 1872) concludes from the different shape of the female skull and the smaller weight of the female brain that they possess only small capability in mental endeavor and therefore are not able to undertake university studies. Also Paul Möbius built his theory of the "weak-mindedness" of women on the "results" of investigations of brain anatomy (*Uber den physiologischen Schwachsinn des Weibes* [Halle: Carl Marhold, 1900]). It was because of the objections and prejudices of this and similar kinds against the intellectual development of women that women were not officially admitted to the universities of Germany until the beginning of this century (in Baden in 1901, in Prussia in 1908). (See the *Handbuch der Frauenbewegung*, Helene Lange and Gertrud Bäumer, eds., [Berlin: W. Moeser, 1901-1906], 5 vols. 1:72ff., 95f.) According to a questionnaire answered by university professors and docents in 1953-1955 concerning their attitude towards women students, belief in the intellectual inferiority of women was at that time by no means overcome. See Hans Anger, *Probleme der deutschen Universität. Bericht über eine Erhebung unter Professoren und Dozenten* (Tübingen: Mohr [Siebeck]. 1960). The verdict given here (473-494)—e.g., that in women "pure intellectual ability" is smaller or less often present, that "abstract thinking" or "any thinking at all" is less possible for them, that they have less "inventive faculty," etc.—even if there were any empirical support, completely overlooks the fact that the centuries-old exclusion of women from intellectual nurture has postponed their intellectual and personal development.

255. A classic parallel is the denigration of blacks because of cultural backwardness and lack of cducation. See W. T. Reich, "Kämpferische Gewaltlosigkeit. Ethische Probleme des Kampfes urn die Gleichberechtigung in den USA," in *Orientierung* 32 (1968): 226-228.

256. "Adam was deceived by Eve, and not Eve by Adam. The woman summoned him to sin; it is just that he take on the guidance of her, lest he be ruined again by female recklessness." *Corpus*, ed. Friedberg 1:1255.

257. This chapter has been referred to already, p. 30, in showing that the subjugation of woman under man, besides its source in her alleged principal offense in original sin, is also derived from her supposed not-in-the-image-of-God status.

258. The *Editio Romana* still presupposes the authorship of Ambrose. Cf. the *Notatio Correctorum* to c. 19 (*Corpus*, ed. Friedberg 1:1256; it attributes to Augustine the remaining pseudo-patristic chapters [13, 17]). Even Friedberg still seems to presuppose the authorship of Ambrose for c. 19; at any rate he raises no objection at this point. *Corpus*, ed. Friedberg 1:1255, n. 188.

259. *Corpus*, ed. Friedberg 1:1255.

260. See Hermann Fitting, *Die Anfänge der Rechtsschule zu Bologna*

(Berlin-Leipzig: J. Guttentag, 1888), pp. 1f., 100f.; Rudolf Sohm, *Institutionen. Geschichte und System des römischen Privatrechts,* 17th ed. (München: Dunker & Humblot, 1923),140ff.

261. Cf. Schulte, *Die Geschichte der Quellen*, 1:98; J. Gaudemet, "Das römische Recht in Gratians Dekret," in *OAKR* 12 (1961): 182; H. E. Feine, "Vom Fortleben des römische Rechts in der Kirche," in *ZRG* Kan. Abt. 42 (1956): 1, 14, *et passim.*

262. Cf. Sohm, *Institutionen. Geschichte und System*, 143f.; Feine, "Vom Fortleben des römische Rechts," lff. *et passim*; also by Feine, *Kirchliche Rechtsgeschichte* 65-134.

263. Cf. Gaudemet, "Das römische Recht," 188ff. Different legal historians, who have studied the use of Roman law in the *Decretum* on the basis of early, handwritten materials, have reached the conclusion "that Roman law was used increasingly step by step in the *Decretum*, and that this happened during the earliest period of its composition" (Gaudemet, 179). The incipient rejection of Roman law, Gaudemet maintains, was seen to be untenable in the long run, after the great triumph of Roman law—as proved by the history of the progressive formulation of the *Decretum* (188f.). The canonists understood "how to place the superior juridical technique, available to them in the burgeoning school at Bologna, in the service of church law" (182).

264. *Corpus*, ed. Friedberg 1:19. The self-sufficiency and independence which Gregory VII had won for spiritual and particularly for papal power, as over against secular, found in this sentence authoritative statement as well as theoretical and legal support. Cf. Schulte, *Die Geschichte der Quellen*, 1:93ff.

265. *Corpus*, ed. Friedberg 1:20. This principle is repeated and used concretely in the *dictum Gratiani, p.c.* 4 in *causa* 15, *questio* 3 (*Corpus*, ed. Friedberg 1:752), almost word for word with specific reference to *distinctio* 10 ("around the beginning of this work").

266. Cf., e.g., the summaries at cc. 9, 12 and 13: "The laws of the emperors ought to be maintained." "The laws are served by all the leaders of the Romans." "Roman law ought to be corrupted by no one's indiscretion." *Corpus*, ed. Friedberg 1:2lf.

267. Cf. Gaudemet, "Das römische Recht," 177f.; Schulte, *Die Geschichte der Quellen*, 1:93.

268. According to Thraede, "Frau," 216 and 246, no direct conclusions about the position of women in Roman society can be drawn from the regulations of Roman law, since Roman law because of its conservative character was burdened with "inconsistencies between legal ideal and reality." But whatever may have been the relation between the legal situation of women and their societal situation in the Roman empire, it was the conception of women in Roman law which was decisive for the place of women in church law, rather than the possibly more progressive situation of women in Roman society (Thraede, 246, 265f.).

269. Cf. Sohm, *Institutionen. Geschichte und System*, 500f.; Weber, *Ehefrau und Mutter*, 158ff.

270. H. Krüger in *Gleichberechtigungsgesetz. Kommentar* by H. Krüger, E. Breetzke, K. Nowack (Munich, 1958), 45.

271. Cf. Sohm, *Institutionen. Geschichte und System*, 500f., 510; Weber, *Ehefrau und Mutter*, 161; Max Kaser, *Das römische Privatrecht*. (Munich: Beck, 1955-1959), 1:70 ("The wife . . . lives . . . in the family of the husband '*filiae loco* [in the place of a daughter]).'" Krüger rightly emphasizes: "Only a family law so contrary to nature, as the Roman could succeed in making the father the power-holder—although the relation to children is naturally determined by their need to be taken care of—and to leave the mother under the husband, along with her (agnate) children as if she were one of them" (45).

272. See on this Sohm, *Institutionen. Geschichte und System*, 504f.; Eduard Heilfron, *Röminisches Rechtsgeschichte und System des römischen Privatrechts*, 7th ed. (Mannheim: J. Bensheimer, 1920), 515; Weber, *Ehefrau und Mutter*, 161.

273. "The *manus mariti* [hand of the husband] . . . is a form of authority by the master of the house over those who belong to the house, a counterpart of the *patria potestas* [power of the father]. "Sohm, *Institutionen. Geschichte und System*, 510.

274. In principle the right of punishment also includes the authority to kill the wife, e.g., in case of adultery. Cf. Sohm, *Institutionen. Geschichte und System*, 510, 531; Fritz Schulz, *Prinzipien des römischen Rechts, Vorlesungen* (Leipzig: Dunker & Humblot, 1954), 113; Kaser, *Das römische Privatrecht*, 1:52f. Weber, *Ehefrau und Mutter*, 161, points to the power of the husband to sell his wife into slavery, which, it is true, was considered as a crime against the sacred, since about the second century B.C. See also Schulz, *Prinzipien des römischen Rechts*, 131.

275. Cf. Sohm, *Institutionen. Geschichte und System*, 510, 531; Weber, *Ehefrau und Mutter*, 161. It was furthermore the duty of the censor to avenge the misuse of family authority. See Kaser, *Das römische Privatrecht*, 1:53. But according to Schulz, *Prinzipien des römischen Rechts*, magistrates did not make great use of their power of coercion.

276. Cf. Sohm, *Institutionen. Geschichte und System*, 510, 512; Schulz, *Prinzipien des römischen Rechts*, 113f.; Weber, *Ehefrau und Mutter*, 162.

277. Sohm, *Institutionen. Geschichte und System*, 508; Weber, *Ehefrau und Mutter*, 165; Kaser, *Das römische Privatrecht*, 1:239f.; Thraede, "Frau," 211f.

278. According to the law of the Twelve Tables, the posession (*usus*) of *manus* over the wife (within a year after marriage) could be prevented by the so-called *trinoctium*, that is, the annual absence of the wife for three nights. Cf. Weber, *Ehefrau und Mutter*, 164f.; Sohm, *Institutionen. Geschichte und System*, 506; Kaser, *Das römische Privatrecht*, 1:68f.

279. Cf. Sohm, *Institutionen. Geschichte und System*, 508; Schulz, *Prinzipien des römischen Rechts*, 131; Weber, *Ehefrau und Mutter*, 165; Weber, *Ehefrau und Mutter*, 165, 195; Heilfron, *Röminisches Rechtsgeschichte*, 516.

280. Sohm, *Institutionen. Geschichte und System*, 512.

281. Cf. Weber, *Ehefrau und Mutter*, 169; Heilfron, *Röminisches Rechtsgeschichte*, 517f.; Sohm, *Institutionen. Geschichte und System*, 511f.

282. According to Schulz, *Prinzipien des römischen Rechts*, 132, such violation is "never adultery, even in the law of the empire." Weber, *Ehefrau und Mutter*, 175, remarks about the marriage laws of Caesar Augustus (*lex Iulia de adulteriis*, eighteen B.C.): The laws are regulated "only against the wife and those guilty with her, while unfaithfulness of the husband remained unpunished, except in the case of the *stuprum*, i.e., the seduction of a reputable free female citizen." Cf. also Theodor Mommsen, *Römisches Strafrecht* (Leipzig: Duncker & Humblot, 1899, reprint Graz: Akademische Druck-U. Verlagsanstalt, 1955), 638f.: "The free Roman wife is obliged by moral law to have no sexual relationship before her marriage and afterward only with her husband. But the husband is subject to similar moral law only in so far as injury to the chastity of a virgin or the wife of someone else makes him a partner in guilt." Concerning the Roman concept of adultery and the different penalties for it, in the case of men and women, see Hans Bennecke, *Die strafrechtliche Lehre vom Ehebruch in ihrer historisch-dogmatischen Entwicklung* (Marburg: R. Friedrich, 1884; reprint Aalen: Scientia Verlag, 1971), 2-33.

283. Cf. Weber, *Ehefrau und Mutter*, 188. (Even so only one who is "guilty with a married woman" is called an adulterer.) See also Bennecke, *Die strafrechtliche Lehre*, 22-24; Kaser, *Das römische Privatrecht*, 1:73; Heilfron, *Röminisches Rechtsgeschichte*, 529.

284. Cf. Sohm, *Institutionen. Geschichte und System*, 513f.; Weber, *Ehefrau und Mutter*, 194f.; Schulz, *Prinzipien des römischen Rechts*, 100; Heilfron, *Röminisches Rechtsgeschichte*, 516.

285. According to Theodor Mommsen, *Römisches Staatsrecht*, 3rd ed. (Leipzig: Hirzel, 1887-1888; reprint, Graz: Akademische Druck-U. Verlagsanstalt, 1952), 3:9, women were always granted citizenship in Roman theory; the lack of political rights did not exclude them from citizenship. Nevertheless he says (201): "Giving an individual a first name . . . is in the highest sense the distinctive feature of a citizen, since a slave or a woman does not legally have a first name but only a male citizen as he puts on the clothing of a man. . . . " Similarly (201, n. 4): "Ancient sepalchral inscriptions teach us that for the full name of a woman, the sex and the family to which she belongs are sufficient. Of course a woman always had a first name too."

286. Cf. Heilfron, *Röminisches Rechtsgeschichte*, 111.

287. *Corpus Iuris Civilis*, 1:868. ("Females are removed from all civil or public offices and therefore are able to be neither judges nor to conduct nor to seek the office of magistrate nor to intervene for another nor to act as procurators") *Dig*. 50, 17, 2.

288. Cf. Mommsen, *Römisches Staatsrecht*, 1:493. It is clear from the classification of the three factors named, which all lead to official incompetence, that the female sex in Roman law is considered to be inferior. This is proved by the attributes and characterizations of women which are repeatedly alleged in connection with the legal limitations (or rather the causes of such limitations): "*infirmitas sexus*" (*Dig*. 22, 6, 9 pr.; *Dig*. 49, 14, 18 pr.) and "*imbecillitas sexus*" (*Dig*. 16, 1, 2, 2, and in other places), the meaning of which is not weakness of the

body but weakness of the mental power of women. The latter meaning refers especially to lack of "judgment and experience" (= *infirmitas*), of "will power and power of judgment" (= *imbecillitas*). Cf. Hermann Heumann and Emil Secker. *Handlexikon zu den Quellen des römischen Rechts*, 10th ed. (Graz: Akademische Druck-u. Verlagsanstalt, 1958), 246, 265. See also Metz, "Statut," 78, n. 3, who notes that women are labeled as inferior in these and other characterizations in Roman law.

289. Cf. Schulz, *Prinzipien des römischen Rechts*, 141.

290. Cf. Heilfron, *Röminisches Rechtsgeschichte*, 111; Max Kaser, *Das römische Zivilprozessrecht* (*Rechtsgeschichte des Altertum* 3, 4) (Munich: Beck, 1966), 150; Schulz, *Prinzipien des römischen Rechts*, 141. A very characteristic though not entirely convincing explanation of the basis and causation of this standard rule of the *praetor* is given in *Dig*. 3, 1, 1, 5: "The reason given by some why this is prohibited is lest contrary to the modesty that is proper to their sex they should become involved in inappropriate affairs, or perform the office of males: truly, is the origin due to Carfania, a most wicked female, who shamelessly prosecuting and disturbing the magistrate, gave cause for this law." *Corpus Iuris Civilis*, 1:35.

291. Cf. Schulz, *Prinzipien des römischen Rechts*, 141 with n. 127.

292. Mommsen, *Römisches Staatsrecht*, 1:369.

293. Cf. Heilfron, *Röminisches Rechtsgeschichte*, 111; Schulz, *Prinzipien des römischen Rechts*, 142.

294. Cf. Heilfron, *Röminisches Rechtsgeschichte*, 552; Kaser, *Das römische Privatrecht*, 2:163; Weber, *Ehefrau und Mutter*, 193.

295. Cf. Kaser, *Das römische Privatrecht*, 1:575.

296. Heilfron, *Röminisches Rechtsgeschichte*, 111.

297. See similar evidence in n. 20, above.

298. "In fact witnesses can be used whom the will concerns, but neither a woman nor a child nor a servant nor a mute nor a deaf person nor a mad person nor anyone who has been prohibited by good people nor any one whom the laws judge to be wicked and unable to be a witness, are able to be summoned among the number of witnesses." *Inst*. 2, 10, 6; *Corpus Iuris Civilis*, 1:17.

299. Cf. Heilfron, *Röminisches Rechtsgeschichte*, 144f.; Sohm, *Institutionen. Geschichte und System*, 539f.; Kaser, *Das römische Privatrecht*, 1:75.

300. "Guardians are established for both males and for females, but for underaged males merely because of their state of weakness; [guardians are established] for both underaged and mature females both because of the weakness of their sex and because of their ignorance of public affairs." *Ulp. tit.* 11, § 1; quoted from Sohm, *Institutionen. Geschichte und System*, 540. The *tutela mulierum* serves as protection of the guardian's own interest as the woman's closest heir. Cf. Heilfron, *Röminisches Rechtsgeschichte*, 144. Actually in some situations it was possible to circumvent the agnate tutelage arrangement, which was very disadvantageous for women (ibid., 145).

301. Heilfron, *Röminisches Rechtsgeschichte*, 145; Kaser, *Das römische Privatrecht*, 1:313.

302. Cf. Heilfron, *Röminisches Rechtsgeschichte*, 145; Schulz, *Prinzipien des römischen Rechts*, 141f.; Kaser, *Das römische Privatrecht*, 1:313; Sohm, *Institutionen. Geschichte und System*, 539.

303. Cf. Schulz, *Prinzipien des römischen Rechts*, 142; Sohm, *Institutionen. Geschichte und System*, 540.

304. Cf. Heilfron, *Röminisches Rechtsgeschichte*, 111, 149; Kaser, *Das römische Privatrecht*, 2:81.

305. Cf. Weber, *Ehefrau und Mutter*, 194f.; Kaser, *Das römische Privatrecht*, 2:80f.

306. Schulz, *Prinzipien des römischen Rechts*, 141; cr. also Thraede, "Frau," 216.

307. "Those who retain in marriage a wife taken in adultery commit the crime of pandering, but not those who have a wife suspected of adultery." Cod. 9, 9, 2; *Corpus Iuris Civilis*, 2:374. In reference to the question raised (in *causa* 32, *questio* 1) it is concluded from this regulation of *Corpus Iuris Civilis* "If therefore it can be gathered from these authorities that no one is permitted to keep his adulterous wife, how much less would it be allowed to take in marriage one who has no hope of chastity. . . ." *Dictum p.c.* in *causa* 32, *questio* 1; *Corpus*, ed. Friedberg 1:1118.

308. "This does not apply to women. It is not permitted to them to accuse their husbands of adultery. As is held in the same book and title (Cod. 9, 9, 1): 'The law of Julius decreed that women cannot bring an accusation of adultery in public judgment, however much they wish to question the violation of matrimony; and that the power of accusing a spouse is granted to males by law; the same privilege is not granted to females.'" *Corpus*, ed. Friedberg 1:1118. The *Glossa Ordinaria* (*ad v. accusationem*) qualifies the statement of Gratian by affirming that women may accuse their husbands of adultery according to church law as well as secular law. Of course, it is said, a husband has a privileged right of complaint according to secular law: "A male can accuse a woman of adultery by marriage law, that it is to say without a written accusation and without fear of false accusation within the proper forty days . . . that a woman cannot do. Otherwise a man and a woman would be judged equally." Furthermore, according to the gloss, secular law has been changed by the ecclesiastical to the extent that only the ecclesiastical punishment for adultery is still in effect. It is true that *ad v. "Privilegium"* the gloss indicates that there is no clear agreement about the complainant rights of women in cases of adultery. (Cf. *Corpus Iuris Canonici Gregorii Papae XIII.* Lyon: I. A. Hvgvetan & G. Barbier, 1671, [hereafter cited as *Corpus*, ed. 1671], 1:1596f.) See also Freisen *Das Eheschliessungsrecht*, 841, 843ff.

309. Plöchl, *Das Eherecht* 104, also confirms that there has been an influence from Roman legal conceptions on Gratian at this point. These conceptions picture man as the head of woman.

310. *Corpus*, ed. Friedberg 1:1118.

311. To be sure, we gather from c. 23 in *causa* 32, *questio* 5 (cf. also *causa* 32, *questio* 5, cc. 19 and 20) that church law, in contrast to the secular, grants to

women as well as to men the right of complaint because of adultery, and that there is equality of punishment. (In the *dictum* we have treated Gratian does not mention c. 23, although such a reference would have been obvious.) But even c. 23 leaves no doubt that despite this equalization in law there was no equalization of husband and wife in practice. The *Glossa Ordinaria ad* v. "*Christiana*" (in agreement with the content of the chapter) states the reasons as follows: "It is shown in this chapter that a wife is able equally to accuse her husband (*vir*) and vice versa; but this does not customarily happen frequently for three reasons, that is because of shame, or because of fear or because the man sins more cautiously, and thus is not easily apprehended." *Corpus,* ed. 1671, 1:1631. Not least important of the causes for the disadvantageous and humiliating situation of wives described here is the obligation of subordination according to classic canon law, as also their disadvantaged position in the secular realm.

312. The reference is to canon 7 of the first Council of Toledo (A.D. 400), which Gratian gives as c. 10 in *causa* 33, *questio* 2. Cf. Hefele, *Conciliengeschichte* 2:78.

313. *Dict. p.c.* 9 in *causa* 33, *questio* 2; *Corpus*, ed. Friedberg 1:1154.

314. According to Freisen, *Das Eheschliessungsrecht*, 842, ecclesiastical litigation is "secular litigation to which the church has made modifications."

315. In *dictum p.c.* 4 in *causa* 15, *questio* 3 (*Corpus*, ed. Friedberg 1:752) Gratian expressly declares that according to canon law no one has the right of complaint who does not have that right in secular law. Gratian extends this rule, which goes back to Pseudo-Isidore (d. *causa* 3, *questio* 5, c. 11: see *Corpus*, ed. Friedberg 1:517, n. 101) by making it into a positive formulation: anyone is competent to act as complainant who has such competence in secular law, if no contrary canons provide otherwise. Cf. on this E. Jacobi, "Der Prozess im Decretum Gratiani und bei den ältesten Dekretisten," in *ZRG* Kan Abt. 3 (1913): 252f.

316. The ecclesiastical legal sources that Gratian appeals to here (a regulation of the Council of Carthage in 419) repeat the Roman legal explanations concerning the witness. Cf. Gaudemet, "Das römische Recht," 186.

317. In this connection the statement of Ambrosiaster (*causa* 33, *questio* 5, c. 17; cf. 36f.), which was also influenced by Roman law, should be remembered, to the effect that a woman cannot be a witness. The regulation of canon 20 of the Synod of Compiègne, A.D. 757 (c. 3 in *causa* 33, *questio* 1 in Gratian) proves that this Roman viewpoint influenced ecclesiastical marital law: "If anyone takes a wife and has her for some time, and this same woman says that he never had intercourse with her, and the husband (*vir*) says that this did happen, the husband's (*vir*) statement is considered true, because a man is the head of a woman." *Corpus*, ed. Friedberg 1:1150.

318. Cf. Jacobi, "Der Prozess," 258, n. 3: "By *iudices* (judges) Gratian is also thinking of advocates, a fact which is explained by the common identification of *iudices* and *advocati* in Italy." See also Jacobi, 245, with n. 4.

319. "The dominant sex characteristics demonstrate whether an hermaphrodite is permitted to be summoned as a witness." *Causa* 4, *questio* 2/3, § 22; *Corpus*, ed. Friedberg 1:1150.

320. The *dictum Gratiani, causa* 15, *questio* 3 *princ*. (*Corpus*, ed. Friedberg 1:750f.) which treats of the exclusion of women from church offices (diaconate and presbyterate), offers a clear example of the mixing up of (deutero-) Pauline quotations with Roman legal regulations for women. Cf. pp. 24ff.

Chapter 2

Subsequent Influence of Gratian's *Decretum* on the Place of Women in the Church

Its Authority

In addition to the discussion of the texts of Gratian's *Decretum* which concern our subject, the question of the authority of the book, and its influence on the subsequent development of law, presents itself. Students of the history of law assign great significance to this work, both for the subject of canon law itself—founded by Gratian as an independent branch of theology[1]—as also for the formation and development of canon law.[2] As a collection of the older law[3] and in serving the purpose of "bringing conformity into church law"—which had existed as a parallel of old and new, general and particular regulations, with resulting contradictions[4]—Gratian's *Concordia* soon (by the end of the 12th century) displaced all older law collections.[5] It became the essential collection of sources of canon law.[6] This great respect was in large part the result of the reception of the work by the school for canonists founded in Bologna by Gratian.[7] In this school the *Decretum* formed the basis and the subject of teaching and of scholarly study.[8] Of course, as a whole, it never achieved the status of law, since it was actually the work of a private person, and the individual sources in it have that authority "which belongs to them in and for themselves,"[9] apart from their acceptance by Gratian. Even when Popes Pius IV and V arranged for an official text of the *Decretum Gratiani* (*Editio Romana*), its nonofficial character remained. The purpose of this edition was simply to prepare a reliable text for the widespread use of the work in school and court.[10] This text of the *Editio Romana* was declared authentic by the constitutions of Gregory XIII, *Cum pro munere* (A.D. 1580) and *Emendationem decretorum* (A.D. 1582), and any alteration was forbidden. Yet that act did not lend the *Decretum* more authoritative legal status.[11] On the other hand, the unassailed valuation and the great respect accorded it as source of ecclesiastical law are attested by the fact that Gregory XIII made it the first part of the *Corpus Iuris Canonici*.[12]

On the basis of its own authority the *Decretum* exercised a significant influence on ecclesiastical practice and on the further development of law. The evidence shows that besides its use in the "school," it was used in the papal chancery and thus in the legislative work of the curia.[13] It was cited at various times by ecumenical councils[14] and it influenced numerous synodal decrees.[15] Out of some regulations in Gratian's *Decretum*, which were themselves of the nature of particular law, universal law developed.[16] Likewise, common law statements were abstracted from papal decretals (issued for individual cases) which Gratian embodied in the *Corpus* as *auctoritates*.[17] Even the *dicta* of Gratian, the authority of which was only "doctrinal" although "important,"[18] have had influence in many directions on scholarly work and practice, so that prescriptive laws have grown from them.[19] The *Decretum*, and thus the opinions of the Magister, created the real basis for the absolute legislative power of popes, which came to full strength immediately after Gratian.[20] In view of these facts and of the general importance of the *Decretum*, it is highly significant that Gratian accepted the Pseudo-Isidorian decretals as papal authority for his source book, without recognizing them as forgeries but simply going along with the judgment of his time, which attributed them to Isidore of Seville.[21] Thus it was an unavoidable consequence of the great respect shown to Gratian's *Decretum* that the forged legal materials were widely taken over into church practice and influenced the development of church law.[22] This was especially unfortunate since the *Correctores Romani*, who arranged for the *Editio Romana*[23] of the *Decretum*, maintained the genuineness of the Pseudo-Isidorian decretals as late as A.D. 1580,[24] although repeated doubt had been expressed about their authenticity and the proof of the forgery had already been advanced by the Magdeburg Centuriators.[25]

It is clear from the application of this discussion to the problem before us that the *Decretum* had a negative influence on the evaluation and the position of women in the church. The ritual regulations for women, which consist exclusively of prohibitions—including the Pseudo-Isidorian decretals and texts (*Statuta Ecclesiae Antiqua*) falsely attached to an important council—have established or at least confirmed a status of legal deprivation and inferiority for women in the ecclesiastical sphere. (Assisting in the process were genuine and nongenuine patristic citations, which were used in the Middle Ages as legal sources,[26] and the accepted opinions of Magister Gratian.) This status became a generally accepted and permanent condition, which is still determinative[27] for the law of the *Codex Iuris Canonici.*[28]

The Decretists

The *Decretum* formed "the basis of the whole instruction in canon law" in the new school of Bologna "up to the last decade of the 12th century."[29] The so-called decretists thoroughly explained and commented on the work in lectures and writings.[30] Especially important for canon law, the result of these writings is the extensive literature on the *Decretum*, consisting of glosses,[31] apparatus and *Summas*.[32] The literature of the decretists exercised a great influence on the further development of canon law in the period between Gratian and Pope Gregory IX (1227-1241),[33] for the papal decretals which formed the primary foundation of church law, originated in close connection with the school and the works which issued from it. "The most famous law-givers of the 12th and 13th centuries" (Alexander III, Innocent III Gregory IX, Innocent IV) were themselves "educated in the schools of the glossators."[34] "Everything set down in the writings [of the canonists], in the nature of new ideas, explanation of sources and hints for living, was used in the decretals,"[35] which since the time of Alexander III were normative for the legal affairs of the church. For the doctrines of the canonists "claimed to work in practice, to be usable in legal affairs, in lawsuits '*quoad causarum tractatum*' in a word, to be '*ius.*'"[36]

The writings of the decretists on the texts of Gratian's *Decretum* discussed above are thus not simply of interest for the subject before us, but must be taken into account for the investigation of the development of the legal history of this problem up to the "decretals of Gregory IX."

The *Summa* of Gratian's pupil Paucapalea, which appeared between 1140 and 1148,[37] was the first work of the Bologna school on the *Decretum*, but it does not contribute much to our question, because it is only "in a minor way an independent exegetical work"[38] and often simply repeats the wording of Magister Gratian's *dicta*.[39] Paucapalea ignores the prohibition of liturgical-ecclesiastical activity for women which we have studied, and he ignores the question of deaconesses. He merely explains the concept *presbytera*, from chapters 18 and 19 in *distinctio* 32, and presents two meanings for it: she is either the wife of a priest whom he had married in minor orders—which would correspond to the wording of c. 18—or a cloistered nun (*conversa ecclesiae*), who was also called *matricuria* because she took care of those things mothers usually take care of (washing altar cloths, baking bread and preparing food).[40] But this explanation cannot in any way be applied to the original Greek form of canon 11 of Laodicea, given by Gratian as chapter 19 in *distinctio* 32. For although the import of the concepts πρεσβύτιδες and προκαθημέναι in this canon are debatable,[41] there can be no doubt that they connote an ecclesiastical function, an office. The meaning given by Paucapalea is thus incorrect. The designation *matricuria* for *presbytera* is taken by Paucapalea from the Latin version (the *Hispana*) of canon 11 of Laodicea which Gratian had used. Apparently the concept *presbytera* in the Latin church had a different and more varied form than in the Greek church. This is indicated by the majority of the designations for *presbyterae* in the Latin version: *viduae*, *seniores*, *univirae* and *matricuriae*.

When Paucapalea comes to the question of *distinctio* 5—whether a woman may come to church during menstruation and after a birth—to which Gratian depending on a decretal of Gregory the Great (cc. 2, 3) had given a positive answer,[42] he equivocates. He seems to give credence, more than Gratian does, to the completely unchallenged superstitious and unenlightened attitudes of the age regarding sexual behavior, particularly of women, which contributed significantly to the exclusion of women from the cultic sphere. Following Isidore of Seville,[43] Paucapalea describes in detail the allegedly devastating effect of menstruation blood: "For only a woman is a menstrual animal by contact with whose blood fruits do not produce, wine turns sour, plants die, trees lack fruit, rust corrupts iron, the air darkens. If dogs eat [the blood], they are made wild with madness."[44] Opposing Gratian's acceptance (in c. 2) of the authoritative statement of Gregory, according to which a woman may enter the church immediately after giving birth, Paucapalea refers to a contrary opinion in the *Penitential* of Bishop Theodore of Canterbury (born in 690).[45] However,

Paucapalea is able to harmonize the mutually contradictory statements only by an interpretation of Theodore which misuses the sources: he says that in contrast to Gregory, Theodore is speaking of a woman who does not come into the church to pray but happens to enter it for some other reason.[46] This solution of the problem makes it quite clear that the idea that menstruation and giving birth lay a burden of stain on women has not been overcome.[47] For according to Paucapalea and his times, only an attitude of humility can be somewhat compensatory: "And so a menstruating woman is not prohibited from entering a church in order to pray."[48]

Paucapalea fully accepts the viewpoint of Gratian that women must be subordinate to men in marriage and in the other areas of life. In his discussion of *causa* 33, *questio* 5, he uses word for word the *dictum Gratiani, p.c.* 11, which makes a woman as "the body of the man" subject to the man as her "head," "because of her situation of servile subjugation."[49] The only exception is in the sexual relationship. The legal consequence of this status in the public sphere is characterized by Paucapalea in the following manner: "She is not able to teach, nor to be a witness, nor to make a promise, nor to judge."[50] In this declaration he takes over from Ambrosiaster, almost word for word, a statement strongly marked by the regulations of Roman law for women. (Cf. *causa* 33, *questio* 5, c. 17.)

Rolandus Bandinelli, the later Pope Alexander III (1159-1181), remarks in his *Stroma* to *causa* 27, *questio* 1, c. 23 (= canon 15 of the Council of Chalcedon), which he composed before 1148[51] in Bologna, that in ancient times it was doubtless customary to ordain deaconesses in the churches, though only after age forty, who were then sternly forbidden to marry.[52] Roland defines the deaconess as *evangeliorum lectrix*, that is, as lector, a person commissioned with the reading of the Gospel. But there is very little evidence that the deaconess had exercised this function.[53] As we have already noted (p. 21), other tasks in community worship were usually assigned to the female diaconate, especially assistance in immersion baptisms, instruction of female catechumens, the job of door keeper, and also, in part, the distribution of Holy Communion to women and children. So Kalsbach[54] assumes that Roland came to the idea of identification of *diaconissae* (deaconesses) and *evangeliorum lectrices* (readers of the Gospel) because of the similarity of the names, deacon and deaconess. On the other hand, Freisen sees in Roland's remark only a "conjecture thrown out at random."[55] In any case, such a definition shows that by the time of Roland there was no longer any clear perception of the deaconess and her tasks, because the institution especially in the Latin church belongs to the past. From the same confused understanding comes also, perhaps, the identification of deaconess and abbesses[56] that often occurred in the early Middle Ages and later and also in the works of decretists we shall soon study. It is possible that an identification of deaconesses and abbesses lies behind Roland's characterization of deaconesses as *evangeliorum lectrices*, since abbesses of the Carthusian order, which had received a consecration ritually similar to that of the subdiaconate, sang the Epistle or Gospel at high mass, during the Middle Ages.[57] Nevertheless, the very vague conception of the deaconess—completely inadequate for an evaluation of the office, its characteristics and the functions assigned to it[58]—seems to have led Roland to a certain reserve in his statement about the incapacity of women to fill clerical offices. Thus while Gratian (*causa* 15, *questio* 3 *princ.*) objects to the entrance of women to the office of the priesthood as well as to the diaconate, though without giving reasons ("Furthermore women are not able to advance not only to the priesthood, but not even to the diaconate"), Roland limits women's incapability to the priestly office, or at least he does not specifically mention the diaconate in this connection.[59] But otherwise, Roland's judgment of women and their legal position in other areas is exactly the same as that of Gratian. At the end of the explanation of *causa* 15, *questio* 3 *princ.*, which we have just mentioned, he emphatically stresses the exclusion of women from accusation and witnessing, with the exception of cases like simony, heresy, and *lése majesté*—as provided in Roman law—as well as cases having to do with marriage.[60] Because of the patristic authorities whom Gratian cites, Roland thinks that the Magister's belief that wives must be fully subject to their husbands, even in their relation to God (*dictum v. c.* 11 in *causa* 33, *questio* 5), is sufficiently and definitively supported.[61] He also offers no objection to the authority granted to husbands (i.e., to clerics) to punish their wives (cf. *causa* 33, *questio* 2, c. 10).[62]

More thoroughly than Roland, Rufinus in his extensive *Summa decretorum* written between 1157 and 1159,[63] a work that became normative[64] for the subsequent decretists literature, analyzes the problem as in his discussion of *causa* 27, *questio* 1, c. 23 on canon 15 of Chalcedon. He expresses his surprise that the Council could direct that women under forty should not be ordained as deaconesses, since according to Ambrose any ordination of a deaconess was contrary to an authoritative regulation. Ambrose in his commentary on 1 Tim. 3:11 had appealed to (apostolic) authority against the Cataphrygians (Montanists), who derived from this biblical passage the right and duty to ordain deaconesses.[65] The allegedly Ambrosian commentary quoted by Rufinus is in reality the *Glossa Ordinaria*[66] to 1 Tim. 3:11; the gloss in turn is a short summary of the Ambrosiaster commentary[67] on the passage.[68] This explains the attribution of the text of the gloss to Ambrose, who in the Middle Ages was considered to be the author of the Ambrosiaster commentary.[69] In solving the problem of the conflict between Chalcedonian regulation and the (earlier) statement of "Ambrose," Rufinus sees the latter as "the authority of the Father" to be determinative. He makes a distinction between sacramental ordination, which relates to services at the altar, and an ordination (better, benediction) for some other ecclesiastial service. As sacramental, the diaconate ordination for women would be contrary to the authoritative prohibition, and canon 15 of Chalcedon is understood to permit only the second form, the nonsacramental ordination. But even the deaconesses consecrated in this way are no longer in existence in the church and it may be, Rufinus thinks, that abbesses were ordained in their place.[70]

But the deaconess' ordination of canon 15 of Chalcedon is hardly only an ordination "to some other ministry" in the sense of a simple benediction, as Rufinus maintains. For as we have already determined in the discussion of canons (p. 20f.), the technical term used for clerical consecration is χειροτονειν and the consecration (χειροτονία) of deaconesses in Byzantium, together with the ceremonies accompanying it is structured parallel to that for deacons.[71] The presentation of stole and chalice indicates the liturgical character of the office. In addition, the deaconess, on the basis of her consecration—like the clergy of higher orders—was obligated to remain celibate, as the regulation of Chalcedon clearly shows. It is thus rash and unfounded to characterize the ordination of the deaconess, administered according to the canon mentioned, as a nonsacramental consecration,[72] a characterization to which Rufinus has apparently been led by the Ambrosiaster commentary (to 1 Tim. 3:11) and by ignorance of the sources about the deaconess. Besides, this commentary and the *Glossa Ordinaria* supported by it by no means present an exegesis faithful to the text. 1 Tim. 3:11 is not referring to woman in general, as Ambrosiaster supposes, when it says: "Women must likewise be honorable, not slandering, sober, true in all things." The context of v. 11 in the midst of regulations about deacons (1 Tim. 3:8-13) undoubtedly forbids such an interpretation. Also the γυναῖκες named in v. 11 cannot be the wives of the διάκονοι in vv. 8-10, 12f., for the expected αὑτῶν is lacking and furthermore the family relationships of the deacons are treated separately in v. 12.[73] It would indeed be surprising if an admonition like that of v. 11 applied only to wives of the deacons and not at all to those of the bishops (cf. 1 Tim. 3:2),[74] whose prominent position in the community would rather lead us to expect the admonition for them, and to feel that they might need it more.

Accordingly, v. 11 of 1 Tim. 3 must be interpreted as, among others, Kalsbach does[75] (taking account of the context):

> This parallel [in language and content] to v. 8,[76] together with the subject of the whole section 3:1-13, which has to do only with ecclesiastical offices, compels us to explain the 'women' of v. 11 as follows: the Apostle is finding a place for women in the congregation to conform to that of the male diaconate.

So v. 11 has to do with guidelines for the deaconess in the early church, just as they are given for the deacon in v. 8. (Of course no further information is given in v. 11 and likewise in v. 8ff. about the type of consecration or the extent of authority of the office.) Thus we have shown that the supposedly erroneous exegesis of the Cataphyrgians, which derived their call for deaconess' ordination from 1 Tim. 3:11, is in fact a very good interpretation of v. 11, while the exegesis of Ambrosiaster, who tried to counter that argument by noting that (in Acts 6) only seven male deacons were chosen, is not valid. Ambrosiaster does not understand that the action of the apostles (Acts 6) was conditioned by the circumstances of the time and its cultural relationships, and as a result he arbitrarily raises that action to a timeless principle, misusing the text of 1 Tim. 3:11. Actually underlying this text is a more developed understanding of office than that of Acts 6, an understanding which includes women in the role of ecclesiastical officeholder, despite all the remaining reservations towards women inspired by rabbinic unspirituality (1 Tim. 2:llff.). These reservations challenged the office of deaconess from the outset and in later times. It was especially because of this anti-feminist manner of thinking,[77] but probably also because of his ignorance of the Eastern deaconess office, that Ambrosiaster in his commentary on 1 Tim. 3:11 argues against the female diaconate, though accurate exegesis would have supported it. For Rufinus the high authority of Ambrose was simply determinative and apparently it did not seem necessary to him to undertake an investigation of the validity of the Ambrosiaster commentary. At the end of his discussion of *causa* 27, *questio* 1, c. 23, Rufinus draws a parallel between deaconess and abbess which often appears in decretist literature and which presumably is dependent upon a regulation of Gregory the Great: the regulation derives the age limitation from the so-called deaconess law (1 Tim. 5:9) and sets it also as the norm for the virgin abbess.[78] Rufinus' parallel is also dependent upon the fact that the structure of the consecration of the canoness-abbess was analogous to that of the diaconate.[79] Thus simply on the basis of the age limitation (age forty) of the Council of Chalcedon, Rufinus thinks he sees in *causa* 20, *questio* 1, c. 13, a directive for the deaconess,[80] although the wording of the chapter[81] gives no occasion to do so. This interpretation, according to which "nun" (*sanctimonialis*) is equated with deaconess and "veiling" with "ordination," obviously betrays lack of clarity about the deaconess office that we have already observed in Roland.

Concerning the distribution of communion to the sick, which is limited to priests in *distinctio* 2, *de consecratione,* c. 29, Rufinus foresees the possibility of distribution by a boy,[82] in case the priest himself is detained by sickness. Thus a (still underaged) boy is trusted with such a duty but not an (adult) woman, who—whether a lay person or a nun—is not even considered by Rufinus for this task. The complete exclusion of women from ritual functions is not surprising in view of the fact that Rufinus, even more than Paucapalea, is prejudiced by Old Testament ideas about purity and the denigrating judgment of sexual actions accompanying them. Following Julius Solinus,[83] he speaks of "detestable and unclean" menstruation blood and he develops in detail a conception of its effects[84] which for modern enlightened thinking is strange and even absurd. In contrast to Gratian and Paucapalea, Rufinus nullifies the permission of women to enter church immediately after giving birth, a permission granted by Gregory the Great (cf. *distinctio* 5, c. 2) but which Rufinus rejects on the basis of contrary custom and especially on the basis of the regulation in Theodore's *Penitential.*[85]

Appealing to the statement of Ambrosiaster (*causa* 33, *questio* 5, c. 17), according to which a woman may not be a witness, Rufinus denies the competence of women as complainant or witness in criminal cases but not civil cases, except in matters relating to wills.[86] Although in Roman law women may perhaps act as witness in secular criminal cases—this relates to exceptional cases provided for in Roman law (cf. *causa* 15, *questio* 3, c. 1)—canon law on the contrary refuses to accept their witness in ecclesiastical criminal cases.[87] Rufinus is here more strict than Roland, who permits a woman to be a complainant in the so-called *crimina excepta* and in marital cases. (On *causa* 15, *questio* 3, cf. p. 80.)

Stephan of Tournay, whose *Summa*,[88] written in the 1160s, depends largely on Rufinus *Summa* and Roland's *Stroma*, follows their lead in general, in his conception of the female diaconate and in fact of any acceptance of women in the clergy. Concerning *causa* 27, *questio* 1, c. 23 *ad v. Diaconissam*, Stephan writes that deaconesses were at one time ordained in the church and given the task of reading the Gospels, but that now since we do not find them in the church any longer, we may assume that they are today called abbesses, who may not be ordained until forty years of age.[89] The identification of deaconesses with lectors is taken from Roland[90] and the parallel of deaconess and abbess goes back to Rufinus.[91] Stephan gives a similar definition of deaconess on *causa* 11, *questio* 1, c. 38: in the early church certain nuns who were called deaconesses were permitted to read the Gospel, which now no longer happens.[92] The identification of nuns and deaconesses clearly reveals an insufficient knowledge of the female diaconate. The latter disappeared exactly because of the advances of ascetic monasticism, so that the deaconess was brought into the convent and in this way completely excluded from congregational service.[93] This parallel of nuns and deaconesses (like the parallel mentioned above between deaconess and abbess) should probably be explained by an attempt to replace a lesser-known concept by a well-known modern one.[94] In contrast to Rufinus, Stephan does not comment on the character of the deaconess' ordination—that is, whether it should be understood as sacramental or nonsacramental. Clearly his idea on this point is not to be taken from his interpretation of the *dictum Gratiani causa* 15, *questio*. 3 *princ*. (women cannot become priests or deaconesses), although here the status of a clerical order is recognized for the early church female diaconate. That is to say, Stephan remarks about the passage *ad v. nec ad diaconatum*, that the same thing could be said about any lower order—that women have no admission it—but that Gratian names the diaconate because this order seemed to be a possibility for women since there were deaconesses earlier; but it no longer exists.[95] Thus it is admitted that early church law in contrast to medieval law recognized the membership of women in the clergy. This means, then, that a change in church discipline to the disadvantage of women had taken place. So Stephan's observation, that women have no place in the diaconate nor anywhere else in the clergy, may have been meant and should be understood not in the sense of a fundamental incapacity of women, but rather in the sense of an exclusion of women from the clergy simply because it is so prescribed in the statute law of the church.

The commentary to *distinctio* 2, *de consecratione*, c. 29 is taken literally from Rufinus.[96] No woman, but in cases of necessity a boy, may bring communion to the sick. The only task remaining for women—and it does not have a close connection with the liturgical service—is, according to Stephan's comment on *distinctio,* 1 *de consecratione*, c. 40, § 1—the washing and mending of palls and linens used in the services and also the preparation of hosts for the sacrifice of the mass. This was the activity, for instance, of the so-called Veglonisses nuns (religious women) of the Milan church. But that is not compatible with the prescription contained in the relevant chapter, which assigns the washing of palls and cloths within the sanctuary to the deacons and subordinate helpers.[97] But, Stephan notes,[98] this regulation has been rescinded by general custom. Furthermore, Stephan finds nothing inappropriate or unfitting in giving to nuns the task of preparing objects required for the liturgical celebration and keeping them clean, but—and there is no real change in this today—that is the extent of women's activity in the ritual-liturgical sphere.

Another product of the Bologna school is the *Summa* of Joannes Faventinus,[99] a compilation of the works of Rufinus and Stephan of Tournay.[100] So also is his commentary to the passages of Gratian's *Decretum* which concern us at this point. He takes over literally Stephan's treatment of the *dictum Gratiani causa* 15, *questio* 3 *pr. ad v. nec ad diaconatum*,[101] and he uses Rufinus as a model in his discussion of *causa* 27, *questio* 1, c. 23 *ad v. Diaconissam.*[102] Likewise, he depends on Rufinus in his interpretation of *causa* 20, *questio* 1, c. 13, in relating the chapter to the deaconess, although the chapter is really about nuns (*sanctimoniales*). Joannes thinks that the consecration rite consisted of the presentation of the veil to the deaconess.[103] But according to the sources, the essential characteristics of the deaconess consecration were the imposition of hands by the bishop in connection with a special prayer of consecration during the holy mass and the presentation of the stole and in some areas of the chalice.[104] Nevertheless, knowledge of the actual ordination rites of the deaconess had already disappeared from the knowledge of the times, as shown by the identification of ordination and veiling as equivalent, which Joannes also adopted from Rufinus.

Among all the Bologna *Summas* before Huguccio, the *Summa* of Joannes Faventinus was the most widely known. It more and more supplanted the Rufinus and Stephan models upon which it was based because it was found to be a handy compilation of the teachings of its precedents.[105] In relation to our problem, the great influence of the *Summa* of Joannes Faventinus brought with it this consequence, that through it the doctrinal opinions of Rufinus about the prohibition of the sacramental ordination of deaconesses—a prohibition supported by the authority of Ambrose—and about the nonsacramental consecration of deaconesses supposedly decreed by Chalcedon, were effectively disseminated, as can be proven by the later decretists (especially Huguccio).

The *Summas* of the French school of decretists, which were in part contemporary with those we have studied and in part somewhat later, and which exhibit an internal relationship to the works of the Bologna school,[106] contain some, but not many, productive discussions.

The *Summa Parisiensis*,[107] which is dependent on the Bologna decretists Paucapalea and Roland Bandinelli,[108] gives no reason for their comment on *distinctio* 32, c. 19:[109] "Women ought not be ordained like the clergy." Apparently the operative legal norm is simply accepted as if it contained no problems. According to the author, the *dictum Gratiani* about the exclusion of women from the priesthood and from the diaconate (*causa* 15, *questio* 3 *princ.*) indicates that there are no longer any deaconesses as there were in the early church.[110] However, the *Summa* contains no further consideration of this early church office. The author understands by *presbytera (distinctio* 32, c. 18) either a nun who lives by an ecclesiastical benefice, or the former wife of a priest.[111] When in *distinctio* 23, c. 24, reference is made to the consecration of women, one must not conclude from that, he declares, that they were *for this reason* permitted to touch the holy vessels and altar cloths; this was granted them *only for the purpose* of cleaning the cloths and getting them ready for use and of decorating the altar.[112] When the author watches over women in such a petty fashion, to be sure they do not overstep the bounds set up for them, the inconsistency and logical deficiency of his statements apparently completely escape him: when it is a question of cleaning and caring for the altar and liturgic utensils, the prohibitions set up for official church services suddenly become inoperative! As in the ritual-liturgical activity of women, public teaching by women—perhaps of men in a congregational assembly—is without exception an error which must be removed, according to the author in agreement with Gratian. Such instruction in spiritual matters by a woman, for example an abbess, can only be given to members of her own sex.[113]

The *Summa Parisiensis* agrees entirely with the teaching of Gratian about the subordination of women (*distinctio p.c.* 11 in *causa* 33, *questio* 5) and with the authority of the Church Fathers which serves as support for the teaching of Gratian.[114] However the author seems to limit the statement of Ambrosiaster (c. 17, *ibid.*), that women may not be witnesses, to the case of drawing up a will:[115] The reason for the rejection of women as witnesses is said to be that they could have had no experience with wills. No account is taken of the fact that women's lack of knowledge and education, thus unmistakably brought to light, is determined by their inferior position. In other (contract) agreements, on the other hand, women are said to be competent as witnesses, even though they are excluded from public office "because of the weakness of their sex."[116] Following this principle of Roman law, the author justifies the exclusion of women from judgeship, despite Old Testament evidence for the execution of this office by women (cf. Judges 4). He thinks, with Gratian,[117] that this Old Testament tradition—although its historicity can hardly be denied[118]—is simply an astounding miracle with no real significance.[119] Thus a legitimate conclusion is not drawn from this tradition—in contrast to the Yahwistic narration (Gen. 2:21 ff.), which has a mythic background without any historical nucleus.

The *Summa Monacensis*, written between 1175 and 1178[120] and also a product of the French school, differentiates, as does Joannes Faventinus, several kinds of veils.[121] The veil of orders is said to have been at one time presented to deaconesses (who have now however disappeared from the scene) though not before their fortieth year.[122] Once again, in dependence on Joannes and thus on Rufinus, the deaconess' ordination is mistakenly called a veiling. Moreover, since the author of the *Summa* differentiates several kinds of laying-on of hands—he calls the consecratory imposition of hands on religious women given to the God-dedicated virgins a sacrament, just like the consecratory imposition of hands of orders for priests and deacons (deaconess consecration is not mentioned!) and the consecratory imposition of hands of dignity for bishops[123]—it becomes clear that the concept of sacrament was not well-defined at the time and not exclusively reserved to the sacred signs today regarded as sacraments. We notice here also a difference between the *Summa Monacensis* and the viewpoint of Rufinus, who had already made a distinction between sacramental and nonsacramental ordination, in order to have a category for the consecration of deaconesses.[124]

One of the most important works of the French school is the *Summa Decretorum* of Sicardus of Cremona,[125] which appeared between 1179 and 1181[126] and which exhibits a certain amount of dependence on the *Summa Monacensis* as well as an influence from the older decretists. More than some of the writings we have studied, this one has a typical *Summa* character: There is considerable "lack of commentary and gloss."[127] Material is treated in part in generalizing formulations, so that we find only succinct observations relating to our problem.

In discussing the question (*causa* 15, *questio* 3) whether a woman can go to court against a priest Sicardus, depending on Gratian, makes the counterargument: "Those who are not able to be priests, are not able to accuse priests nor to testify against them."[128] No reason is given for the supposed incapability of women to be priests—their exclusion from the diaconate (as in Gratian) is not even mentioned. But his further counter-arguments, which bear the imprint of a patristic manner of thinking, show clearly a denigrating opinion of women. It can only be concluded that Sicardus, constrained like his predecessors by that kind of bias, sees the practice of ecclesiastical office as incompatible with the position and character of women. For example, in dependence on the statement of Ambrosiaster (*causa* 33, *questio* 5, cc. 17, 19), he remarks: "A woman ought to cover her head for two reasons: because of original sin and because of reverence for the bishop; she does not have the power of speaking in front of the bishop. Furthermore, she is not able to teach or [do] similar things."[129] Clearly influenced by Old Testament conceptions of ritual purity,[130] Sicardus says in another place (on *distinctio* 1, *de consecration*) that women (including nuns) may not touch the consecrated ceremonial vessels because of the reverence due to them. Only "consecrated men" are worthy enough to do so.[131] It is hardly surprising that Sicardus, burdened with such a heavily prejudicial view of women, thinks an actual ordination of a woman would be ineffectual,[132] which means that women are on the same level as the unbaptized.

As in the ecclesiastical sphere so in the marital: Sicardus places women in a substantially subordinate position. He sets up a hierarchical model for marriage, in which man is the principle and the origin of woman[133]—a conception later undergirded philosophically and then expanded by Thomas.[134] In working out this creaturely dependence, which was undoubtedly derived from Gen. 2:21ff., woman is so subjugated to man, according to Sicardus, that she must accommodate herself unresistingly to his will, yes even to his caprice. Like a reed in the wind she must give way before him and humble herself.[135] Only a ruthless will to oppress, which seeks self-affirmation in mastery and power over woman, can make such a demand, despising as it does the personal worth of woman. It thoroughly prevents woman from attaining the liberty of personal decision and control, since it places her under the authority of another human and therefore imperfect, being.

It remains to note that Sicardus goes along with the *Summa Monacensis* completely in his understanding of the different kinds of veils (among others the veil of ordination, which is not presented until age forty).[136] The same is true for his understanding of the sacramental character of the laying-on of hands granted to the God-dedicated virgins.[137]

The Bologna pupil of Gratian, Simon de Bisiniano, produced a *Summa* perhaps between the years of 1177 and 1179,[138] shortly before Sicardus's work, which is dependent upon it. It itself depends in many ways on Joannes Faventinus in its treatment of our subject.[139] To solve the problem of the contradictions arising from the inconsistent dates used in chapters 12-14 in *causa* 20, *questio* 1, Simon points to the different kinds of veils. Thus like Joannes and Sicardus he refers mistakenly to the deaconess, understanding her ordination as a veiling.[140] He seems to answer in the negative the question of the possibility of ordination of women, in agreement with *distinctio* 32, c. 19.[141]

Besides his *Summa* and even before writing it, Simon was active in glossing.[142] His gloss on chapter 12 in *causa* 20, *questio* 1, mentioned above, is important for our question and at the same time characteristic of the theological thinking of that time. He refers to the regulation in the chapter, which says that an abbess, but not a bishop, must be virginal. The justification for this is, he says, that the abbess represents the virgin church and the bishop represents Christ; but at the same time, it is as though Christ has had two wives:[143] first, the church that has come from the Jewish people and then the church that has come from the pagans.[144] Here the questionable manner by which Simon seeks to justify the differing presuppositions for the assumption of the office of bishop and the office of abbess does not concern us as much as the symbols he uses. The bishop is the embodiment of Christ and the abbess—that is, the female—is the representative of the church, a symbolization based on an interpretation of Eph. 5:22-23. The result has been a decisive imprint on Catholic thinking about ecclesiastical office,[145] creating a foundation for opposition to the admission of women to church office.[146] Of course, an objective exegesis of Eph. 5 will not yield any such symbolization.[147] Besides it needs to be pointed out that in the New Testament the relationship between the bishop (or officeholder) to the Christian congregation is never described in terms of bridegroom-bride. That is a relationship obtaining only between Christ and Church.[148] In the scriptural passage used in the gloss, 2 Cor. 11:2,[149] Paul does not see himself as the bridegroom of the congregation but rather, at most, as the one who brings the bride to bridegroom, thus as the one who leads the congregation to Christ,[150] a function which by its very nature is not reserved to the male sex.

The *Summa* of Huguccio, which was not finished before 1188[151] is considered to be the most important work of the Bologna school, because of its extensiveness, its detailed treatment—never before achieved—of the *Decretum*, and its critical evaluation of the older decretists.[152] As one might expect, it is more thorough than its predecessors in discussing the question of women and church office, although it is still to a large extent dependent on them.

In his exposition of chapter 23 in *causa* 27, *questio* 1, concerning canon 15 of the Council of Chalcedon, which gives rules for the deaconess ordination, Huguccio—like Rufinus—favors instead the statement of "Ambrose" that the deaconess ordination is contrary to authority.[153] This statement, it is particularly emphasized, preceded the Council decree. In solving the contradiction, Huguccio too accepts the Ambrosiaster passage as normative: the ordination of deaconesses consisted simply in the fact that they were chosen and appointed in a certain ceremonial form for any services that belonged to the deacons. Perhaps what they did was to sing the gospel and recite prayers during matins and this function was characterized as diaconal.[154] Like the earlier decretists, Huguccio takes the duty of the abbess as criterion for the female diaconate, which he himself expresses as the practice of abbesses (described above) in many communities. Deaconesses of this kind, he continues, no longer exist, unless one could say that the abbesses take their place, and that is the sort of ordination the Council of Chalcedon is referring to, while Ambrose, on the contrary, refers to ordination for the various levels of Holy Orders[155]—i.e., to sacramental ordination. This, or a similar understanding of a deaconess, is expressed in other passages of the *Summa*, where the deaconess is often simply identified with a nun, who is ordained "not in regard to orders but in regard to a certain ministry"—for instance, to recite the Gospel during matins.[156] It is worthy of note here that besides the conception of the nature and tasks of the female diaconate already described, there was another, though not so common conception, so Huguccio tells us. According to it, married women were ordained up to the diaconate; later, during the time of Ambrose, this ordination was forbidden; still later, at the time of the Council of Chalcedon, women were again ordained, which now of course, says Huguccio, no longer happens.[157]

Thus the deaconess' ordination of the early Christian age and of Chalcedon was even in the Middle Ages not regarded as simple benediction. The prevailing opinion, which however thinks of it as such, rests for proof on the Ambrosiaster passage and thus on an untenable foundation.

Huguccio's attitude to the whole question of ordination of women agrees with his conception of the female diaconate. In the context mentioned, to *causa* 27, *questio* 1, c. 23, he declares that women are incapable of ordination and he brings forward a justification for this contention that is new in decretist literature. The incapacity of women for ordination, he says, rests on an ecclesiastical decree pronounced on account of their sex. A factual ordination would therefore have no spiritual validity. For this reason and in conjunction with a reference to the Pseudo-Isidorian decretal *distinctio* 23, c. 25, Huguccio says that women are also forbidden to exercise the related functions of office.[158] In accordance with Huguccio's interpretation, male sex is thus the most important presupposition not only for the validity of ordination but also for the practice of church office in medieval canon law. The unlimited acceptance of this principle becomes particularly clear in the treatment and arrangement of a special case, that of the hermaphrodite: if in the hermaphrodite the male sex predominates, he may in theory be ordained, although in actuality he cannot be because of his deformity. So the ordination would be valid, though not permitted. But if the female sex predominates, the hermaphrodite would not be ordained even if a factual ordination takes place. That would be true also in case neither sex predominates. As Huguccio remarks, Roman legal regulations for hermaphrodites (in matters connected with wills) were normative for the formation of canon marital law on this issue.[159] This clearly pronounced dependence of canon law on Roman law continued to be determinative, even during the subsequent period down to the law in force today. (Cf. canon 968, § 1.)[160]

The viewpoint represented by Huguccio and his epigones, that male sex is the *conditio sine qua non* for the validity and effectiveness of ordination as well as for the exercise of the functions of clerical office, is based in the first place on a fundamental misunderstanding of ordination. As official commissioning and spiritual preparation for ecclesiastical service, ordination can never have sex as essential presupposition for its validity and operation: it is always directed toward a *human* being. In the second place and especially, Huguccio's viewpoint is based on disrespect for woman, her baptism, and her personal and religious worth, all of which qualify her as well as man for receiving ordination and for the exercise of the functions of clerical office. Therefore it must be emphatically emphasized that the church opposes the ethos of the Christian message in an essential point, as long as it preserves this viewpoint and elevates it to a legal norm.

Huguccio himself furnishes ample proof that the law of the church made because of sex—the regulation which he says excludes women from ordination because of their sex—is the consequence of a massive denigration of women. Using the text of Ambrosiaster, which Gratian takes over as c. 13 in *causa* 33, *questio* 5—the text in turn finds support in the Yahwistic creation narrative of Gen. 2—Huguccio affirms in agreement with the prevailing opinion of his time the dependence of woman on man and her subjugation to his authority. The subjugation is a matter of essence and finds its basis therefore in the creation. The result is that she partakes of the dignity of the image of God in far less measure than man. In three respects it is claimed that man but not woman is the image of God and Christ: just as all life has its source in God, so all those who follow the first man (i.e., male) have their source in him; just as out of the side of the crucified Christ the church has come forth under the sign of water and blood, so out of the side of sleeping Adam his bride Eve was formed; finally, just as Christ administers the church and leads it, so the husband rules and leads his wife. For this reason a man must not—like a woman—bear a sign of subordination, but rather a sign of freedom and authority. Only for one reason could a woman also be considered as in the image of God: if as a being endowed with spiritual understanding and reason she had access to knowledge of the being of God.[161] Analogically Huguccio sees the glory and honor of God embodied only in man: by making man, God has shown himself more powerful and more glorious, for only man has come immediately and originally from the hand of God, while woman on the contrary is formed from man. Only man glorifies God principally and directly, while woman on the contrary only does so through the mediation of man, if she is first directed and taught by him to praise God.[162]

The woman as a derived being, who has her origin in man and therefore depends upon him and remains subject to him, who lacks direct access to God in her being and her religious life and is thus deprived of full independent personhood—that is the view of women we get from Huguccio and his times, mainly as the final consequence of the Yahwistic Creation account and of certain passages from the New Testament (1 Cor. 11; 1 Tim. 2:11ff.). This view, together with the prejudicial conception of women that lies at the basis of Roman law, brought about their exclusion from orders. It would certainly be a mistake to suppose that the decree of law in effect today (can. 968, § 1) rests on other presuppositions and foundations, since the continuity between the old and the new law was in this respect definitely maintained.[163]

It is difficult to overestimate the influence of Huguccio on the canonists of later time and thus on the later development of law.[164] As the most complete commentary to Gratian's *Decretum*, his *Summa* became the essential foundation of the great gloss apparatus of Laurentius and also that of Joannes Teutonicus.[165] "The following age needed only to use it as source, not much more had to be done."[166] Consequently its sharply formulated thesis about the incapacity of women for ordination because of their disdained sex had a strong influence on subsequent canonical theory and practice.

Although Robert of Flamesbury's *Poenitentiale* represents a "special category only bordering on genuine canonistics,"[167] it should be considered because already there is a clear dependence on Huguccio.[168] There is the same unconditional presupposition of the necessity of male sex for ordination. It is, according to Robert, the first factor of the substance of orders, i.e., it sets forth the essential requirement for the validity of ordination. Baptism is named only in second place, followed by further prerequisites.[169] In accordance with this premise, Robert declares definitively: "Woman [in principle] are only blessed, not ordained." It is not prejudicial to this premise, he says, that deaconesses once existed, for the designation deaconess had another meaning than the designation deacon in his (Robert's) time. A woman never had the office that the deacon now holds.[170] Huguccio had judged just as sharply the early church office of the deaconess. Compared to Roland and Stephan— less so to Rufinus—a strengthening of the tendency to deny woman any capacity for ordination is apparent.

At the end of the decretist literature stands the *Apparatus ad decreta* by Joannes Teutonicus published soon after the fourth Lateran Council (1215).[171] It became the *Glossa Ordinaria* (ordinary commentary) of the *Decretum*. Besides the work of the previous decretists, especially Huguccio, the more recent legislation of popes (especially Alexander III)[172] is assimilated into the Joannine gloss. In the following age it becomes the real foundation for the study and usage of the *Decretum* and is evaluated as almost itself the fountainhead of law.[173] This explains its great significance. Its definitive revision was made by Bartholomaeus Brixiensis in the 1240s,[174] and in this revised form it became the basis for subsequent research.[175]

The statements of the *Apparatus* on *causa* 27, *questio* 1, c. 23 are especially important for our question. First of all, the deaconess of canon 15 of Chalcedon is interpreted as abbess without further explanation—which not only misses the meaning of the canon but also disregards the degree of uncertainty that still clung to the judgement of the decretists before Huguccio about equating deaconess and abbess. Over against the Council's decree on ordination Joannes—clearly following Huguccio (cf.

p. 90, above)—places the earlier statement of "Ambrose," which opposes ordination of deaconesses.[176] This statement seems to be determinative for the position of Joannes himself, agreeing as it does almost verbatim with Huguccio's statement: "Women do not receive the [sacramental] character [of orders] by impediment of sex and the law of the church."[177] Joannes draws two conclusions from this alleged incapability of women to receive ordination. (1) Women can exercise no function that requires a consecration; the Pseudo-Isidorian decretal *distinctio* 3, c. 25 is added as proof. (2) The ordination of deaconesses of Chalcedon was not a sacramental ordination but only a benediction, on the basis of which some special kind of duty was assigned, perhaps the reading of homilies or of the Gospel at Divine Office, which was not permitted to other (nuns).[178] When it deals with the relevant chapters from Gratian, the gloss emphasizes the exclusion of women from the offices of the ordained or from the duties connected with them. Joannes justifies the prohibition of teaching in *distinctio* 23, c. 29, by pointing out that teaching is the responsibility of the priesthood; besides, *causa* 33, *questio* 5, c. 17 (Ambrosiaster) rejects any possible teaching right of women because of their subordination to men.[179] Baptizing by women (*distinctio* 4, *de consecratione* c. 20) is regularly prohibited, according to Joannes—agreeing with Gratian—but in cases of necessity an exception is permitted.[180] The gloss on *distinctio* 2 *de consecration*, c. 29, allows for distribution of communion to the sick if the priest is prevented, by a deacon or a *laicus catholicus*.[181] (Of course this means a male layperson, as already mentioned, pp. 10f., above; however the gloss, in contrast to Rufinus and Stephan, does not specifically mention the possibility that a boy could also act as deputy for the priest.)

The reason for the exclusion of women from the functions just mentioned—especially from orders that according to contemporary opinion alone make these functions possible—lies, for Joannes (as we have noted) in the sex of women, which means it lies in their inferiority. Many passages in the gloss are quite candid about this. We have already shown that such a denigrating opinion of women goes back in part to the considerable influence of Roman law on medieval canonistics, a fact clearly discernible in Joannes Teutonicus. Whether a hermaphrodite can be a witness in a will or before a court, whether he can be ordained, depends entirely, according to the gloss, on the predominance of the male sex.[182] Like Gratian the gloss accepts uncritically the rigid role differentiation that Roman law prescribes for the sexes: It grants a free and honorable position to the male but requires an oppressive dependency relationship for the female. For Joannes, too, all public offices and functions[183] are considered male positions (*officia virilia*). The spiritual office and the duties relating to it stand on the same level with these public offices and functions,[184] which results in the exclusion of women not only from ecclesiastical offices but also from the practice of judgeship,[185] from being witnesses in wills and in criminal cases,[186] and from being plaintiffs (except in cases involving judicial punishment for injustice against them or their families).[187] Instead of these, the principal duty of women, according to the gloss in agreement with Roman law and with Ambrose (cf. *causa* 32, *questio* 2, c. 1), is the preservation and propagation of the species: to be childless is a disgrace for (married) women.[188] This narrow definition of existence [*Daseinsbestimmung*] gives woman an exclusively biological reality; it does not value her as a person and individual. In addition, it necessarily prevents her development to full humanity. According to the view of Joannes—which is informed by old Roman, extremely patriarchal family law and the teaching of the Fathers[189]—a (married) woman is denied independent existence to such a degree that a slave-like position is expected of her as a matter of course. She is obligated to serve her husband—her lord and master—in two ways: she must be sexually compliant and she must also serve him in the home.[190] If she fails this obligation, or if she should even be faithless to her marriage vows, the husband as "head of the wife" is empowered to pass judgment on her and reprimand her. Joannes says he may also punish her but not strike her too hard. The law gives him the opportunity to treat her as the master treats his slaves or day laborers.[191] From such classification of women it of course follows necessarily that they are unfit to receive ordination and to carry out ecclesiastical offices.

It is true that the viewpoint of Joannes Teutonicus, that women are unfit for ordination because of their sex, did not remain completely uncontested, although it was doubtless the prevailing opinion of his time. We may gather this from his concluding discussion of *causa* 27, *questio* 1, c. 23: "Some (i.e., those who don't agree with him) say that if a nun is ordained, she truly receives the character (of orders), since being ordained is a question of fact and anyone is able to be ordained after baptism."[192] The indispensable presupposition for valid ordination, according to this variant (from traditional thinking) conception, is not male sex but only baptism: if ordination is granted on the basis of being baptized, then the validity of ordination is acknowledged *eo ipso* with its factuality (after baptism anyone—i. e., everyone, man or woman—is able to be ordained. The proof offered here is a decretal of Innocent III (*Extra* 3.43.3), which says that an unbaptized person cannot be ordained and, if he is factually ordained, he does not actually receive the character of ordination. Thus the question of the conditions requisite for valid ordination is objectively, if not quite fully,[193] answered: the only foundation, or the necessary presupposition, for the validity and efficacy of ordination, as well as for the exercise of ecclesiastical office, is the baptized and believing person (to which may be added, a person with a particular qualification, i.e., charisma for his vocation). The sex of the ordinand is irrelevant.[194]

The *Rosarium Super Decreto*, written between 1296 and 1300[195] by Guido de Baysio, who was already one of the decretalists, takes account of materials not used in the *Glossa Ordinaria* and of literature written after Joannes and is thus a kind of supplement to the gloss.[196] It presents a clear confirmation of the fact we have already noted in discussing the major works of the decretists, that the conviction that women are unfit for ordination rests on a belief in their inferiority. In his treatment of the chapter (*causa* 27, *questio* 1, c. 23) that regulates the ordination of deaconesses, Guido shows his agreement with the view of Joannes Teutonicus, that women are unfit for the sacramental character of ordination, by arguing as follows: "orders is for the more perfect members of the church since it is given for the distribution of grace to an other. A women however is not a perfect member of the church, but a male is."[197] The imperfection here attributed to women is understood by Guido as substantial, in accordance with creation. For in agreement with Huguccio[198] he says that woman in contrast to man is not the glory of God, bccause she did not come into existence immediately from the hand of God, but rather was formed from man and has a relationship to God only through man. Guido, supported by some of the patristic texts (*causa* 33, *questio* 5, cc. 18, 19) discussed above (p. 33-34), finds further reasons for the exclusion of women from ordination in their alleged moral inferiority: as the principle of sinfulness and the tempter of Adam, woman has become the effective cause of damnation; accordingly she cannot also be, by virtue of the grace-mediating power of ordination, the effective cause of salvation.[199] Thus Guido derives the exclusive fitness of men for the priesthood—for the "distribution of grace to an other"—from the substantial and ethical perfection ostensibly characterizing only the male. This kind of justification betrays not only a considerable amount of hubris and arrogance, but also makes clear to what extent the truth has disappeared from view—the truth that the ministry of the church is based on the priesthood of Christ and permanently remains in relationship to it alone, and that therefore a purely creaturely perfection or any kind of "merit" on the part of human beings can never serve as a sufficient prerequisite for the priesthood. Just as untenable is the opinion of Guido that woman's alleged stain of having been the "effective cause of damnation" cannot be eradicated even by the redemption offered by Christ. Guido says that the extent of Eve's guilt cannot be balanced even by the fact that Mary is the Mother of God, since Mary was only the "material cause of salvation." Because woman was created from man, Guido allows the female sex in general only the ability to be the material cause of salvation,[200] though, paradoxically she can be the only effective causation for sin, according to Guido. The method of the whole abstruse argumentation makes it especially clear that the negative understanding of women based on certain scriptural passages and considerably strengthened and shored up by patristic and pseudo-patristic exegesis and scholastic speculation, fully repressed the statement in Gal. 3:28 about the fundamental parity of male and female in Christ. This negative judgment became, consequently, the sole determination of the value and place of women in the church.

Guido comments about *distinctio* 32, c. 18 *ad v. presbyteram* that one must not conclude that this word [*presbytera*] has to do with a female priest, for if a woman should be ordained she would still not receive the (sacramental) character of ordination "by impediment of her sex and the law of the church" (here Guido takes over the formulation of the *Glossa Ordinaria*). He admits that some of the rules are contradictory to this—referring to the objection to the traditional point of view mentioned by Joannes Teutonicus (p. 95). *Presbytera*, according to Guido, means rather the wife of an ordained man.[201]

Following Joannes, Guido maintains that by deaconess we must understand an abbess, or perhaps it was once the designation for a woman who served the priest as acolyte. But this form of female diaconate no longer exists in the church.[202]

Notes

1. Cf. Schulte, *Die Geschichte der Quellen*, 1:95; Feine, *Kirchliche Rechtsgeschichte*, 276f.

2. Cf. Schulte, *Die Geschichte der Quellen*, 1:94f.; Wasserschleben-Schulte, "Kanonen-und Dekretalensammlungen," in *Realencyklopädie für protestantische Theologie und Kirche*, Albert Hauck, ed., 3rd ed., 24 vols. (Leipzig: J.C. Hinrichs,

1896-1913) (hereafter *RE*) 10:11f. Sägmüller, 1:237f.; Feine, *Kirchliche Rechtsgeschichte*, 276f.; Stickler, *Historia iuris canonici*, 1:201f., 211f.

3. See Schulte, *Die Geschichte der Quellen*, 1:68; Feine, *Kirchliche Rechtsgeschichte*, 276f.

4. Sägmüller, 1:235; cf. Schulte, *Die Geschichte der Quellen*, 1:60.

5. Cf. Schulte, *Die Geschichte der Quellen*, 1:67f.; Feine, *Kirchliche Rechtsgeschichte*, 277; Stickler, *Historia iuris canonici*, 1:211.

6. Cf. Schulte, *Die Geschichte der Quellen*, 1:67; Plöchl, *Das Eherecht*, 2:470; Stickler, *Historia iuris canonici*, 1:211.

7. Cf. Schulte, *Die Geschichte der Quellen*, 1:95; Sägmüller, 1:237; Feine, *Kirchliche Rechtsgeschichte*, 277; Stickler, *Historia iuris canonici*, 1:219.

8. Cf. Feine, *Kirchliche Rechtsgeschichte*, 279; Schulte, *Die Geschichte der Quellen*, 1:67, 212. According to Plöchl, *Das Eherecht*, 2:499, Gratian's collection spread from the new school of church law in Bologna to the schools in Pavia, Paris, Toulouse and Valencia.

9. Schulte, *Die Geschichte der Quellen*, 1:68f.; cf. Sägmüller, 1:238f.; Stickler, *Historia iuris canonici*, 1:210ff.; Feine, *Kirchliche Rechtsgeschichte*, 277. In his preface to the Code, Cardinal Gasparri points to the private character of Gratian's collection.

10. Cf. Schulte, *Die Geschichte der Quellen*, 1:68; Stickler, *Historia iuris canonici*, 1:211.

11. Cf. Sägmüller, 1:238; Philipp Schneider, *Die Lehre von den Kirchenrechtsquellen*, 2nd ed., (Regensburg: Pustet,1892) 124.

12. Cf. Plöchl, *Das Eherecht*, 2:486; Feine, *Kirchliche Rechtsgeschichte*, 293.

13. Cf. W. Holtzmann's investigation, "Die Benutzung Gratians in der päpstlichen Kanzlei im 12. Jahrhundert," *Studia Gratiana*, 1 (1953), 325ff., esp. 345-349. See also Wasserschleben-Schulte, 11: The authority of the *Decretum* "had to be increased and strengthened all the more because the popes themselves used it and cited it in their decretals."

14. Cf. Plöchl, *Das Eherecht*, 2:473.

15. Ct. Artonne, "L'influence du Décret de Gratien sur les statuts synodaux." *Studia Gratiana*, 2 (1954), 645ff.

16. Cf. Feine, *Kirchliche Rechtsgeschichte*, 277; Freisen, *Das Eheschliessungsrecht*, 10; Schulte, *Die Geschichte der Quellen*, 1:68.

17. Cf. Albert Michael Koeniger, *Grundriss einer Geschichte des katholischen Kirchenrechts*, (Cologne: F.P. Bachem, 1919), 39; see also Schulte, *Die Geschichte der Quellen*, 1:86.

18. Schulte, *Die Geschichte der Quellen*, 1:70; cf. Plöchl, *Das Eherecht*, 2:473.

19. Cf. Schulte, *Die Geschichte der Quellen*, 1:68, 94 with n. 8; Feine, *Kirchliche Rechtsgeschichte*, 277; Plöchl, *Das Eherecht*, 2:473; Stickler, *Historia iuris canonici*, 1:211.

20. Cf. Schulte, *Die Geschichte der Quellen*, 1:94ff.; Feine, *Kirchliche Rechtsgeschichte*, 277; G. Le Bras, "Les écritures dans le Décret de Gratien," *ZRG*

Kan. Abt. 27 (1938), 80 ("Le décret est une justification de l'oeuvre, de l'autorité de l'Eglise et plus solide point d'appui du système des décretales.")

21. Cf. Sägmüller, 1:225; E. Seckel, "Pseudoisidor," in *RE*, 16:267, 284; R. Grand, "Nouvelles remarques sur l'origine du Pseudo-Isidore, source du Gratien," *Studia Gratiana*, 3 (1955), 3, 5.

22. Cf. Freisen, *Das Eheschliessungsrecht*, 7; Feine, *Kirchliche Rechtsgeschichte*, 277; Seckel, "Pseudoisidor," 292.

23. Concerning the work and worth of the *Correctores Romani*, see Schulte, *Die Geschichte der Quellen*, 1:72f. Freisen, *Das Eheschliessungsrecht*, 12, remarks that "the *Correctores* did not consistently carry out their plan to establish a critically satisfactory text" and thus did not accomplish their purpose (11).

24. Cf. Seckel, "Pseudoisidor," 292f.; Schulte, *Die Geschichte der Quellen*, 1:73.

25. Cf. Seckel, "Pseudoisidor," 292f.; Schulte, *Die Geschichte der Quellen*, 1:73 with n. 34; Sägmüller, 1:225; H. Fuhrmann, "Pseudoisidor," in *LThK* 8:864-866.

26. Cf. pp. 33f. Munier, *Les sources patristiques*, 167, remarks:"Les textes des Pères . . . ont servi directement à l'élaboration du droit classique. La doctrine canonique proposée par le Maître de Bologne se fonde simultanement sur les canons patristiques et sur les décisions émanant des organismes législatifs; Gratien continue de recourir ax témoignages patristiques pour fixer les règles de la législation." Similarly also Freisen, *Das Eheschliessungsrecht*, 6f. Of course the authority of the Fathers (*auctoritas patrum*) is repressed by the decrelists in favor of papal authority. Cf. Munier, in the precis of *Les sources patristiques* in *Revue de Droit Canonique* (hereafter *RDC*) 4 (1954):191f. (Note there also a reference to the fact that the theoretical basis for this repression of the authority of the Fathers (*auctoritas patrum*) had already been given in *distinctio* 20.)

27. As one can see from the Code, Fontes IX (*Tabellae*), cols. 13f., many of the texts of Gratian's *Decretum* which we have discussed have influenced (or as we have often pointed out, stamped their impression on) the canon law operative today:

distinctio 23, c. 25 and dist. 1 *de consecratione*, c. 41-43
    can. 1306 § 1, Code
distinctio 4, *de consecratione*, c. 20
    can. 1342 § 2, Code
distinctio 2, *de consecratione*, c. 29
    can. 845 § 1, Code
causa 33, *questio* 5, c. 11
    can. 1312 § 2, Code
causa 33, *questio* 5, c. 19
    can. 1262 § 2, Code

Besides Munier *RDC* 4 (1954):191f., R. Metz also points out the strong influence of the Church Fathers, especially Augustine, on the Code law through the medium of the *Decretum* of Gratian. See his "Saint Augustine et le Code de Droit Canonique de 1917," in *RDC* 4 (1954):405ff.

28. On this see Metz, "Statut," 97-108.

29. Thus Schulte, *Die Geschichte der Quellen*, 1:212; cf. also Stickler, *Historia iuris canonici*, 1:20lf., 211.

30. Cf. Feine, *Kirchliche Rechtsgeschichte*, 279. For the teaching method used in the Bologna school, see Schulte, *Die Geschichte der Quellen*, 1:212ff. According to Schulte a greater significance for canon law appears in those writings which by the way included everything "which had usually been presented orally." (*Ibid.*1:215f.)

31. The glosses are prior in time to the *Summas* and the apparatus. So Schulte, *Die Geschichte der Quellen*, 1:216; J. Junker, "Summen und Glossen. Beiträge zur Literaturgeschichte des kanonischen Rechts im zwölften Jahrhundert," in *ZRG* Kan. Abt. 14 (1925):386, 403ff. See also Stephan Kuttner, *Repertorium der Kanonistik (1140-1234)* (Vatican City: Biblioteca apostolica vaticana, 1937) 1:3ff., 124.

32. Cf. Schulte, *Die Geschichte der Quellen*, 1:215ff.; Feine, *Kirchliche Rechtsgeschichte*, 279.

33. Cf. Schulte, *Die Geschichte der Quellen*, 1:95 with n. 11.

34. Freisen, *Das Eheschliessungsrecht*, vi; cf. *Die Summa magistri Rolandi, nachmals Papstes Alexander III*, Friedrich Thaner, ed., (Innsbruck: Wagner, 1874; reprinted Aalen: Scientia Verlag, 1962), IV.

35. Paucapalea. *Summa über das Decretum Gratiani*, Johann F. Schulte, ed., (Gießen: E. Roth, 1890; reprinted Aalen:Scientia Verlag, 1965) iii; Thaner, *Die Summa magistri Rolandi*, ivf. ("The formation of canon law took place in the reciprocal feedback between school and papacy.") Similarly, Freisen, *Das Eheschliessungsrecht*, vi.

36. Thaner, *Die Summa magistri Rolandi*, iv.

37. Cf. Kuttner, *Repertorium der Kanonistik*, 126; Alphonse van Hove, *Prolegomena ad Codicem Juris Canonici*, 2nd ed. (Rome: H. Dessain, 1945)1/1:433f.

38. Kuttner, *Repertorium der Kanonistik*, 126f.

39. Cf. Schulte, *Die Geschichte der Quellen*, 1:113; Kuttner, *Repertorium der Kanonistik*, 126.

40. "his *presbyterae*, that is, wife, whom he had been taken in minor orders. . . . Or we understand *presbyterae* to be those dedicated to the church, and who are called little mothers (*matricuriae*) because they perform the chores which mother are accustomed to perform; for they wash vestments, make bread and prepare the cooking." Paucapalea, *Summa*, Schulte, ed., 26.

41. See the discussion on pp. 18f.

42. See chapter 1, n. 36.

43. *Etymologiarum libri* 9, 1 (*PL* 82, c. 414); Paucapalea. *Summa*, Schulte, ed., 11, n. 4. According to Browe, *Beiträge zur Sexualethik*, 2, Isidore took the idea from J. Solinus' 3rd century *Collectanea rerum memorabilium* (Theodor Mommsen, ed.[Berlin: In aedibus Friderici Nicolai, 1864]), 17, which is in large measure dependent on Plinius' *Natural History and Mela's Chorography*. (Cf. the article, "Julius Solinus," in *Pauly's Realencyclopädie der classischen*

Altertumswissenschaft [Stuttgart: Alfred Druckenmuller, 1918] 10/1:823-838) Rufinus of Bologna follows Solinus immediately and explicitly. (See n. 84, below.)

44. On *distinctio* 5 *pr.* §2 v. "item mulier que menstrua patitur," Paucapalea, *Summa*, Schulte, ed., 11.

45. "But against this it is read in the penitentials of Theodore that if a woman would dare to enter a church before the prescribed time, she should do penance on bread and water for the same number of days that she ought to have abstained from church." Paucapalea, *Summa*, Schulte, ed., 11. Schulte refers (*ibid.*, n. 9) to the regulations of Theodore which Paucapalea probably has in mind. *Theod. poen.* 1, 14, §17f. (in Hermann Wasserschleben, *Die Bussordnungen der abendländischen Kirche,* [Halle: C. Graeger, 1851; reprint, Graz: Akademische Druck- u. Verlagsanstalt, 1958], 199): "Moreover women, neither religious nor lay, ought to enter a church during the time of menstruation, nor receive communion. If they dare to do so, they should fast for three weeks" (§ 17). "Similarly they should do penance who enter a church before they are clean of blood after birth, that is, forty days" (§ 18).

46. "Blessed Gregory said that she does not sin in this, who, going to give thanks, humbly enters a church. Theodore truly said of her who enters timidly, not because of prayer, but drawn by some other necessity." Paucapalea, *Summa*, Schulte, ed., 11.

47. Despite his generally progressive and humane attitude on the subject—for the time in which he lived—Gregory the Great calls menstruation "a defect . . . that [women] are weakened by the defect of their nature." *Corpus*, ed. Friedberg 1:8, Palea § 1.

48. Paucapalea, *Summa*, Schulte, ed., 11.

49. *Ibid.*, 133f.; see also the discussion 27f.

50. Paucapalea, *Summa*, Schulte, ed., 134.

51. Cf. Kuttner, *Repertorium der Kanonistik*, 128, with reference to Thaner, *Die Summa magistri Rolandi*, xxxiii (see also xli).

52. "In ancient times, there is no doubt that deaconesses, that is readers of the gospel in church, were customarily ordained. She ought to be ordained before forty years of age, nor should she be allowed for any reason to contract a marriage after ordination." *Summa magistri Rolandi*, ed. Thaner, 121.

53. Only the Monophysite deaconess, as far as I could determine. Cf. Kalsbach, *Die altkirchliche Einrichtung*, 58; Funk, "Klerikale Frauen?" 278. But the Monophysite deaconess had other functions as well.

54. Kalsbach, *Die altkirchliche Einrichtung*, 94.

55. Freisen, *Das Eheschliessungsrecht*, 700.

56. So Kalsbach, *Die altkirchliche Einrichtung*, 88f., 112. While Kalsbach sees in the *diaconissa* and the *abbatissa* two completely different and independent offices, Schäfer, in *Kanonissenstifter*, 51ff. and in his "Kanonissen und Diakonissen," 58ff. assumes the identity of the canonical abbess (director of canonesses, not to be confused with the monastic abbess) and the deaconess, implying a development of the deaconess to the canonical abbess, in whose office

the deaconess office continues to exist. According to this suggestion, the title deaconess was "gradually suppressed by the subsequently more common name of abbess, a result of the victorious spread of monasticism in the east and in the west," *Kanonissenstifter*, 55. Nevertheless, Schäfer (*ibid.*, 58) expressly emphasizes that "the functions of the diaconate in the early church" extended quite far "beyond the direction of the (God-consecrated) women."

57. Cf. Franz Diekamp and Klaudius Jüssen, *Katholische Dogmatik nach der Grungsätzen des heiligen Thomas*, 12th ed. (Münster:Aschendorff, 1954), 3:373. See also Van der Meer, "Priestertum der Frau?" 87, n. 7 who (with a reference to Schäfer, "Kanonissen und Diakonissen," 60 with n. 1) refers to the fact that Carthusian nuns still receive stole and maniple in the consecration of virgins, although they are permitted to sing only the Epistle; the stole, however, indicates that they formerly sang the Gospel also. (When the bishop says to them, at the time of the maniple investiture, "Act manly!," the absurd idea is suggested that actions like the reading of the Gospel and the Epistle are in themselves beyond the nature of women and really should be reserved for men, who are thus "complete human beings.")

58. This will be considered in the treatment of the statements of the later decretists about the deaconess.

59. "Women however are not nor are they able to be of the order of these [priests]" on *causa* 15, *questio* 3, *princ.*, *Summa magistri Rolandi*, ed. Thaner, 33.

60. "We say therefore that by no means should the voice of a women be admitted in an accusation or in a testimony, unless for the crime of simony or for heresy or for lèse-majestè, or in marriage cases." *Summa magistri Rolandi*, ed. Thaner, 34.

61. On *causa* 33, *questio* 5, c. 11: "In this chapter it is held that if a wife would vow to abstain from food or drink or clothing or anything else with the exception of the carnal debt with the consent of her husband (*vir*), she ought not to observe the vow if he orders her to the contrary. This understanding and also the law are clearly proved by the present chapter. A women ought always to be subject to a man, that is her head, which these five chapters clearly teach." *Summa magistri Rolandi*, ed. Thaner, 199.

62. "For no reason should a superior consign his wife to death, nevertheless they are to be delivered over to prison for penance without danger of death." *Summa magistri Rolandi*, ed. Thaner, 191.

63. Cf. *Summa decretorum des Magister Rufinus*, Heinrich Singer, ed., (Paderborn: Ferdinandi Schoeningh, 1902; reprinted Aalen: Scientia Verlag, 1963), cxvi-cxvii; Kuttner, *Repertorium der Kanonistik*, 132.

64 Cf. *Summa des Rufinus*, Singer, ed., lxxx, lxxxvi; Kuttner, *Repertorium der Kanonistik*, 132.

65. "We are lead to sufficiently wonder how a council ordered that deaconesses ought to be ordained after forty years of age, when Ambrose said that to ordain deaconesses is against authority. Indeed, he said on the first Letter to Timothy on that place 'Women similarly respectable' etc.: 'Using the pretext of

these words, the Cathafrigians said that deaconesses ought to be ordained, which is against authority.'" *Summa des Rufinus*, Singer, ed., 437.

66. Cf. *Summa des Rufinus*, Singer, ed., 437, n. f. According to J. Schmid, "Glossen," in *LThK*, 4:968ff., the *Glossa Ordinaria* to the New Testament was written by Anselm of Laon at the beginning of the 12th century. Its usage was widespread in the 12th and 13th centuries, which explains its name.

67. That is to say, the *Glossa Ordinaria* to the Bible depends mainly on the works of the Church Fathers; it is to a large extent only an extract from their exegesis. Cf.. Schmid, "Glossen," 968ff.; A. Kleinhans, "Exegesis," in *LThK*, 3:1284.

68. Cf. *Summa des Rufinus*, Singer, ed., 437, n. f. Ambrosiaster's commentary on 1 Tim. 3:11 reads as follows: "'Women similarly chaste,' etc. (cf. 1 Tim. 3:11). Because he ordered a person made a bishop to be holy and equally a deacon, he certainly did not wish the common people to be different. . . . And he therefore wishes women, who are seen to be inferior, likewise to be without fault in order that the church of God might be clean. But the Cataphrygians, seeking a pretext for their errors, maintain by groundless presumption that these same deaconesses ought to be ordained because women are addressed after the deacons, even though they know the apostles to have chosen seven deacons. Were there then no suitable woman to be found even though we read that there were holy women among the eleven apostles? But in order that the heretics might seem to ascribe their own mind to these words, not in the understanding of the law, they depend on the words of the Apostle against the sense of the Apostle; since he ordered that a woman ought to be silent in Church, and they on the contrary lay claim to the authority of ministry." *PL* 17:496f.

69. Cf. chapter 1, n. 204.

70. "But it is one thing for women to be ordained by ritual (*sacramentum*) as far as the office of the altar is concerned, as deacons are ordained; this is somewhat prohibited. It is another [to ordain] in another way to some other ministry in the church which is permitted here. Today however deaconesses are not found in the church in this way, but certainly abbesses are ordained in place of them." *Summa des Rufinus*, Singer, ed., 437.

71. Cf. Kalsbach, *Die altkirchliche Einrichtung*, 69f. 109; Funk, "Klerikale Frauen?" 278.

72. Because of the indicated characteristics of ordination, several writers come to a conclusion opposite to that of Rufinus. Cf. chapter 1, p. 21, with n. 159.

73. Cf. Kalsbach, *Die altkirchliche Einrichtung*, 11.

74. So too Max Meinertz, *Die Pastoralbriefe des heiligen Paulus* (*Die Heilige Schrift des Neuen Testaments*, 7), 4th ed. (Bonn: Hanstein, 1931), 46.

75. Kalsbach, *Die altkirchliche Einrichtung*, 11 (who refers in n. 2 to Belser, Meinertz, Wohlenberg); Cf. Schäfer, *Kanonissenstifter*, 65. The most recent exegesis comes to the same conclusion: cf. Gottfried Holtz, *Die Pastoralbriefe* (*Theologischer Handkommentar zum Neuen Testament*, 13) (Berlin: Evangelische Verlagsanstalt, 1965), 85.

76. "Deacons must likewise be honorable, not double-tongued, not addicted to much wine, not greedy for gain."

77. Cf. n. 68, above: ". . . women, who are seen to be inferior." Note there also the reference to Paul's command of silence for women (1 Cor. 14:34f.). Of course Ambrosiaster overlooks the fact that Paul himself permitted women helpers in his missionary activity, who could not have been on principle excluded from the ministry of the word. (Cf. Rom. 16:1, 3, 12; 1 Cor. 16:19, among other references.) So too Holtz, *Die Pastoralbriefe*, 73, who also (72, n. 88) points to the fact that grave doubts have been raised—from the standpoint of textual criticism—in regard to 1 Cor. 14:34-36. See also chapter 6, n. 158.

78. Cf. Kalsbach, *Die altkirchliche Einrichtung*, 89, 94.

79. Cf. Kalsbach, *Die altkirchliche Einrichtung*, 90f; Schäfer, "Kanonissen und Diakonissen," 57; Funk, "Klerikale Frauen?" 281£. According to the Code, consecration of abbesses is rated as simply benediction, i.e., as a sacramental. Cf. Honorius Hanstein, *Ordensrecht: ein Grundriss für Studierende, Seelsorger, Klosterleitungen und Juristen* (Paderborn: F. Schöningh,1953), 244; J. Baucher, "Abbesses," in *DDC*, 1:65f., where it is specifically emphasized that the *benedictio* of the *abbatissa* confers no special authority in comparison to the consecration of abbots, which according to canon 625 of the Code gives authority to confer minor orders and public blessing.

80. "In the second chapter (*causa* 20, *questio* 1, c. 13) it speaks of deaconesses, who ought not be veiled, that is, ordained before forty years of age as below in *causa* 27, *questio* 1, c. 23." *Summa des Rufinus*, Singer, ed., 382.

81. "Holy women ought not be veiled before their fortieth year." *Corpus*, ed. Friedberg 1:846.

82. "Unless he (the priest) is sick, then if a great need occurs, the sick person is able to receive communicate even from a boy." *Summa des Rufinus*, Singer, ed., 554; on this question Rufinus refers specifically to Burchard. Cf. *Summa des Rufinus*, Singer, ed., 554 with n. h.

83. Cf. n. 43, above. According to Singer, *Summa des Rufinus*, cxxiv, the work of Solinus given there belonged "to the 'school authors' who were used in the Middle Ages for instruction in geography and natural science."

84. "And in fact this blood is so detestable and unclean that, as Julius Solinus said in his book on the marvels of the world, through contact with it fruits do not produce, wine turns sour, plants die, trees lack fruit, the air darkens; if dogs eat [the blood], they are then made wild with madness." Sexual intercourse during menstruation could cause abortions: "Indeed is desire kept away not only because of the uncleanness of the menstrual flow, but also lest a defective progeny is born from that intercourse." *Summa des Rufinus*, Singer, ed., 16; in *ibid.*, p. 17, more precise statements are made about this and additional very strange viewpoints of medical "science" of the time. Cf. also the statements of Paucapalea, *Summa*, Schulte, ed., 48.

85. "Truly this (teaching) concerning the childbirth by a woman is voided today because of the contrary custom of the church and most strongly because of

the (teaching) of the penitential of Theodore. . . ." *Summa des Rufinus*, Singer, ed., 16 with n. a; cf. p. 78-79, with n. 45, above.

86. On *causa* 33, *questio* 5, c. 17: "A woman, (etc.) is able neither to be a witness in a criminal case, nor able to be a witness in a civil case; except in a will." *Summa des Rufinus*, Singer, ed., 506f.

87. On *causa* 33, *questio* 2/3: "Now is it asked in the second (question) in what way it might be generally true that someone who is prohibited from making an accusation, is prohibited from witnessing to an accusation, as women are not able to accuse according to the law, however they are able to be witnesses as below in *causa* 15, *questio* 3, c. 1 (concerning public crimes). But women surely are able to be witnesses in civil cases, however in criminal cases in which the accusation is made by one person alone, they are not capable of being witness as below in *causa* 33, the last question, the last chapter (17). If anyone nevertheless wished to content that in criminal cases the testimony of women is still accepted, it is answered that, even if they are admitted clearly according to the law in secular crimes, according to canon law on the other hand the testimony of a woman is never allowed in an ecclesiastical crime." *Summa des Rufinus*, Singer, ed., 274. Yet Rufinus allows women complainant rights in case of adultery, though they are clearly not as favorable as those granted to men. Rufinus (*Summa des Rufinus*, Singer, ed., 491), following *causa* 32, *questio* 5, c. 23: "Here is it clearly taught that women are able to accuse men of adultery, but not easily, that is, males are able (to accuse) based on suspicion and without fear of false accusation." *Summa des Rufinus*, Singer, ed., 491.

88. Cf. Kuttner, *Repertorium der Kanonistik*, 135; Hove, *Prolegomena*, 1/1:434.

89. "In ancient times, deaconesses were ordained in the church, that is, readers of the gospel, who because now they are not in the church perhaps we call them abbesses, and they ought not be ordained before forty years of age." Ms. Bamberg Patr. 118 (B. ID. 21), fol. 225rb, quoted from F. Gillmann, "Weibliche Kleriker nach dem Urteil der Frühscholastik," in *AkKR*, 93 (1913):244, n. 3; this passage is lacking in the Schulte edition of Stephan's *Summa* which is likewise the case in some of the following statements by Stephan on the question before us.

90. See p. 79.

91. See pp. 82-83.

92. "In the primitive church it was permitted to certain holy women who were called deaconesses to read the gospel, which today is not done." Ms. Bamberg Patr. 118 (B. ID. 21), fol. 199va, quoted from Gillmann, "Weibliche Kleriker," 244, n. 4. We may gather this from his concluding discussion of *causa* 27, *questio* 1, c. 23: "Some (i.e., those who don't agree with him) say that if a nun is ordained, she truly receives the character (of orders), since being ordained is a question of fact and anyone is able to be ordained after baptism." 192.

93. See Schäfer, *Kanonissenstifter*, 55, 60, 272f.; Zscharnack, *Der Dienst der Frau*, 53ff.

94. Similarly, Kalsbach, *Die altkirchliche Einrichtung*, 88f.

95. "It is also possible to say this of some of the lesser orders. But this is said since clearly it is seen that there were deaconesses in ancient times, an order which is not in the church today." Ms. Bamberg Patr. 118 (B. ID. 21), fol. 206vb, quoted from Gillmann, "Weibliche Kleriker," 244, n. 5.

96. Cf. *Die Summa über das Decretum Gratiani*, Johann F. Schulte, ed. (Gießen: E. Roth, 1891; reprinted Aalen: Scientia Verlag, 1965), 272; see n. 82 above.

97. "The palls and the coverings that are in the sanctuary would have become dirty . . . the deacons with a lower ministry within the sanctuary wash the coverings of the Lord's table, lest the crumbs from the Lord's Body accidentally improperly drop off." *Corpus*, ed. Friedberg 1:1304. The chapter is taken from Letter 2 of Pseudo-Clemens, which in part existed before the Pseudo-Isidore collection (cf. Friedberg 1:1304, n. 404), and supports canon 1306, § 2, the Code (445, n. 2). See chapter 1, n. 45.

98. On *distinctio* 1, *de consecratione* c. 40, § 1: "Today by general custom this is rescinded. Perhaps nonetheless this [law] is not inconveniently stated, for this washing is intrusted to holy women, as in the church of Milan where the *Veglonissae*, that is certain religious women, prepare the offerings for the sacrifice of the altar. And in this way the *Veglonisae* wash the furnishings of the church, fix the rips, and, as we have said, prepare the offerings for use in the sacrifice." *Die Summa*, Schulte, ed., 267.

99. The *Summa* was completed after 1171; cf. Kuttner, *Repertorium der Kanonistik*, 145; Hove, *Prolegomena*, 1/1:434f.

100. So Kuttner, *Repertorium der Kanonistik*, (who refers in n. 1, p. 145, to Maasen, Schulte, Singer, Gillmann). Joannes Faventinus himself acknowledges this in his preface. Cf. *Summa des Rufinus*, Singer, ed., xlvi, with n. 4.

101. Cf. Gillmann, "Weibliche Kleriker," 245 with n. 3 (Gillmann is dependent on Ms. Miinchen lat. 3873, fol. 81vb); see p. 84f.

102. Cf. Gillmann, "Weibliche Kleriker," 245f.; see pp. 82-83f.

103. "This is the veil of ordination that is given to deaconesses of forty years of age." Ms. Miinchen lat. 3873, fol. 95va, quoted by Gillmann, "Weibliche Kleriker," 246, with n. 2. The same view is expressed in a gloss which, as Gillmann (345, n. 1) notes, is added by a later hand in the margin of the Bamberg manuscript of Stephan's *Summa* on *dict. Grat. p.c.* 10 in *causa* 20, *questio* 1 *ad v. velamen*: "There are many veils, as we are able to find in different chapters of this book. There is indeed the veil of conversion . . . There is the veil of consecration . . . There is the veil of ordination, which is now obsolete, which was placed on deaconesses but not until after forty years of age. . . ."

104. So Schäfer, "Kanonissen und Diakonissen," 62, 64 (with sources). There is no mention of veil presentation to the deaconess in the consecration formulary of the *Apostolic Constitutions* (8, 20), and also none in the formulary recorded by Assemani, *Codex liturgicus*, 9:115—although there it is presupposed that the ordinand is wearing a veil: the stole is placed under the veil. It is true that the presentation of the veil is specifically mentioned in the consecration ritual recorded by M. Blastares, *Syntagma alphabeticum*, lit. Γ, c. 9 (*PG* 144:1175), yet

the presentation of the veil is not the core of the ordination ritual but rather the laying on of hands during the consecration prayer.

105. Cf. *Summa des Rufinus*, Singer, ed., xlvif.; Kuttner, *Repertorium der Kanonistik*, 145.

106. Cf. Hove, *Prolegomena*, 1/1:436f.; Kuttner, *Repertorium der Kanonistik*, 169. (It can be assumed that the Frenchman Stephan of Tournay, educated in Bologna, stimulated *Decretum* studies in France). Kuttner, *Repertorium der Kanonistik*, 169, with n. 5 and p. 135.

107. On the basis of his investigations, T. P. McLaughlin, *The Summa Parisiensis on the Decretum Gratiani* (Toronto: Pontifical Institute of Mediaeval Studies, 1952), xxxif., places the origin of the *Summa* as early as about 1160—in contrast to previous researchers: Schulte (1160s or 1170s), Gillmann and Kuttner (about 1170).

108. So McLaughlin, *Summa Parisiensis*, xxvii. Against Schulte and Kuttner (who refers to Schulte), McLaughlin disputes the dependence of the *Summa Parisiensis* on Rufinus. *Ibid.*, xxviif., xxxiii.

109. *Summa Parisiensis*, McLaughlin, ed., 32; see also the discussion on pp. 18f.

110. "This indicated that there are not now deaconesses as in the early church." *Summa Parisiensis*, McLaughlin, ed., 175.

111. "Or a religious woman who lives from the benefice of a church or who was the wife of him who is a priest." *Summa Parisiensis*, McLaughlin, ed., 32.

112. On *dict. Grat. p.c.* 24 in *distinctio* 23 *ad v.* "*Vasa*": "And granted that you hear a woman to be consecrated, you should not understand that a woman on that account would be allowed to touch the vessels or vestments. Understand that in other respects the furnishings around the altar are entrusted to them. This is allowed out of the need of the vestments, that is, for washing or cleaning." *Summa Parisiensis*, McLaughlin, ed., 24. Stephan of Tournay writes in similar fashion (see p. 84-85).

113. On *distinctio* 23, c. 29, *ad v.* "*Mulier*": "Concerning women he (that is Gratian) has said that they ought not offer incense around the altar, etc. and in this case he removes another obstacle, lest of course she should teach men, for an abbess is able [to teach] women." *Summa Parisiensis*, McLaughlin, ed., 24f.; also on *causa* 33, *questio* 5, c. 17, *v.* "*Mulierem constat, nec docere potest*": "It is not permitted for women to teach men in an assembly. But it is not contrary [to this] that women are able to teach holy women." *Summa Parisiensis*, McLaughlin, ed., 255.

114. "The master concludes that this was said because a husband [*vir*] is able to annul the vow of abstinence before it has been undertaken if he should so wish. On the other hand it is held otherwise for the vow of continence since once she should take a vow of continence with the consent of her husband [*vir*], thereafter he is not able to recall her to her abandoned servitude. Yet in this yet they are not to be judged as inequitable, although in other matters, the man is the head of the women." *Summa Parisiensis*, McLaughlin, ed., 254.

115. *Ad v.* "*nec testis esse*": "[The statement] 'Indeed from the fact that the Julian Law concerning adultery prohibits a wronged women to testify, it can be held that a women who has not been wronged is able to testify' seems to nullify this decree. But a women is not able to stand as a witness for wills, for in wills seven witnesses are preferred; mature, male and Roman citizens. Males certainly are called as witnesses where witnesses exist. A women is not able to understand a will, so a solution has been made; a women ought not to add anything." (The last sentence is corrupt.) *Summa Parisiensis*, McLaughlin, ed., 255 with n. 46.

116. "In other contracts, just as in buying, selling, leasing, hiring, a women is able to be a witness, although they are exempted from civil offices because of the weakness of their sex." *Summa Parisiensis*, McLaughlin, ed., 255.

117. Cf. p. 25.

118. Cf. H. W. Hertzberg, "Debora und Deboralied," in *RGG*, 2:52f.

119. On *causa* 33, *questio* 5, c. 17 *ad v.* "*nec iudicare*": "nor [is this] in disagreement with women who in the Old Testament are read to have judged. And in fact the miracles of the Old Testament are more to be admired than to be considered as an example for human action." *Summa Parisiensis*, McLaughlin, ed., 255.

120. Cf. Kuttner, *Repertorium der Kanonistik*, 180 (who refers to Gillmann, "Die Heimat und die Entstehungszeit der *Summa Monacensis*," in *AkKR* 102 (1922):25-27); Hove, *Prolegomena*, 1/1:437.

121. Cf. on this Gillmann, "Weibliche Kleriker," 245, with n. 1; see also p. 85, with n. 103, above.

122. "Formerly the veil of orders was given to deaconesses, who are not now in the church, but not before forty years of age." Ms. München, lat. 16084, fol. 25ra; quoted from Gillmann, "Weibliche Kleriker," 245 with n. 1.

123. "The consecratory (imposition of hands) on religious [women] is appropriate only for the bishop and is a *sacramentum* and ought to be done at certain times. . . . As it is a sacrament (*sacramentum*), it cannot by law be repeated." Ms. München, lat. 16084, fol. 7vb; quoted from Gillmann, "Weibliche Kleriker," 245, n. 2; also by Gillmann, "Die Siebenzahl der Sakramente bei den Glossatoran des Gratianischen Dekrets," in *Der Katholik* 89 (1909), 190, n. 1.

124. Cf. the discussion on p. 81. Concerning Rufinus's concept of sacraments, see also Gillmann, "Die Siebenzahl der Sakramente," 184ff.

125. Cf. Kuttner, *Repertorium der Kanonistik*, 151. (Here the *Summa* is considered the work of the Bologna school; but see Kuttner, "Réflexions sur les Brocards des Glossateurs," in *Mélanges Joseph de Ghellinck, S.J.*, [Gembloux: J. Duculot, 1951], 2:783-787.) The text of the sources from the *Summa* has been graciously made available to me by my teacher, Prof. Dr. P. J. Kessler, who is engaged in the preparation of the edition of Sicardus's *Summa*.

126.Cf. Kuttner, *Repertorium der Kanonistik*, 151; Hove, *Prolegomena*, 1/1:435.

127. Kuttner, p. 151; cf. Schulte, *Die Geschichte der Quellen*, 1:144.

128. Ms. München lat. 4555, fol. 46r.

129. Ms. München lat. 4555, fol. 46r.

130. One gathers from another, liturgical work by Sicardus, the so-called *Mitrale*, that he, like Rufinus, agrees with the views of Solinus (see n. 84, above) about the impurity and harmfulness of menstruation blood. Sicardus gives a remarkable justification for the regulation of Lev. 12:1ff., which he considers equally binding in the New Covenant (the regulation makes woman unclean and unable to enter the temple for forty days after the birth of a son and, eighty days after the birth of a daughter): "Two things were enjoined in the law; one of which pertains to the one giving birth, the other to the one born. As to the one giving birth, if a woman should bear a male, she should abstain from entering the church for forty days as one unclean since an infant conceived in uncleanliness is said to be unformed for forty days; and if [a woman bears] a female, the period of time is doubled. The menstrual blood which accompanies the child, is held to be unclean since up until that time, as Solinus said, by its touch fruit withers and plants die. But why is the time doubled for females? Answer: because two-fold is the curse of the birth of a female; she has of course the curse of Adam, and over and above that 'in sorrow are you born,' or because, as the knowledge of the physicians states, women remain unformed in conception twice as long as men." *Mitrale* 5, c. 11, *PL* 213:242. It is true that in his *Summa* (on *distinctio* 5) Sicardus—in agreement with the viewpoint of Gregory the Great (*distinctio* 5, c. 2)—remarks as follows: "While it is held in the law concerning a woman who bears menstruating that she is prevented from entering a church, today she is not blamed for entering out of humility." Ms. München lat. 4555, fol. 3r; yet the limitation "for entering out of humility" remains characteristic of his attitude toward this question!

131. "Reverence for utensils consists in using and in not using . . . In not using . . . Furthermore utensils should not be touched except by a consecrated man [*hominis*], they should not even be touched by a religious woman as in *distinctio* 23 (Ms:42), c. 25." Ms. München lat. 4555, fol. 74r. Thus Sicardus agrees here with this Pseudo-Isidorian decretal. A conception of respect which ignores essentials in favor of superficialities also lies at the basis of the passage about the proper attitude toward the sacrament of the altar (on *distinctio* 2, *de consecratione*): "Reverence is discussed here, that priests or other pure persons make pure hosts, and preserve them once they are made so that they have no impurities. Similarly for the wine and water as Burchard [says in] book one, chapter '*panis*.'" Ms. München lat. 4555, fol. 76r. Such an "impurity" arises, in the judgment of the times, when women touch the host. In the passage from Burchard (*Decretum*, book 5, c. 29, *PL* 140:758B) to which Sicardus refers, besides clergy only boys may therefore take charge of the (unconsecrated) hosts. Cf. also Rather of Verona (890-974): "No female may approach the altar lest the she touch the chalice of the Lord. The corporal must be the most clean." *PL* 136:559.

132. In its context the following passage must be understood in that sense: "What if a Jew or pagan would accept orders or consecration to an office? Some answer that he would be a bishop. And on the contrary, what if a woman were consecrated? Again how could that which is outside be ordained? Further would

not it be retracted if a servant would give an ruling?" Ms. München lat. 4555, fol. 12r.

133. "Besides there is in marriage a certain vestige of the trinity. The husband [*vir*] is certainly the foundation, from which [comes] the woman and from the foundation of both of them [comes] the progeny." Ms. München lat. fol. 60v.

134. "A male is the beginning and end of woman, as God is the beginning and end of every creature." *Summa Theologiae* 1, q. 93, a. 4 and 1. [For a convenient English edition of these references, see *St. Thomas Aquinas, Summa theologica*, Fathers of the English Dominican Province, translators (New York: Benziger Brothers, 1947-1948), 3 vols., 1:469-470; 471-472.]

135. This attitude of submissiveness is demanded from women in all spheres, except, apparently, that of marriage intimacy: (on *causa* 35): "Spouses are equal in continence. . . . In other things the husband [*vir*] is truly the head of the wife; thus it follows the husband [*vir*] can take a vow of abstinence without the consent of his wife, on the other hand a wife cannot [do so] without [the consent of] her husband [*vir*]. Indeed as it says in the chapter, if it would happen that after the husband [*vir*] had accepted [her vow], if he wishes he can change [his decision]. In short, if he denied what he first approved, thus a female yields to a man like a reed in the wind." Ms. München lat., fol. 70r.

136. On *causa* 20, *questio* 3:

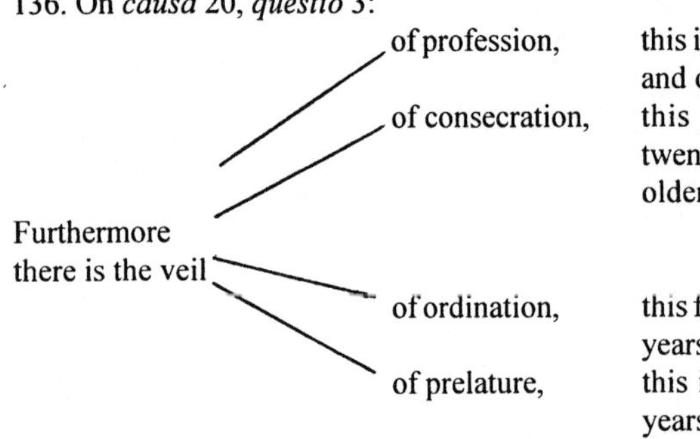
Furthermore
there is the veil
of profession,
this is for all twelve years and older
of consecration,
this is only for virgins twenty-five years and older
of ordination,
this for deaconesses forty years and older
of prelature,
this is for abbesses sixty years and older

Ms. München lat., fol. 51r. But that is, as far as I know, the only place where Sicardus mentions the deaconess.

137. Cf. Gillmann, "Die Siebenzahl der Sakramente," 199, n. 2.

138. Cf. Kuttner, *Repertorium der Kanonistik*, 149; Hove, *Prolegomena*, 1/1:435.

139. According to Schulte, *Die Geschichte der Quellen*, 1:141, Simon repeatedly refers to Joannes Faventius and considers his work to be the perfect *summa*.

140. "And there is the veil of ordination that once was give to deaconesses forty years of age . . ." Bs. pag. 71a, Rs. fol. 66r Iv; quoted from J. Juncker, "Die Summa des Simon yon Bisignano und seine Glossen," in *ZRG* Kan. Abt. 15 (1926):474; Gillmann, "Weibliche Kleriker," does not deal with Simon's statement on *causa* 20, *questio* 1, c. 13.

141. On dist. 32, c. 19 *ad v.* "*tanquam ordinatas constitui*": "as of course in so far as she has an income supplied from a church. Of course she is also able to receive charity from it. Or an abbess ought not be established or consecrated among the holy virgins." Ms. Bamberg Can. 38 (*distinctio* 2, 20), fol. 5ra; quoted from Gillmann, "Die Siebenzahl der Sakramente," 245, n. 2.

142. Cf. J. Juncker, "Die Summa des Simon," 479; also see Juncker, "Summen und Glossen" in *ZRG*. Kan. Abt. 14 (1925):474.

143. *Ad v.* "*virginem*": "It is fitting for an abbess to be a virgin since she prefigures the virgin church. The bishop on the other hand signifies Christ hence virginity of the body is not required of him. For Christ is read to have had two wives . . . Simon." Ph. fol. 162ra; quoted from Juncker, "Die Summa des Simon," 474.

144. On *distinctio* 26, c. 2, *ad v.* "*sicut femina*": "It is asked why an impure woman is not able to be advanced as abbess and how even a soldier corrupted by fornication is able to be advanced as bishop. I answer: The bishop bears the form of Christ; the abbess represents the form of the church. Christ divided himself in some sense; first by joining himself to the church of the Jews in the apostles; then through the apostles to the peoples; who were however one and united. Thus the apostle: 'I betrothed you to one husband, in order to bring you as a pure virgin to Christ.' Therefore you have here what is no surprise, that he is advanced and she however is not. According to Simon." Ms. Bamberg, can. 17, fol. 77rb; quoted from Juncker, "Die Summa des Simon," 471. As Juncker (471ff.) has been able to show, Simon's glosses on *causa* 20, q. 1, c. 12—quoted in the previous footnote—form the basis for this text (which carries the symbol "secundum *Si*") from the *Distinctiones Bambergenses*.

145. See the discussion on p. 205.

146. Cf. Van der Meer, "Priestertum der Frau?" 128ff; R. A. van Eyden, "Die Frau im Kirchenamt. Pädoyer für die Revision einer traditionellen Haltung," in *Wort und Wahrheit*, 22 (1967):355.

147. As will be shown in chapter 6, pp. 181-182, Eph. 5 is a marriage exhortation marked by the patriarchal conceptual level of the author; no conclusions about clerical office can be drawn from it.

148. Cf. Van der Meer, "Priestertum der Frau?" 132f.; van Eyden, "Die Frau im Kirchenamt," 355. The insignia of the bishop, the ring, which the abbess also wears, has no biblical basis.

149. "I betrothed you to one husband, in order to bring you as a pure virgin to Christ."

150. So too Van der Meer, "Priestertum der Frau?" 133.

151. Cf. Hove, *Prolegomena*, 1/1:436; Schulte, *Die Geschichte der Quellen*, 1:161 (not before 1187). The *Summa* has not yet been edited, but through mediation of my teacher Dr. P. J. Kessler, Prof. A. M. Stickler has graciously placed at my disposal a microfilm of Mss. Münich lat. 10247 and Vatican lat. 2280. In this way it was possible for me to take into account several texts not used by Gillmann in "Weibliche Kleriker," 246-249.

152. Cf. Schulte, *Die Geschichte der Quellen*, 1:163ff.; Kuttner, *Repertorium der Kanonistik*, 157f.; Hove, *Prolegomena*, 1/1:435f.

153. "But how can the Council of Calcedon say that deaconesses ought to be ordained when Ambrose who preceded [the council] said this to be contrary to authority [commenting] on that place in the first letter of the apostle to Timothy, 'similarly, women ought to be respectable' etc. He said in fact that using the pretext of these words, the Cathafrigians said that deaconesses ought to be ordained, which is against authority." Ms. München lat. 10247, fol. 229ra.

154. "But deaconesses were ordained, that is, chosen and through a certain ceremony established in some office that belonged to deacons. They perhaps sang and said the gospel and prayer at matins and such office and such prelature were said to be in the diaconate." Ms. München lat. 10247, fol. 229ra.

155. "Abbesses now fill such an office in some places and such deaconesses are now not found among us, unless one says that abbesses took their place and the Council of Calcedon spoke of such an ordination; Ambrose spoke of ordination to orders." Ms. München lat. 10247, fol. 229ra.

156. Thus on *causa* 20, *questio* 1, c. 13 *ad v.* "*ut non velentur*": "Concerning the veil of ordination, that is, they are not ordained as deaconesses would be. Certain nuns were accustomed in the past to be ordained as deaconesses, not in regard to orders but in regard to a certain ministry as they proclaim the gospel in the readings at matins or similar things. But now this is not done, however some nuns, without a special installation, still proclaim the gospel at matins in some places." Ms. Vatican lat. 2280, fol. 233 rb; similarly on *causa* 11, *questio* 1, c. 38 *ad v.* "*diaconissam*": "Formerly some nuns were so called due to a certain office. Perhaps now they are not, however the name is retained now so that a nun is sometimes called a deaconess." Ms. Vatican lat. 2280, fol. 170 vb. By the *diaconissa* of c. 30 in *causa* 27, *questio* 1 Huguccio likewise understands any God-dedicated woman or nun: "'deaconess' is understood to stand for any nun or woman dedicated [to God]" "Ms. Vatican lat. 2280, fol. 258rb. Huguccio, like his predecessors, relates c. 13 in *causa* 20, *questio* 1, which concerns veiling of dedicated virgins, to the deaconess and therefore mistakenly equates the subject of this chapter with that of canon 15 of Chalcedon": "The veil of ordination, which at one time was given to deaconesses of forty year of age, as in the above chapter (c. 13) and in *causa* 27, *questio* 1, c. 23." Ms. Vatican lat. 2280, fol. 233rb.

157. "Others say that formerly a woman was ordained as far as the diaconate. Later during the time of Ambrose, this was prohibited. Again later at the time of this council they were ordained. Now they are not ordained. But the first explanation prevails." Ms. München 10247, fol. 229ra.

158. "But I say that a women is not able to accept orders. What impedes this? The law of the church and sex, that is, the law of the church made on account of sex. If therefore a female is in fact ordained, she does not receive orders, and hence is forbidden to exercise the offices of orders as in *distinctio* 23, c. 25." Ms. München 10247, fol. 229ra.

159. On *causa* 27, *questio* 1, c. 23 *ad v.* "*ordinari*": "What if the person is an hermaphrodite? A distinction should be made concerning the reception of orders as it is concerning the testimony given in a will as in *causa* 4, q. 3, cap. 3, par. 22, § *item Hermafroditus*. If therefore the person is drawn to the feminine more than the male, the person does not receive the order. If the reverse, the person is able to receive, but ought not to be ordained on account of deformity and monstrosity. *distinctio* 36, c. 11 defends this. What if a person is equally drawn to both? The person does not receive orders." Ms. München 10247, fol. 229ra. Huguccio expresses the same point of view to *causa* 4, I. 2 and 3, c. 3, 22 *ad v. sexus incalescentis*: "If someone has a beard and always wishes to act like a man (*excercere virilia*) and not like a female, and always wishes to keep company with men and not with women, it is a sign that the male sex prevails in him and then he is able to be a witness, where a woman is not allowed, that is, in a will and in final wishes, and then, of course, he is able to be ordained. If truly a person lacks a beard and always wishes to be with women and act like a female (*exercere feminea opera*), the judgment is that the female sex prevails in that person and then they are not allowed as a witness, where a female is not allowed, that is for a will, but neither then is the person able to be ordained because a female does not receive orders." Ms. Vat. 2280, fol. 140va. For example, Huguccio includes in *virilia opera* (*officia*) touching the consecrated vessels and cloths during the church services. For that reason women, even nuns, he says, are to be excluded from such duties. Thus on *distinctio* 1, *de consecratione* c. 41: ". . . nor is it allowed for them [that is, to nuns blessed and consecrated to God] to produce or touch, but I understand by ministering that this is an office of men as in *distinctio* 23, c. 25. In fact they should be censured here in this matter since they are practicing male offices (*virilia officia*), at another time it was permitted for them to touch and properly produce them [that is the holy vessels and vestments]." Ms. Vat. 2280, fol. 331va. It is quite clear from Huguccio's discussion of *distinctio* 23 that these and other so-called *virilia officia* and also the *feminea opera* have nothing to do with essential male and female functions but are simply the kind of discussion he gives the following justification for the prohibition of women's preaching and teaching in a gathering of men: "Finally it should be noted that therefore women are forbidden to teach men, lest they think they should be held in esteem." Ms. München 10247, fol. 25rb.

160. Even in modern canonical literature, for instance, the question whether a hermaphrodite can be consecrated is solved in exactly the same fashion used by Huguccio (and thus by Roman law). Cf. Heribert Jone, *Gesetzbuch der lateinischen Kirche*, 2nd ed. (Paderborn, F. Schöningh, 1950-1953), 3 vols., 2:191; A. Lanza, "De requisita sexus virilis certa determinatione et distinctione ad ordines," in *Apollinaris* 19 (1946):49-66. Phillips, *Kirchenrecht*, 1:451, expresses the most extreme consequence of this principle, that only man is fit for ordination: "Male sex is so important for ordination that whenever a person belongs to the male sex and is baptized" (characteristically, being baptized is put in second place!), "he is fit for ordination under any circumstances except his own clearly

expressed will, so that a male child, a sleeping or even an insane man is preferred in this respect to the most saintly women."

161. "For three reasons a male and not a female is said to be the image of God. First because as God is the one from whom all other things [came], thus one man [*homo*] was made from the beginning from whom the rest exist and thus in this he has a similarity with God in that as all things from that one [came], thus from one man [*homo*] all the others [came] . . . Second because as from the side of Christ in death sleeping on the cross the beginning of the church flowed, that is, blood and water by which are signified the symbols [*sacramenta*] of the church through which the church subsists and has its beginning and the spouse of Christ was produced, thus from the side of Adam sleeping in paradise his wife was formed from him since a rib was taken from him from which Eve was formed. Third because as Christ rules the church and governs her thus a husband [*vir*] rules his wife and therefore he ought not to have a sign of subordination like a female but [a sign] of freedom and authority.—The fourth way both a male as well as a female is certainly said to be the image of God, whence that [passage] 'we make man [*homo*]' that is 'we make him in our image and our similitude' that is capable of the divine essence through reason, through the intellect, through memory, through ingenuity, and this is said both of a female as well as of a male." Ms. München 10247, fol. 266rb.

162. "Furthermore a male and not a female is said to be the glory of God for three reasons. First because God appeared more powerful and more glorious in the creation of males than of females, for the glory of God was manifested principally through man [*homo*] since [God] made him *per se* and from the slime of the earth against nature, but the female was made from the man [*homo*]. Second because the man [*homo*] was made by God with nothing mediating which is not the case for the female. Third because [a man] principally glorifies God, that is with nothing mediating, but a female [glorifies God] through the mediation of a male since a male teaches and instructs the female for the glorification of God." Ms. München 10247, fol. 266rb. Similarly, later on, concerning c. 13 (ibid.) *ad v.* "*vir non debet velare*": "[a male would not to cover (his head)] when he prays, that is, to have a sign of subjugation; in some sense he is not open to God, that is in some sense not close to Him in an unmediated way." München 10247, fol. 266rb. Huguccio's statement that only man is "*gloria dei*" is taken over verbatim by Guido of Baysio in his *Rosarium* ([Strassburg: Johann Mentelin, 1473; reprinted Lyon, 1549.] fol. 373v) on *causa* 33, *questio* 5, c. 13 ad v. "*mulier non est gloria dei*" (cf. p. 96) and also by Aegidius Bellamera in his commentary on Gratian's *Decretum* (*Remissorius, qui primus est tomus in duas partes dictus ad Commentaria in Gratiani Decreta.* 3 vols. [Lyons: Apud Sennetonious fratres, 1550] 3, fol. 89r).

163. The position taken by Concetti against the priesthood of women (see Heinzelmann, *Schwestern*, 89-101) implies very consistently an understanding and evaluation of women which is strikingly similar to that of Huguccio. He affirms, p. 99, that in accordance with the order of creation, primacy belongs to man; Christ has therefore not granted the priesthood to women, "in order to respect the order of creation and the plan of salvation, both of which require the dominance

of the male: of the old Adam and the new Christ." "The role of mediator" belongs "in accordance with the will of God and of Christ to man because of his superior position and because of his natural capabilities to represent Christ, the highest mediator, in concrete forms of expression." It is true that at one point, characteristically, there is a difference in the argumentation: while Huguccio unhesitatingly presents his conviction of the inferiority of women—the viewpoint of his times agreed with him—Concetti, taking account of the different outlook of modern times, affirms that this "dominance" of man does not impair "the equality and worth of the sexes," since "different functions" are allotted to men and to women. Since the ground has been cut from under the idea of women's inferiority, the attempt is made by using such threadbare arguments to conceal and minimize the legal situation of women, which is still disadvantageous despite the continuing emphasis today on equality of the sexes.

164. Cf. Schulte, *Die Geschichte der Quellen*, 1:167ff.

165. Cf. Stephan Kuttner, *Kanonistiche Schudlehre von Gratian bis auf die Dekretalen Gregors IX* (Vatican City: Biblioteca apostolica vaticana, 1935), X; Kuttner, *Repertorium der Kanonistik*, 158.

166. Schulte, *Die Geschichte der Quellen*, 1:168.

167. Kuttner, *Kanonistiche Schudlehre*, XIII. The *Poenitentiale* was written, according to Kuttner, between 1207 and 1215; according to Gillmann, "Wiebliche Kleriker," 250, n. 1, it was not completed before 1208.

168. According to Schulte, *Die Geschichte der Quellen*, 1:210, Robert uses and quotes from Huguccio and Joannes Faventinus, among others.

169. "Of the substance of orders are sex, baptism, first tonsure, [the foundation] of the other orders, the power of the one ordaining and his intention and perhaps the intention and words of the one ordained. . . ." Ms. Bamberg Patr. 132 [Q. VI. 42], fol. 13v, quoted from Gillmann, "Weibliche Kleriker," 250, n. 1.

170. ". . . Sex is of the substance of orders since women are blessed, not ordained. Granted that it is found that at one time there were deaconesses, but they were called deaconesses in another sense than a deacon today. A female certainly never had that office in the way a deacon has." Ms. Bamberg Patr. 132 [Q. VI. 42], fol. 13v, quoted from Gillmann, "Weibliche Kleriker," 250, n. 1.

171. See Kuttner, *Repertorium der Kanonistik*, 93; Hove, *Prolegomena*, 1/1:431.

172. Cf. Schulte, *Die Geschichte der Quellen*, 1:173f.; Hove, *Prolegomena*, 1/1:431.

173. So Schulte, *Die Geschichte der Quellen*, 1:175.

174. See Kuttner, *Repertorium der Kanonistik*, 103; Hove, *Prolegomena*, 1/1:431f.

175. The edition containing the *Glossa Ordinaria* and used in the following discussion: *Corpus Iuris Canonici Gregorii Papae XIII* (Lyons: I.A. Hvgvetan & G. Barbier, 1671) (hereafter *Corpus*, ed. 1671)

176. *Ad v. "ordinari"*: "Ambrose who precedes this council seems to oppose this. He certainly said, on that passage of the apostle in the First Letter to Timothy, 'similarly, women ought to be respectable,' 'using the pretext of these words, the

Cathafrigians said that deaconesses ought to be ordained, which is against authority.'" *Corpus,* ed. 1671, 1:149b.

177. "I answer that women do not receive the character [of orders] by impediment of sex and the law of the church." *Corpus,* ed. 1671, 1:149b.; cf. also on *causa* 15, *questio,* 3 *princ. v.* "*Tertio*": "A cleric is not able to be convicted of a crime by the testimony of a woman, since a woman is not then, nor is able to be, of the same order." *Corpus,* ed. 1671, 1:149b 1:1073; *causa* 33, *questio* 5, c. 17, *ad v.* "*nec testis*": ". . . nor [is a woman able to be a witness] against a cleric in a criminal case since she is not able to be what they are." *Corpus,* ed. 1671, 1:149b 1:1827.

178. ". . . Thus they are neither able to exercise the office of orders as in *distinctio* 23, c. 25 nor is she here able to be ordained, but some blessing surely can be bestowed upon her from which some special office follows that is not allowed to others, perhaps the reading of homilies or the Gospel at matins." *Corpus,* ed. 1671, 1:149b 1:1496. Joannes speaks similarly in other places about the office of the deaconess, as on *causa* 20, *questio* 1, c. 13 *ad v.* "*non velentur*": ". . . the veil of ordination, as a deaconess might be [veiled], not for orders, but for a certain ministry by proclamation the Gospel in the readings at matins." *Corpus,* ed. 1671, 1:149b 1:1122; on *dict. Grat. p.c.* 10 in *causa* 20, *questio* 1 *ad v.* "*velamen*": ". . . the veil of ordination which formerly was put on deaconesses of forty years of age, as above in the same *questio*, c. 13." *Corpus,* ed. 1671, 1:149b 1:1221.

179. *Ad v.* "*docere non praesumat*": "This certainly is a sacertodal office as in *causa* 16, *questio* 1, c. 19. Further you have fuller [evidence] in *causa* 33, *questio* 5, c. 17." *Corpus,* ed. 1671, 1:149b 1:115. On *causa* 16, *questio* 1, c. 19 *ad v.* "*sacerdotes*" Joannes, it is true, declares that a woman may preach if she has permission of the priest: "Or through a sacerdotal licence . . . Similarly the laity and women preach by the license of the priest as above in *distinctio* 23, the last chapter." *Corpus,* ed. 1671, 1:149b 1:1097f. However, Joannes misunderstands the authority alleged in *distinctio* 23, c. 29: it maintains on the contrary an express prohibition against teaching by women. Added is a prohibition against teaching by a layman, which is however limited: the male lay person, but not a woman, may teach when requested by the clergy. (Cf. p. 11.)

180. *Ad v.* "*mulier*" he refers to *causa* 33, *questio* 5, c. 17—i.e., to the statement of Ambrosiaster, who says that women are excluded from all public functions. Reference is also made to the prohibition of teaching in *distinctio* 23, c. 29. Permission to baptize in cases of necessity is supported (following *dict. p.c.* 20 in *distinctio* 4 *de consecratione*) by the decretal of Urban I in *causa* 30, *questio* 4, c. 4 (*Corpus,* ed. 1671, 1:149b 1:1983).

181. In *distinctio* 2, *de consecratione*, c. 29, *ad v.* "*peruenit*": "Some foolish priests have sent the body of the Lord through the laity or women; that is forbidden here, nor ought it be done, but if these same ones continue who have acted so contrarily, they are to be deposed."; *ad v.* "*per semetipsum*": "Or through the deacon, if it is necessary . . . or though a lay catholic [male]." *Corpus,* ed. 1671, 1:149b 1:1924f.

182. On *causa* 4, *questio* 2/3 c. 3 § 22 (*Hermaphroditus*): "It was asked whether an hermaphrodite, that is who appears to have the sex of a man and a female, is able to be a witness in a will? And it is answered that if the person seeks more the things which are male, the person is able; otherwise not . . ." *ad v.* "*ad testimonium*" Of course in a will where a woman is not able to be a witness according to law as in the *Institutes*, 2,10,6; (*Corpus Iuris Civilis* 1:17) she is also not able to be in a trial, *causa* 15, *questio* 3, c. 1. But what if there is equality in everything? Again should not such a person be able to be ordained? . . . Johannes. But certainly among all the things to be considered the sex which is more attractive should be included . . . "Hug." *Corpus,* ed. 1671, 1:773. The symbol "Hug," indicates that the application of this principle of Roman law to canon law, especially to the law of ordination, goes back to Huguccio.

183. On *causa* 33, *questio* 5, c. 17 *ad v.* "*auctoritatem*": "All male offices are to be removed from women, *causa* 33, *questio* 7, *p.c.* 1; *Digest* 16,1,1,2" *Corpus,* ed. 1671, 1:1827. On *causa* 15, *questio* 3 *princ. ad v.* "*legibus*": "*Dig. de reg. iur.* 1. [*si*] *foeminae*" ("Females are removed from all civil or public offices.") D.50,17,2; *Corpus Iuris Civilis* 1:868), *Corpus,* ed. 1671, 1:1073.

184. See n. 182 above.

185. On *causa* 15, *questio* 3 *princ. ad v.* "*mulieres*": "Females are not able to be judges *de jure* as in *causa* 33, *questio* 5, c. 17 and *causa* 3, *questio* 7, *p.c.* 1, *Digest* 50,17,2, unless the leader knowingly delegates the case as in *causa* 2, *questio* 5, c. 7 and *causa* 23, *questio* 4, c. 47, *causa* 12, *questio* 2, c. 8. Or unless this was done in previously written custom, as in *Extra* 1,43,4. Further she is not able to teach as in *causa* 23, c. 29." *Corpus,* ed. 1671, 1:1073.

186. On *causa* 33, *questio* 5, c. 17 *ad v.* "*nec testis*": "They are not admitted in criminal cases, except in those cases in which disreputable people are admitted, nor in a will, *Institutes*, 2,10,6, nor against clerics in a criminal case because she is not able to be what they are, as above, *causa* 2, *questio* 7, c. 38, nor even against laymen as noted in *causa* 15, *questio* 3. c. 1," *Corpus*, ed. 1671, 1:1827.

187. On *causa* 15, *questio* 3, c. 2 § "*Non est permissum*": "A women is not able to accuse someone in a public court, unless prosecuting injury to herself or to one of her own." *Corpus,* ed. 1671, 1:1074.

188. On *distinctio* 56, c. 5 *ad v.* "*quod suum est*": "Nature in fact produced women for this, in order to bear offspring . . . and it is shameful for married females not to have children," *Corpus,* ed. 1671, 1:293. The gloss takes over fully the conception in Roman law of the nature and vocation of woman. Cf. *causa* 6, 40, 2 ("Of course nature produced women for this, in order to bear offspring, and desire was especially established in them for this. . . ," *Corpus Iuris Civilis* 2:271); *Dig*. 21, 1, 14 ("The function of females, of course, is to accept and to care for the greatest number of children conceived." *Corpus Iuris Civilis* 2:271). Chapter 5 in *distinctio* 56 mentioned above, which is taken from the letter of Jerome to Pammachius (cf. *Corpus*, ed. Friedberg 1:221, n. 45), expresses clearly the understanding of the procreation process in antiquity and in the Middle Ages: the vulva of women is equated with the earth, which receives the seed: "Thus earth, that is the vulva, received the species of humans; [the earth] fostered that received

from him, fashioned into a body that which was fostered, distinguished them bodily. . . ." *Corpus*, ed. Friedberg 1:221.

189. Joannes, like Gratian, is strictly limited by a narrow concept of the doctrine of the Fathers about the derivation of woman from man and about woman as the originator of sin. This is obvious from the gloss to the patristic texts in cc. 11-20 in *causa* 33, *questio* 5; on c. 12, *ad v.* "*est ordo naturalis*" Joannes remarks: "that is, arising from the birth and origin; for a female is from the body of a male." *Corpus,* ed. 1671, 1:1825; on c. 13 *ad v.* "*ut unus*": "that is, man himself (*homo*) is said to be the image of God since as water flowed from the side of the Lord, thus Eve from the side of Adam." *Corpus*, ed. 1671, 1:1825; on c. 13 *ad v. mulier*: ". . . God is not glorified through her as through a male, for through her the first lie was introduced." *Corpus*, ed. 1671, 1:1825; on c. 19 *ad v.* [*peccatum*] "*originale*": " that with respect to humans had its [original sin's] origin from her." *Corpus*, ed. 1671, 1:1827.

190. On *causa* 33, *questio* 5, c. 4 *ad v.* "*hunc*": ". . . a husband (*vir*) has a twofold submission from his wife; one in regard to the debt to be yielded [to him] and the other in regard to the service to be shown to him." *Corpus*, ed. 1671 1:1821; also cf. the gloss on c. 12 *ad v.* "*ut serviant*": "It is indeed is true, that a guardian (*patronus*) by allowing freedom to enter into a business agreement, allows to her works as ought to be in the office of males." *Corpus*, ed. 1671, 1:1825.

191. On *causa* 7, *questio* 1, c. 39 *ad v.* "*iudicari*": "A husband is able to judge a wife, correcting her, . . . But not beating her . . . but he is able to chastise with moderation since she is of his family . . . as lord his servant . . . and likewise his hired hand." *Corpus*, ed. 1671, 1:836; also cf. the gloss on *causa* 27, c. 26, *ad v.* "*receperint*": "Wives are subjects to their husbands and children to their parents and servants to their lords, hence they are to be restrained by them and according to the law ought to be rebuked lest they enter into an offense worthy of excommunication." *Corpus*, ed. 1671, 1:1497; *causa* 33, *questio* 5, c. 14 *ad v.* "*ut pene famulas*": "not that they should be beaten immoderately however." *Corpus*, ed. 1671, 1:1825. The gloss on *causa* 33, *questio* 2, c. 10 *ad v.* "*Placuit*" concerns the clerics' right to punish their wives: "It is stated here that if the wives of clerics should sin, they should not kill them, but guard them lest they have the opportunity of sinning in something else, weakening them by beatings and hunger, but not to death." With reference to *causa* 7, *questio* 1, c. 39, the gloss *ad v.* "*potestatem*" expressly grants also to male laypersons the right to punish their wives (*Corpus*, ed. 1671, 1:1656).

192. On *causa* 27, *questio* 1, c. 23 *ad v.* "*ordinari*" (*in fine*), *Corpus,* ed. 1671, 1:1496. Concetti, "La donna," 94, quotes only the negative position of Joannes Teutonicus on the problem of ordaining women, without mentioning the opposite opinion in any way. He also ignores Joannes' prejudicial thinking about the female sex, which makes it in his opinion unfit for consecration. In other passages also Concetti is careless about "traditional proofs," which he gathers together without noting their time-conditionedness or investigating their validity.

193. One viewpoint is especially ignored by the argument of Joannes, which represents the opinion of the time, although it is also ignored by the opposing position. This is the viewpoint that an ordination is meaningful and finally also valid only when the ordinand has the charisma required to carry out his office. The narrower view results from the fact that the sacramental character of ordination—corresponding to scholastic thinking—is excessively and one-sidedly emphasized, while the spiritual quality of the ordinand is largely overlooked.

194. Representatives of the traditional ecclesiastical doctrine involve themselves in contradictions when they claim that both baptism and male sex are required for ordination. For example, Phillips gives the following justification for these two requirements, appealing to texts of the *Corpus Iuris Canonici* that we have already discussed: "First, concerning the necessity of baptism for the reception of ordination, it is the gateway and the foundation for all other sacraments. . . . One must first be born through baptism in order to be able to act and in order to be able himself to give birth" (*Kirchenrecht*, 1:444f.). But then Phillips suddenly forgets this fundamental importance of baptism for ordination, when he seeks to justify the requirement of male sex and in connection with it the unfitness of women for ordination: "But even the strongest faith of a baptized woman is never strong enough to empower her to receive ordination. . . . In accordance with divine command woman is subject to man and not called to authority. Adam was created before Eve, but Eve sinned before Adam, and therefore she is rightly subject to his sovereign authority. . . . Christ is the bridegroom of the church and like him the priesthood is mysteriously wedded to the church. Only men can procreate, only priests can create priests. Therefore a woman cannot ascend to even the lowest steps of authority; she may not receive the royal distinctive marks of the priesthood. . . ." (*Kirchenrecht*, 1:446f.). Apart from the inconsistency and the completely perverted understanding of ecclesiastical office ("sovereign authority"), it is clear from such language that the conception of women as unfit for ordination because of their sex implies an opinion of women as inferior human beings—in fact is identical with such an opinion.

195. Cf. Plöchl, *Das Eherecht,* 2:510; Kuttner, *Repertorium der Kanonistik*, 87.

196. Kuttner, *Repertorium der Kanonistik*, 87; Schulte, *Die Geschichte der Quellen*, 2:188.

197. "Add this: you say that [a women] is not able to be ordained as has been said above and this is the reason because orders is for the more perfect members of the church since it is given for the distribution of grace to an other. A women however is not a perfect member of the church, but a male is." *Rosarium* (Strassburg: Johann Mentelin, 1473; reprinted Lyon, 1549) fol. 329r; the edition I have used adds as "*Additio*": "Add this: that a woman is not the image of God, but a male is"; among evidences given are Gen. 1; Wisdom 2 (23); 1 Cor. 11; *causa* 33, *questio* 5, cc. 13 and 19).

198. On *causa* 33, *questio* 5, c. 13 *ad v. gloria* (*Rosarium*, 373v), Guido takes over, word for word, the statements of Huguccio (pp. 92f. with n. 162).

199. "Furthermore a woman was the effective cause of damnation since she was the origin of lying [text: of deprivation] and Adam was deceived through her, *causa* 33, *questio* 5, cc. 18 and 19, and therefore she was not able to be the effective [cause] of salvation since orders effected grace in another and thus salvation." *Rosarium*, 329r.

200. "But the material cause of salvation was able to be a woman, more precisely, materially as she had been taken from a male because a woman had been made from the side of Adam, *causa* 33, *questio* 5, c. 20; the Virgin Mary ought to have been [the cause] of salvation, and it is true that the sex of women was the material cause of our salvation, that is, the Blessed Virgin from whom Christ our salvation came forth materially. . . ." *Rosarium*, 329r. In referring to Guido, Aegidius Bellamera, on *causa* 27, *questio* 1, c. 23 *ad v.* "*characterem*," simply copies Guido's justification for the unfitness of women for ordination (*Remissorius* 3:28r).

201. ". . . you say that this *presbytera* is not so called because she had been ordained; for if a women would be ordained, she would not receive the character by impediment of her sex and the law of the church, although some disagree insofar as noted in *causa* 27, *questio* 1, c. 23. But in this case she is so called because she is the wife of an ordained man." *Rosarium*, 43r.

202. On *causa* 11, *questio* 1, c. 38 *ad v.* "*diaconissam*": "concerning that spoken of in *causa* 27, *questio* 1, c. 23, Joannes explains here that a woman who ministered to priests was at one time called an abbess or deaconess, of whom the law speaks here . . . today [such a woman] is not in the holy church." *Rosarium*, 205v.

Chapter 3

Decretals as Source for Sex Discrimination in the Priesthood

The Decretals of Gregory IX

Gratian's establishment of universal papal legislative authority resulted in the promulgation of a large number of papal decretals, especially by Alexander III and Innocent III, which claimed universal recognition.[1] These so-called *decretales extravagantes*—i.e., they circulated outside the *Decretum*—were brought together in separate collections, five of which, the *Quinque compilationes antiquae*, were everywhere accepted in the schools.[2] In 1230 Pope Gregory IX (1227-1241) commissioned his chaplain and confessor, the Dominican monk Raymond of Pennaforte, to complete the compilations of decretals with new additions, to eliminate both the inconsistencies between texts and also some material that would prove to be extraneous, and to create a unified composition.[3] Raymond's methodology was hardly scientific: He eliminated inconsistencies by suppressing decretals or changing them and he often shortened them by eliminating some of the evidences (the so-called *pars decisa*). Consequently the decretals do not appear in anything like their original form.[4] Gregory published the *Compilatio nova* (the so-called *Liber Extra*) on September 5, 1234, and sent them to the universities of Bologna and Paris with the mandate to use only this collection of decretals in the ecclesiastical courts and schools. "In this way the collection became an official, authentic, consistent, universal, and (vis-à-vis the *Compilationes antiquae* but not the *Decretum*) exclusive book of law."[5] The result is that all chapters of the compilation have legal authority in the form in which they appear, without regard to the original wording.[6]

Only a few of the large number of decretals that Gregory's compilation contains deal specifically with our problem, which is perhaps evidence that the subordinate position of women in the church had hardened considerably[7]—not the least reason for which was the antecedent collection of Gratian's. Of particular importance is the decretal of Innocent III, *Nova quaedam*[8] (*Extra* 5.38.10), which was sent in 1210 to the bishops of Burgos and Palencia (Spain) and also to the abbot of a Cisterian monastery. It sharply condemns the practice of certain abbesses in these dioceses of giving ecclesiastical, and thus priestly, blessing to nuns under them,[9] of hearing their confessions,[10] of reading the Gospel and preaching publicly. The practice of these abbesses obviously aroused the ire and the disapproval of the Pope, for he calls it incongruous and absurd, thus showing unmistakably that such practice is thoroughly incompatible with his narrow view of women. Here too, then, the motivation of the prohibition is the pejorative view of women as conditioned by the times. Moreover—of course not without inner connection with this traditional motivation, which was already evident in Gratian's *Decretum*—a "theological" reason appears now for the first time: reference to Mary who in contrast to the apostles did not receive the power of the keys.[11] This argument, which some even today like to raise against the admission of women to ecclesiastical position,[12] calls to mind the objection of Epiphanius of Salamis (died 403)[13] to the priestly office of women: God did not even give Mary the authority to baptize—Jesus did not have himself baptized by her but by John—not to mention the office of the priesthood. The kind of theological thinking which underlies such argumentation is of course completely untenable, but it is nonetheless accepted by many today, and therefore we cannot entirely avoid a discussion of it.

Obviously we cannot go deeply into the question of the priesthood of Mary in the framework of the present investigation. This would require a separate Mariological study, and we must content ourselves with a few hints and observations. First of all, in regard to the objection that Mary never received priestly ordination and the "power of the keys" (*potestas clavium*) established by it, H. Van der Meer[14] has already noted recent publications on this issue and has emphasized that the question of the priesthood of the Mother of God is far from solved—even if one does not misunderstand this priesthood as parallel to the priesthood of Christ and independent of it. It is true that Mary is granted priesthood in a certain sense by theological writers but not the priesthood of office (*sacerdotium ministeriale*)—which is mistakenly understood as priesthood in the full sense. The reason for this rejection, as R. Laurentin has shown,[15] is that Mary was not fit to receive the sacrament of ordination, according to these theologians, because she was a woman. This kind of reasoning certainly raises questions and leads to the conclusion that the denigration of the female sex on the one hand, and the overemphasis on the sacramental priestly office on the other, could have brought about a falsification and distortion of Mariology in this respect. H. Van der Meer[16] rightly points out that the argument—Mary was not a priest because a woman cannot be a priest—can no longer be used as proof for the thesis that a woman may not be a priest. For this unproved thesis is being used as basis for the statement that Mary is not a priest: one cannot at the same time prove the first by the second and the second by the first.

But beyond this, other criticism can be made of the traditional assumption that rejects the priesthood of Mary. There is not the slightest reason to confine to the so-called lay aspect of the church the predicate applied to Mary by tradition, and also by the Constitution of the Church of Vatican II,[17] that she is the archetype of the church. Such a conception, represented for instance by O. Semmelroth and R. Laurentin,[18] suggests a truncated understanding of the function of Mary in salvation history, as well as a remarkably exaggerated understanding of priestly office—which does not conceive ministry in terms of the whole church and its charismatic essence but rather as isolated from them.[19] Mary is not only the image of the receiving and believing church—loving as a bride[20]—she is also, and for this very reason, just as much the image of the church proclaiming the Gospel and conferring the grace of salvation in sacramental signs. This is, in traditional terms, the church of priestly office and Mary is the one who bestows upon the world the gift of the eternal Word of the Father, the redeemer and the source of salvation, after she had conceived him in her free consent. It is not legitimate to sever the two aspects of the church—on the one hand, receptive attitude toward God and his grace, and on the other hand active extension of salvation as deputy of Christ—nor is it legitimate to identify these two aspects with the church of the laity, on the one hand, and with the church of priestly office, on the other. The church's (active) work of salvation in the name of Christ and at his behest inevitably presupposes the ("passive") reception and assimilation of the grace of salvation.

Insofar as Mary can rightly be called model of the church her priestliness cannot be taken from her. Of course her priesthood must not be understood as a limitation of the one, highest, only-effective priesthood of Christ. It is rather a participation in his priesthood—by grace and at the same time the result of her free decision—just as the priesthood of the whole church (in the sense of 1 Peter 2:9; Rev. 1:6; 5:10) does not infringe or obscure the independence and the sole effectiveness of Christ's redemptive act. Such a misunderstanding is completely excluded—if one thinks of the ministry as charged with the duties of universal priesthood for the "upbuilding of the body of Christ" (Eph. 4:11f.)[21] when it is remembered that the New Testament avoids using the concept ἱερεύς for officeholders and simply characterizes their activity as διακουία.[22] From the fact that Mary is not numbered among the twelve apostles and was not given the power of the keys we must not conclude that she is not a priest. Her priesthood is realized in the acceptance and birth of the Son of God and in the complete giving of herself in participation in his passion and death. This brings her into God's redeeming act itself and links her most closely to the priesthood of Christ. Just as the priesthood of Christ did not come about through an act of ordination and yet ecclesiastical office was only made possible and legitimized by it, so the priesthood of Mary did not require establishment by a sacramental ordination or by apostolic office, since it had its source in the immediate election and calling by God.

Considering then the place of Mary in the salvation activity of God, it seems clear that the Mariological arguments of the *Nova quaedam* decretal has little merit. Therefore, the prohibition of blessing, hearing confession and preaching cannot be justified by reference to Mary and her position. On the contrary, it is weakened by such reference.

The medieval abbess was not only forbidden these liturgical and pastoral functions, which are partly dependent on ordination, but also the *potestas iurisdictionis* (power of jurisdiction)[23] linked to her office was limited, so that, although it is true that in this sphere she had considerable authority, one cannot speak of any equal authority with the abbot in regard to jurisdiction. Again the reason is certainly to be found in her exclusion from the sacrament of ordination.

This situation is evident in the decretal *Dilecta*[24] written in 1222 by Pope Honorius III (*Extra* 1.33.12) to the abbot of Michelstein (Halberstadt diocese).[25] The Pope refers to a request he has received from the abbess of Quedlinburg, relating that she had suspended from office and benefice a number of canonesses and clergy because of disobedience and certain offenses, but that since she could not excommunicate them they ignored the suspension. The Pope accordingly commissions the abbot to force the canonesses and clergy, if necessary by an ecclesiastical censure, to obey the regulations and show proper deference to authority.

From this decretal it is quite clear that the Pope recognizes and confirms the authority of the abbess of the Quedlinburg foundation over the canonesses and clergy who belong to it. In general, the abbess of a foundation of canonesses[26] had considerable official authority; she had charge of all foundation property; she distributed prebends, benefices, churches and offices in the churches.[27] Beyond this, she was especially responsible for the care of the canonesses and their moral education.[28] All who lived in the convent owed her obedience. The foundation clergy, too—canons who had charge of the services in the foundation's churches and were responsible for pastoral care—had to take an oath of obedience when they were received into the foundation chapter.[29] On the basis of her position the abbess exercised a certain amount of discipline over the canonesses and foundation clergy. She could admonish, suspend, demote and even dismiss them for carelessness or infraction of rules.[30]

Now, according to the decretal the Pope does not indeed dispute this authority, but nevertheless he does limit it. The abbess, in contrast to the abbot, is not empowered to impose ecclesiastical censure—specifically mentioned is excommunication[31] as the most severe censure—in order to lend greater emphasis to her disciplinary measures. Because of this fact, that the right to use censure as punishment is reserved to the abbot, it is clear that the abbess' suspension of duties and incomes should not be understood as censure[32]—which per se it could be except in case of vindictive punishment[33]—but rather as a disciplinary measure (without the punishment aspect)[34] permitted to the abbess on grounds of her administrative powers.

In harmony with the fact that the abbess does not have the authority to inflict ecclesiastical censure, the so-called "bowing" punishment, she does not have the right to absolve from such a punishment. We learn of this from the decretal of Innocent III, *De monialibus*[35] (*Extra* 5.39.33), in A.D. 1202, in which it is decreed that nuns may be absolved by the local bishop, if they have been excommunicated because of a violent act (involving physical injuries) against a fellow sister, lay brother or lay sister or against clerics commissioned for pastoral care in their cloister. Such authority is not given to their immediate superior, the abbess.

As in the decretal we have just discussed (*Extra* 1.33.12), failure of her subordinate clerics to recognize the superior position of the abbess forms the background and occasion for the decretal *Dilecta* of Honorius

III (*Extra* 5.31.14), directed to the prior (? *praepositus*) and archdeacon of the city of Soissons. Although only the abbess as presiding officer of the foundation chapter and as representative of the whole foundation had the right to use her seal[36] in certification of foundation documents, the clerics of an abbey church in the diocese of Meaux demanded the right to use their own seal. This demand was contrary to regulations—they were a part of the cloister chapter and so did not constitute an independent collegium—and they were acting against the will of their superior. The Pope empowers the prior and the archdeacon of Soisson to forbid these clergy the right to prepare and use their own seal under threat of censure. Here is explicit recognition of the abbess' position as *caput et patrona* of the clergy involved.[37]

The outstanding position of the abbess (or also of the secular female ruler)—outstanding at least in comparison with the general situation of women in that time—brought with it the attendant result that the normal hindrances which women experienced in lawsuits were sometimes breached. We learn from the decretal of Innocent III *Quum dilecta* (*Extra* 2.30.4), of the year 1206, that the abbess of Gandersheim,[38] contrary to canon law derived from Roman law,[39] was appointed by the Pope to be procurator—i.e., plaintiff in a case at law. She was to represent him in defending the rights of her cloister before the Dean of Paderborn who was acting as judge.[40] (Her abbey had been given exemption privileges by Innocent III's predecessors, which were however being disputed as superannuated by canons of the Hildesheim bishopric.)

In another case a principle of canon law that also agrees with Roman law—a woman cannot function as referee in a court of arbitration—is breached by customary legal practice: the judicial decision of a Frankish queen is accepted as valid in the decretal *Dilecti filii* of Innocent III (*Extra* 1.43.4), in A.D. 1202. (It concerned the usage of a piece of forest territory disputed by the Cistercian convent of Eschailly[41] and the Hospitalers[42] of the Sens diocese in France.) In considering the fact that the Hospitalers contested the decision of the Queen, the Pope points out that female rulers in Gaul—in contrast to general secular law which excludes women from such public office and from any judicial function—are permitted normal jurisdictional authority over their subordinates in accordance with recognized custom. So he orders the Hospitalers to submit to the Queen's decision, especially since it was strengthened by the presence and advice of bishops.[43]

We may conclude from a number of the decretals discussed that a limited jurisdictional authority of women is recognized and protected by the official church, but it is also clear how much this authority needs such protection since it is often seriously contested and endangered by limitations of right and freedom that burden women in the secular as well as the ecclesiastic sphere. Not least injurious for women is the prejudice against them as inferior by reason of sex, a prejudice that more than any other factor conditions the legal limitations of women. The decretals of Gregory IX are not free from it. According to *Extra* 5.40.10, an excerpt from the *Etymologies* of Isidore of Seville, in judging the qualifications of a witness one must be sure that the witness is of the male sex.[44] The reservations applied to the testimony of a woman result from the idea that her statements are always untrustworthy and fickle.[45] As absurd and contrary to Christian thinking as such an understanding is, that a person should have a higher credibility because he belongs to the male sex, it still was bound to work a great hardship on women especially in an unfriendly environment and historical period, when they tried to carry out any official office they may have had.

Although decretal law allows important women, such as abbesses or regents, a certain amount of independence and responsibility in the jurisdictional sphere—except for authority in punishment and in absolution—comparable opportunities in the ritual-liturgical sphere are denied (even to the abbess). This is proved—besides the decisive decretal *Nova Quaedam* we have discussed on p. 123, which forbids the abbess essential functions despite her office—by canon 3 (used in expanded form as *Extra* 3.2.1.) of the Synod of Nantes in A.D. 658 (A.D. 895 is also a possible date).[46] This canon makes general judgments against women and excludes them entirely from the chancel during mass. The wording of this chapter presents no difficulty in understanding the motive that lies at the basis of the prohibition. First of all, a priest is firmly forbidden to live in the same house with a woman not closely related by blood. But in order to prevent any possible incestuous relationship, even the mother, sister, or aunt of the priest is prohibited from living in the same house with him, although disciplinary council decrees in general permit this. Similar to these regulations is the liturgical prohibition: added to the immediately preceding, it appealed to the authority of the canons[47] with increasing insistence in the following words—including a part of a sentence omitted by Raymond of Pennaforte: "But according to the authority of the canon it is also completely prohibited that any female presume to approach the altar or to minister to a priest or to stand or even to sit within the chancel."[48] The basis for this strict ruling is again to keep a woman away from the priest in order to prevent any possible illicit relationship.[49] The prohibition thus serves to protect celibacy, like the preceding regulations about living arrangements. The forceful denial of liturgical function to women within the area of the altar, as it was ordered in the cited *capitulum*, shows, however, to what degree priestly celibacy—zealously promoted and finally required by law in the medieval church—was enacted at the expense of women; through what degradation and legal deprivation of women it was purchased and supported. A law which requires such coercive means to keep it in operation only brings upon itself the suspicion it deserves and finally a fundamental doubt of its reasonableness.

Particularly mentioned in the *capitulum* as a generally forbidden liturgical function of women at the alter is that of acolyte, which according to decretal law[50] even male children may perform. It is thus clear that religious aptitude does not count as the determinative criterion for this duty, nor does appropriate age, but merely sex. This regulation discriminating against women is still in effect. The chapter mentioned (*Extra* 3.2.1) supports canon 813, § 2, of the Code of Canon Law,[51] which decrees that a woman may not be an acolyte, except when a man—or else a boy—is not available and there is a legitimate reason. Even in this case she must give the responses from a distance and in no case approach the altar.[52]

The official post-conciliar still holds in principle to the traditional discipline. In a circular of the post-conciliar Liturgy Commission, dated January 25, 1966, the practice of sometimes using girls and women as acolytes in the Netherlands and in the United States was characterized as a serious offense against church discipline and strictly forbidden.[53] (The practice had been introduced in accordance with art. 14 of the *Constitution on the Sacred Liturgy*,[54] which encouraged all members of the people of God toward conscious and active participation in liturgical celebration and, in fact, said that they were obligated to participate.) Even quite recently, November 5, 1970, the prohibition was again expressly enjoined by the Third Instruction concerning the orderly implementation of the *Constitution on the Liturgy*.[55] Although, to be sure, this kind of regulation is likely to lead to the gradual formation of its very opposite in prescriptive law, nevertheless the fact that official church regulations declare a woman to be “such an unworthy being” that “every service near the altar must be forbidden” to her,[56] is a scandal. As long as such regulations belong to operative ecclesiastical law, the statement of the *Constitution on the Church* of Vatican II (art. 32)[57] that there is no inequality in the church based on sex, remains an untrue affirmation.

The Decretalists

A great many canonists, the "decretalists," made a thorough study of the Gregorian collection of decretals, so that one can speak of a blossoming time of canon law in this period.[58] The canonical works of the first period—from Gratian to Gregory IX—consisting of the *summas* and glosses of the decretists, were exploited by the new generation of decretalists and in this way were gradually pushed into the background.[59] In treating the decretals that concern the object of the present study, the decretalists also follow to a great extent the writings of the decretists.

Raymond of Pennaforte (see p. 121) takes a negative attitude to the ordination of women, in his *Summa de poenitentia* which appeared[60] before the promulgation of the decretals of Gregory IX, i.e., before A.D. 1234.[61] He depends mostly on Huguccio, which means on the *Glossa Ordinaria* of Joannes Teutonicus on the *Decretum*, but he also partly includes the more recent decretal legislation and affirms, with reference to the Ambrosiaster passage rejecting ordination of women, that women cannot receive the sacred character of any clerical order because their sex is against it and also the laws of the church are against it. For this reason, in his opinion, even abbesses cannot preach,[62] bless, excommunicate,[63] absolve, assign penance, judge,[64] nor exercise any office connected with any order, no matter how learned, saintly or religious they may be. Several of the texts of the *Decretum* treated above are used as proof-texts for this position, plus the Mariological argument which Raymond takes from the decretal *Nova quaedam*.[65] (We have already given this argument, pp. 123ff.) In concluding his own position on the question, Raymond rejects the opinion of those who accept the fitness of women for ordination both in reference to the diaconate and the presbyteriate, and who support their opinion, he says, by reference to *causa* 27, *questio* 1, cc. 23 and 30 for the diaconate, and by *distinctio* 32, c. 18 for the presbyterate. Raymond is hasty and without justification in accusing the representatives of this position of lying; he places them on the same level with Montanists. He seeks to minimize their evidences—which at least for the female diaconate are considerable—as did Huguccio and Joannes Teutonicus, by interpreting the diaconate ordination as a simple benediction which qualifies for special duty, for instance reading the homily[66] in matins or something similar. (As already mentioned, such an understanding of the female diaconate cannot be harmonized with our sources; the uncritical copying of previous writers ensures the continuation of error and mistaken interpretation.) Raymond understands *presbytera* to be the wife of a priest, which accords with the content of *distinctio* 32, c. 18, or rather one of the persons named in *distinctio* 32, c. 19 (see p. 18)—a widow, or the so-called *matricuria*. This of course does not agree with the meaning of *presbytera* in canon 11 of the Council of Laodicea, by which the (female) bearer of an ecclesiastical office is designated.

Goffredus de Trani, in his *Summa super titulos decretalium*, written between 1241 and 1243,[67] produces an almost literal excerpt from Raymond's *Summa*. Like the latter, he affirms that women called deaconesses had no diaconal orders but that they apparently simply had the privilege of reading the homilies during matins.[68]

In his important *Apparatus in quinque libros decretalium*—completed[69] immediately after the first Council of Lyon, in 1245—Pope Innocent IV, formerly Sinibald Fieschi, presents, in contrast to Raymond and Goffredus, no more exact reason for the *Nova quaedam* (*Extra* 5.38.10) prohibition of liturgical participation by abbesses. He simply adds to functions already prohibited in the decretal (of preaching, reading the Gospel, blessing and hearing confessions) the declaration of absolution (from ecclesiastical censures), teaching, acting as judge and the giving of the veil to nuns by the abbess.[70] All of these, says Innocent, are also precluded by canon law. Among other supports, these prohibitions are supported by those texts of the *Decretum* that clearly express the conception of the inferiority of women and of the *status subiectionis* (state of subjugation) which must consequently be required of them—which shows that Innocent could not harmonize these ecclesiastical functions with the ideas of women he had absorbed from his age. Thus Innocent's reason for the regulation (*Extra* 5.39.33) that nuns cannot be absolved from a censure by their abbess but only by the local bishop is that "this is not suitable for the sex of women."[71] This is a reason that could apply to a prohibition of all pastoral and liturgical functions. The only liturgical activity Innocent considers to be congruous with the nature of women is the reading of the Gospel, or Divine Office.[72] The reference in this connection to *causa* 27, *questio* 1, c. 23 (*Diaconissam*) shows clearly that Innocent understands the deaconess—exactly as Raymond, Goffredus and previously the decretists did—as nuns. That fact is also apparent in his discussion of the decretal *Presbyter* (*Extra* 3.41.1): He remarks that cultured women of orders like priests have the right and even the duty to pray the *officium*, because they too, it might be said, receive through benediction a kind of orders, and this is the reason some of them are deaconesses—again referring to *causa* 27, *questio* 1, c. 23, which is canon 15 of Chalcedon. However, he says, even if this ordination should extend to saying the office, it still doesn't belong to the seven ecclesiastical orders.[73]

Innocent takes from the decretal *Dilecta* (*Extra* 1.33.12) the fact that the abbess may suspend the clerics under her from office and from their benefices. He understands the reason to be that she has official jurisdictional power through customary right. Innocent however emphasizes specifically, referring to a Roman legal regulation, that this is an exception from ordinary law,[74] and he doesn't forget that the abbess had no right to excommunicate, to interdict or to absolve.[75]

Bernard of Botone's *Apparatus ad decretales Gregorii IX*, written in 1245,[76] presents a more detailed treatment of our problem than the commentary of Innocent IV. Because of its completeness, its thorough treatment of the material and its consideration of previous literature, it was soon accepted as the *Glossa Ordinaria* to the *Liber Extra*.[77] Not surprisingly it retains the traditional doctrine on our question; viewpoints already expressed appear, expanded by new viewpoints taken from decretal law.

Concerning the decretal *Nova quaedam* (*Extra* 5.38.10), which should be especially noted here, Bernard like Innocent remarks that perhaps abbesses had been permitted to read the Gospel during matins and for this reason were also called deaconesses.[78] Again, incorrectly and contrary to the sources, *causa* 27, *questio* 1, c. 23 is cited as evidence. Thus in the judgment of medieval canonists, the office and tasks of the deaconess shrink to this one scanty liturgical function. Joined to the preaching prohibition of the decretal, which is applicable to the abbess and to women in general, the gloss lists a whole catalogue of liturgical functions and other offices from which women are excluded because of their sex—e.g., touching sacred vessels, teaching activity, judgeship, acting as arbitrator, being a plaintiff in a lawsuit, and performing as counsel in court. For this, Bernard refers in part to the already recognized texts of Gratian's *Decretum* and in part to the new decretal law. He describes the legal situation of women in its dependence on Roman law and concludes that, in principle, women are forbidden the practice of every official function that is intended for the male (*viri officium*).[79] Bernard himself brings up the question whether an abbess may install and suspend in office—e.g., clerics—and this leads him to the decretal *Dilecta* (*Extra* 1.33.12), where this problem (*ad* v. *iurisdictioni*) is especially treated.[80] In dependence on the wording of the decretal, in which the pope gives the abbess jurisdictional authority over the clerics under her, the gloss here accepts that authority—despite contrary legal norms which forbid women to judge or to hold any official office. But at the same time the gloss adds a not inconsiderable limitation: In contrast to the male person (abbot) the abbess possesses only an incomplete jurisdictional authority. It is true that in cases of disobedience she can suspend from office and from benefice her nuns and the clergy under her—in accordance with the content of the decretal—since she is responsible for management of temporal and spiritual things. Also because of her administrative authority she has, like the abbot, the right to assign churches and benefices and to install clerics in the churches of her cloister. But she does not have the authority to excommunicate and to absolve (from an ecclesiastical censure). One could also say that she cannot punish by suspension[81] and by interdiction, since these also belong to the power of the keys; but they are not assigned anyhow to the female but only to the male sex. (Here the gloss repeats the argumentation of the decretal *Nova quaedam* word for word.) For even if the Blessed Virgin Mary were more exalted than all the apostles, the Lord did not nevertheless give to her but to them the keys of the kingdom.

In other respects, woman may not have such great authority because she is not created in the image of God[82]—only man is the image and reflection of God. The woman must rather be subject to the man and be at his service as a maid, since the man is head of the wife and not the contrary. The foregoing gloss expresses most clearly the causal relationship between the serious denigration of women as human beings (denial of their image-of-God status) and their exclusion from the power of the keys by their lack of ordination. The argument is supported by Gratian's *capitulum* 13 and *capitulum* 15 in *causa* 33, *questio* 5, which themselves depend on Pauline statements informed by the rabbinic spirit. Other passages indicating a denigration of the feminine sex, mixed with untenable theological argument, show clearly that such contempt is the only reason for denying women access to orders and the liturgical and jurisdictional functions connected with them. For example, just as in the gloss, Bernard in explaining the decretal *De monialibus* (*Extra* 5.39.33) remarks that feminine sex must be understood as the main reason for the fact that the abbess cannot absolve the nuns under her, that furthermore she cannot hear their confessions, give them her blessing or expound the Gospel. All this, which the decretal itself indicates, results from women not receiving the power of the keys.[83]

With similar bias the gloss finds a basis for the status of women's inferiority in areas beyond the liturgical and jurisdictional. Thus the extent of disdain and contempt of women—in an environment which made them vulnerable to inhumane situations and stunted their personal development—is clear from a blatant commentary on the reason for the classic canon law which excluded women from the function of witness in criminal cases and cases of wills and testaments.[84] The commentary is as follows: "What is lighter than smoke? A breeze. What [is lighter] than a breeze? The wind. What [is lighter] than the wind? A woman. What [is lighter] than a woman? Nothing!"[85] A similar tendency to masculine arrogance is expressed in gloss to the decretal *Duo pueri* (*Extra* 4.2.12), which says because the man has the "headship," as in *causa* 33, *questio* 5, 15, he should be believed before a woman.[86] This absurd principle of canon law—to bind credibility to the masculine sex—is contrary to human experience and to the Christian spirit, yet it is uncritically taken over and even supported the gloss.

Henricus de Segusio, who later became cardinal-bishop Ostia and was therefore called (Cardinalis) Hostiensis, was one of the most important canonists of his time[87] because of his thorough comprehension of both [Roman and church] laws. In his *Summa super titulis decretalium* (*Summa aurea*), which was probably written between 1250 and 1253,[88] he takes up the question of the particular requirements for valid ordination, one of which is masculine sex of the ordinand.[89] Depending closely on Raymond and Goffredus, he declares that, following the comments of Ambrose (Ambrosiaster) on 1 Tim. 3:11, rites of consecration are only for men, not for women. For women could not be tonsured and their hair could not be cut.[90] Besides they could not exercise the power of the keys and also could not serve at the altar—a large number of texts we have already considered are added to prove the latter. Like Innocent IV and Bernard of Botone, Hostiensis also names the reading of the Gospel at matins as the only liturgical activity possible for women, and like them he mistakenly refers to *causa* 27, *questio* 1, c. 23, as support. It is true, writes Hostiensis, that some others understand the deaconess mentioned in this canon as abbess and understand the concept *ordinari* to mean the bestowing of the veil.[91] But Hostiensis sees no argument against his thesis that women cannot be ordained, either in the legal sources which speak of the deaconess, or in *capitula* 18 and 19 of *distinctio* 32 which mention *presbytera* and which he interprets exactly as his authorities Raymond and Goffredus.

In another important work, *Commentaria in quinque decretalium libros*, completed after 1268,[92] Hostiensis, referring to the relevant decretals—and here more in the form of commentary and gloss—gives his opinion about the legal status of women in the church, often clearly depending on the *Glossa Ordinaria* of Bernard of Botone. Like Bernard, Hostiensis remarks about the decretal *Nova quaedam* (*Extra* 5.38.10) that the prohibition of the abbess reading the Gospel probably concerns high mass; she could perhaps read it during Divine Office, for which reason she is also called deaconess (once again reference is made to *causa* 27, *questio* 1, c. 23). Hostiensis thinks the purely private instruction of nuns concerning the rules of their order, etc., is compatible with the prohibition of public activity on the part of abbesses.[93] Besides the activity of preaching, he also sets forth other functions that are forbidden to women: teaching and touching liturgical vessels—not even masculine laypersons are permitted that. (It is surely in keeping with Hostiensis' manner of speaking to add—then certainly not women!) He justifies the fact that the decretal characterizes the practice of such activities by women as intolerable and absurd by insisting that such activities apply to public functions and therefore—according to the viewpoint of that age—are exclusively masculine functions. It is clear from the assertion of the Roman legal source *Dig.* 50, 17, 2—that women are to be kept from all public offices—that this very principle of Roman law was applied without reservation to canon law and so barred women's entrance to all ecclesiastical official functions. Because of this legal principle, Hostiensis maintains, an abbess cannot bestow the veil on her nuns or absolve them—in addition to the already mentioned prohibitions. She cannot act as judge nor arbitrator, unless she has this office by succession or custom. Likewise she cannot appoint or suspend clerics.[94] Hostiensis is more strict about the latter than Innocent IV (see p. 131) and even more strict than the *Glossa Ordinaria*.[95] This is clear from his discussion of the decretal *Dilecta* (*Extra* 1.33.12) which treats the place of the abbess in jurisdictional matters. *Ad v. suae iurisdictioni*[96] he accepts in essential points the justification of the gloss for the exclusion of the abbess from the so-called power of the keys and from the functions that depend upon it: not to Mary but to the apostles were the keys of the kingdom given; besides, woman in contrast to man is not made in the image and likeness of God and so she stands in a sort of servant relationship to man, her head. Because of the modest reserve required of her, a woman may not interfere in the affairs of men—a viewpoint which Hostiensis takes from Roman law. The abbess, he thinks, is simply in possession of a spiritual and temporal administration on the basis of which she may grant benefices but which do not give her the right to suspend.

This contention, that the abbess does not have power to suspend, differentiates Hostiensis[97] from other canonists. His reasoning is that suspension is to a certain extent the consequence of the power of the keys and, together with excommunication and interdiction, comes under the rubric of ecclesiastical censure, a means of punishment not granted to the abbess according to the decretal. It is not necessary to consider what actually happens—the suspension of clerics by the abbess as mentioned in the decretal—but only what may rightly happen. Above all, since this kind of function is generally forbidden to women, it is always forbidden, if not expressly declared. And since the law contains no express declaration that a woman can suspend *de jure*, Hostiensis says, one may not conclude it from the opinion expressed above. Her office allows the abbess only to admonish and to hand out assignments, but not to punish.[98]

In his discussion of *Extra* 1.43.4, Hostiensis presents a thorough and comprehensive description of the legal situation of women according to classic canonical and secular law. He comes to this by the decretal's reference to Roman law, according to which women are excluded from public office. He finds eighteen points in which a woman is legally disadvantaged in comparison to a man and thus demonstrates the authority of the Roman legal maxim (*Dig.* 1, 5, 9),[99] which says that the position of women is in many ways worse than that of men, and this includes the sphere of the church. (Of the many examples, which in each case are documented by the corresponding ecclesiastical or Roman legal sources, only the most important can be given here.)[100] The inferior status of women, according to Hostiensis, is expressed, for example, in the fact that teaching and preaching as well as the functions resulting from the power of the keys are forbidden her, and that she may not be ordained—which would give basis for the other functions. (For the last named point the Pseudo-Isidorian decretal *distinctio* 23, c. 25 is used as evidence, although in fact it has no historical source value.) Hostiensis refers to the contradictory canon *causa* 27, *questio* 1, c. 23, and solves the opposition of the canon, as Raymond of Pennaforte does: either the concept *diaconissa* is used in the canon only in an inexact way or else it is considered as a deaconess' ordination to indicate not that the deaconess is ordained like the deacon and receives the character of orders, but simply so that she may read the Gospel during matins, not, to be sure, in a solemn form but as a simple recitation. Some of the further examples which Hostiensis uses of the disadvantageous situation of women in the ecclesiastical as well as the secular realm are: their exclusion from judgeship and from arbitration functions, and from the right to present a case and enter complaints in courts and to act as counsel or, in wills and testaments, as witness. Finally in point eighteen, Hostiensis refers to the neglect of women which to a certain extent constitutes the basis for all the particular legal limitations: their state of subjugation (*status subiectionis*) under men and their alleged inferiority (not made in the image of God), reinforced by the three already discussed chapters of Gratian's *Decretum*, *causa* 33, *questio* 5, cc. 13, 15, 17.

As contrast to the many examples of women's disadvantages, Hostiensis presents three examples of the advantages which he says women have, all of them taken from Roman law. One point concerns a concession to women, that of ignorance of the right and of laws in specific cases.[101] But when one realizes that this privilege is granted to women, according to the relevant Roman legal regulation (*Dig*. 22, 6, 9) "because of the weakness of their sex" and, as Hostiensis remarks in another place, "not only through ignorance, but also through simplicity,"[102] then it is apparent that a deep contempt for women lies behind such ostensibly preferential treatment.

If Hostiensis suggests the method for demonstrating the position of women consisting of balancing their legal limitations with their so-called privileges, one of the following canonists, Aegidius de Bellamera, develops the method in almost exaggerated form. In his *Praelectiones in libros decretalium*[103] he presents thirty-one examples of the disadvantages of women in comparison with men. As in the case of Hostiensis, there is the exclusion of women from public teaching and preaching, from jurisdictional authority and from orders, also denial of their entrance into the altar area, their supposed lack of the image-of-God and their subordination to men.[104] Insofar as these many disadvantages do not contain in themselves the viewpoint that women are inferior, they are explained in a manner unmistakably implying a contempt for women. For instance, women cannot be entrusted with the office of judgeship because they are "fickle and fragile," besides, they do not possess the required intelligence and education.[105] Concerning the sixteen alleged privileges of women suggested by Aegidius, R. Chabanne has already noted[106] that they are hardly recognizable as such. Like the legal limitations, they are deduced from the supposed ontic and ethical inferiority of women. For example, Guido explains the earlier physical development of women, on the basis of which they attain maturity earlier than men, by noting that weeds are known to grow rapidly.[107] He also thinks that the fact that in certain cases women receive easier treatment in court is justified by their "fragility [and] imbecility" as well as the "less natural constancy and discernment of women"[108]

The manner in which Hostiensis and, following him, Bellamera characterize the position of women is especially instructive and important for our problem because it shows clearly that the exclusion of women from orders and from the consequent functions of teaching, preaching, pastoral care—as well as the status of subordination of women in general—is an unfortunate and unfavorable legal situation. On the contrary, today—since the question of admission of women to church office is conditioned by social evolution—we often find the opinion expressed that the exclusion of women from the office of the priesthood and the functions connected with it are neither disadvantageous nor any kind of discrimination.[109] This kind of argument, however, reflects a lack of knowledge or a failure to observe the historical sources and developmental interrelationships upon which ecclesiastical church law for women is based. For it is exactly these sources and relationships which prove that the position of women in the church—despite asseverations of equivalence with men—is today in main features still identical with their status in medieval canon law, a status described by Hostiensis and other canonists as "a worse situation than that of men." It is nothing other than the direct consequence of a contempt for women of their alleged exclusion from the image-of-God status.

The important commentary by Joannes Andreae, his *Novella in decretales Gregorii IX*, completed in 1338,[110] in large part makes use of the canonical literature at hand, including that of Hostiensis. In doing so, Joannes has the intention of supplementing by use of various works available to him the *Glossa Ordinaria* of Bernard of Botone.[111] With this goal in mind we would expect that Joannes would continue the direction taken in regard to the present question by his predecessors, if necessary adding a few new viewpoints to strengthen it.

Supplementing the *Glossa Ordinaria* treatment of the decretal *Nova quaedam*—which contains the prohibition of blessing, preaching and hearing confessions by the abbess—Joannes refers to the argumentation of several decretalists against the ordination of women. Thus he alludes to the view of Goffredus Tranensis who (in reference to the decretal mentioned as well as to *distinctio* 23, c. 29 and *causa* 33, *questio* 5, c. 17) goes back to the formulation of Huguccio and of Joannes Teutonicus[112] in declaring that a woman may not receive the (sacramental) character of ordination because of her sex and because of the regulations of the church against it. In refutation of the chapter about the deaconess and the *presbytera* which contradicts that position, Joannes points to Joannes Teutonicus' comments on the chapter, not omitting Ambrose's statement against ordination of deaconesses[113] with which Raymond of Pennaforte had supported his argument. But in addition to these well-known viewpoints he adds a new argument against the ordination of women, which reveals an influence of scholastic theology on sacraments and may have been taken from Thomas Aquinas: Because of the subjection of woman to man, she does not have the capability to mark out for herself a prominent position, and thus she lacks the adequate and necessary presupposition for the reception of the sacrament of orders, which involves such a prominent position.[114] Thus it is from the subordination of woman—which Joannes Andreae grounds in the Genesis passage, 3:16, and the rabbinically influenced passage, 1 Tim. 2:11ff.—that he concludes the unfitness of women for ordination. The lack of verisimilitude in the argumentation reveals itself especially in the fact that the Bible passages used as support are not convincing.[115] But apart from that, a viewpoint about ordination is apparent in the discussion that is characteristically exaggerated and marked by scholastic understanding of sacrament. It tends toward a misunderstanding of the priestly office as a kind of domination. Joannes Andreae's concluding argument also implies such a distorted understanding of office: "Clerics ought to wear the crown [i.e., tonsure] which is not allowed to women. . . ."[116] Here Joannes refers not only to 1 Cor. 11 but also to *distinctio* 30, c. 2, which speaks of: "the hair which God gave as her veil and as a memorial of her subjugation."[117] Of course the unfitness of women for ordination established in this way draws with it the consequence, according to the viewpoint of Joannes Andreae, that no woman may minister in the sanctuary.[118]

In interpreting the decretal *Dilecta* (*Extra* 1.33.12), which has to do with the extent of the jurisdictional authority of the abbess, Joannes Andreae for the most part follows Hostiensis. Like him, he denies the abbess' authority to suspend the clerics under her from their office, because the use of censure as means of punishment—which includes suspension along with excommunication and interdiction—is not permitted her.[119] He mentions in this connection the teaching of a certain Vincentius, according to which while the abbess does not have the right to inflict suspension, in the sense of a canonical punishment—in which the celebrant or the father confessor brings upon himself an irregularity because of a violation of suspension[120]—she does have the right to forbid clerics to celebrate mass and the right to cut off their income.[121] This differentiating interpretation may more accurately reflect the true state of affairs than the all too one-sided viewpoint of Hostiensis (see pp. 134f.).

Explaining Bernard's reasons for female exclusion from full jurisdictional powers—it is due, he had said, to the fact that woman is not made in the image of God—Joannes Andreae refers to the Old Testament narrative about the creation of the woman from Adam (Gen. 2:21f.), misunderstanding it in the way Ambrosiaster did (*causa* 33, *questio* 5, c.

13) as historical account and expounding it as proof of the inferiority of woman as a human being.[122]

The *Commentaria in decretales* by Peter of Ancharano (1330-1416) is a comprehensive work that widely uses the preceding literature[123] and depends especially on Hostiensis and Joannes Andreae in dealing with the object of our study.

Repeating the argumentation of Joannes Andreae—which had been influenced by Huguccio, Joannes Teutonicus and then by Thomas Aquinas—Peter gives a negative answer to the question raised by the decretal *Nova quaedam* (*Extra* 5.38.10) concerning women's fitness for ordination.[124] Concerning the decretal's prohibition of blessing, hearing confessions, preaching, etc., Peter, like Hostiensis, soberly considers that a woman is not as well adapted to these functions as a man.[125] He thinks that the alleged unfitness of women to receive ordination is the reason for the regulation of the decretal *Extra* 3.2.1, that no woman may approach the altar as acolyte.[126] Actually this interpretation, which agrees with that of Joannes Andreae, does not accord with the tendency of the decretal (cf. pp. 127ff.).

From the decretal *Dilecta* (*Extra* 1.33.12) Peter draws the following conclusions concerning the position of the abbess:[127] 1. The clerics, the canonesses and all persons belonging to the convent are obliged to obey the abbess; thus a woman can be in charge of churches, but only as abbess—because of the honor of her position she is granted management rights—but not simply as a woman. Peter notes that in this way the situation of a woman is less fortunate, since she cannot be a judge, an advocate or manager—in the sense of one who engages in business. 2. The abbess has jurisdictional authority, but it does not extend to punishment by ecclesiastical censure for disobedience on the part of those under her. This is the obvious result of the fact that the pope has commissioned someone else, the abbot, with that authority. From the decretal it is not possible to decide surely, Peter thinks, whether the abbess has authority to suspend from office. He refers to the opinion of Vincentius on this problem (cf. p. 138), already expressed by Joannes Andreae, and then goes on to agree with Hostiensis' view that a woman cannot rightly inflict the punishment of suspension from office—in the form of an ecclesiastical censure. The circumscribed jurisdictional authority of the abbess is also the object of the discussion of the decretal *De monialibus* (*Extra* 5.39.33). Peter notes that in contrast to the abbot the abbess is not empowered to absolve her nuns from a censure, since she is unable to use the power of the keys, which of course has not been transmitted to the female sex.[128]

Peter also sees a secondary position of the abbess in contrast to the abbot, in the difference between the consecration of the abbot and abbess, from which authority arises. Although the abbess receives the same benediction as the abbot, it does not have the same effectiveness: In contrast to the abbess the ordained abbot has the capability of bestowing the ecclesiastical blessing and the minor orders on the monks under him.[129] The reason given for the limitation of these functions to the abbot—that they are, without any qualification, male functions—is again typical of the narrow viewpoint about women which one has come to expect from those times.

The extensive commentary on the decretals of Gregory IX by Antonius de Butrio (1338-1408) exhibits, like that of Peter of Ancharano, a strong dependence on the earlier decretalist literature.[130] This is true of the treatment of decretals we will now discuss. In an almost word-for-word copy of Joannes Andreae, Antonius answers the question of the fitness of women for ordination that had been asked in connection with the decretal *Nova quaedam* (*Extra* 5.38.10).[131] Depending on the *Glossa Ordinaria* of Bernard of Botone and referring to the Pseudo-Isidorian decretal *distinctio* 23, c. 25, he finds reason for the decretal's explicit prohibition of preaching in the argument that the function of preaching is incompatible with the nature of women.[132] It is true that such a judgment reflects the outlook of the times, but on a more profound level it also reflects the extent of women's lack of freedom, for the boundaries of their activity possibilities are laid down, without regard to their own wishes and capabilities, by thc arbitrary determination of men, to the detriment of any development beyond these narrow boundaries.

Antonius handles the question raised especially by the decretal *Dilecta* (*Extra* 1.33.12), the question of the jurisdictional authority of the abbess, mainly in the form of a detailed discussion of what the gloss has to say on the subject. Expanding the gloss' position—that in contrast to men, women do not have full authority—he remarks that a woman as private person and as an individual cannot act as judge nor in any way carry out male functions, but as a person in a high position she can do these things. For, in this case, it is not she herself who carries out these functions but rather the dignity of her office, so to speak, is doing them.[133] This point of view again documents very clearly the fact that female sex in itself was considered as fundamental disqualification for the exercise of public office. According to the outlook of the times, such disqualification could apparently receive some alleviation in a high position. Naturally with such a narrowing and denigrating view of women, Antonius denies their capability of possessing and using the power of the keys just because of their sex. He finds the reason given by the gloss—Mary in contrast to the apostles was not given the "keys to the kingdom of heaven" and women could not have such authority because they are not created in the image of God and because they are in subjection to men—quite binding and sufficient. Influenced by Hostiensis and other decretalists as well as by the gloss, he maintains that the abbess has no right to excommunicate or to suspend from office—both rights come under that of censure and both depend on the power of the keys. However, he allows the abbess the right to suspend from benefice, since this is an administrative authority.[134]

Similarly to the exclusion of women from the exercise of ecclesiastical disciplinary authority, Antonius also explains the fact—decreed in the decretal *De monialibus* (*Extra* 5.39.33)—that the abbess is not authorized to absolve her nuns from a censure. He declares that the basis for these and other relevant limitations of rights (prohibition of hearing confession, giving blessing and reading the Gospel) consists likewise in the supposed incapacity of women for stewardship of the power of the keys because of their sex.[135]

Finally we must consider the *Lectura in decretales* of Nicolaus de Tudeschis (1386-1445 or 1453),[136] who is accounted one of the most important canonists of the Middle Ages. He utilizes the previous decretalist literature but supplements it, as far as that was possible after the writings of Joannes Andreae, on which he depends. Von Schulte says that later canonists did not go beyond him but simply exploited his materials.[137]

Writing about the prohibitions contained in the decretal *Nova quaedam* (*Extra* 5.38.10)—mainly prohibitions of hearing confessions—Nicolaus agrees that an abbess or another woman in high position may have jurisdictional authority as special right *in foro contentioso*, i.e., in the realm of law suits; proof texts for this are given, among other sources, in the two decretals (*Extra* 1.43.4 and *Extra* 5.31.14) we have considered above. But, he declares, this authority does not apply in the area of penance, for the jurisdiction in this realm is a consequence of the power of the keys and the power of ordination, for the possession of which a woman is completely unfit. This is so true that even in the case of a factual ordination a woman would not receive the character of orders, according to general opinion, which, indeed, represents the *Glossa Ordinaria* (of Joannes Teutonicus) to *causa* 27, *questio* 1, c. 23.[138] This sharp judgement is also apparent in Nicolaus' view of the nature of women. It is a narrow and negative view consistent with the outlook of his times. Thus is considering the fact that the decretal characterizes blessing, hearing confessions and public preaching[139] on the part of abbesses as incongruous and absurd and consequently condemns them, Nicolaus agrees, noting that in order to oppose any opinion or action it is sufficient to indicate the resulting absurdity, the argument *ab absurdo*.[140] On this theme he remarks in another place—in explaining the requirement of *Extra* 5.40.10 that witnesses be male—that when women are permitted to be witnesses they are not as credible or trustworthy as men and therefore the testimony of men must be preferred when two men and two women disagree as witnesses. The concept *mulier* (woman) is not derived, he claims, from the female sex but from the softness and weakness of feminine character. The concept *vir* (male), on the other hand, is also not a denotation of sex but is derived from the constancy and virtue of man.[141] (There is internal evidence that this judgement of women has been taken from the *dictum Gratiani causa* 32, *questio* 7, *p.c.* 18, discussed on pp. 26f.).

Following the decretal *Dilecta* (*Extra* 1.33.12), Nicolaus describes and circumscribes the abbess' area of competence in jurisdictional matters—including the power to punish—in the same fashion as his predecessors. The abbess does have the authority to grant benefices and so she possesses the right of conferring and installing which belong to spiritual jurisdiction but not the jurisdiction of orders. As woman she is excluded from all rights and authorities which depend upon the power of the keys—itself connected with orders. For this reason an abbess cannot grant her nuns absolution from sins, nor can she excommunicate, although she is a religious. Nicolaus notes that the canonists do not generally grant the abbess the right, in the strict sense of the word, to interdict and to suspend from orders—i.e., to forbid the exercise of the power of orders bestowed in the rite of ordination—so that a violation of the suspension brings upon itself an irregularity. So he too denies the abbess this authority, following the reasoning of his predecessors.[142]

Notes

1. Cf. Sägmüller, 1:239f.; Feine, *Kirchliche Rechtsgeschichte*, 283.

2. Cf. Sägmüller, 1:240; Feine, *Kirchliche Rechtsgeschichte*, 284. The *Quinque compilationes antiquae* (ed. by Friedberg, Leipzig, 1882) contain no material on our subject which is not also in the decretals of Gregory IX.

3. Cf. Sägmüller, 1:242; Feine, *Kirchliche Rechtsgeschichte*, 287.

4. Cf. Sägmüller, 1:243; Feine, *Kirchliche Rechtsgeschichte*, 287; Stickler, *Historia iuris canonici*, 1:245ff. The critical editions of the *Corpus Iuris Canonici* by J. H. Böhmer (1747), E. L. Richter (1839) and E. Friedberg (1879-1881) reconstruct the original text of the decretals as far as possible by restoring the "*partes decisae*." (Cf. Sägmüller, 1:243.)

5. Sägmüller, 1:243; cf. also Feine, *Kirchliche Rechtsgeschichte*, 287; Stickler, *Historia iuris canonici*, 1:247ff.

6. Feine, *Kirchliche Rechtsgeschichte*, 287; Stickler, *Historia iuris canonici*, 1:247f.

7. The following contain no further important texts on the subject before us: the collections of decretals which appeared after the Gregorian collection and which like the latter belong to the *Corpus Iuris Canonici*—i.e., the so-called *Liber Sextus* of Boniface VIII, the *Constitutiones* of Clement V and the *Extravagantes* of John XXII (which in contrast to the compilations named have a purely private character) and the *Extravagantes Communes*.

8. The text of the decretal reads as follows: "News of certain things recently have reached our ears, about which we are not a little amazed, that abbesses, namely those constituted in the diocese of Burgos and Palencia, bless their own nuns, and hear the confessions of sins of these same, and reading the Gospel presume to preach publicly. Since then this is equally incongruous and absurd (nor supported by you to any degree), we order through the apostolic writing at your discernment so that, lest this be done by others, you take care by the apostolic authority firmly to prevent [these actions] because even though the most blessed virgin Mary was more worthy and more excellent than all of the apostles, yet not to her, but to them the Lord handed over the keys to the kingdom of heaven."

9. The protest of the Pope can only refer to a blessing used in official-liturgical form, as, for instance, in the consecration of virgins. Against that, a claim is also made in a capitulary of Charlemagne (from 789): "It has been heard that some abbesses, against the custom of the holy church of God, give a blessing with the imposition of hands and the sign of the holy cross on the heads of males and also veil virgins with a sacerdotal blessing. You should know that to be altogether forbidden to you in your parishes, most holy fathers" *MGH*, Capit. I 60.

10. Confession of sins, as a statement of conscience before the abbess, was a regulation for nuns in many monastic rules and thus was not unusual in actual practice. (See B. Poschmann, *Die abendländische Kirchenbusse im frühen Mittelalter* [Breslau, 1930]:72; P. Browe, "Die Kommunionvorbereitung im Mittelalter," in *Zeitschrift für katholische Theologie* [hereafter cited as *ZkTh*] 56 [1932]:399f.) Now the Pope bases the prohibition of this and other functions named on the contention that Mary did not possess the *potestas clavium* (power of the keys), which in the Middle Ages was understood to mean mainly the power of binding and loosing acquired by ordination. (Cf. L. Hödl, *Die Geschichte der scholastischen Literatur und der Schlüsselgewalt*, Part 1 [Münster, 1960]:381ff.) Therefore, it must be presumed that the reference here is not only to such a devotional confession, but to a kind that makes confession before a priest—and the resultant absolution—dispensable. M. Bernard, *Speculum virginum*.

Geistigkeit und Seelenleben der Frau im Hochmittelalter (Cologne, 1955), 115f., is apparently correct in seeing in the prohibition the outcome of developing theological reflection about the sacrament of penance and thus regards it as a preventive measure against the extensive practice of confession to laypersons.

11. See L. Hödl, "Schülsselgewalt," in *LThK*, n. 9, and n. 10 above.

12. E.g., by Concetti, "La donna," 89f.; quoted in Heinzelmann, *Schwestern*, 89f.

13. *Adversus haereses*, 1.3, t.2 (*PG* 42:743); cf. Concetti, "La donna," 91 with n. 3.

14. Van der Meer,"Priestertum der Frau?" 151f. with n. 171.

15. *Marie, l'Eglise et le Sacerdoce II. Etude thèologique* (Paris, 1953), 38f. ("On n' jamais produit qu'une seule raison: Marie n'ètait pas capable du sacrament de l'ordre: 'propter femineum sexum'").

16. Cf. Van der Meer,"Priestertum der Frau?" 152.

17. Cf. the *Dogmatic Constitution on the Church*, chapter 8, 63-65 (*AAS* 57 [1965], 64f.; Abbott, *Documents of Vatican II*, 92f.).

18. So Otto Semmelroth, for instance, *Maria oder Christus/ Christus als Ziel der Marienverehrung*, (Frankfurt: J. Knecht, 1954) 131: Mary is, "to speak exactly, not simply the image of the church. . . . Mary is rather the image of the church insofar as the latter—as 'Laós,' as lay community receiving and offering together—encounters Christ, who through the office meets with his people." (Cf. also *ibid.*, 145.) Similarly, Laurentin, "Marie et l'Eglise dans l'oeuvre salvifique," in *Marie et l'Eglise II* (1952), p. 55: Mary is called type of the church but not of the church in its hierarchical functions. Contrariwise, M. J. Scheeben, *Die Mysterien des Christentums*, 2nd ed. (Freiburg, 1951), 449f., saw in Mary exactly the type of the "official" church, of its authority in ordination and jurisdiction. According to Scheeben, the grace-giving motherhood of the church, patterned after and based on the spiritual motherhood of Mary, receives full development and expression in the so-called office-priesthood of the church. Of course the viewpoint of Scheeben did not remain undisputed: see on this and on Scheeben's Mariology in general cf. Dillenschneider, *Maria im Heilsplan der Neuschopfung* (Colmar-Freiburg, 1960), 271ff.; also, *Die heilsgeschtliche Stellvertretung der Menschheit durch Maria*, ed. by C. Feckes (Paderborn, 1954), 308-322, 360-367.

19. See pp. 204ff., for further (critical) discussion about the traditional understanding of church office.

20. So Semmelroth, for instance, *Maria oder Christus*, 130f. His identification of this church with 'Laós,' (see n. 18 above) excludes the office holders from the "people of God." Opposing this view is the concept of church and office in *Lumen Gentium* of Vatican II, which is certainly a sign of progress insofar as all members of the church, and thus also the office holders, belong to the "people of God."

21. Cf. Adolf M. Ritter, and Gottfried Leich. "Wer ist die Kirche/Amt und Gemeinde im Neuen Testament," in *Der Kirchengeschichte und Heute* (Göttingen: Vandenhoeck & Ruprecht, 1968), 68.

22. Cf. K. H. Schelke, *Jüngerschaft und Apostelamt. Eine biblische Auslegung des priesterlichen Dienstes* (Freiburg, 1957), 125-132; Ritter and Leich, 60.

23. According to the prevailing opinion of theologians and canonists, abbesses, including those of the Middle Ages, possess, in fact, no jurisdictional power; the authority of their office is characterized as simple *potestas dominativa*. (Cf. J. Baucher, "Abbesses," in *DDC* 1, 67ff.; Pie de Langogne, "Abbesses," in *Dictionnaire de théologie catholique*, A. Vacant, and others, eds., 15 vols. and indexes, [Paris, Letouzey and Ané, 1930-67] (hereafter *DTC*) 1:18ff.). This point of view is critically investigated by Van der Meer, "Priestertum der Frau?" 115-128, who (like other writers, e.g., Metz, "Statut," 99; cf. also Schäfer, *Kanonissenstifter*, 140ff., 152) comes to the conclusion that historical facts refute the presupposition that the abbess' authority is only a quasi-jurisdiction or *potestas dominativa*. Van der Meer says that only on the basis of this presupposition—that the abbess as woman cannot possess jurisdictional authority—could one deny that she has such authority—a position, however, that cannot withstand an unbiased view of the facts. (My own position on this question cannot be given within the framework of this study.) In an investigation worth noting in this connection, Th. J. Bowe, *Religious Superioresses. A Historical Synopsis and Commentary* (Washington, D. C.: Catholic University of America, 1947), 27-30, presents the work of a number of writers, from the 15th to the 19th centuries, who affirm that a woman may have jurisdictional power in the church by means of special authorization by the Pope.

24. "The daughter beloved in Christ, abbess of Bubrigen, (According to *Corpus*, ed. Friedberg 2:201, n. 4, the original form was Quedlinburg) having sent us a request, has made known to us that when she herself suspended most of her canonesses and her clerics subject to her jurisdiction from their offices and benefices on account of disobedience and sins, these same, confident in the belief that this abbess was not able to excommunicate them, did not observe the suspension, on account of which their excesses remains uncorrected. On account of which, at your discretion, the ecclesiastical opinion mentioned earlier being cancelled on advice of the appeal, we order in regard to the aforementioned canonesses and clerics that you compel that they observe his healthy admonitions and orders, paying the obedience and reverence owed to the aforementioned abbess. *Corpus*, ed. Friedberg 2:201.

25. Cf. *Corpus*, ed. Friedberg 2:201, n. 2 and n. 3.

26. The so-called cannonesses formed a community that did not live according to strict monastic rule; they were not bound by ceremonial vows, having the right to reenter the world freely, and they retained their own property and foundation benefices. Foundation clergy (*canonici*), who were commissioned with pastoral care and divine services in the foundation churches, were also attached to the foundations which usually were established in the neighborhood of already existing parish churches. Cf. Schäfer, *Kanonissenstifter*, 11ff. *et passim*.

27. Cf. Schäfer, *Kanonissenstifter*, 143.

28. *Ibid*., 142f.

29. The canons had to promise obedience, according to Schäfer, *Kanonissenstifter*, 103, not only to the abbess but also to the bishop and the foundation chapter.

30. Cf.Schäfer, *Kanonissenstifter*, 143f; and his "Kanonissen und Diakonissen," 54.

31. In the canonist and dogmatic theology of the Middle Ages, the power of excommunication was understood as a manifestation of the power of the keys. See Hödl, "Schülsselgewalt," 184, 382.

32. So too Bowe, *Religious Superioresses*, 24 ("In view of the fact that in using the words 'ecclesiastical censure' the pope at the same time restricted to the abbot the right to invoke this penalty, he appeared to regard the act of suspension as something distinct from this penalty.")

33. Cf. Mörsdorf, *Lehrbuch des Kirchenrechts*, 3:395.

34. Perhaps we may use for this the term "provisional suspension" (see Mörsdorf, *Lehrbuch des Kirchenrechts*, 2:116, and 3:354). See also the interpretation of the decretal by the decretalists, p. 138 with n. 121 of chapter 4 and p. 142 with n. 142 of chapter 4.

35. "Concerning nuns, your fraternity has inquired of us through whom the benefit of absolution may be extended if they seize violently either one of their own or lay brothers or lay sisters or even clerics serving in their monasteries in order to defile them. About this [issue] of your consultation, accordingly, we respond in the following way that by our authority they are to be absolved through the bishop in whose diocese their monastery was." *Corpus*, ed. Friedberg 2:903.

36. According to Cf. Schäfer, *Kanonissenstifter*, 154, abbesses "since the 13th century at the latest used their own seals for confirmation of foundation documents." The authentication of solemn decisions of the whole chapter, since the second half of the 12th century, according to Schäfer, 161, took place in German foundations "under the great seal (*sigillum maius ecclesiae N. N.*) of the church in question," along with the seal of the abbess; who earlier was often alone responsible for the seal (*ibid.*, n. 7).

37.Cf. *Corpus*, ed. Friedberg 2:841.

38. Cf. *Corpus*, ed. Friedberg 2:445, n. 4.

39. See *causa* 3, *questio* 7, c. 2 (2), *Corpus*, ed. Friedberg 1:525.

40. The decisive excerpt of the decretal reads: "Since the aforesaid monastery has been shown to be subject to the law and ownership of the apostolic see through the privilege of our predecessors, lest the law of the Roman church remain unprotected, we have disposed this same abbess to have been established as procurator of this same [monastery] in order that, as an exception against the possessions and law of the Roman church does not apply not except for a long standing prescription, this same [abbess] should govern in our place in this and other matters that were advanced before you in court." *Corpus*, ed. Friedberg 2:445f.

41. Cf. *Corpus*, ed. Friedberg 2:231, n. 3.

42. An order that cared for the sick. Cf. K. Hofmann, "Hospitaliter," in *LThK*, 5:492f.

43. Cf. *Corpus*, ed. Friedberg 2:231. The decretal's section on discipline is summarized by Raymond of Pennaforte as follows: "For a single woman as for a female ruler it is not possible to accept the decision of a court; it is different if a woman has another jurisdiction from common law or custom. For then it would be possible for her validly to promise to accept the decision of a court over the temporal things of the church." *Ibid.*

44. "Witnesses, moreover, are to be considered by condition, nature and life. Condition, if free, not a slave . . . Nature if a male, not a female." *Corpus*, ed. Friedberg 2:914.

45. "For a female always produces untrustworthy and fickle testimony." (*Corpus*, ed. Friedberg 2:914; according to Friedberg, n. 41, this concept is taken from Vergil, Aen. *N,* 569, where the reading is: "a female always untrustworthy and fickle. . . .")

46. The rubric attributes the chapter to a council of Mainz, contrary to *Corpus*, ed. Friedberg 2:454, n. 1 (canon 4 of the Synod of Nantes, A.1, n. 36), according to Hefele, *Conciliengeschichte* 3:104, it is from canon 3 of the A.D. 658 Synod of Nantes, which reads as follows: "not even mother, sister or aunt may stay in the house with the priest, since there have been cases of terrible incest. Also no woman may serve at the altar."

47. Note especially canon 44 of the Synod of Laodicea (between A.D. 347 and 381), which forbids women access to the altar, and which is repeated by many later synods. Cf. chapter 1, n. 36.

48. *Corpus*, ed. Friedberg 2:454. The part of a sentence omitted by Raymond of Pennaforte (cf. p. 121), which must be added, reads as follows: "but according to authority of the canon . . . completely"; it is clearly the connecting term between the two textual excerpts of the decretal, not only in form but also in content.

49. This is also the sense in which Van der Meer, "Priestertum der Frau?" 96f., understands the canon. However, he does not take into account the omitted sentence fragment (see n. 48, above) and thus he overlooks the inner connection already present in the text between the two prohibitions—which are in themselves dissimilar—and so his comments remain conjecture. W. Hellinger, "Die Pfarrvisitation nach Regino von Prüm (part 2)," in *ZRG* Kan. Abt. 49 (1963): 98f. also interprets the prohibition as a measure to protect celibacy. In this connection reference should also be made to *causa* 18, *questio* 2, c. 25 (cc. 26 and 27 of the Second Lateran Council, A.D. 1139), since this chapter shows a construction very similar to *Extra* 3.2.1: certain women in orders (presumably canonesses) are forbidden to have their own guest rooms or private quarters where under pretext of hospitality they might receive male guests, contrary to good morals. Immediately after this statement, the following regulation for the liturgical Divine Office is added: 49. "In the same way we prohibit even women religious to be gathered together with canons and monks in one chorus for the singing of psalms in church." *Corpus*, ed. Friedberg 1:836.

50. Cf. *Extra* 1.17.15 (*Corpus*, ed. Friedberg 2:140), according to which it is merely prohibited that the illegitimate son of a priest serve him as acolyte.

51. Cf. Code, 273, n. 3.1. The first of the sources cited there is *Extra* 3.2.1

52. "The server of the Mass may not be a woman except for a just cause, a man being unavailable, and by the same law that [if she is a server] a woman should answer from a long way off lest through some agreement she approach the altar" in *AkKR* 81 (1901):163 ("Whoever would disobey this prohibition of the church would not be free from mortal sin, as all writers confirm who mention it. 'Therefore Laymann says rightly,' declares St. Alphons, 'that the priest should rather celebrate without an acolyte than that he should permit a woman to approach the altar.'") Similarly, Jone, *Gesetzbuch* 2:70.

53. The text reads: ". . . Jusqu'où peut aller le munus liturgicum des femmes, des femmes, dont le bapteme leur donne droit et devoir (Const. art. 14), ce sera à étudier de près; mais, que dans l'organisation actuelle de la liturgie, les femmes n 'aient pas a. remplir un ministerium auteur de l'autel, cela est certain. Car le ministerium dépend de la volonté de l'Eglise, at l'Eglise catholique n'a, en fiat, jamais confié le ministerium liturgique â des femmes.—En conséquence, toute innovation arbitraire en ce domaine sera considérée comme une infraction grave â la discipline ecclésiastique et devra être éliminée avec fermeté." *La Documentation catholique*, Paris, 1er mai 1966, 807 quoted from Heinzelmann, *Schwestern*, 19f., n. 18.

54. *AAS* 56 (1964), 104; Abbott, *Documents of Vatican II*, 156f.

55. "According to the liturgical norms handed down in the Church, women (girls, married women, religious) are forbidden to serve at the altar of a priest, not in any church, house, convent, college or institution of women." *AAS* 62, 1970, p. 700.

56. *Herder Korrespondenz*, 24 (1970), 559.

57. *AAS* 57 (1965) 38; Abbott, *Documents of Vatican II*, 58.

58. Cf. Plöchl, *Das Eherecht*, 2:517; Feine, *Kirchliche Rechtsgeschichte*, 290; Hove, *Prolegomena*, 1/1:472.

59. Kuttner, *Kanonistiche Schudlehre*, xiiif.; Feine, *Kirchliche Rechtsgeschichte*, 290.

60. Cf. Kuttner, *Repertorium der Kanonistik*, 445 (the Summa was not completed before 1227); likewise, Hove, *Prolegomena*, 1/1:513.

61. "It should be noted that a female is not able to receive the character of any clerical order. Ambrose on that saying of the apostle in the first letter to Timothy, 'similarly, women ought to be respectable,' said 'using the pretext of these words, the Cathafrigians say that deaconesses ought to be ordained, which is against authority,' since women do not receive the character by impediment of sex and the law of the church. Hence even an abbess, however learned, holy or religious, is not able to preach, nor to bless, nor to excommunicate, nor to absolve, nor to give penance, nor to judge, nor to exercise the office of any order, as in *distinctio* 23, c. 29 and c. 25; *causa* 33 c. 17; *Extra* 5.39.33. Furthermore granted that the most blessed Virgin Mary was more worthy and more excellent than all the apostles, not however to her, but to them the Lord committed the keys of the kingdom, as in *Extra* 5.38.10. Some now, as the Cathafrigians, still consider females to receive even the diaconal and presbyteral character introducing in support of this *causa* 27, c. 23 and c. 30, in which it seems expressly to demon-

strate the diaconal order, the presbyteral order is shown through *distinctio* 32, c. 18, but those chapters (*causa* 27, c. 23 and c. 30) call a deaconess those over whom some blessing was clearly bestowed by reason of which some special office followed, clearly the reading of the homily at matins or some other [service] not allowed to other nuns; in that chapter (*distinctio* 32, c. 18) a *presbytera* is so named since she was the wife of a priest, or perhaps a widow, or a 'little mother' (*matricuria*), that is, having care of the things of the church as after the fashion of the mother of a family (*materfamilias*) . . ." Raymund of Peñaforte. *Summa de poenitentia et matrimoni cum glossis Joannis de Friburgo*, (Rome: Sumptibus Ioannis Tallini, 1503) 316f. Gillmann, "Weibliche Kleriker," 252, n. 1, remarks that Vincent of Beauvais in his *Speculum historiale* (1254) 1.8, c. 70, treats the subject in question by a word-for-word excerpt from Raymond's *Summa*; also that Johannes of Freiburg in his *Summa confessorum* (1280-1298) 1.3, t.23, q.1, takes the whole title "*De impediments sexus*" literally from Raymond—with explicit reference to him—making only a few additions himself.

62. *Ad v. "praedicare,"* William of Rennes, from whom (according to Schulte, *Die Geschichte der Quellen*, 2:240, n. 7, and Gillmann, "Weibliche Kleriker," 252) the glosses have come in the edition of Raymond's *Summa* that I have used, observes that the preaching prohibition applies to the public proclamation in the church or in a synod but not to the teaching and admonition of nuns within the cloister. He rejects public preaching (*Summa de poenitentia*, 316) by referring to what Augustine says—"a woman taught one time and the whole world was overthrown"—in which the negative consequences of the Yahwistic narrative of the Fall on the evaluation of women in the church become obvious.

63. *Ad v. "excommunicare,"* William, referring to the decretal *Dilecta* (*Extra* 1.33.12) and the teaching of some canonists, does allow the abbess the right to suspend from office and benefice the clerics under her, and this means a certain amount of jurisdictional authority ("they have of course as I say a certain kind of jurisdiction"), *Summa de poenitentia*, 316.

64. The exercise of the function of judge in spiritual matters (*de spiritualibus causis*) is in principle denied to women, according to William (*ad v. "iudicare," Summa de poenitentia*, 316), but not in secular affairs, when and where prescriptive law permits it. (As verification William offers *Extra* 1.43.4.)

65. See n. 8, above.

66. Ad v. "*homiliam,*" William remarks that besides the homily, deaconesses may have recited the oration in matins, but now this is done by all nuns because of the lack of clerics. But, he says, the deaconesses about whom the chapter "*Diaconissam*" is speaking (*causa* 27, *questio* 1, c. 23) do not exist any longer; their installation in the offices mentioned (reading the homily, etc.) may have been called "ordination" but not a conferring of a (consecration) character or ecclesiastical orders (". . . the ordination of whom is called an installation to the aforementioned office, not the acquisition of any character or ecclesiastical order." *Summa de poenitentia*, 317). William follows Huguccio completely (see p. 90) in the question whether and under what circumstances a hermaphrodite may be ordained (*ad v. "mentiuntur," Summa de poenitentia*, 316).

67. Cf. Schulte, *Die Geschichte der Quellen*, 2:90; Hove, *Prolegomena*, 1/1:476.

68. ". . . nor is what is read in *causa* 27, c. 23 and c. 30 opposed by the [laws] mentioned earlier, these laws certainly speak of deaconesses, not those who have the diaconal order, but those who had obtained some prerogative among the other nuns, perhaps concerning the homilies read at matins . . ." Goffredus de Trani, *Summa super titulis decretalium* (Lyon, 1519; reprinted Aalen: Scientia Verlag, 1968.), fol. 30 v.

69. Cf. Schulte, *Die Geschichte der Quellen*, 2:93; Hove, *Prolegomena*, 1/1:477.

70. *Ad v.* "*benedicunt*": "that they are not able [to bless], *causa* 3, *questio* 5, c. 17, nor to veil, *causa* 20, *questio* 2, c. 3, nor to absolve, *Extra* 5.39.33, nor to teach *distinctio* 23, c. 29, nor to judge *causa* 33, *questio* 5, c. 17." Innocent IV (Sinibaldus Fliscus). *Apparatus in quinque libros decretalium* (Frankfurt, 1570; reprinted Frankfurt: Minerva, 1968), fol. 544v.

71. *Ad v.* "*episcopum*": "of course this is not suitable for the sex of women," *Extra* 5.38.10. *Apparatus*, fol. 551v.

72. On *Extra* 5.38.10 *ad v.* "*publice*": "at matins, however, they are able to read *causa* 27 (Text: 38) *questio* 1 c. 25." *Apparatus*, fol. 544v.

73. ". . . The laity, however, are certainly able to say the psalms which are said at hours, but not in the manner of an office . . . however literate nuns say the offices since they are able to be said to accept a certain order by blessing, whence some among them are even deaconesses, *causa* 27, *questio* 1, c. 23, which order, although it is sufficient for saying the offices, [is] nevertheless not one of the seven orders of the church." *Apparatus*, fol. 453r.

74. Similarly also on *Extra* 2.30.4 *ad v.* "*procuratricem*" (in reference to the competence of the abbess to act as deputy in a lawsuit): "*Dig.* 1, dist. 3.3.41 opposes, but this is special for women established in a dignity. . . or according to which this is an abbess, she is able to be a procurator for the things of a monastery . . . or this was by a special favor which is not allowed to another." *Apparatus*, fol. 347r.

75. *Ad v.* "*suspendat*": "It should be noted here that an abbess is able to suspend her clerics from an office and a benefice. And this is for that reason since by custom she has ordinary jurisdiction according to ruling below, *Extra* 1.42.4, in another case, however, this is against the common law . . . they are not able to excommunicate, however, as here, nor to absolve as below in *Extra* 5.39.33, you will find a reason below in *Extra* 5.8.10." *Apparatus*, fol. 158v/159r.

76. Cf. Hove, *Prolegomena*, 1/1:474. But according to Schulte, *Die Geschichte der Quellen*, 2:115 and Hove, *Prolegomena*, 1/1:473, the author was writing up to the very end of his life (1263).

77. Cf. Schulte, *Die Geschichte der Quellen*, 2:115.

78. *Ad v.* "*Evangelium*": "At matins of course they were able to read the gospel, from which they are even called deaconesses," *causa* 27 [Test 17], *questio* 1, c. 23 *Corpus,* ed. 1671, 2:1869f.

79. *Ad v. "praedicare"*: "A woman in fact is able neither to preach, nor to teach because this office is foreign to women, nor to touch the sacred vessels . . . nor are they able to veil nuns . . . nor to absolve them . . . nor to judge, unless clearly some noble [woman] has this from custom . . . nor to take authority upon themselves . . . nor is she able to be a procurator in court . . . nor is she able to plead in court . . . and generally the office of males is forbidden to women." *Corpus*, ed. 1671, 2:1869f.

80. "Thus a women then has jurisdiction, below *Extra* 1.43.4. But that a woman is not able to judge, *causa* 33, *questio* 5, c. 17, nor can she discharge civil offices, *Codex* 1.2.12.18, Dig. 1.2.50.17.2 seems to contradict this. You say that an abbess has some sort of jurisdiction, although not full [jurisdiction] as a male does. You say then that she is able to suspend her nuns and clerics from office and benefice if they were disobedient, according to that which is indicated sufficiently here; she has in fact temporal and spiritual administration. . . . Further, by reason of her administration and after her confirmation, she is able to bestow churches and benefices and install clerics in the churches of her monastery . . . as abbots . . . Just as an abbot, in fact, they act with the consent of the chapter . . . an abbess in the same way. She is not able to excommunicate or absolve, below *Extra* 5.39.33. And it is able to be said that neither is she able to suspend nor to interdict since this pertains to the keys . . . and the pope did not say here that she is able to do so since the keys of the kingdom of heaven were handed over not to the feminine sex, but the masculine: granted of course that the most blessed Mary was more excellent than all the apostles, it was not however to her, but to them that the Lord committed the keys of the kingdom, as in *Extra* 5.38.10, nor is she able to veil nuns, *causa* 20, *questio* 2, c. 3. Besides a women ought not have such power since she was not made in the image of God, but a male who is the image and glory of God [was so made]; and a woman ought be subject to a male and to be somewhat like handmaid to males, as a male is the head of a woman and not the contrary, *causa* 33, *questio* 5, c. 13 and c. 15." *Corpus*, ed. 1671, 2:431f.

81. There seems to be here a contradiction to previous statements according to which, on the basis of the content of the decretal, the abbess is granted authority to suspend from office and benefice. But apparently the power of suspension referred to above should be understood as the consequence of the abbess' administrative authority, *potestas dominative*, which allows her a certain right of punishing those under her, whereas here on the contrary reference is made to the right of censuring, which only higher ecclesiastical authority possesses. (Cf. p. 74.)

82. The edition (col. 432) has the following marginal reading *ad v. "imaginem"*: "Blessed Thomas proposes how this should be understood that a woman was not made in the image of God in [*Summa theologiae*] 1, *questio* 93 [Text: 51 art. 4 *ad* 1. *argum*[*entum*]." Allusion is made to the following statement of Thomas: "In relation to that with which the meaning of an image principally has to do—that is, in relation to spiritual nature—the image of God is in man and also in woman. . . . In relation to something secondary, it is true that the image of God is in man in a way not found in woman. For man is beginning and end of woman,

just as God is beginning and end of the whole creation. Therefore the Apostle adds to the words, 'Man is the image and reflection of God but woman is the glory of man,' the reason for this (1 Cor. 11:8f.): 'For the man does not come from the woman but the woman from man. Neither was man created for woman but woman for man.'"

83. *Ad v. "per episcopum"*: "The sex of a woman impedes [this]; nor is an abbess able to absolve nuns, as this makes clear, nor to hear their confession, nor to bless them or to read the gospel since the keys of the church were not entrusted to the feminine sex." *Corpus*, ed. 1671, 2:1905.

84. Cf. p. 76; also gloss on *Extra* 5.40.10 *ad v. "non foemina"*: "Understand this for criminal cases in which case a woman is not able to be a witness according to the laws, *causa* 33, *questio* 5, c. 17, but in civil and matrimonial [cases] she certainly gives testimony. . . . Further a woman is not permitted [to testify] for wills." *Corpus*, ed. 1671, 2:1936.

85. On *Extra* 5.40.10 *ad v. "varium"*: "What is lighter than smoke? A breeze. What [is lighter] than a breeze? The wind. What [is lighter] than the wind? A woman. What [is lighter] than a woman? Nothing." *Corpus*, ed. 1671, 2:1936.

86. "As *causa* 33, *questio* 5, c. 15 [on the words "as head"] whence he is more to be believed than the wife." (two references are given for this: *Extra* 4.2.6 and *causa* 33, *questio* 1, c. 3, *Corpus*, ed. 1671, 2:1455).

87. Cf. Schulte, *Die Geschichte der Quellen*, 2:127; Plöchl, *Das Eherecht,* 2:520.

88. Cf. Hove, *Prolegomena*, 1/1:476.

89. "But over and above the rules already stated, [the correct] sex is required; orders are conferred on men [*homines*] not of course on women as Ambrose says on Timothy on that passage, 'similarly, women ought to be respectable,' etc. since they ought not to be tonsured . . . nor should the hair of women be cut off, *distinctio* 30, c. 2, nor are they able to exercise the power of the keys, *Extra* 1.3.12 and expressly in *Extra* 5.38.10, nor even ought they serve at the altar, below *Extra* 3. 2. 1, *distinctio* 23, c. 29 and c. 25, *de consecratione, distinctio* 1, c. 41, *causa* 33, *questio* 5, c. 17, however they are able to read gospel at matins, *causa* 27, *questio* 1, c. 23, although some explain the deaconess here to be an abbess; ordained, that is to be veiled; nor does *distinctio* 32, c. 18 disagree since here "*presbytera*" [means] in some sense "presbyteral," not that she would be ordained, but the wife of one ordained, hence in the following chapter where such females are called elders, having one husband or *marticurie*, that is having maternal care of the church, as is said of the mother of a family (*materfamilias*)." Hostiensis (Henricus de Segusio), *Summa aurea*, (Venice: Apud Iacobum Vitalem, 1574; reprinted Turin: Bottega d'Erasmo, 1963),188.

90. Authority used for this is *distinctio* 30, c. 2 (canon 17 of the Synod of Gangra/Asia Minor, between A.D. 325 and 370): "Any woman who, judging this to be fitting for devotion, has cut off the hair which God gave as her veil and as a memorial of her subjugation, as if annulling the law of subjugation, let her be anathema." *Corpus*, ed. Friedberg 1:107. The stipulation is clearly influenced by

the Pauline passage 1 Cor. 11:5ff.—and therefore by rabbinical viewpoints, which in this way have had influence on ecclesiastical legislation.

91. Hostiensis also in another place (*Summa aurea*, 173)—following many of his predecessors—understands the ordination of the deaconess as bestowing the so-called "the veil of ordination which formerly given to deaconesses of forty years of age."

92. According to Schulte, *Die Geschichte der Quellen*, 2:125, he worked on the book to the very end of his life, (A.D. 1271); cf. Hove, *Prolegomena*, 1/1:479.

93. "Understand [this to mean] in a solemn mass; in matins of course they certainly are able to read it [the gospel] hence they are called deaconesses, *causa* 27, *questio* 1, c. 23; *ad v.* "*publice*": "as if he said if privately in the chapter she would explain the rule to her nuns alone or offer some good examples for moral instruction or other simple words, this is not condemned." Hostiensis (Henricus de Segusio), *Commentaria in quinque libros decretalium*, 5 vols. (Venice: Apud Juntas, 1581; reprinted Turin: Bottega d'Erasmo, 1965), 5:101r.

94. "And this is the fourth abuse . . . a woman of course is able neither to preach nor to teach nor even to touch the sacred vessels, *distintio* 23, c. 25 and c. 29, *causa* 33, *questio* 5, c. 17, since not even a layman is able to exercise this office."; *ad v.* "*id absonum sit*": "On the contrary, those things which are omitted and which are considered to be male offices (*virilia officia*) from which women usually have been excluded as *Dig.* 50.17.2 demonstrates . . . hence they [women] likewise are able neither to veil their own nuns . . . nor to absolve . . . nor to judge, nor to receive a judgment unless some noble woman had this clearly through succession or custom . . . but they are not able to install nor suspend . . ." *Commentaria,* 5:101r.

95. While Bernard of Botone is of the opinion that the abbess by reason of her administrative authority can appoint clerics and suspend them from office and benefice (cf. pp. 139f., above), Hostiensis grants her only the right to grant benefices and to withdraw them on *Extra* 1.33.12 *ad v.* "*suae iurisdictioni*": ". . . She is able to bestow a benefice"; *ad v.* "*excommunicare*": "[to excommunicate] nor to suspend, granted *de facto* she might be able to withdraw his prebend, although some say that she is able to suspend . . ." *Commentaria,* 1:173v.

96. "Thus therefore a woman has jurisdiction as here and below in *Extra* 1.43.4. But on the contrary, since a woman is not able to judge, *causa* 33, *questio* 5, c. 17 . . . nor to perform male offices (*virilibus officiis*), *Dig.* 50.17.2. Solution: what the contradictions say usually prevails. This is misleading in regard to noble women . . . This is misleading also in regard to women in authority (*praelata*) for the same reason, so that this is such that she does not have full spiritual jurisdiction, since she is able neither to hear confessions or absolve, nor to exercise other things which pertain to the keys of the church, no matter how great and noble she is. And this is the reason since granted that the most blessed Virgin was more excellent than all of the apostles, it was not however to her, but to these that her Son turned to hand over his keys, below *Extra* 5.38.10. Nor was a woman made in the image and similitude of God as a male [was], and therefore she is a sort of handmaiden to males since a male is the head of a woman, *causa* 33, *questio* 5,

c. 13 and c. 15 according to Bernard. But also she ought not to mix with the company of males on account of feminine modesty, *Cod.* 2.44.2. . . . Therefore she is able neither to veil nuns nor to excommunicate as was said . . . she is able to have spiritual and temporal administration as here . . . and she is able to grant benefices from which she has this administration . . . Her same subjects are also held to show obedience and reverence and to fulfill her admonitions and beneficial commands . . ." *Commentaria,* 1:173 r/v.

97. "Nothing is said concerning a sentence of suspension, therefore are they obliged to serve it? Yes, according to some, since she herself suspends . . . This is true *de facto*, but it does not say in another place in this letter that she is able to do this *de jure*, on the other hand, what should be considered is not what is done, but what ought to be done. . . . And therefore whatever others say, you say that at least she is not able to suspend from office since this is a kind of key, and is contained under the name of ecclesiastical censure which, since an abbess is not able to exercise this [censure], [it] is committed to judges to whom she has recourse as follows. As in fact to excommunicate, to suspend and to interdict are connected, and are effected from the same and to the same person, by which reasoning a lack of jurisdiction is denied [in] one [case], it is to be denied in the rest [of the cases]. . . . Especially since from which such things are usually forbidden to women . . . they are always forbidden unless they are found to be expressly granted, but you do not find expressed in the law that a woman is able to suspend *de iure*, therefore you ought not to supplement this from the opinion of the glossators . . ." *Commentaria*, 1:173v.

98. *Ad v.* "*compellas*": "as if he said that admonition, command but not punishment belong to the abbess." *Commentaria*, 1:173v.

99. "In many articles of our laws, the condition of females is worse than that of males."*Corpus Iuris Civilis*, 1, 7.

100. "The condition of females is in fact worse that males in many things. . . . First because a women is not able to judge . . . unless a ruler entrusts this to her . . . Or unless custom agrees with this for her . . . Second because she is not able to receive a judgement for herself. . . . Third because she is not able to teach, publicly preach, hear confessions, nor to exercise other things which pertain to the keys, below *Extra* 5.38.10. Fourth because she is not able to receive orders, *distinctio* 23, c. 25. But on the contrary, *causa* 27, *questio* 1, c. 23 [on deaconesses]. Solution: this is speaking improperly. Or she is said to be a deaconess not that she is ordained in the way a deacon [is], nor does she receive a character, but in order to be capable of reading the gospel at matins, not in magnificence or solemnly, but simply in the style of a reading. Five because she is not able to prosecute . . . Eight because she is not able to accuse . . . Nine because she is not able to adopt . . . Fourteen, the condition of women is worse in testifying in wills. . . . Fifteen in supervision, because she is not able to exercise the office of procurator . . . unless perhaps appointed by the ruler . . . Eighteen in subjugation to males and the covering of her head and in formation in similitude of the image of God, *causa* 33, *questio* 5, c. 13, 15 and 17." *Commentaria*, 1:204v.

101. "The [condition of females] is better . . . since it is allowed for them to be ignorant of the law . . . but only in specific cases of the law . . . " *Commentaria*, 1:204v.

102. On *Extra* 5.3.40 *ad v.* "*excusare*": ". . . nuns truly not only through ignorance, but also through simplicity, [ought to be excused] for it is permitted for women to be ignorant of laws." *Commentaria*, 5:25v. Similarly on *Extra* 2.22.10 *ad v.* "*Tantum venditio*": ". . . the sex of women was to be spared on account of fragility and most strongly when pursued by a swarm of laws." *Commentaria*, 2:118r. Quite clearly a mental weakness and frailty is meant. Of course Hostiensis shares the universally held view of the physical weakness and inferiority of woman. For instance, on *Extra* 4.2.4 (*ad v.* "*complesset*") he presents the following reason, among others, for the earlier female puberty: ". . . the sex of women is naturally worse, hence commonly she lives less [long] since she also has less natural heat and therefore as she is more quickly ended, so she naturally ought to come to completion more quickly. . . . Plato truly said that therefore this is so since weeds grow more quickly than good plants but it is also able to be said that it is easier to endure women than to lead men hence a woman always is spared, not the same for men. . . ." *Commentaria*, 4:11r.

103. On this see Hove, *Prolegomena*, 1/1:495f.; Schulte, *Die Geschichte der Quellen*, 2:274 (there is no indication of the date of composition; which is also true for A. Lambert, "Bellemère," in *DDC*, 2:296f.—according to Lambert, Bellamera died in A.D. 1407).

104. On *Extra* 1.43.4: "Six, it is asked and we proceed with the case in which the condition of women is worse . . . Sixteen is because she is not able to teach publicly, or preach, or hear confessions, nor exercise the other things which pertain to the keys of the church . . . or to administer the rituals [*sacramenta*] . . . Seventeen is because she is not able to receive orders." (as evidence for this, *distinctio* 23, 25, is given, as in Hostiensis; Aegidius refutes—similarly to Hostiensis—the contradictory authority of *causa* 27, *questio* 1, c. 23; we have already, chapter 2, n. 200, dealt with his reasoning for the exclusion of women from Holy Orders, a crass denigration of women taken from Guido of Baysio). "The thirty-first is in subjugation to males, in the covering of her head, in the formation in the similitude and to the image of God, *causa* 33, *questio* 5, c. 13 and 15 . . . and entrance to the sanctuary when the divine [rites] are celebrated and approaching the altar . . . and thus the law is understood that says the condition of women is worse in many articles of the law." Aegidius Bellamera. *Praelectiones in decretalium libros*, 6 vols. (Lyon, 1548-1549) 3:141v/142r.

105. "But why are women removed from civil and public offices? The reason is because they are fragile and usually less discerning . . . Again especially in making judgements the reason is because a judge ought to be constant and unchanging . . . but a woman is fickle and fragile . . . again because she is not prudent nor learned as a judge ought to be in himself." *Praelectiones* 3:141r. The right of adoption is denied to women for the following reason: "The reason of reason, because the power of the father [*patria potestas*] is good, worthy and holy

. . . but females do not have worth from themselves, but from a male." *Praelectiones* 3:141v.

106. "Réflexions sur la condition canonique de la femme, d'aprés l'oeuvre de Gilles Bellemère (1337-1407)," in *Bulletin des facultés catholiques de Lyon*, 76e année, new series no. 16 (1954):9.

107. "And the reason is because weeds grow quickly" *Praelectiones* 3:142v. This comparison is presumably taken from Hostiensis (cf. n. 102, above) as well as the explanation added: "Another reason because it is natural that insofar as whatever being tends to its end more quickly, the more quickly it is completed as is apparent in flies." *Praelectiones* 3:142v.

108. "The reason for the difference is on account of the fragility, imbecility and less natural constancy and discernment of women." *Praelectiones* 3:142v/143r.

109. E.g., M. Schmaus, *Katholische Dogmatik*, 6th ed. (Munich, 1964), 4/1:754: "The limitation of ordination to men . . . does not mean any disregard for or denigration of women in the church. It is only an expression of the dissimilarity of man and woman. . . . A woman remains empowered for and obligated to the ministry conferred by universal priesthood." (It is not evident how the "dissimilarity of man and woman" should be expressed in this case: of course there is no area of tasks in the church which men do not share with women!) 89f.; similarly, Remberger, "Priestertum der Frau?" 131f. and Concetti (quoted by Heinzelmann, *Schwestern*) "La donna" 99, agree with Schmaus.

110. Cf. Gillmann, "Zur Frage der Abfassungszeit der Novelle des Johannes Andrea zu den Dekretalen Gregors IX," in *AkKR* 104 (1924):261-275; Hove, *Prolegomena*, 1/1:479.

111. Cf. Schulte, *Die Geschichte der Quellen*, 2:220f.; Hove, *Prolegomena*, 1/1:479.

112. On this see p. 93 with chapter 2, n. 177.

113. See p. 129 with n. 61 above.

114. On *Extra* 5.38.10: ". . . beyond what is established that the signified [*res*] and sign are required in a sacrament . . . but no prominent position is able to be signified by the female sex as she has the status of subjugation—1 Timothy 2: 'I do not permit a woman to teach nor to rule over a male' because of course in equality she acted badly, therefore she was subjugated, Genesis 3 'you will be under the power of a male'—therefore she does not receive the character of the sacramentum that has prominence." Johannes Andreae, *Novella Commentaria in quinque libros decretalium*, 5 vols., (Venice: Apud F. Fransicum 1581; reprinted Turin: Bottega d'Erasmo, 1963), 5:125v. Quite similarly Thomas says (S.T., Suppl. q., a.1): ". . . since as a sacrament is a sign in which those things are done in sign [*sacramento*], not only a signified [*res*] but also a sign of that signified [*signum rei*] . . . As therefore no prominent position is able to be signified by the feminine sex since a women has the status of a subject, therefore she is not able to receive the sacrament of orders." *Summa theologiae*, cura et studio P. Caramello, Turin/Rome, 1948, vol. 4, p. 773.

115. See chapter 6, pp. 175ff.

116. "Clerics ought to wear the crown [i.e., tonsure] which is not allowed to women . . ." *Novella* 5:125v. This ridiculous objection is also made by Phillips, *Kirchenrecht*, 1:446f.: she may not receive the royal sign of differentiation of priesthood—cutting her hair would be a disgrace to her.

117. See n. 90, above.

118. On X 3.2.1 *ad v.* "*ministrare*": "as a [female] is not capable of receiving orders." *Novella*, 3:7r.

119. *ad v.* "*monita*": " . . . according to Hostiensis, it is held therefore that at least she is not able to suspend from office since of course excommunication, suspension and interdict are contained under censures, one being prohibited, by the connection of the law, the rest are prohibited and it is sufficient that this is not expressly permitted to women . . ." *Novella* 1:267 v.

120. Cf. Mörsdorf, *Lehrbuch des Kirchenrechts*, 2:111, 116.

121. *Ad v.* "*ab officio suspendere*": "Hence Vincentius said that an abbess is not properly able to suspend so that by her suspension one celebrating during which [suspension] commits an irregularity as does a penitential confessor, it is permitted that she would fully be able to interdict, for example for chaplains, they cannot celebrate or collect their income for that day and are held to obey." *Novella* 1:267v.

122. *Ad v.* "*imago*": "as all creatures come forth from God, thus all humans come forth from Adam, and from him alone, but not from Eve alone as Eve herself came forth from Adam and thus she herself is not the image of God in creation." *Novella* 1:267v.

123. Cf. Schulte, *Die Geschichte der Quellen*, 2:281; Hove, *Prolegomena*, 1/1:496 (neither writer gives the date of composition).

124. Petrus de Ancharano, *Commentaria in quinque libros decretalium*, 5 vols., (Bologna: Apud societatem Typographiae Bononienis, 1581), 5:196r; cf. p. 88 with n. 114, above.

125. "Note that the condition of women is worse than males in this . . ." *Commentaria* 5:196r.

126. "Note that a female is forbidden to minister at the altar and even to approach, understand that even if she were a nun . . . , for she is incapable of receiving ordination." *Commentaria* 3:9r.

127. "First note that clerics, female canons and everyone at the monastery is held to obey the abbess; therefore a female is able to be the administrator of churches, which you should understand as [being] an abbess, since then administration is granted to her by reason of dignity, [it would be] otherwise if a simple female as in the *Digest* 3.3.41 (concerning administrators) in which of course the condition of females is worse since they are not able to be judges, advocates or administrators . . . Note that an abbess has jurisdiction . . . note that the pope orders to another, through ecclesiastical censure, that he compel monks and clerics to obey the abbess, and thus is it given to understand that she herself is not able to punish through a sentence of censure those resisting her . . . clearly it is not said here that the suspension holds. Vincentius says . . . (cf. p. 138 with n. 121). The gloss and also Hosteiensis and hold this opinion that she is not able

to suspend from office . . ." (for continuation, see n. 119, above); *Commentaria* 1:309r.

128. "It should be noted . . . that the privilege granted to monks that they are able to be absolved by the abbot if they should fight among themselves, does not hold for nuns that the abbess is able to absolve them, on account of incapacity the keys are not granted to the female sex . . . the bishop therefore absolves." *Commentaria*, 5:217r.

129. On *Extra* 5.1.13: "note that the abbess is also blessed as an abbot . . . the blessing of an abbess does not however have the same effect as the blessing of an abbot. A blessed abbot of course blesses . . . and confers minor orders . . . which an abbess does not do as this is a masculine act (*actus virilis*), *Extra* 1.33.12, and *Extra* 5.38.10." *Commentaria* 5:7r. Current law (the Code, canon 964, n 1) also provides that regular abbots who are priests, after receiving consecration as abbots, may bestow tonsure and minor orders on those of their subjects having at least simple vows. (Cf. Mörsdorf, *Lehrbuch des Kirchenrechts,* 2:96.)

130. Cf. Schulte, *Die Geschichte der Quellen*, 2:293; Hove, *Prolegomena*, 1/1:497. (There is no indication when it appeared.)

131. Antonius de Butrio, *In quinque libros decretalium commentaria*, 7 vols., (Venice: Apud Juntas, 1578; reprinted Turin: Bottega d'Erasmo, 1967), 7:111r; see p. 137.

132. "You say that this office is foreign to them [women]." *In quinque libros*, 7:111r.

133. "The gloss concludes a woman to have a certain jurisdiction . . . granted not as full as that of males, such that she is able to suspend nuns from benefices as is said here. You say, granted the teachers do not say, as a woman and individual and considered privately, she is not able to judge nor to administer the duties of males, but by reason of her dignity this is so, since this is said to be done not by her herself, but by her dignity as it is here. . . . And the gloss wishes to say this when it says, 'And she has temporal and spiritual administration which she conducts, this she is able [to do] . . .'" *In quinque libros*, 2:89r.

134. "According to the aforesaid, the gloss says that this same abbess is not able to excommunicate, nor to absolve since she does not thus have full power as a man [does]. But this is called into doubt as she is able to suspend through her office since is it clear that [she does] so . . . On the contrary since to suspend from office depends upon the power of the keys . . . which power does not fall to a woman . . . The power of the keys, of course, was not handed over to women, but to Peter. Granted that the Virgin Mary was certainly more excellent than all of the apostles, it was not to her, however, but to the apostles that the keys of the kingdom of heaven were handed over, *Extra* 5.38.10. Again, she ought not to have the power of the keys since she was not made in the image of God, but a male alone who is the glory and image of God [was so made]. Again a women ought not to rule over a male and in some sense ought to be a handmaiden to the male and not the contrary, *causa* 33, *questio* 5, c. 13. Through the above, it can be adduced that . . . she is able . . . neither to suspend nor to excommunicate . . . but in this case it is to be referred to the superior [authority] as the text says here since she

will have to make this to be observed; the teachers hold that she does not suspend through her office and it is evident through reason since she is not able to excommunicate, as was said above, therefore neither is she able to suspend from office. The logical consequence proceeds in a similar way, as both concern the keys . . . An abbot says that a female is not able to make a suspension from office by which one having been suspended, but not observing it, incurs an irregularity, but she is clearly able by so doing to introduce a kind of suspension in order to prohibit so they cannot celebrate on certain days, and cannot collect their daily incomes, and so she is able to suspend from benefices and prebends. . . . And Hostiensis indeed holds this, namely that she is not able to suspend since excommunication and suspension are encompassed by the term censure. Prohibited from one, and the rest are considered prohibited. Again it suffices that it does not seem to be permitted . . ." *In quinque libros*, 2:89r.

135. "Here then, since an abbess is unfit for the power of absolving by reason of her sex as she is unfit for the power of the keys . . . from this it follows that she does not hear confessions nor bless her [nuns] nor read the gospel." *In quinque libros*, 7:127v.

136. Cf. Hove, *Prolegomena*, 1/1:497; Schulte, *Die Geschichte der Quellen*, 2:312. (There is no indication of the time of writing.)

137. Cf. Schulte, *Die Geschichte der Quellen*, 2:312.ff.

138. "Note first from the text that granted an abbess is able to have jurisdiction in court disputes as in *Extra* 5.31.14 and the same for other women in *Extra* 1.43.4 and here in *causa* 12 *questio* 2, c. 8 it is noted; she is not able to have jurisdiction, however, in penitential judgment. And the reason is from diversity since the jurisdiction of the penitential courts proceeds from the power of the keys and orders of which a woman is totally incapable, so true is this that according to common opinion, if a woman is ordained *de facto*, she does not receive the character, which the gloss holds on *causa* 27, *questio* 1, c. 23." Nicolaus de Tudeschis, *Lectura in decretales*, vols. 1-3 (Lyon, 1534), vols. 4-5 (Venice: 1504), 5:110r. The edition I used (Venice, 1504) indicates, in a footnote supplementing the prohibition of hearing confessions, that according to the opinion of Guido of Baysio male sex is required for reprimanding another person, because a woman cannot be allowed to do this kind of thing "on account of inconstancy and fickleness."

139. The prohibition of public preaching leads Nicolaus, as Hostiensis and others, to the supplementary remark that, however, the abbess is permitted to give private admonitions to her nuns: " . . . she is able therefore to admonish her nuns in private by giving good example and by explaining sacred scripture." *Lectura*, V, 5:110r.

140. "Third, note here 'incongruous and absurd' because for opposition to any statement or act, it suffices to prove the absurdity which follows [from it], therefore the argument from the absurd is valid." *Lectura*, V, 5:110r.

141. "Note that a female is not of such credibility as a male, thus he is better able to persuade . . . since in cases in which a female is admitted, she does not produce as much faith as a male, and therefore if two males are on one side and

two women on the opposite side, the witness of the males is preferred; for a woman (*mulier*) is so-called, not from her sex, but from the softness of her mind (*a mollitiale mentis*) while a male (*vir*) [is so-called], not from his sex, but from the constancy and virtue of his soul (*a constantia et virtute animi*) . . ." *Lectura*, 5:13 4r.

142. "Note first from this gloss that an abbess is capable of conferring of benefices, she is able therefore to have the duty of conferring and of establishing; they of course belong to spiritual jurisdiction, not jurisdiction of orders.—Secondly note that, in other cases certainly having spiritual jurisdiction, those things which derive from the power of the keys do not fall to a woman, hence an abbess is not able to absolve nuns from their sins as in *Extra* 5.38.10 nor to excommunicate as here. From which note that not having orders she is not able to excommunicate, granted that she is a person with vows. . . . The gloss says the same concerning suspension from office and concerning the power of forbidding from entering a church and from the divine office, and this opinion the teachers follow here saying that granted an abbess is able to suspend from a benefice, to take away prebends and to interdict in the broad sense and to suspend from orders, as when having clearly ordered her subjects, they cannot celebrate until they have made satisfaction; strictly and properly however she is not able to interdict or suspend from orders, namely by making that suspension and interdiction which would result in irregularity for offenders; this is proved by that, since excommunication, suspension and interdict are contained under the heading of ecclesiastical censures. . . . As therefore one of them is forbidden by the reason of incapacity, the rest are understood to be forbidden as all derive from orders." *Lectura*, 1:128r/v.

Chapter 4

Summary of the Most Significant Conclusions

The fixed status of subordination of women in operative ecclesiastical law—more particularly their exclusion from office and from every official pastoral and liturgical function connected with it—has its foundation in the corresponding decrees of classical canon law contained in the *Corpus iuris Canonici*. The decisive bases of the contemporary legal situation of women in the church were already set forth in the source-collection of Gratian about the middle of the 12th century. It contains various stipulations taken from older law collections, which prevent women from the exercise of every cultic-liturgical function within the altar area, the taking of communion to the sick, public teaching as well as baptizing (cf. p. 7). The theme of these prohibitions—which come partly from excerpts of the Pseudo-Isidorian decretals and partly from Council decrees or texts mistakenly attributed to Council decrees (*Statuta ecclesiae antiqua*)—clearly reveals a pejorative conception of women because of their sex, a conception strongly conditioned by the continuing influence of Old Testament ideas about cleanness as well as by exaggerated sacralization of the cult connected with this influence (cf. pp. 8f., 9f.) As an addition to the regulations mentioned, Gratian's understanding of the substantial and ethical inferiority of women and the state of subjugation deduced from it provide a negative reinforcement. This inferiority is derived from particular Pauline passages or passages attributed to Paul (1 Cor. 11:3ff.; 1 Tim. 2:11ff.) that were influenced by a rabbinical type of thinking, but especially from patristic and pseudo-patristic texts as well as Roman legal regulations for women (cf. pp. 24ff., 38ff.). Although the doctrine of Gratian achieved no legal but only doctrinal authority, it nevertheless achieved considerable importance for the further development of law.

In their scholarly studies of the texts of the *Decretum* of Gratian, the decretists for the most part adopted his doctrines. However, while Gratian simply states, concerning the question of the ordination of women, that they can never attain the diaconate nor the presbyterate (p. 23)—he fails to give any reasons and ignores the early church office of deaconess, apparently thinking, one gathers from his arrangement of texts about the deaconess, that this office has no great importance—some decretists present a more detailed treatment of the office of deaconess as well as of the question of ordination of women in general. Yet it must be clearly noted that although these scholars are familiar with the existence of this early church office, they are not clear about just what it was and they have some mistaken impressions about it. They place the deaconess parallel to the abbess or identify her with an ordinary nun. They think her office consisted merely in reading the Gospel or a homily during matins, and they understand the ordination of deaconesses as bestowing of the veil (cf. pp. 83, 84, 90). This contra-historical judgment about office and ordination of the deaconess, in connection with the increasingly clear tendency—especially since Rufinus—to deny women any ordination qualifications, may be traced back to a statement of Ambrosiaster mistakenly attributed to Ambrose, as well as to a lack of knowledge of historical evidence. This statement of Ambrosiaster, as the result of a mistaken interpretation of 1 Tim. 3:11, sharply condemns the ordination of deaconesses. (cf. pp. 81ff.). Under the weight of this "authority of the Fathers," Rufinus, and then the important decretists who followed him (Joannes Faventinus, Huguccio, Joannes Teutonicus) interpret as simple benediction the ordination of deaconesses of canon 15 of the Council of Chalcedon (*causa* 27, *questio* 1, c. 23). The benediction supposedly authorized the function mentioned above. The result of this interpretation is the exclusion of women from sacramental ordination.

However, an actual rationalization of the exclusion of women from clerical orders is made for the first time in decretist literature, by Huguccio. He contends that women's unfitness for ordination is determined by church decree and by the feminine sex—or, more exactly, by church decree drawn up because of feminine sex (see p. 90). This explanation is accepted by the *Glossa Ordinaria* of Joannes Teutonicus and later also by several decretalists. As shown by the formulation itself ("the law of the church made on account of sex"), the reasoning presupposes an inferiority of women, which has its foundation in patristic and pseudo-patristic exegesis of particular Bible passages (cf. pp. 91f.) and beyond this in Roman law. Thus in approximation to the regulation of Roman law, according to which women must be kept from all offices and public functions, women in the church are denied competence for official activity (cf. pp. 90, 94). The application of this principle of Roman law to canonical ordination law remains, especially since Huguccio, a determinative feature of decretist and decretalist literature.

There is evidence in the *Glossa Ordinaria* of Joannes Teutonicus that some decretists,[1] finding support in the above mentioned Chalcedonian canon (*causa* 27, *questio* 1, c. 23), opposed the prevailing opinion and recognized the fitness of women as well as men for ordination on the basis of their baptism (cf. p. 95). But this position was not strong enough to maintain itself. That it did appear so early in history, however—a correctly established theological position opposing a prevailing tradition based on untenable arguments—is noteworthy.

The decretals of Gregory IX (cf. p. 121) supplement the basic precepts, already given in Gratian's *Decretum*, for the ecclesiastical position of women in the Code of Canon Law, by adding a few more. Thus the decretal *Nova quaedam* (*Extra* 5.38.10) of Innocent III is especially significant in its strict prohibition of public preaching or Gospel reading by an abbess, of her giving the (ecclesiastical) blessing to her nuns or hearing their confessions (cf. p. 122). Further, the decree of a Synod of Nantes, recorded as *Extra* 3.2.1, in general forbids women to enter the sanctuary during divine services and act as acolyte for the priest (cf. pp. 127f.). The indication that not Mary but the apostles were given the "keys to the kingdom of heaven" serves as basis for the prohibitions of the decretal *Nova quaedam*—an argument without validity, to be sure, in light of its inadequate understanding of the position of Mary in the story of redemption (cf. pp. 126ff.). In contrast to the cultic-liturgical realm, a woman—as abbess or regent—is granted in the jurisdictional realm certain powers over persons under her, in recognition of the authority belonging to her office. Nevertheless, the position of the abbess is in no way comparable to that of the abbot, since, as the decretals *Dilecta* (*Extra* 1.33.12) and *De Monialibus* (*Extra* 5.39.33) indicate, she has no authority to inflict specific ecclesiastical punishments and to absolve from them, because of her exclusion from orders (cf. pp. 124f.).

The treatment of the Gregorian material by the decretalists follows closely the teaching of the decretists, especially the *Glossa Ordinaria* of Joannes Teutonicus and thus the writings of Huguccio. Substantial support for the prevailing viewpoint that women are not qualified for ordination, and therefore must be excluded from the liturgical and jurisdictional functions dependent on ordination, is provided for the decretalists by the statement of Ambrosiaster (see p. 162) which has the consequence that the ordination of deaconesses is interpreted as simple benediction and the office of deaconess simply as the privilege of reading the homily during matins. With this argument the decretalists commonly suggest the additional argument of the decretal *Nova quaedam*, that the power of the keys was not extended to Mary—and thus not to feminine sex. As the evidence of many sources would show, the judgment of the decretalists in this question, like that of the decretists, rests on a narrow and negative conception of the nature of women. In keeping with the outlook of the times in which they lived, they reserve liturgical and jurisdictional functions in principle and exclusively to men (*virilia officia*), considering the inferior nature of women to be inconsistent with the exercise of such functions (cf. pp. 134, 142). The statement of the *Glossa Ordinaria* of Bernard of Botone—woman does not have the power of the keys because she is not in the image of God and must serve man in in subjugation—is often repeated by subsequent decretalists and is to a certain extent symptomatic of the causal relationship between the denigration of women and their exclusion from church office. This causal relationship is also determinative for the relevant regulations of the *Corpus Iuris Canonici* and the current law built upon them.

Notes

1. The relevant passage of the gloss (on *causa* 27, *questio* 5, c. 23 *ad v.* "*ordinari*") does not tell us which of the decretists or theologians are referred to; also the literature of the decretists and the decretalists used provides no indication.

Chapter 5

Exegetical Excursus on the (Patristic) Scriptural Proof for the Subordination of Women

In consideration of the fact that the Church Fathers (and in agreement with them, Gratian—and, following him, the great majority of decretists and decretalists) derive from particular scriptural passages of the Old and New Testaments the inferiority of women and as a consequence their distinct limitations of freedom and law, an investigation of the validity of the scriptural proofs given is necessary. The question also arises how binding are the passages used as proof, especially since the patristic authorities in Gratian's *Decretum* constitute an essential source for the law currently in effect[1] and have placed their mark on the regulations for women in that law.[2]

The scriptural proof given by Gratian (cc. 13 and 19, *causa* 33, *questio* 5 in his *Decretum*) for the statement of Ambrosiaster—that women are not in the image of God—is Gen. 1:27 (also Gen. 2:7-24) and 1 Cor. 11:6f.[3] Let us first of all investigate the dependability of the Old Testament proof. Gen. 1:27a is quoted almost literally in c. 13;[4] since Ambrosiaster explains the expression *homo* (human) exclusively in the sense of *vir* (male), Gratian derives from v. 27a the Godlikeness of man alone. But is it permissible to understand the Hebraic concept ādām in this way—since it is necessary of course to go back to the Hebrew—and thus to limit it exclusively to man? According to the present position of exegesis, the question must be answered in the negative. Investigations of the concept ādām have shown that a collective meaning of the word is the original,[5] and that this meaning is present in Gen. 1:26f.[6] Accordingly it is the judgment of the commentators that Godlikeness of woman is likewise asserted, since precisely the species "mankind"—to which, as expressly emphasized in v. 27b ("he created them as male and female"), both sexes belong—is created as God's image.[7]

It is true that J. Boehmer[8] notes the alternation between singular and plural object in the text of Gen. 1:27, which reads:

וַיִּבְרָא אֱלֹהִים אֶת־הָאָדָם בְּצַלְמוֹ בְּצֶלֶם אֱלֹהִים בָּרָא אֹתוֹ זָכָר וּנְקֵבָה בָּרָא אֹתָם

"And God created man (ādām) in his image, in the image of God he created him; as male and female he created them." From this alternation Boehmer concludes that hā ādām in v. 27a should be limited to man—i.e., to the male sex—and is that it is about him alone that Godlikeness is affirmed: "According to the image of God 'man' κατ' ἐξοχήν (= the man) is created, not the woman (cf. 1 Cor. 11:7): he is the one indicated as *he* in אתו . As a secondary element it is added that mankind is divided in a male and a female part: this reality is expressed in אתם and it is exactly in this plural form that the illusion is prevented, that man and woman might share an equal status. Thus אתם refers to the male and female halves of humanity." The restriction of Godlikess to the male follows, according to Boehmer, from the circumstance that the Old Testament narrator could not be expected to attribute to woman as to man the analogous lordship over the animal world (c. v. 26), which is an expression and consequence of Godlikeness. For this the Old Testament with its view of women is evidence:

> A religion whose adherents still pray:
>
> ברוך אתה יי אלהינו מלך העולם שלא עשני אשה[9]
>
> (Sachs, *Gebetbuch der Israeliten*, 6) and in this point resemble Plato's deathbed prayer; a religion whose cult sign is circumcision and in which woman is rated one way or another like animals as helpmates for man, in accordance with Gen. 2:18ff.—to mention only a few characteristics; which has branches running into the New Testament, e.g., 1 Cor. 7 and 11:7-10: for such a religion the idea that woman is in the image of God and shares in the lordship of the world is absolutely impossible. Anyone who thinks otherwise, in fact all those who consider women to have a rather high place in the Old Testament, are caught in the bonds of a

> traditional Christian-idealizing exposition of Gen. 1 and 2, especially in the explanation of Jesus in Mt. 19:4-6 and similar passages. After every ירדו,[10] [Let them have dominion, Gen. 1:26], the narrator refers to אדם, i.e., to a group of men, to all men—many or few—existing at that time. The totality of the then contemporary male world is called to lordship over animals and plants, and that is attributed in Gen. 1:26 to the original will of God.[11]

In a monograph that takes account of the latest research, W. H. Schmidt criticizes Boehmer's position.[12] First, he agrees with Boehmer that according to Gen. 1:26 humanity created, not a human pair (as in Gen. 2:7, 21f.).[13] He says,

> While אדם in the Yahwistic creation narrative of Gen. 2-3 and in the priestly Toledot book (Gen. 5:la, 3-5) refers to an individual, the meaning in Gen. 1 is obviously a plural—'the human race.' This is indicated by the plural of the verb in v. 26b ('in order that they may have dominion') and the introduction of the benediction of v. 28. Also in Accadian creation narrative it is likewise 'humanity' which is created . . . .[14]

The pluralistic meaning as "humanity" is implied, he thinks, despite the use of the article with ādām in v. 27 (diverging from v. 26).[15] Perhaps the article is used in v. 27 because the word has already been used in v. 26.[16] The אתו (him) of v. 27a, Schmidt continues, refers to הָאָדָם, "the man" of v. 27a, which is to be understood as collective; the plural אֹתָם (they) in the (secondarily added) part of the verse, 27b, refers to the duality of the sexes and thus the two singular and plural suffixes are not inconsistent with each other.[17] Schmidt thinks that v. 27b ("as male and female he created them") seems unnecessary, since "man" in Gen. 1:26f. stands for mankind collectively and thus already contains the plural indicated in v. 27b. The type of language, style and meter of v. 27b proves that this part of the verse is in fact a secondary addition. As the priestly document, having in mind cultic prescriptions, adds to the reference to plants and animals "each according to its kind" (Gen. 1:1lf., 21, 24f.), so it inserts in the reference to mankind the sentence "He created them as male and female." (Cultic laws required this differentiation.)[18] Thus it is stated, according to Schmidt, that humanity consists "from creation on, of both sexes."[19]

Thus in contrast to Boehmer, Schmidt sees in v. 27 (creation of mankind according to the image of God) a statement of the priestly narrator which includes women. It is true that he adds the limitation that in v. 27b ("male and female he created them") it is not a question "of an equalization of man and woman through creation"; and although v. 28 refers to both—i.e., blessing and dominion[20] are promised to mankind, not only to man— v. 27b names man before woman. Thus Schmidt thinks that although the preeminence of man is by no means so sharply emphasized in the priestly document as in the Yahwist document (Gen. 2:7, 18-25), it is nevertheless not absent there (in this connection he also refers to Num. 1; 3:15ff.).[21]

Besides what Schmidt says about Boehmer's exposition of Gen. 1:26f., the following critical comments may be made. It seems to me that Boehmer, in finding reference only to man in the Godlikeness and dominion rights of Gen. 1:26f., entirely overlooks the fact that woman is included in the dominion mandate and privilege repeated in v. 28. For immediately preceding, in v. 27b, the sexual differentiation of mankind is indicated: "as man and woman he created them," from which follows in v. 28: "God blessed them and said to them: 'Be fruitful and multiply and fill the earth and make it submissive to you and have dominion over the fish of the sea . . . and over every creature. . . .'" Very probably the Old Testament narrator wants the charge of procreation to be understood as directed to both sexes,[22] especially since the sexual differentiation of the human species has just been mentioned. The further imperative, "bring the earth in subjection to you," and "have dominion," follows then immediately and speaks of the same subject: "mankind," consisting of men and women. But now since the lordship over nonhuman creation is the consequence of Godlikeness (cf. Gen. 1:26),[23] the statement about the creation of ādām as image of God (1:26f.) must be applied to woman also.[24] Of course, it still remains true that the priestly document, as well as the Old Testament in general, undoubtedly sees in man the more valuable human being[25] and therefore recognizes in him preeminently the dignity of the image of God. In indicating this situation Boehmer has touched upon a decisive point—with which Schmidt agrees, although he does not formulate it so sharply—that has been given too little attention up to now in both Old Testament and New Testament exegesis, insofar as the latter, especially in the apostolic letters, is based on the Old Testament point of view regarding women. The position which the Old Testament accords to women in the social and cultic realms must be appreciated and taken into account as the context for special statements about women. Thus a brief discussion of this position is needed.[26]

Since earliest times the patriarchal large family was the exclusive societal form in Israel.[27] It must be assumed that the Israelites brought the patriarchate with them when they entered the Promised Land, especially since they came from a nomadic life.[28] The consequence for women was that they were inferior to men in social and religious relationships. In marriage, which often had a polygamous structure, a woman was legally considered the property of her husband,[29] who as her "baal" ruled over her[30] and to whom she was obligated to be obedient. Only the husband had the right of divorce (cf. Deut. 24:1). Her task as wife consisted mainly in the exercise of sexual and procreative functions. The Old Testament genealogies[31] show clearly that in accordance with the outlook of the times her role in reproduction was considered to be a purely passive one: she, "received" the "seed" of her husband and "bore" him children.[32] The real begetter of new life was thought to be only the man. Male progeny was particularly desired and valued.[33] The denigration of women articulated in these facts is further evident in the estimated value of women in Leviticus 27:1-7, which is about half that of men.

The social position of women in Israel, which was marked by the laws and customs of the ancient Orient, was matched by their religious-cultic position. The oldest cult law[34] had to do with men only and demanded of them alone an appearance in the sanctuary three times a year. Women were not obliged to share in pilgrimages or in the Passover meal. They were in principle excluded from priestly function, i.e., from serving in the sacrifices and in the temple.[35] Although women had a closer relationship to religion in early Israel—as charismatic prophets and judges[36]—they were increasingly forced out of official cultic activity by the progressive strengthening of the priesthood and the development of legal emphasis in religion. A not unimportant aspect of this process must have been the laws of purification (Lev. 12; 15:19ff.). Thus the official practice of religion and the fulfillment of the law were essentially the prerogative and duty of the free Israelite male, who bearing the sign of the covenant, circumcision, was, in contrast to the female, the only "fully authorized member" of the covenant people.[37]

It is in the context of this given situation, especially of the position given the Israelite woman of Old Testament times in the social sphere, that the Yahwistic creation narrative (Gen. 2:7-24) must be understood and judged: in the patristic and pseudo-patristic statements accepted by Gratian the inferiority of woman as not God's image (Ambrosiaster) is derived from this narrative, as well as from other sources.[38] The so-called biblicistic understanding of Gen. 2 clearly underlies these patristic maxims and indicates the untenability of their reasoning.[39] The Fathers considered it a historical fact that the man "Adam" was the first created human being, in whom all others have their origin—in the first place, woman.[40] In keeping with this historical interpretation, the consequence drawn by the Fathers from Gen. 2:22ff. is a thoroughly real consequence, which has defined the life of woman: the *status subiectionis* (state of subjugation) to man. Modern theology has not yet divorced itself completely from this patristic exegesis—which is supported by Pauline interpretation—and patristic evaluation of the Yahwistic creation narrative. Even today, Gen. 2:21ff. is considered to some extent the *locus classicus* for the subjection of woman to man, supposedly set forth and founded on the order of Creation.[41] Strengthened by the Pauline statements (1 Cor. 11:3ff.; 1 Tim. 2:11ff., among others) that go back to it, this passage from Genesis has become authoritative for the position of women in current church law. The decree of the Bible Commission of June 30, 1909, "On the Historical Character of the First Three Chapters of Genesis" (Denz. 2121-2128), strengthened the almost literal understanding of Gen. 2:21ff. Paragraph 3 of this decree sets forth the exegetical principle that where the Genesis chapters have to do with "facts which touch upon the fundamentals of the Christian religion," there must be no questioning of "the literal historical sense."[42] In this context a few examples are given which are to be understood as facts connected with doctrine, among others "the formation of the first woman from the first man" (Denz. 2123). H. Renckens, who thinks that the Bible Commission was unfortunate in the treatment of paragraph 3, describes the influence of the decree on the exegesis of Gen. 2:21ff. in the following manner: "Without apparent motivation the unanimous but contrived conclusion was thus reached that the rib belongs to the symbolic wording of the report but that the physical derivation of woman from man is taught as historical fact."[43] Even after the relaxation of the decree by a letter from the secretary of the Commission to Cardinal Suhard in 1948,[44] and even after and despite the statement of the Commission itself that its earlier decrees are to be understood as conditioned by the times,[45] Catholic exegesis retained in large part the traditional explanation of Gen. 2:21ff. Yet in relation to other aspects of the Yahwistic creation narrative, Catholic exegesis very easily shed its literalism. Thus in more recent publications of Catholic writers—from the 1950s and the 1960s—the doctrine of evolution is by no means rejected, although a literal interpretation of Gen. 2:7ff. would exclude it. At the same time, they follow the Bible Commission in finding woman's origin in man.[46] The conclusion of natural science that woman cannot be derived from man[47] demands, however, a decisive break with a biblicistic interpretation of the text.[48] The latest exegesis is today largely ready for this break, since it ascribes only symbolic and etiological significance to the Yahwistic description of the creation of woman. But once again the result of this exegesis is often the deduction from the alleged allegorical form of the text, that subordination of woman to man is the divine order of creation[49]—completely ignoring the longstanding patriarchal milieu of the author.

Renckens reasonably suggests that the Bible Commission had its eye on the New Testament texts 1 Cor. 11:7-12, 1 Tim. 2:31 and Eph. 5:28-30, in explaining the "formation of the first woman from the first man" as an historical fact consistent with doctrine. For these texts refer to Gen. 2:21ff. (creation of woman from man) as factual event.[50] Further explanation for the position of the Bible Commission, Renckens thinks, may be found in the place Gen. 2:21ff. has in church tradition, which wanted to see in the creation of Eve a model for the birth of the church from the side of Christ.[51] In addition, Renckens has the following comment on the reasons for the Commission's decree:

> No matter how important a New Testament fact that has a typological relation with an event of the Old Testament may be, and no matter how urgent the reference to the Old Testament may be, one cannot therefore conclude that the Old Testament event is a *historical* fact. A *literary* fact is obviously sufficient. . . . The Old Testament is for them [i.e., the New Testament writers, especially Paul] a storehouse from which they unhesitatingly take whatever meets their needs, sometimes whatever happens to come to mind. . . . Thus, where Holy Scripture so often quotes itself, comments on and reinterprets itself, we seem to be led to the exegetical principle—in seeking to answer the question, what has happened objectively—that the oldest scriptural passage, which became the source of a whole series of quotations and allusions, has a certain primacy before the whole tradition which resulted from it. . . . In other words, the later data, which in dependence upon Genesis speak about the appearance of the first woman, are of such a nature that our conclusion could be: Genesis must have the last word.[52]

Thus we are left with the text itself, for the objective understanding of which reference to the time of writing of the Yahwistic creation narrative—in contrast to the priestly narrative some 500 years later—may be helpful: the Yahwist probably lived after David's death, i.e., in the 10th to 9th century B.C., and presumably in the neighborhood of Solomon's residence.[53]

From a literary standpoint, Genesis 2 and 3 were put together into a unified whole by the Yahwist who had at his disposal two originally independent documentary themes. It has been called a "well constructed anthropological *aitologumenon*" because it answers the question, "How did empirical-historical mankind come to its present *miseria conditionis humanae* status?"[54] Thus the fall of man is the real theme of Gen. 2:4b-3:24.[55] Into this central theme of the narrative, various peripheral themes—etiological myths in literary form—are woven, one of which is the creation of woman in Gen. 2:21ff.[56] Haag convincingly suggests the likelihood that the account of the creation of man (Gen. 2:7—ādām) originally included both sexes, but that as the author worked a folktale of the creation of woman into the story, he decided to limit the first account to the creation of the male,[57] who was thus placed alone at the beginning of the human race. Thus it is in accordance with the strongly monogenetic thinking of the Yahwist—which means of his Israelite ancestors—that he not only appoints a particular progenitor for each tribe[58] but also traces back the whole of mankind to one beginning and source, concretized in one single man (ādām). This is the way he explains the unity of mankind.[59] It is incontestable that this person, who "as the absolute beginning point is carrier of the fullness of everything human"[60] could only be, and must be—in the conceptual world of the Yahwist as of the Old Testament in general—a male. According to J, the originators of various peoples (Israel, Edom, Moab, Ammon, etc.) are not tribal parents but tribal fathers, which corresponds to the general position of the Old Testament, that only the male can beget offspring.[61] Following this understanding of reproduction—specifically, monogenetic thinking about ancestors which was conditioned by his understanding of reproduction—the first woman must come from the Adam-man,[62] the Yahwist believes, in order that all men may originate from him. The Yahwist could explain this event only by an unmediated intervention of God, since a normal reproduction was of course excluded.

In this connection it is worth noting that the idea of a derivation of woman from man is not found only in the Old Testament: there are similar myths in other patriarchal cultures.[63] The Old Testament narrative (Gen. 2:21ff.) should be read in the framework of this mythic viewpoint: it adopts a very old tradition with strongly marked characteristics.[64] Of course the Yahwist utilizes this available motif about the origin of woman from man not only to trace the whole of humanity—not excluding the woman—back to one ultimate origin and ancestor, but also, surely, in order to explain why man finds in woman, and not in animals, a being profoundly close to him (v. 23a),[65] and especially why love binds the two sexes to "become one flesh."[66] But the narrow horizon of patriarchal thinking is clearly shown by the use of the mythic derivation of woman as explanation of love between man and woman. Love thus goes back to the original unity of the sexes, yet the author finds the unity embodied only in man (v. 21). The primacy of the male according to J is also expressed by the fact that the man alone is the name-giver, not only for animals (v. 19f.) but also for woman (v. 23; Gen. 3:20).[67] Many exegetes find further confirmation of the secondary significance and position of woman in contrast to man (according to J in Jahweh's formation of woman from the rib[68] of man in order to provide him "a helper fit for him" (v. 18). This is the line of approach taken by Gunkel: The myth does not mean "that woman originally is 'coordinated' with man, that she is 'under him,'" but rather that woman is only a "help" for man and man (the male) is "the human being" per se. The myth does not present the ideal, according to Gunkel; it intends to explain facts.[69] Opposing this interpretation, other expositors lay more weight on the phrase כְּנֶגְדּוֹ, which more carefully defines the concept "help" and from which they conclude that man, according to J, finds in woman "his opposite number, his complement."[70] An equal partner,[71] and thus, in this view, any derogation of woman is excluded.[72] Taking into account the conceptual horizon of the Yahwist, Renckens paraphrases the content of the concept "help" in the following way: "The hagiograph refers to the social phenomenon of the family in general; one misunderstands the universal import of the account if one is thinking here only of the sexual act. At the same time it is even less possible to exclude it. The passage itself makes that fact abundantly clear."[73]

In conclusion, it may be said about Gen. 2:21-24 that it should be understood *not as historical fact*.[74] but, as Renckens says, as an etiological explanation and interpretation of the following empirical phenomena: "1. the absolute unity of the human species; 2. the relationship between man and woman [as the Yahwist views it]; 3. the Hebraic expression for blood relationship: 'to be of someone's flesh and bones'; 4. the Hebrew words for man and woman: *isch* and *isschah*."[75] But the etiological character of the Yahwistic creation narrative, into which mythic materials are clearly assimilated, forbids us to draw any dogmatical or legal consequences to the effect that woman is not made in the image of God, that she is inferior in accordance with the order of creation and therefore that she is rightly subordinate to man.[76] An exegesis that does not avoid drawing such conclusions from Gen. 2 completely ignores the time-conditioned horizon of the biblical writer—a practice inadmissible in every respect.[77] Or such exegesis may actually be based upon the same or similar sociological structure as that of the biblical writer, and thus lack any critical objectivity toward him—as in the case of the Church Fathers (cf. the discussion of the Gratian chapter, pp. 29ff.). But in any case a misunderstanding results and false conclusions are drawn about the right classification and evaluation of women. It may be added that the priestly account of Genesis 1 supplies a kind of correction and relativization for the Yahwistic creation narrative which is often wrongly taken in an absolute sense[78] or as if it were a more exact explanation of Genesis 1[79]—a process that is bound to work out to the detriment of a true view of women. The relationship between the two accounts is rather the following: "The second chapter [i.e., of Genesis] is . . . older than the first and adds no historical detail to it. The relationship is the reverse of the biblical order. That is, Genesis 1 is later, presents a further stage of development and is therefore theologically more cautious: *Gen. 1 directs the anthropological pictures of chapter 2 to their root, to its doctrinal content.* The same thing is true concerning the origin and equivalence of the two sexes (Gen. 1:27; cf. 5:lf.)."[80]

Favorable to this evaluation of Genesis 1—with its more timeless and thus more valid formulation, in comparison with Genesis 2—is the fact that Jesus specifically, in Mt. 19:4-6, refers to the priestly account and only uses chapter 2 in the reference to man and wife "becoming one body." Jesus says nothing about the origin of woman in man nor about any derived, inferior existence of women. On the contrary, he rejects as illegitimate and as inconsistent with the divine order of marriage, any one-sided right of divorce for the husband resulting from such a view of women and from hardness of heart (Mt. 19:3-9). Thus it becomes very clear that Jesus wants women to be regarded as independent, free, and equal persons having a claim on equal rights[81] and thus neither possessions of men nor in any way subject to their domination.

Besides using the two creation narratives, especially the Yahwistic, the Church Fathers, followed by Gratian—who, however, is even more dependent on Paul—make use of the story of the Fall (Genesis 3) as support for the *status subiectionis* (state of subjugation) of women. They see in Eve, and thus in woman in general, the originator of sin, who as such must remain under the dominion of man. (Cf. *causa* 33, *questio* 5, cc. 18 and 19 as well as the *dictum Gratiani, causa* 15, *questio* 3 *princ.*) A principle objection to such an interpretation of Genesis 3 and the conclusion drawn from it is that the Fall narrative should not be taken as an historical account.[82] It should be understood as etiology that makes use of mythic representation to answer the question about the origin of evil and suffering in the world. The answer it gives is: "They do not come from God but rather solely from the sin of man. . . . In this way sin is defined as man's disregard for the will and order of God. If that is true, it is quite irrelevant what the concrete form of sin was."[83] The writer worked various materials together that tell in several differing forms of the original sin of man.[84] According to J. Begrich, the so-called Paradise or Fall narrative is a composite of two differing sources. The one dealt with the offence of a primeval man, which he committed in the Garden of Eden and for which he was punished by being driven by God out of the Garden. The other source tells of the woman and the serpent (Gen. 3:1-6a): the woman was punished for the transgression of a particular prohibition and the serpent for tempting to the transgression.[85] The story of primitive man was reduced because of its strongly mythological coloring, according to Begrich: he thinks that combining the two sources of traditional materials resulted in the elimination of the cause of the anathema against primeval man, in place of which the redactor has the man (ādām) share in the offence of the woman[86] (cf. Gen. 3:6).

The temptation story (Gen. 3:1-7), in the middle of which we find the serpent and the woman, is of Canaanite origin and contains an emphasized polemic against the Baal cult of the serpent for which Palestinian archeology has provided evidence.[87] The actual theme is fertility:

> The figure that looms behind the serpent in Gen. 3 is the Canaanitic Baal, appearing in the guise most tempting to Israel, that of a serpent. For in this particular shape he was the life-giver, the life-renewer, the phallus. As such he belonged especially to the Canaanitic autumn and New Year feast, with its sexual excitement and frenzy. But to the prophets and their circles this 'renewal of life' was simply and solely immorality and sensuality (cf. Hos. 4:12b-14).[88]

The conception that the woman succumbs first to the temptation of the serpent and then tempts the man is found in similar form in several Fall myths in patriarchal cultures: The woman is blamed for transgressing a prohibition and for the loss of life and paradise in connection with that act.[89] The writer's willingness to accept such mythic explanation and to use it in the setting of Israelite milieu and history may have been the result of the common Old Testament experience: Israelite women felt themselves drawn to the neighboring foreign cults—not least because of the purely masculine character of the Yahweh cult—and thus threatened the latter.[90] The idea in Gen. 3 is not that the woman led the man astray and therefore is the one more easily tempted—thus proving, as so often happens, her ethical inferiority[91]—but rather that because she is excluded from the Yahweh cult, and thus lacks possibilities for sufficient religious development, she herself is led astray into a surrogate religion.[92] According to the text of Gen. 3:8-19, Yahweh's penal sentence does not distinguish which of the two human beings first fell into sin—no matter how the role of woman may be described by the narrator for the reasons mentioned above. Both are personally and directly addressed by God, brought to judgment and punished.[93]

In content, the punishment gives religious meaning to concrete empirical reality as the Yahwist understands it—reality burdened by the many sufferings and troubles of both women and men. The hagiograph traces this distress in human life back to an anathema, to a divine, punishment meted out to mankind as consequence of an original sin.[94] It is clear from the threat of divine vengeance, which is directed against the woman, that the Yahwist sees her as being ruled by man as a consequence of her sin (Gen. 3:16), in addition, to the grievances of pregnancy and the pains of childbirth, while the punishment for the man is carried out in the area of his life and work as the Yahwist portrays this area—curse of the field, toil of earning a living (Gen. 3:17ff.). The Palestinian coloring is sharply reflected in the sentences meted out.[95] The sentence ". . . He [the man] shall rule over you" וְהוּא יִמְשָׁל־בָּךְ (Gen. 3:16), has long been understood as divine command in the sense of a decree. This interpretation seems to be present in the New Testament[96] and some of the passages from the Church Fathers quoted by Gratian appear to understand Gen. 3:16 as divine decree.[97] But the passage cannot legitimately be taken in this way (as one could gather from the context): ". . . The words 'he shall rule over you' are not a commandment but a threatening announcement of the consequences of human disobedience. . . . Here the position of women as it really was in the ancient Near East—in contrast to the will of the creator—is conceptualized: no order is proclaimed."[98] The author of Gen. 3 was obviously a witness to the rulership of men over women and it seemed to him like the misfortune of destiny, so that he was moved to seek the cause and explanation—as for the other plagues which afflict mankind—in an original sin. But if we ignore this clearly etiological character of the story—which also characterizes the myths of the Fall among primitive people[99]—then we do arrive at the misguided interpretation of Gen. 3:16 as divine command or punishment which is not supposed to be annulled. Besides its untenability, such an interpretation, which even today has legal consequences in the church, demonstrates a no less heartless and inconsiderate position than that of the ultra-conservative

Calvinists which "on the basis of Gen. 3:16 rejects modern, painless 'natural childbirth' and on the basis of Gen. 3:17-19a refuse to permit innoculation against disease, even for animals!"[100]

The New Testament, especially the Pauline passages presented—in patristic statements used by Gratian—as proof for the *status subiectionis* (state of subjugation) of women, are dependent upon the Old Testament passages we have just considered. In chapter 13 of *causa* 33, *questio* 5, which is dependent upon Ps. Augustine (Ambrosiaster), 1 Cor. 11:7a is cited (along with Gen. 1:27) as scriptural proof for woman's supposed lack of the image of God: "Therefore the apostle says: 'For a man ought not to cover his head, since he is the image and glory of God'"; Ambrosiaster continues: "A woman, however, must cover her head, because she is neither the glory nor the image of God."[101] If the scriptural text itself does not draw this conclusion, it must still be granted that the sentence added by Ambrosiaster corresponds at least to the sense of the Apostle's words. It does say in 1 Cor. 11:7b that "woman is the glory of man." It is clear from this and from the whole context that for Paul the image of God status is limited to man, as will be shown in more detail below. This consequence is also drawn from 1 Cor. 11 in chapter 19 in *causa* 33, *questio* 5 which is taken from the Corinthian commentary of Ambrosiaster.[102] For Paul the limitation to man of the image of God status also implies man's position of rulership over woman (cf. 1 Cor. 11:3; Eph. 5:23) and her subordination to him (cf. Eph. 5:22, 24), as also discussed in some patristic statements used by Gratian (cf. cc. 15 and 19 in *causa* 33, *questio* 5). Paul presents the following justification of the preferential position of man: "For man is not made from woman but woman from man. Neither was man created for woman but woman for man." (1 Cor. 11:8f.; [cf. 1 Tim. 2:13: "For Adam was created first, then Eve"]). Obviously, reference is made here to the Yahwistic creation narrative (especially to Gen. 2:21-24), which Paul understands as an account of a factual event.[103] 1 Cor. 11:8f. also shows that Paul views the Yahwistic creation narrative as interpretation of the priestly narrative: in 1 Cor. 11:7a he assigns the narrow meaning "man" to the collective concept אָדָם (ādām) in Gen. 1:26f.—which leads to the limitation of the image-of-God concept to man (male): "For it is the man who need not cover his head because he is the image and reflection of God."

In order to understand 1 Cor. 11, one must observe that Paul stands entirely within the Jewish-rabbinical tradition of Genesis interpretation as exegesis research has proved incontestably.[104] Following this tradition he accepts Genesis 2:21ff. as completely historical and thus arrives at the position that a "difference of essence,"[105] a difference in hierarchal classification, exists between the two sexes, since man appeared first and without mediation from the hand of God but woman was formed later and in fact from the man. Such thinking is clearly marked by the rabbinical and generally Oriental conception, "Everything good comes first" (or "The older is the more valuable").[106] The earlier and unmediated creation of Adam by God implies, according to late Jewish conceptualization, that he alone is the reflection of God;[107] woman is a "derived, secondary being" and therefore is denied participation in this evaluation: "Eve is not created according to the image of God but her existence is derived from Adam."[108] When Paul in 1 Cor. 11:7b characterizes woman as δοξα ἀνδρός "reflection of man"—in contrast to his characterization of man in rabbinical language[109] as εἰκών καὶ δόξα θεοῦ—he is saying that the relation of woman to man is like the dependent relationship between a reflection and the (real) picture. The real picture is man, the reflection is woman.[110] Here too Paul stands within the framework of rabbinic tradition.[111] Without doubt, it is not woman but man alone who is the true image of God, according to Paul, although there is doubt about the nature of a Godlikeness that is established in creation and limited to the male. (Jervell[112] notes that late Jewish conceptualization emphasizes the dominion status of man, especially his religious prerogatives.) In any case, from the limitation of Godlikeness to man—i.e., from his primary creation—late Judaism, and Paul following it, derives man's position as "head" vis-à-vis woman, as 1 Cor. 11:3 says. What Paul is doing here—in dependence on rabbinic tradition[113]—is setting forth a descending classification: God—Christ—man—woman, in which each preceding member of the series is "head" (κεφαλή), in the sense of "master," or the establishing beginning or source[114] of the following member. Johannes Weiss comments on this:[115] "The climax: God (Christ), man, woman assigns to woman a status not only underneath man but also distant from Christ and God . . . We must admit that v. 3 [of 1 Cor. 11:3] remains below the level of Gal. 3:28 in typical Jewish-rabbinic derogation of woman." By the argumentation of 1 Cor. 11:3ff. Paul attempts to establish theologically the custom taken over into the Christian community from Judaism, requiring women to wear a veil in congregational assembly, at prayer and in prophesying. For Paul this custom has the signification of indicating the inferior position of women in accordance with the "order of creation."[116] Closely related is the further signification that Paul (v. 10) gives to the veil: It serves as a protective device against demons. The explanation is as follows: Late Judaism thought of Godlikeness as present in the head or perhaps even more in the face (πρόσωπον) of the male[117] and that this constituted a protection against attacks and temptations from the demons.[118] The reason for this was that dominion status was connected with Godlikeness: possession of ἐξουσία over animals, demons and the other creatures.[119] Now since woman as only δόξα of man is helpless before the demons, she must wear διά τοὺς ἀγγέλους,[120] (v. 10) a substitute protection, a sign of power (ἐξουσία) in the form of a head covering.[121] As Jervell rightly remarks,[122] this obligation excludes the possibility that Paul grants woman Godlikeness, even if it be only secondary, for in this case the veiling would be superfluous. It is, according to Paul, not only the fact that women are not created in the image of God that requires her to wear an ἐξουσία, a sign of power, on her head, but also the fact of her "weakness," her "religious-ethical inferiority."[123] This point of view goes back to a late Jewish exposition of the origins narrative (Gen. 3), according to which only Eve, not Adam, sinned.[124] The serpent was not able to touch Adam; the power of Satan came through the woman.[125] Evidence of this tradition besides 1 Cor. 11:10 is found especially in 2 Cor. 11:1-4[126] and 1 Tim. 2:14,[127] which expressly states: "and Adam was not deceived but the woman was deceived and became a transgressor." (This line of thought becomes, as in 1 Tim. 2:11ff., the justification for the subordination of woman in the patristic passages used by Gratian: cf. cc. 18 and 19 in *causa* 33, *questio* 5.) In 1 Cor. 11:10 the rabbinic interpretation of Gen. 3 is combined with Jewish speculation about Gen. 6:1ff. (intercourse of the sons of God[128] with the daughters of men). J. Weiss interprets the allusion of Paul to this passage in 1 Cor. 11:10 as follows:

> As according to Gen. 6:1ff. the sons of God, charmed by the beauty of the daughters of men, seduced them . . . , so the danger is always present that the lust of angels (i.e., spirits, demons) will be aroused when a woman in prayer approaches the heavenly realms. This is why she must cover herself, in order by wearing the veil to hold off the attacks of angels, which could not happen to a man.[129]

since according to Paul he alone is the image of God. As evidenced in rabbinic sources, the veil serves in general to keep woman in subordination to man,[130] which is also the significance of the veil for Gratian.[131] Jervell explains the connection between the two functions involved in covering the head—on the one hand, it is a means of protection against demons, on the other hand, it is symbol of subordination—as follows:

> One may understand . . . the ἐξουσία (cf. 1 Cor. 11:10) as a kind of head covering which, exactly because it represents the secondary position of woman in subordination to man, also serves as protection against demons or apostate angels. By covering her head she shares in the protection against demons which man has because of his image-of-God status. Since she is not Godlike, she must have a head covering.[132]

In one way Paul weakens his statement (1 Cor. 11: 3ff.) concerning female inferiority in terms of Creation—using this inferiority to justify wearing the veil—by explaining in v. 11f.: "Nevertheless, in the Lord man is not independent of woman nor woman of man; for as woman was made from man, so man is now born of woman. And all things are from God." This could mean that man and woman are bound together "in the Lord"[133] and that neither of the sexes receives any preferential status before God.[134] Yet the statement must not be read as abrogating previous statements that have placed women in essence below men.[135]

A passage in Ephesians, chapter 5:22-33, is clearly influenced by the Yahwistic creation narrative about the creation of women (Gen. 2:2lff.) and the Jewish-rabbinic interpretations of it. Depending on patristic authority, which he cites (e.g., in *causa* 33, *questio* 5, c. 15), Gratian (*dictum p.c.* 11 in *causa* 33, *questio* 5) takes from this Ephesians passage the statement about woman as "body of a male" (*corpus viri*) and the statement about man as "head of woman" (*caput mulieris*). (In connection with 1 Cor. 11:3 we have already discussed the characterization of man as "head of woman" and traced it back to Gen. 2:21ff. See pp. 177f.)

Paul makes use of a common Jewish formula in calling woman σῶμα or σάρξ of man in Eph. 5:28, 29.[136] This formula goes back to the Yahwistic narrative about the generation of woman from the body of men,[137] which is itself to be taken as an etiological explanation for the presumably existing formula "to be someone's flesh and bones" (cf. Gen. 2: 23)—indicating blood relationship—and for the formula for the sexes "to become one flesh" (cf. Gen. 2:24).[138] Since Paul in Eph. 5:31 quotes Gen. 2:24 word for word, many exegetes conclude that Paul's characterization of the wife as σάρξ of the husband has come from this verse.[139] Yet in the Yahwistic narrative, both events, the formation of woman from man and the sexes becoming one body, stand in correlation to each other so that it is sufficient to take Gen. 2:21, 24 in general as the source of the concept "body" or "flesh" applied to woman in Eph. 5.

More important for us is the fact that in using this concept, Paul characterizes woman less as an independent self-responsible person than as the possession and property of man, as a being subordinate to him, who for direction is referred to him as her "head."[140] Now of course it must not be forgotten that the word σῶμα "always means for Paul the whole person, not a part of the person;" it indicates the person "vis-à-vis God or another person."[141] Thus it practically means "person." However, it is noteworthy that σῶμα (or σάρξ) is never used for man in his relationship to woman—which should also be possible in view of the sexes "becoming one flesh"[142]—but in Paul the man is always the "head" of the woman and never (or never also) her "body."[143] He is given the power-of-command over her (Eph. 5:22) because he is "head."[144] But beyond this position, man is called upon to love his wife—indeed "as his own body,"[145] since the marriage relationship of man and wife stands parallel to the relationship between Christ and the church. Contrariwise the wife must subordinate herself to the husband "in everything" (ἐν παντί), v. 24; in fact, she must fear him, v. 33. From this classification of higher and lower—man and wife, "head" and "body"—and from the differentiation in the demands made on each in relation to the other, it is clear that strictly speaking Paul considers only the male human being to be a free, independent person. (As already mentioned, the reason for this evaluation is the Pauline concept that the male is the source of existence for the female, the origin of her being—in accordance with the literal interpretation of the Yahwistic narrative in Gen. 2:2ff.)[146] This leaves the woman in a dependent, relative and subordinate position.[147] Thus it must be affirmed that Paul in 1 Cor. 11 and Eph. 5 has not advanced very far beyond the Old Testament appraisal and position of women,[148] except that in Eph. 5 the relationship between husband and wife—allegorically related to the bond between Christ and church—has received a religious deepening, spiritualization and durability.[149]

The analogy between marriage and the paradigmatic relation between Christ and his church—an analogy that underlies the admonition to married couples in Eph. 5—originates in a particular kind of rabbinic exposition of Gen. 2:21ff.: a typological transference of the relationship Adam-Eve to the relationship Adam-Israel. This means that Israel comes from Adam[150] and thus Eve is equated with Israel.[151] Gen. 2:24 is quoted in Eph. 5:31f.[152] and the typology Adam-Israel is transferred to the relationship Christ-church[153] in which Christ is understood as eschatological Adam[154] and the church as the "new Israel."[155] Paul's analogical methodology implies an uncritical, biblicistic understanding of Gen. 2:21ff. The parallel between Christ-church on the one hand and man-wife on the other is only possible if the Yahwistic narrative of the creation of woman from man is misunderstood as literal history. It is also this narrative so understood which explains the demand—based on the place of the church in relation to Christ—that woman be unconditionally submissive to man. As probably no other Pauline passage, it is exactly because of Eph. 5—and indeed on the basis of this analogy—that Paul's understanding of the structure of marriage and the subordination of women was accepted as dogma and is considered even today as divine decree.[156] Regardless of the fact that the man does not always—and alone—possess the higher ethical and spiritual qualities[157] required for a function as "head," such a function is attributed to him simply because he is male. Such an "order" is not only absurd, it also omits needed respect for the freedom and independence of the personhood of woman. It is true that marriage as analogue of the relationship between Christ and the church can and even must be used, but only in a limited way, since in marriage—as different from the bond between Christ and church—the partners have equal worth and equal rights. Accordingly, in marriage a true and deep relationship must exclude the domination of one partner over the other.

Our critical investigation of the Pauline and deutero-Pauline statements (1 Cor. 11:3ff.; 1 Tim. 2:11-14 [to which cf. 1 Cor. 14:34f.];[158] Eph. 5:22-33)—which give "proof" for the *status subiectionis* (state of subjugation) of women by authority of the Fathers as quoted by Gratian and in Gratian's *dicta* themselves as well as in the literature of the decretists and decretalists depending on Gratian—has shown that these passages are characterized by a clear denigration of women in ontical as well as in religious-ethical terms. As we have indicated, this negative evaluation of women must be traced back to the strong dependence of Paul and the writer of the pastoral letters on the late Jewish rabbinical tradition,[159] from which the rabbinic interpretation of Genesis and other scripture was taken.[160] Just as the conception of women in the Pauline and deutero-Pauline passages—characterized as it is by rabbinic thinking—cannot claim to be binding, so also are the legal consequences unjustified which Paul (or whoever wrote the pastoral letters),[161] as well as Gratian supported by the authority of the Fathers, have deduced for women. Such consequences are devoid of any true foundation.

Notes

1. See Munier, *Les sources patristiques*, 205ff. R. Metz, "Saint Angustin et le Code de droit canonique de 1917," *RDC* 4 (1954):405-419.

2. See pp. 87f. with chapter 2, n. 27.

3. See pp. 30f. Against the possible objection that the statements of Ambrosiaster have nothing to do with the teachings of genuine Church Fathers and that therefore no weight should be given to his idea that women are by nature not made in the image of God, it must be pointed out that the influence of Ambrosiaster on church doctrine and law can hardly be overestimated, since his writings were associated with those of Ambrose and Augustine over the centuries. Besides, the God-likeness of woman is a highly debated truth, in part denied, among the genuine Church Fathers. (Cf. Van der Meer, "Priestertum der Frau?" pp. 61f. and Elisabeth Schüssler Fiorenza, Der vergessene Partner, Grundlagen, Tatsachen und Möglichkeiten der beruflichen Mitarbeit der Frau in der Heilssorge der Kirche. [Düsseldorf: Patmos Verlag, 1964], 72.) Also according to Thomas, woman is in one sense not the image of God. (See chapter 3, n. 82) This point of view is likewise found in contemporary theologians: e.g., H. Doms,"Zweigeschlechtlichkeit und Ehe," in *Mysterium salutis, Grundriss heilsgeschichtlicher Dogmatik*, vol. 2, ed. by Johannes Feiner and Magnus Löhrer, eds., (Einsiedeln, Benziger 1965) 730f., 734f.; also by Doms, "Ehe als Mitte zwischen ihrem Urbild and ihrem Nachbild," in *Ehe im Umbruch*, Albrecht Beckel, ed., (Münster, Regensberg, 1969), 241, 243.

4. " . . . As the [scripture] certainly says: And God make a human [*homo*]; in the image of God, God made him." Ambrosiaster omits Gen. 1:27b—"male and female he created them"—this part of the verse would have made his argument quite impossible.

5. Cf. Wilhelm Gesenius, *Hebräisches und aramäisches Handwörterbuch über das Alte Testament*, (Leipzig: F. C. W. Vogel, 1921), 10; Lexicon in Veteris Testamenti libros, Ludwig Köhler and Walter Baumgartner, eds., (Leiden: Brill, 1953), 12: "אָדָם all is collective and means mankind, people" (may be combined with plural and singular); "later and isolated, אָדָם may mean a single person. . . . in Gen. 2:5-5:5 there is a mixture of the collective אָדָם = man and w(omen) m(asculini) Adam. Thus we have הָאָדָם, e.g., in Gen. 2:7, 8, 19 and 4:1—the (type) man = Adam; but אָדָם in Gen. 5:la = mankind." Cf. also F. Stier, "Adam" in *Handbuch theologischer Grundbegriffe*, 2 vols., (Munich: Kösel-verlag, 1962), Heinrich Fries, ed., 1:13.

6. Cf. Paul Heinisch, *Das Buch Genesis*, (Bonn, Hansstein, 1930), 101; Otto Procksch, *Die Genesis*, 2nd ed. and 3rd ed., (Leipzig: A. Deichert, 1924) 1: 449f.; Gerhard von Rad, *Genesis: A Commentary*, (Philadelphia: Westminster Press, 1961), 55; Werner H. Schmidt, *Die Schöpfungsgeschichte der Priesterschrift*, 2nd ed., (Neukirchen-Vluyn: Neukirchener-Verlag des Erziehungsvereins, 1967), 144f. (references to further literature are found on this p. 145, n. 1).

7. Cf. Procksch, 450; von Rad, 46f.; Eichrodt, Walther. *Theologie des Alten Testaments,* part 2/3, 5th ed., (Götingen: Vandenhoeck & Ruprecht, 1964), 81; Oswald Loretz, *Schöpfung und Mythos. Mensch und Welt nach den Anfangskapiteln der Genesis,* (Stuttgart: Katholisches Bibelwerk, 1968), 87; Wolfgang Trilling, *Im Anfang schuf Gott . . . :eine Einführung in denSchöpfungsbericht der Bibel,* (Freiburg: Herder, 1964), 8; H. Wildberger, "Das Abbild Gottes" (Gen. -1:26-30) I, *Theologische Zeitschrift,* 21 (Basel, 1965):249.

8. Julius Boehmer, "Wieviel Menschen sind am letzten Tage des Hexaemerons geschaffen worden?" *Zeitschrift für die alttestamentliche Wissenschaft* (hereafter cited as *ZAW*) 34 (1914):34. F. Schwally, "Die biblischen Schöpfungsberichte," *Archiv für Religionswissenschaft* (hereafter cited as *ARW*) 9 (1906): 172-175, sees in v. 27 the idea that Gen. 1 originally had to do with an androgynous mythos—an idea that P. Winter, recently, shares (*ZAW* 68 [1956]: 78f.; 70 [1958]: 260f. In v. 27b Schwally wants to replace אֹתָם by אתו. Against this, see Eichrodt, 2: 81 with n. 35, and von Rad, 58. "The plural in v. 27 ['he created them'] is intentionally contrasted with the singular ['him'] and prevents one from assuming the creation of an originally androgynous man."

9. Translated: "Blessed art thou, Yahweh, our God, King of eternity, who has not made me a woman!"

10. I.e., let them have dominion . . . (Gen. 1:26).

11. Boehmer, 33.

12. Cf. Schmidt, 145, n. 1.

13. Agreeing with this opinion rejected by Schmidt are, for instance, Hans Gunkel, *Genesis*, 6th ed., (Göttingen: Vandenhoeck & Ruprecht, 1964), 11; likewise Heinisch, 101 and Peter Morant,. *Die Anfänge der Menschheit. Eine Auslegung der ersten 11 Genesis-kapitel*, (Lucerne: Räber & Cie, 1960), 61. Boehmer, 33, rightly remarks about this interpretation: "It seems that unconsciously and unintentionally the Paradise narrative of Gen. 2f.—where apparently a human pair, and otherwise no human beings, are presented—has become a model for the understanding of 1:26-30 and thus has suggestively influenced the exposition of this passage. Conceivably enough—when the whole weight of century-old, even millenia-old tradition has hindered objective research . . . "

14. Schmidt, 145.

15. Schmidt, 145, n. 1, refers to numerous parallels, including Gen. 8:6, 5; 6:6f.; 7:23.

16. The appropriate parallel may be found in 'light," Gen. 1:3-4 (Schmidt, 145, n. 1).

17. Schmidt, ibid.

18. Schmidt, 146, n. 1, gives numerous illustrations of this—for instance, the Levitical cleanliness regulations that differentiate between men and women.

19. Schmidt, 145f.; cf. also Claus Westermann, *Genesis*, (Neukirchen-Vluyn: Neukirchener-Verlag des Erziehungsvereins, 1966-), 221.

20. Like many other commentators, Schmidt sees in the dominion status of mankind a consequence of the Godlikeness of men (142); see also n. 23, below.

21. Schmidt, 146f. with 147, n. 1.

22. Jervell, Jacob. "*Imago Dei.* Gen 1, 26f. im Spätjudentum," in *der Gnosis und in den paulinischen Briefen*, (Göttingen: Vandenhoeck & Ruprecht, 1960), 94, 110, demonstrates that in late Judaism the idea arose that the procreation charge (Gen. 1:28) was given to the man alone; the man would diminish his Godlikeness if he did not procreate. Cf. also J. B. Schaller, *Gen. 1:2 im antiken Judentum*, unpublished dissertation, (Göttingen, 1961), 156 ("It is occasionally admitted that the command of Gen. 1:28 is intended for woman too [cf. Strack and Billerbeck, *Kommentar zum Neuen Testament*, 2:372f.], but this has not been a generally accepted point of view. Actually, reference of this command to the man alone corresponds to Israelite marital law.") Of course it remains a question whether the rabbinical interpretation really corresponds with the content of the statement of Gen. 1:28. But since the Old Testament regarded reproduction as the exclusive province of the male, the rabbinic exposition of Gen. 1:28 is not completely impossible. Cf. Gen. 9:1,7 ("God blessed Noah and his sons and said to them: 'Be fruitful and multiply, and fill the earth. . . . And you, be fruitful and multiply, bring forth abundantly on the earth and have dominion over it.'") The similar charge—to that of Gen. 1:28—is here directed exclusively to men.

23. Cf. Friedrich Horst, *Gottes Recht; gesammelte Studien zum Recht im Alten Testament* (München, C. Kaiser, 1961), 226, 23; E. Schlink, "Gottes Ebenbild als Gesetz und Evangelium," *Der alte und der neue Mensch: Aufsätze zur theologischen Anthropologie*, Gerhard von Rad, ed., (München: A. Lempp, 1942), 71; similarly, Loretz, 93 ("Godlikeness is . . . the presupposition of the dominion status of men"); also see Westermann, 213.

24. Perhaps a confirmation of this is to be found in Gen. 5:lb, 2: "On the day when God created man [adam], he made him according to the image of God. Male and female he created them and gave them the name 'man' [adam], on the day he created them." Here the concept "adam" is expressly applied to woman also, but with it also the Godlikeness characterizing adam. Cf. Henricus Renckens, *Urgeschichte und Heilsgeschichte. Israels Schau in die Vergangenheit nach Gen. 1-3*, (Mainz: Matthias-Grünewald-Verlag, 1959), 96F., on the passage: ". . . Man is image of God because he is a human being . . . "; see also Stier, 13. On the contrary, Boehmer, 34, thinks that for text-critical reasons—he refers to a variant reading of the Septuagint and certain commentaries, which he fails to identify—and for objective reasons, "their name" (שְׁמָם) in Gen. 5:2b) should be read as "his name" (שְׁמוֹ), Other commentators, however, keep the reading שְׁמָם (their name) of the Hebrew original text throughout. E.g., John Skinner, *A Critical and Exegetical Commentary on Genesis*, 2nd ed. (Edinburgh: T. & T. Clark 1930), 130; likewise La Sainte Bible, 1/1, (La Genèse, traduite et commentée par Albert Clamer) (Paris: Letouzey et Ané, 1953), 166 ("l'appellation enfin d'Adam des deux représentants d' l'humanités . . . ").

25. Cf. A. S. Kapelrud, "Mensch (im AT)," in *RGG*, 4:862; Ludwig Köhler, *Theologie des Alten Testaments*, 4th ed., (Tübingen: Mohr, 1966), 53.

26. The following literature deals with this problem in detail: Norbert Peters, *Die Frau im Alten Testament* (Düsseldorf, L. Schwann, 1926); Georg Beer, *Die soziale und religiöse Stellung der Frau im israelitischen Altertum*, (Tübingen:

Mohr, 1919); Johann Döller, *Das Weib im Alten Testament*, (Münster in Westfalen: Aschendorff, 1920); Thaddaeus Engert, *Ehe- und Familienrecht der Hebräer*, (München, J. J. Lentner, 1905); Max Löhr, *Die Stellung des Weibes zu Jahwe-Religion und -Kult*, (Leipzig, J. C. Hinrichs'sche Buchhandlung, 1908).

27. Cf. Martin Noth, *Geschichte Israels*, 6th ed., (Göttingen, Vandenhoeck & Ruprecht 1966), 104, 133.

28. Cf. W. Plautz, "Zur Frage des Mutterrechts im Alten Testament," *ZAW*, new series 33 (1962): 10 with n. 3. Plautz shows that "most of the indications of former matriarchy," which some thought could be found among the Israelites (e.g., name giving through the mother, separate living quarters for wives—Gen. 2:24), "do not hold up under investigation and can be equally well explained by other phenomena." Only a particular type of marriage and the (relatively exalted) position of the queen mother in Judah may go back to the influence of an older (Canaanite?) culture on the patriarchal society of the Israelites. (pp. 29f.)

29. Cf. Ex. 20:17; Johannes Leipoldt, *Die Frau in der antiken Welt und im Urchristentum*. (Leipzig: Koehlert & Amelang, 1954), 103; Beer, 6f.

30. Cf. Gen. 20:3; 2 Sam. 11:26; correspondingly the married woman is "be'ula" (past participle of ba'al = to rule, possess; cf. Gen. 20:3; Dt. 22:22; Is. 54:1). which is translated in the Septuagint and in Paul (Rom. 7:2) by ὑπανδρος—subordinate to the authority of man. Cf. Walter Bauer, *Griechisch-deutsches Wörterbuch zu den Schriften des Neuen Testaments und der übrigen urchristlichen Literatur*, 5th ed., (Berlin, A. Töpelmann, 1957-1958), 1657.

31. Cf. , e.g., Gen. 4:17f.; Gen. 5:3ff.; 10; 11:10-26.

32. Plautz, 26, notes that the phrase *jld lo*—"she bore him" children, e.g., in Gen. 30:4f., 17, 19—"is usual in describing birth in marriages which are strongly patriarchal." In Wisdom 7:1f. the Old Testament idea of the reproductive process develops into a theory in which Greek influence may have been effective: "In the womb I was formed into flesh, in ten months by the seeds of man my blood congealed. . . . " On this cf. E. Lesky, "Die Zeugungs- und Vererbungslehren der Antike und ihr Nachwirken," *Abhandlungen der Akademie der Wissenschaften und der Literatur (Geistes- und sozialwissenschaftliche Klasse)*,19, (1950): 1227-1425.

33. Cf. Gen. 29:31-55; 30:1-24; 35:17; Ps. 127:3-5.

34. Ex. 23:17; 34:23; Dt. 16:16; cf. Beer, 34f.

35. Cf. Num. 3; 4; Lev. 1;2;3;4.—Beer, 38; Löhr, 48f, n. 16; Engert, 61, n. 26. According to Ex. 38:8 and 1 Sam. 2:22, women had only certain services to perform at the entrance to the holy tent, but in the later (post-exilic) time even that possibility no longer existed for women. Cf. Beer, 39.

36. Cf. Ex. 15:20f.; Judges 4:4ff.; 5; 2 Kings 22:14ff. See Helga Rusche, *Töchter des Glaubens*, (Mainz: Matthias-Grünewald, 1959).

37. Beer, 37f.; cf.Köhler, 53. From the fact that there is no feminine form in the Old Testament for the characteristics "pious" (חָסִיד') "righteous" (צַדִּיק) and "saintly" (קָדוֹשׁ) (cf. Leipoldt, 72), we may conclude that no active, responsible role was allowed for women in the Yahwist religion. The same conclusion may be

drawn from the fact that the "I" who is the official person praying in the Psalms is a man. (A few characteristic examples: "Blessed is the man who does not walk in the counsel of the ungodly . . . but his delight is in the law of the Lord . . . " [Ps. 1:lf.]; "Let thy hand be over the man at thy right side, over the son of man whom thou didst raise up for thyself" [Ps. 80:18]; "Blessed is everyone who fears the Lord, who walks in his ways! You shall enjoy in truth the fruit of the labor of your hands. . . . Your wife blossoms like a fruitful vine within your house, your sons blossom like olive shoots around your table. Thus shall the man be blessed who fears the Lord" [Ps. 128:1-4].)

38. Cf. cc. 13 and 20 in *causa* 33, *questio* 5.

39. Renckens, 253, is critical of a hasty reference to the teachings of the Fathers because of their scriptural commentaries which are "often slavishly dependent on literal interpretation."

40. Cf. c. 13 in *causa* 33, *questio* 5 (This image of God is in man [*homo*] as he was made the one from whom others come into being, having the command of God, in some sense His vicar . . . "); also c. 20, ibid. (" . . . For this reason from the beginning, two, male and woman, were not made, . . . but first the male, then the woman from him. . . . ")

41. Cf. J. Schildenberger, "Adam" in *LTHK*, 1:126 (From the origin of the first woman [Eve] from Adam [2:21f.] the equal value of woman with man, as well as the coordination and the subordination of woman to man, is established.) Similarly, see Morant, 130; Herbert Muschalek, *Urmensch-Adam, Die Herkunft des menschlichen Leibes in naturwissenschaftlicher und theologischer Sicht,* (Berlin: Morus Verlag, 1963), 7. Concetti, "La donna," 9, very clearly refers to the order of creation as the reason for excluding women from the priesthood: "It is true . . . that in the order of creation—the Bible says this clearly—primacy belongs to the male." Doms, 241-243, argues similarly.

42. Renckens, 208.

43. Renckens, 209.

44. Cf. Renckens, 208f.; likewise, Theodor Schwegler, *Die biblische Urgeschichte im Lichte der Forschung*, (Munich: A. Pustet, 1960), 25.

45. See *Revue biblique*, new series, 62 (1955), 414-419; cf. N. Greitemann, "Rabies theological" in *Wort und Wahrheit*, 16 (1961), 242: "The decrees of the Bible Commission from 1905-1915 and 1932" were "not annulled, it is true, but the administration of their obligatory character has been relaxed since 1955."

46. Thus Morant, 128f. (See also 128, n. 9 [p. 211], where other exegetes, who represent the same position, are mentioned.) Also Morant, 145; and Muschalek, 205ff., 230f.

47. Cf. Schwegler, 90; Muschalek, 204f.

48. Schwegler, 25-28, rightly notes the fateful consequences of uncritical Bible study which have already taken place in the course of church history.

49. Thus Schildenberger, 126; Renckens, 200 and especially 254ff.; Schwegler, 90; also Herbert Haag, "Die biblische Schöpfungsgeschichte heute," in *Evolution und Bibel*, Herbert Haag, Adolf Haas, and Johannes Hürzeler, eds., (Freiberg: Herder, 1962), 49—referring to Schwegler, though with some

reservation: "It should not be taught how she [woman] was created, but what she is: the natural partner of man, who, however, lives in a certain state of dependency on him."

50. More attention will be paid to these texts on pp. 177ff., since they are in part basic to the *auctoritates patrum* (authorities from the Fathers) utilized by Gratian.

51. Cf. Renckens, 213.

52. Renckens, 214f.

53. Thus Hans Walter Wolff, "Das Kerygma des Jahwisten," in *Gesammelte Studien zum Alten Testament*, Hans Walter Wolff, ed., (München, C. Kaiser, 1964), 349f. According to Ernst Sellin, and Georg Fohrer, *Einleitung in das Alte Testament*, 10th ed., (Heidelberg: Quelle & Meyer, 1965),165, the only agreement on this is that J cannot be dated later than 722 B.C. There are differences of opinion about the earliest possible date. Disagreeing with Wolff, Sellin and Fohrer place the appearance of J in the decades between 850 and 800 B.C.

54. Stier, 15; Herbert Haag, "Die Themata der Sündenfall-Geschichte," in *Lex tua veritas*, Heinrich Groß and Franz Mußner, eds., (Trier: Paulinas-Verlag, 1961), 110f.

55. Cf. Haag, "Die Themata," 111.

56. Cf. Stier, 15; F. Hesse "Paradieserzghlung," in *RGG*, 5:99.

57. Haag, "Die Themata," 109f. (It is, however, not clear, according to Haag, whether the Yahwist found the passage about the creation of women already a part of the adāmāh narrative or himself put the two together. *ibid.*, 110.) See also *ibid.*, 2f.

58. Thus the Canaanites are, according to Gen. 9:18, 22, derived from a common tribal father, Ham, the son of Noah; according to Gen. 28:13f. (cf. Gen. 35:10ff.), Jacob is the tribal father of Israel and his brother, Esau, the father of the Edomites (Gen. 36:9ff.); see also the ancestral tree in Gen. 10. In this way the Yahwist explains the forgotten historical origins of particular tribes and clans. See Renckens, 226; Wolff, 360.

59. Cf. Renckens, 198f.

60. Renckens, 199.

61. See p. 169 with n. 32, above. When in the Old Testament certain tribes are named for women and are derived from them (e.g., "Rachel" and "Leah" tribes—see S. Mowinckel in *ZAW*, Beih. 77 (1958), 129-150), the reason may be found in the polygamous structure in the Old Testament, which is characterized, according to Plautz, 15, by the fact that "the relationship between a woman and her own children is closer than that of the husband to all of his children." But that does not change the fact that—as Plautz, 17, says,—"all mothers and children . . . are subordinate to the common spouse and father" and "their names, relationship and children's inheritance are determined by the legal superiority of the father."

62. Thus J. Scharbert (rescension of J. de Fraine, "La Bible et l'origine de l'homme"), *Biblische Zeitschrift* 6 (1962):309 ("The fact that the writers of biblical pre-history, as well as Paul too, recognize Adam as the only first man is

of course due to the Israelite-Judaic thinking about tribal ancestors. Since woman is likewise a human being, she must also, according to this viewpoint, be derived from the Adam-human being, which, however, could then be explained only by a non-mediated intervention of God.") Renckens, 198, says, similarly: "It fits thoroughly into the strongly monogenetic thought structure of the Garden of Eden account . . . that the first woman is formed from the first human being and thus is herself the second human being."

63. Eskimos relate that woman was created from the thumb of man (Westermann, 314); other mythic examples of the derivation of woman from a part of the body (including the rib) of man are given by Josef Leo Seifert, *Sinndeutung des Mythos: die Trinität in den Mythen der Urvölker*, (Vienna: Verlag Herold, 1954), 250f. and also by Hermann Baumann, *Schöpfung und Urzeit des Menschen im Mythus der afrikanischen Völker*, (Berlin, Reimer, 1964), 128, 159, 240, 249. Baumann, 239f., traces this myth cluster, especially the rib motif, to Christian-Islamic influence, although this is disputed by others. It is worth mentioning that a mythic idea often connected with the assumption of a secondary creation of woman is that she is in some way a defective being. Cf. Baumann, 204, 369.

64. Thus Westermann, 313.

65. This perception is expressed by the so-called consanguinity formula in Gen. 2:23 ("bone from my bone and flesh from my flesh"); cf. W. Reiser, "Die Verwandtschaftsformel in Gen. 2:23," in *Theologische Zeitschrift*, 16 (Basel, 1960): 4 ("Despite man's closeness to the animal, he is not profoundly related to the animal. Man is related only to man. That is the meaning of the consanguinity formula in the Yahwistic narrative of the creation of woman.")

66. Thus Gunkel, 13; similarly, von Rad, 68; Renckens, 199f. Referring to Procksch, Plautz opposes the assumption that Gen. 2:24 may reflect an original matriarchy, as Gunkel, 13, affirms. Plautz says, 28: "It is not a matter of a law of custom but of a force of nature."

67. See Westermann, 311 ("In giving names man discovers, conditions and orders his world. In this way a supreme autonomy of man in his circumscribed realm is brought to expression.") Similarly, Loretz, 115; Schmidt, 229, n. 1.

68. There is not yet any agreement among exegetes in the explanation of this motif. According to S. N. Kramer, "Enki and Ninhursag. A Sumerian 'Paradise' Myth," *Bulletin of the American School of Oriental Research*, Suppl. 1 (1945): 8f., the symbol of the rib should probably be traced to a Sumerian play on words; so too Westermann, 314 (in a reference to J. B. Pritchard, "Man's Predicament in Eden," in *The Review of Religion*, 13 (1948-1949):15: ". . . in Sumerian there is established through a play upon words, a definite connection between the rib and 'the lady who makes live'"). Westermann thus has reservations about an etiological view of the rib motif, as we find it, e.g., in von Rad, 82f. According to Hermann Baumann, *Das doppelte Geschlecht; ethnologische Studien zur Bisexualität in Ritus und Mythos*, (Berlin, D. Reimer 1955), 304 (see also 170f. with n. 122), the narration motif—creation of woman from the rib of man—is an abbreviated expression of an underlying mythic understanding according to which woman is formed from the left (in mythical language, the female) side of the

original man Adam pictured as androgynous. Othmar Schilling, *Das Mysterium Lunae die Erschaffung der Frau, nach Gn. 2, 21f.*, (Paderborn, F. Schöningh, 1963) uses a comparison from the history of religions to suggest that the rib is a representation of the moon and thus a fertility symbol. Schilling says that in using this symbol the biblical writer has given the moon idol into the hands of the creator God and thus the creation concept has overcome any kind of physical or mythical self-generation.

69. Gunkel, 13; similarly, Döller, 6, who however, in contrast to Gunkel, treats the passage uncritically: "A certain dependence of woman on man is already expressed in the creation account, in that she is simply there for his sake, as his helper."

70. Loretz, 115f.

71. Thus von Rad, 66f.; similarly, Eichrodt, 2:77.

72. However, many exegetes (e.g., Schmidt, 201—although in contradiction to 147, n. 1—and Westermann, 316f.) succumb to the danger of idealization, in that they dispute any form of a secondary position of woman in the Yahwistic creation account. On the other hand, Ilse Bertinetti, *Frauen im geistlichen Amt. Die theologische Problematik in evangelisch-lutherischer Sicht*, (Berlin: Evangelische Verlagsanstalt, 1965), 88, rightly notes: "No exegetical device can obscure the fact that the second creation account presupposes a clear, if limited, priority of the male."

73. Renckens, 195. According to targum Jeruschalmi 1, the "help" which the woman affords to Adam is exclusively sexual, as also the Aramaic translation of Gen. 2:18 suggests: "It is not right that Adam should sleep alone, I will create for him a woman, who will be as support by his side." (Schaller, 38); Augustine (*De Genesi ad litteram*, 1, 93, in *CSEL* 28/1, 271) similarly interprets the concept 'helper' as simply the contribution of woman to the procreation of offspring ("If it is asked to what this 'help' ought to refer, nothing else credibly suggests itself than for the procreation of sons, as the earth is the help of the seed so that bushes are born from both of them.") Contrariwise, Westermann, 317, maintains: "The phrase 'a helper fit for him' does not mean woman as sexual partner nor woman as helper in the field; any such delimitation destroys the sense of the passage. The personal fellowship between man and wife in the widest sense is intended . . ." Cf. also Westermann, 309.

74. Cf. Renckens, 203, 227f.; Haag, "Schöpfungsgeschichte," 49; Loretz, 120; Westermann, 313.

75. Renckens, 203f.; also see J. Begrich, "Die Paradieserzählung. Eine literargeschichtliche Studie," in *Gesammelte Studien zum Alten Testament*, 28.

76. So too Bertinetti, 88; similarly, Loretz, 28f. with n. 45 and n. 46.

77. Cf. Schwegler, 19f., 86.

78. Especially in the explanation of the Bible Commission (cf. p. 170, above) concerning the historical character of the narrative of the origin of woman from man.

79. This is pointed out by Renckens, 205, and Boehmer, 31ff., who rightly oppose any such interpretation.

80. Thus Renckens, 205; also see Schmidt, 229; similarly Bertinetti, 89.

81. Cf. Metz, "Statut," 62.

82. Cf. Hesse, 99; so also Loretz, 120, 131.

83. Haag, "Schöpfungsgeschichte," 45f.; see also his Haag, "Die Themata," 7.

84. See more on this in Begrich; Haag, "Die Themata," 101ff.; also see Westermann, 258, 265f.

85. Cf. Begrich, 29 and many other places. Also according to Haag, "Die Themata," 5ff., the temptation story (Gen. 3:1-7), which is significant in the context of our discussion, is of independent origin; J has worked it into the "Garden of Eden theme" (which, according to Haag, should be distinguished from the so-called adāmāh theme of Gen. 2-3). Cf. also Westermann, 265f.

86. Begrich, 36f. This explains "the succinctness and plainness in the story of the temptation of the man"; the psychological depth of the temptation of the woman by the serpent is lacking. (29f.) Other exegetes who are not occupied with the problem of source analysis in J too quickly find in the succinctness of the description an opinion of the narrator that woman has a special influence on man toward evil as well as toward good (cf. Begrich, 29). Still others construct from the narration an easier inclination to temptation and thus a moral inferiority of woman in comparison to man. So, e.g., B.K. Budde, "Die biblische Paradiesesgeschichte," in *ZAW* Suppl. 60 (Giessen, 1932): 46: "It [the serpent] proves its cleverness by going to the woman, who is of course considered to be the more unwise and more sensualof the two humans . . ."; a similar judgment is made by Heinisch, 120 and Procksch, 31.

87. Cf. Haag, "Die Themata," 5; Renckens, 247; note especially F. Hvidberg, "The Canaanitic Background of Gen.1-3," *Vetus Testamentum* 10 (1960): 285-294, especially 287: "The Canaanitic Baal appears not only in the form of a man . . . but also in the form of a serpent"; also see Loretz, 117, 121.

88. Hvidberg, 289.

89. Cf. Siefert, 272f., 286 (here the dependence of this mythic motif on the patriarchial culture is expressly indicated); cf. also Ferdinand Herrmann, "Symbolik in den Religionen der Naturvölker," in *Symbolik in den Religionen der Naturvölker*, Ferdinand Herrmann, ed., (Stuttgart: A. Hiersemann, 1961), 9:132.

90. See Gen. 31:19; Judges 17: 4ff.; 1 Kings 15:13; Jer. 7:17; 44:15-19, 25. According to Beer, 41 with n. 2, Israelite women possessed many amulets and statues of gods, including representations of the fertility goddess, Astarte, which were found in Palestinian excavations. Because of the danger of culture corruption and idolatry, marriages of Israelite men with Gentile women were strictly prohibited. Cf. Ex. 34:16; Ezra 9:1ff.; Neh. 13:23ff.

91. Cf. n. 86, above. The statements of the commentators named in no way fall short of those of rabbinic late Judaism, which were influential in the New Testament (cf. 1 Tim. 2:14 and 2 Cor. 11:3) and also in the writings of the Church Fathers. (Concerning rabbinic exposition of Gen. 3, see Egon Brandenburger, *Adam und Christus; exegetisch-religions-geschichtliche Untersuchung zu Röm. 5, 12-21(1.Kor 15)*, (Neukirchen: Kreis Moers, 1962), 39f., 49f., 44f.).

92. Several writers have taken special notice of the negative consequence of the extensive exclusion of women from the Yahweh religion. E.g., Köhler, 53: "Yahweh's covenant with Israel is a covenant with men, for they represent the people. . . . Women have no place in this revelation and therefore in the worship of Yahweh they are a continuing danger." Cf. also Wilhelm Rudolph, *Jeremia*, vol. 12 of the *Handbuch zum Alten Testament: Erste Reihe: [die kanonischen Bücher des Alten Testaments]*, Otto Eissfeldt, ed., 3rd ed., (Tübingen: J. C. B. Mohr (P. Siebeck), 1968), 55: "According to this passage [Jer. 7:16ff.], the worship of the queen of heaven [i.e., the Babylonian-Assyrian Ishtar] is first of all a matter for women, who actually come off somewhat badly in the Yahweh religion." Bertinetti also, 23f., rightly points out this connection: "The lack of the possibility of regular religious activities misled women into unofficial religious practices. Thus the prevention of official cultic practices resulted commonly in the development of a kind of surrogate religion, characterized by men as superstition and idolatry. One may see here the completely natural reaction to an unwarranted exclusion of a whole section of the people from a religious practice which had become the business of the male population alone, yet this reaction could also be seen as continuance of ancient folk superstition carried out by insufficiently enlightened women." The membership of women in Christian heresies (Montanism, etc.) may be similarly explained. See Heinzelmann, *Schwestern*, 50f.

93. Cf. Bertinetti, 93.

94. Cf. Renckens, 256; Bertinetti, 94; von Rad, 75, 81f.; Westermann, 74ff., 266f., who alludes to the etiological character of myths of the Fall outside the Bible, to which the sentences of punishment in Genesis that do not belong to the original part of the Garden of Eden story go back in the final analysis. See also Schmidt, 215, 218.

95. Cf. Stier, 17 ("Old Israelite ears probably wanted to hear, and were supposed to hear, that field and woman are exactly the bearers of fruit upon which the Canaanite fertility cult was to bestow its prosperity").

96. In 1 Cor. 14:34 the subjection of woman is demanded, among other reasons, because of "the law." The commentators often refer to Gen. 3:16. And according to Strack and Billerbeck, 3:468, the Apostle must have had this passage in mind; yet one should not insist on the term law, since traditional custom was often accepted as Torah (= law). Hans von Campenhausen is more cautious (*Die Begründung kirchlicher Entscheidungen beim Apostel Paulus: zur Grundlegung des Kirchenrechts*, [Heidelberg: C. Winter, 1957], 24): "Paul seems to be following [(i.e., in the regulation that women must remain silent)] a practice of the Jewish synagogue which is also attested, he thinks, by ancient 'law' (14:34) but it is not clear what Paul is thinking about here and whether he is thinking at all about a particular passage of the Pentateuch."

97. Cf. c. 15 in *causa* 33, *questio* 5 (Jerome on Tit. 2:5): "The word of the Lord is indeed blasphemed, or the primary purpose of God is even condemned or brought to nothing . . . when, against the law and faith of nature, she who is a Christian and subject to the law of God, wishes to rule over a male." Cf. also cc. 18 and 19.

98. H. Greeven, "Die Frau im Urchristentum," *Sonderdruck des Zentralblatts für Gynäkologie*, 81, (1959), 298; also see Renckens, 255 ("Instead of formulating a law, the judgment is a statement of fact.") Likewise, Van der Meer, "Priestertum der Frau?" 28 ("Nor is Gen. 3:16 a law [in the sense of 'precept'] but an existing fact"). Also see von Rad, 82.

99. On this see Seifert, 259, 262f. Herrmann, 138-141; so, too, Westermann, 74f.

100. Van der Meer, "Priestertum der Frau?" 28f.

101. Gratian also treats this sentence as the Apostle's word, as his punctuation shows. (Cf. *Corpus*, ed. Friedberg 1:1254.) On the contrary, in the *Quaestiones veteris et novi Testamenti* (*CSEL* 50, 243), A. Souter, ed., from which this chapter is taken, only 1 Cor. 11:7a is printed as quotation—not the sentence added by Ambrosiaster.

102. The words used there are in literal agreement with *causa* 13: "a woman ought to cover her head because she is not the image of God." *Corpus*, ed. Friedberg 1:1225.

103. Cf. Jervell, 308: "Paul clearly considers that only the man was created on the sixth day. Only later was the woman created . . . " Cf. also Ernest Findlay Scott, *The Pastoral Epistles*, (London: Hodder & Stoughton 1948), 27.

104. See especially Jervell, 293, 295f., 311; Schaller, 189; Johannes Weiss, *Der erste Korintherbrief*, 10th ed., (Göttingen: Vandenhoeck & Ruprecht, 1925), 270; Heinz Dietrich Wendland, Die Briefe an die Korinther, 12th ed., (Göttingen, Vandenhoeck u. Ruprecht, 1968), 91 ("Paul is doubtless using here a traditional exposition of the creation narrative, an exposition which corresponds to the actual and thorough subordination of women in cultic and legal realms dominant in the world of antiquity").

105. So Jervell, 298f.; similarly, Wendland, 90.

106. Cf. J. Jeremias, "Adam," *Theological Dictionary of the New Testament*, Gerhard Kittel et al., eds., (Grand Rapids, Mich., Eerdmans 1964-1976) (hereafter cited as *ThD*), 1:141; also 1 Tim. 2:13 (reference to the primacy of Adam in creation as explanation of the prohibition against teaching by women) is conditioned by this principle. See Joachim Jeremias, *Die Briefe an Timotheus und Titus*, 8th ed., (Göttingen, Vandenhoeck & Ruprecht, 1963), 19; Norbert Brox, *Die Pastoralbriefe*, 4th ed., (Regensburg, Verlag Friedrich Pustet, 1969), 134f.

107. Jervell, 109ff., presents a great deal of evidence from rabbinic writings of the limitation of image-of-God status to Adam and thus to the male. In addition see Schaller, 113, 152f., 172, esp. 189.

108. Tanch B Tazria 10, in Jervell, 110 (with further references to sources); in summary Jervell, 111, says: "*The tendency of rabbinic theology is not only to deny image-of-God status to Eve*—from the standpoint of salvation history—*but so to every woman*" [emphasis added]. Yet there are other viewpoints in rabbinic writings which grant this status to both man and woman; the married couple is seen as humanity in the image of God. (Evidence is given by Jervell, 111f.) It is true that Paul in 1 Cor. 11:3ff. is not influenced by this viewpoint, though perhaps he is in 1 Cor. 11:11f. See Jervell, 311f.

109. Cf. Jervell, 299; Schaller, 189.

110. Cf. Jervell, 300; H. Schlier, "Κεφαλή" in *ThD*, 3:679.

111. Schaller, 24, 33, points out that the Septuagint, which is influenced by Jewish tradition, translates the expression כְּנֶגְדִּי (= as his—Adam's—complement, Gen. 2:18) with *κατ 'αὐτόν.* Also see Jervell, 300.

112. Jervell, 301 ("A rabbinic reason for denying women the image-of-God status was precisely that they did not have the same religious duties as men"); see also Jervell, 109. Similarly, Schaller, 152: according to one rabbinic tradition image-of-God status consists in circumcision, i.e., in actual membership in the people of God—thus a woman is ipso facto considered to be not image-of-God.

113. According to Schaller, 188f., the series God-Adam-Eve is found in the targum translation of Gen. 1:26f. and 2:18. Since Paul in 1 Cor. 11:7 directly characterizes man as "image of God," contrary to his usual custom and without reference to Christ as mediator, it is practically certain, Schaller says, that Paul's series was also originally God-man-woman and that he simply enlarged it for christological purposes.

114. Cf. Schlier, "Κεφαλή" in *ThD*, 3:678, 33f. ("Κεφαλή means the one who stands above the other in the sense that he establishes the other's being"); Wendland, 90 ("The term 'head' means the outstanding, the superior, especially the head of a community.")

115. Weiss, 270.

116. Cf. Wendland, 91.

117. See Jervell, 303 with p. 114, n. 433.

118. See Jervell, 305ff.

119. Cf. Jervell, 305.

120. Jervell, 307, Weiss, 274 and Hans Lietzmann, *An die Korinther 1-2*, 4th ed., (Tübingen: J. C. B. Mohr [P. Siebeck], 1949), who finds support in Dibelius, understands by τοὺσ ἀγγέλουσ demons and evil spirits; see also n. 128 below.

121. Martin Dibelius, *Die Geisterwelt im Glauben des Paulus*, (Göttingen: Vandenhoeck & Ruprecht, 1909), 18ff. indicates that in widespread popular belief magical power was attributed to the veil.

122. Jervell, 308.

123. Cf. Jervell, 368f.

124. Cf. Jervell, 304 with n. 436; likewise Brandenburger 39f., 44f., esp. 49f. (the last containing numerous references).

125. Cf. Jervell, 305 with n. 442; also see Brandenburger, 49f.: According to *Slavonic Enoch* 31, 6 and *Apocalypse of Abraham* 23, the devil's attack against Adam was possible only through Eve.

126. Paul here compares the Christian people to a virgin, whom he has betrothed to Christ. Christ and the congregation are placed parallel to Adam and Eve. Paul fears that as Eve succumbed to the seduction of the serpent, so the mind of the faithful may be turned away from the sincere and pure devotion to Christ. The comparison is only apt if at its base lies the idea that Eve was led by the serpent to be unfaithful to Adam. As a matter of fact, there is a well-known rabbinic tradition according to which Eve did succumb to sexual seduction by the

serpent. Paul is here dependent on this tradition. Cf. Jervell, 304; Brandenburger, 50; Strack and Billerbeck, 1:138.

127. Jervell, 304f. and Brandenburger, 50, among others, point to the late Jewish tradition as basis for 1 Tim. 2:11ff. So also Brox,134f. who refers to W. Nauck, *Die Herkunft des Verfassers der Pastoralbriefe*, unpublished dissertation (Göttingen, 1950), 96ff., according to whom 1 Tim. 2:13-15a, which underlies the prohibition of teaching in 1 Tim. 2:12, is a short Midrash which leans closely to the rules of rabbinic exegesis. Brox, 133, ṡays that the occasion for the teaching prohibition is an heretical (gnostic) practice which gave women complete liberty to teach in open assembly. No scholarly certainty exists about the authorship of the Pastoral letters: Catholic and some Protestant exegetes hold to their genuineness, but there is a growing inclination, including that of Catholic scholars, to think that "the assumption of genuineness makes it more difficult to explain the meaning of the letters." Brox, 25; see the thorough discussion of the authorship question, Brox, 22-60.

128. The Septuagint translates "sons of God" (Gen. 6:2) with ἄγγεοι τοῦ θεοῦ; cf. the parallels in 1 Cor. 11:10: διὰ τοὺσ ἀγγέλοι.

129. Weiss, 274f.

130. See Strack and Billerbeck, 3:427-437.

131. Cf. cc. 13 and 19 in *causa* 33, *questio* 5; also see *dictum Gratiani, causa* 15, *questio* 3 *princ*. ("to have the head covered as a sign of subjugation").

132. Jervell, 309. (Jervell also, 309, n. 459, notes that in rabbinic understanding the woman was ordered, after the Fall, to wear long hair. Cf. Strack and Billerbeck, 3: 442.)

133. Cf. Wendland, 92.

134. See Lietzmann, 55.

135. Cf. Wendland, 92 ("It should not be claimed that v. 11 annuls all that has previously been said.")

136. See E. Schweizer, "σάρχ," in *ThD*, 7:125; also by Schweizer, "σῶμα" in *ThD*, 7:1078.

137. This could also be inferred from the fact that Eph. 5:30—"For we are all members of his (i.e., Christ's) body"—contains in many mss. the addition "from his flesh and from his bones," a clear reference to Gen. 2:23. In the same way Ernest Best, *One Body in Christ; A Study in the Relationship of the Church to Christ in the Epistles of the Apostle Paul*, (London, S. P. C. K., 1955), 178, says: "The ἐκ (i.e., from his flesh, etc.) suggests, that as Eve came from Adam so the Church comes from Christ; this reproduces the conception of Christ as the ἀρχή of the Church, its originating cause . . . "; cf. also S. F. B. Bedale, "The Theology of the Church," in *Studies in Ephesians*, F. L. Cross, ed., (London, A. R. Mowbray 1956), 72.

138. Cf. Renckens; Gunkel, 13.

139. Thus Schweizer, "σάρξ", in *ThD*, 7:137, 12ff.; Franz Mussner, *Christus, das All und die Kirche, Studien zur Theologie des Epheserbriefes*, (Trier, Paulinus-Verlag, 1955), 150f.: "Of course woman is not literally the 'body' or the 'self' of man, but in marriage she becomes 'one flesh' with her husband,

according to Gen. 2:24, so that love of the husband for his wife meets something in her which belongs to his own (physical) essence." See also Francis Foulkes, The Epistle of Paul to the Ephesians, An Introduction and Commentary, (Grand Rapids, Eerdmans 1963), 160.—"Christ loves her [i.e., the church] as His body. . . . Even so husbands are to love their wives, as their own bodies. It would seem that Genesis 2:24 is already in mind, though it is not quoted till verse 31. . . . Paul . . . comes closer to the terms of Genesis 2:24 when he says, 'For no man ever yet hated his own flesh.'"

140. Fritz Rienecker, *Der Brief des Paulus an die Epheser*, (Wuppertal: R. Brockhaus, 1961), 209, understands Eph. 5:28f. exclusively in this sense, although he fails to take account of its timebound nature. ("The body has not independent will, rather its whole life movement is regulated by the impulse that comes from the head. So it is with the relationship between Christ and his people and thus with the relationship between man and woman.)

141. E. Schweizer, "σῶμα" in *ThD*, 7, 1064.

142. Ibid.; "In sexual intercourse the body of one belongs to the other."

143. Perhaps there is an exception to this in 1 Cor. 6:15f. "Do you not know that your bodies are members of Christ? Shall I therefore take the members of Christ and make them members of a prostitute? . . . Do you not know that he who joins himself to a prostitute becomes one body with her? For it is written, 'The two shall become one.'" (Gen. 2:24).

144. According to Mussner, 148, the extent of this power-of-command is comparable to that of a master over his slaves!

145. This expression in v. 28a and v. 29 ("flesh") has a variation in v. 28b as follows: "He who loves his wife loves himself." Here a certain identity of the married partners is implied (cf. Metz, "Recherches," 381) and the concept "body" is almost given the significance of person. But wife is still seen as dependent on and in relation to husband (as part of himself ["body"] or as himself) and defined more exactly by his person—never the reverse! The objective significance of the concept "body" or "flesh" applied without question to women fits especially well the concept σκεῦος (instrument, vessel), which, in an exclusively sexual sense, is applied to wives in 1 Thess. 4:4 and 1 Peter 3:7—in dependence on late Jewish linguistic usage. Thus this concept—combined with that ofκτᾶσθαι—characterizes the marriage relationship of husband to wife as that of possession, in which the wife has only a passive role and to a certain extent is looked upon as an object to be used. See Ch. Maurer, "σκεῦος," *ThD*, 7, 361f., 365-367.

146. Cf. Bedale, 71.

147. Marianne Weber, *Ehefrau und Mutter in dr Rechsentwicklung*, (Tübingen: Mohr, 1907), 184, remarks aptly about this: "Thus Paul seems to think of the unconditional subjection of the wife as presupposition for the realization of that mystical image in marriage, and apparently for him obedience is much more indispensable than any other attribute on her part [emphasis added]. For he demands of the husband: You men, love your wives . . . just as Christ has loved his church and given himself for it . . . ," but then he says to the wives: 'but the wife must respect the husband.'"

148. Cf. Weber, 182f. But this is not true for 1 Cor. 7 and Gal. 3:27f.

149. Weber, 184.

150. Cf. Schaller, 184, 189. Again, the theory of male procreation, i.e., the Jewish idea of tribal ancestors, lies behind this point of view.

151. Cf. Schaller, 189.

152. "For this reason a man (ādām) shall leave his father and mother and be joined to his wife; and the two shall become one flesh (Gen. 2:24). This is a great mystery, and I take it to mean Christ and the church."

153. Cf. Schaller, 189.

154. See Schweizer, "σῶμα" ThD, 7:1077.

155. Cf. Schaller, 102.

156. According to Mörsdorf, *Lehrbuch des Kirchenrechts,* 2:139, the headship of the husband in marriage (cf. c. 1112 with cc. 93 and 98, § 4) is generally recognized in canonistic studies as a divine principle of marriage. Cf. also Doms, 241-243.

157. E.g., Augustine in two passages quoted by Gratian suggests a higher ethical demand on men because of their supposed superiority: ". . . it belongs to them [men] both to surpass females in virtue and to rule them by example." (*causa* 32, *questio* 6, c. 4); "If the head is man, the man ought to live better and to exceed his wife in all good deeds." (*ibid.*, c. 5). Actually, however, the claim to dominion and power over women and to a privileged position toward them is usually derived from a simple assertion of the superiority of men.

158. Weighty text-critical considerations have been raised against the 1 Cor. 14:34f. passage. See Gottfried Fitzer, *"Das Weib schweige in der Gemeinde:" über den unpaulinischen Charakter der mulier-taceat-Verse in 1. Korinther 14*, (München: Chr. Kaiser, 1963); Hans Lietzmann and Werner Georg Kümmel, *An die Korinther I-II*, 4th ed., (Tübingen: J. C. B. Mohr (P. Siebeck), 1949), 75.

159. See the rabbinic sources and parallels to these passages in Strack and Billerbeck, 3; also Schaller, 187-189; cf. n. 104 above.

160. Cf. Campenhausen, 42; Brox, 134ff.

161. The "Pauline" prohibition of teaching by women (cf. 1 Cor. 14:34f. and 1 Tim. 2:11ff.) already had authoritative influence on early church liturgies. Cf. Walter Lock, *A Critical and Exegetical Commentary on the Pastoral Epistles* (*I & II Timothy and Titus*), (Edinburgh, T. & T. Clark, 1924), 29, which refers to the following liturgies: *Canon. Hippol.* § § 81-88 ("a free woman should not come into the church with colorful garments . . . nor ought they under any circumstances speak in church since this is the house of God." The "justification" ["since this is the house of God"] is very instructive on the question of the valuation of women); *Test. Dom.* 2, 4; *Apostolic Constitutions*, 3, 6.

Part II

Doctrine

Chapter 6

The Traditional Conception of the Priesthood: An Argument for the Exclusion of Women

Doctrinal arguments to justify the exclusion of women from service in ecclesiastical office have often been criticized and thoroughly refuted, in the theological literature of recent years.[1] But several additions can be made to the refutation. Especially the analysis of the conservative understanding of church office, which opposes admission of women to ordination, needs such addition and deepening in regard to one aspect of the concept of office—that of representation. Of course the problem cannot be treated in detail in the framework of this study—only in a preliminary fashion—but some basic reflections may throw light on the questionableness of the traditional understanding of office and representation, insofar as it is directed against the admission of women to church positions.

Traditional Understanding of Ecclesiastical Office

According to the traditional Catholic concept of church office, one who possesses the presbyterial and episcopal office is understood to be the representative of Christ, as one who in his functions of office and especially in the liturgical celebration portrays and represents Christ.[2] Although the representation concept in this crystallized juridical form is not present in the New Testament (more on pp. 207ff.), pointers in this direction developed relatively early,[3] and in the course of time it became an essential characterization of the officeholder in Catholic theology.[4] Several encyclicals of Pius XII[5] made use of this tradition in emphasizing the representative function of the priest as well as of ecclesiastical officeholders in general. This emphasis is expressed repeatedly, especially in his encyclical, "Concerning the Sacred Liturgy" (*Mediator Dei*): "The minister at the altar offering a Sacrifice in the name of all His members represents Christ, the Head of the Mystical Body."[6] "Only to the Apostles, and thenceforth to those on whom their successors have placed their hands, is granted the power of the priesthood, in virtue of which they represent the person of Jesus Christ before their people, acting at the same time as representatives of their people before God."[7] The ability of the priest to represent Christ in this form goes back according to Catholic teaching, to the infusion of grace in the priest's ordination, or more exactly, to the imprint of the sacramental nature of ordination. *Mediator Dei* speaks about this too: Priests alone have "the indelible 'character' indicating the sacred ministers' conformity to Jesus Christ the Priest."[8] Similarly, in another place, Pius says: "The minister by reason of the sacerdotal consecration which he has received, is made like the High Priest and possesses the power of performing actions in virtue of Christ's very Person."[9]

Referring expressly to the encyclical, J. Pascher[10] develops further its concept of representation—which was also expressed by Vatican II.[11] He sees in the eucharist a representation and realization of the historical Last Supper, a sacred drama in which the priest has the task of "conveying the person of Christ"—an expression also used in the encyclical—"or, to speak more exactly, to portray him faithfully."[12] According to Pascher, it is his ordination that gives the priest his ability to do this: "Concerning the priestly actor, it must be said that he is set off from the people by virtue of his elevated position at the altar and his vestments. He portrays Christ. Even theologically, his significance is defined by the categories of the drama in the statement that he and he alone is, in the eucharist, the *persona* of Christ." (In this connection Pascher thinks of *persona* in its old basic meaning of "mask" or "role" in a drama.)[13] ". . . In order to be able to play this role in a religious drama," the priest requires "an inner similarity to Christ impressed upon him by the sacrament of ordination."[14]

Although in this way the ability of the priest to represent Christ is understood as the consequence of the sacrament of ordination and thus as a pneumatic power, nevertheless paradoxically—but undeniably—the male sex of the priest, a biological quality, is considered in traditional Catholic theology to be the foremost presupposition for his representing Christ in the priesthood. It is true that this conception appears only implicitly in the encyclical *Mediator Dei*, and likewise in the texts of Vatican II, but it is clear enough[15] and has exercised a definite influence on the thinking of various Catholic writers about office and representation. One of these writers, O. Semmelroth,[16] says that a continuation and a pictorial representation of the "redemptive encounter" between Christ and humanity takes place in the church. This encounter is realized in the church by the fact

> that her ordained officeholders represent Christ in virtue of the indelible character of orders and in the fact that the Christian community brings to further completion Mary's conception and compassion by hearing the word of the teaching and governing offices and by participating in the sacrifice of the priestly office.[17]

In accordance with this pattern, Semmelroth sees in the sacrifice of the eucharist a sacramental reflection of that "'rite of heavenly sacrifice' in which the sacrifice of Christ and the participating sacrifice of Mary on Calvary has eternal validity before the Father."[18] Even more clearly the exercise of ecclesiastical office is characterized as a male role and the function of the congregation as female. Thus Semmelroth comments:

> What Paul writes in the fifth chapter of Ephesians about the relation of husband to wife is to a high degree valid for the relation between the priest and the congregation, for the latter is a relationship which like that of marriage—yet even more realistically—reflects the relationship between Christ and Mary.[19]

Other writers[20] have a similar point of view about ecclesiastical office and its relation to the Christian community. It is a point of view restricted by categories of sexual polarity, which has of course the obvious result that women are completely denied capability for church office. It is argued, for example, that Christ, the bridegroom and head of the church—the life-giving principle for the church, in fact—could not be represented by a woman, who is subject to man and as a passively receiving being could not be called (like him) the "head." This viewpoint is not seldom the main argument for the exclusion of women from orders. Thus E. Krebs remarks: "As father, spouse and bridegroom Christ stands vis-à-vis his church. . . . But being father and bridegroom is the role of the male. So there is in the priesthood a mystical relationship to maleness, by which we can clearly see that Christ has entrusted this masculine office to the male."[21] M. Schmaus also perceives an inner causal connection between the male sex of the priest and representation of Christ, thus justifying the reservation of the office to males:

> Thus [as in the case of Christ] the fact that the priest is a man is in itself a natural indication of his commission to go out into the world and proclaim the Gospel of the Kingdom of God, to give the sacraments and so to confer divine life in a creativity effected by the power of Christ. The place of women is rather to receive life and to take care of it.[22]

Even in recent publications a similar reasoning is used to deny women admission to service in church office.[23]

A Critique

Apart from an obvious denigration of women—they are allegedly not fit to represent Christ, the head, because they are inferior, etc.—the traditional but also modern viewpoint about representation, on the basis of which women are denied access to ecclesiastical office, implies an understanding of office incompatible with biblical statements about church and office. Thus while church office in the Pauline conception of church as "body of Christ" exists as an organ and a function among other various functions *within* the body (cf., for instance, Rom. 12:4-8 and 1 Cor. 12:27ff.), incorporated in the total organism of the body, office and the bearers of office are placed *over against* congregation and church in the traditional understanding. Office and bearers of office seem to be separated out from the unity of the body and associated with Christ as "head" and "bridegroom" of the church (cf. Eph. 5:23ff.). Also in accordance with this pattern, New Testament statements about church as "body" and "bride of Christ," which in themselves reveal the relationship of the exalted Lord to the church *in its totality*, are erroneously referred in traditional ecclesiology to the relationship between church officials and the lay congregation.[24] This is clear in Semmelroth (as well as in other theologians[25]), who says:

> When tradition as well as Holy Scripture calls the church the bride of the Lord, the church here—strictly speaking—means the congregation in contrast to ecclesiastical office. For in Catholic understanding, office is an exact representation of Christ, the bridegroom. So strictly speaking it must be 'bracketed out' of the church, insofar as the church is the bride. Similarly, in the statement that the church is the body of Christ, insofar as a reality is meant which is placed vis-à-vis Christ, the head, once again we have a bracketing out of the priesthood. For the priesthood is just that—the visible portrayal of the head of the church.[26]

Of course Semmelroth preserves the distinction between Christ and the priest, but Wintersig seems not to do even that: "In a particular way vis-à-vis the church and the soul, to be Christ, the bridegroom, in sacred love and gracious procreation—that is the essence and vocation of the holy priestly order, which stands in contrast to the rank and file of the faithful."[27]

Undoubtedly, an illegitimate transfer of the marriage admonition section in Eph. 5:22-33 to the relationship office-congregation, together with an unbiblical and superficial concept of representation, has made a considerable contribution to the formation of this understanding of church office. True, according to Eph. 5 marriage is a reflection of the covenant between Christ and the church, in which the position of the husband is compared with that of Christ and the position of the wife, with that of the church.[28] As an analogy to this, and on the basis of the representation theory, traditional theology sees the bishop as the bridegroom of the local church. Realization of this fact appears in the giving of a ring to the bishop in the ritual of his consecration as bishop. The ring symbol indicates that the bishop as representative of Christ is being married to the local church.[29] This spiritual marriage was considered so real that from it far-reaching consequences for church law were drawn, in thorough analogy to physical marriage[30]—consequences which are in part still influential today. The relationship of the pastor to the congregation is still expressed as spiritual marriage—in dependence on Eph. 5;[31] the attitude that the husband is expected to take toward his wife, according to Eph. 5, is accepted as the standard and norm for the relation of the priest toward the congregation.[32]

Thus office and representation are understood to mean taking the position of Christ as head and life-giving bridegroom of the church—opposite the church—and so to carry forward his work. Capability to do this, as we have noted (pp. 202ff.) is linked to two presuppositions: male sex and ordination. The more important of the two—for the purpose of representing Christ—is male sex, according to traditional doctrinal belief and operative church law (even today valid ordination is in the first place dependent upon this condition), and the result is that the objective of the office-bearer considered as representative is to portray and to imitate Christ in his earthly existence, as man.[33] Outward, biological likeness to the historical Jesus—from which a spiritual likeness and similarity of nature is too quickly concluded—thus becomes the main requirement for official representation,[34] always of course with the presupposition of sacramental ordination, which in traditional teaching perfects through grace an ability to represent Christ that is thought to be natural to male sex. At the same time this ordination sets a constitutive boundary between clergy and laity.[35] In the Decree on the Ministry and Life of Priests (*Presbyterorum Ordinis*) of Vatican II, this action of the sacrament is described in the following way: "The sacerdotal office of priests is conferred by that special sacrament through which priests, by the anointing of the Holy Spirit, are marked with a special character and are so configured to Christ the Priest that they can act in the person of Christ the Head."[36] This is especially true for the consecration of bishops as the "fullness of the sacrament of orders,"[37] according to the teachings of Vatican II. By virtue of his consecration the bishop becomes immediately the "ambassador" of Christ and even more, the "image of Christ."[38]

> From tradition . . . it is clear that, by means of the laying-on of hands and the words of consecration, the grace of the Holy Spirit is so conferred, and the sacred character so impressed, that the bishops in an eminent and visible way undertake Christ's own role as Teacher, Shepherd and High Priest, and that they act in his person.[39]

Understood in this way, representation comes critically close to an identification of the bishop with Christ, as is evident in the consequences drawn from this point of view for the relationship of church members to the bishop: "The faithful," says the Constitution on the Church, "must cling to their bishop, as the church does to Christ, and Jesus Christ to the Father, so that everything may harmonize in unity."[40] For, "He who hears them [the bishops], hears Christ, while he who rejects them, rejects Christ and Him who sent Christ."[41] Priests "must respect in him [the bishop] the authority of Christ, the chief Shepherd" and they owe him for this reason love and obedience.[42] Of course admonitions that bishops and priests must carry out their office in the spirit of Christ are not lacking,[43] but one certainly gets the impression from the passages quoted that the office-bearer as man and simply because of his ordination is already brought so close to Christ—or even put in his place—that he may to a certain extent lay claim to all the rights of the one he represents. Furthermore, this tendency is strengthened by the application of the concept "father" to the bishop and priest—a concept receiving approval in the texts of Vatican II. Here is another consequence of the traditional idea of representation:[44] the office-bearer is seen as representative of God, the Father, and his office is considered as a paternal function.[45] The duty of obedience on the part of the laity is the exact counterpart to the characterization of the office-bearer as "father."[46]

There are two distinct causes for this traditional understanding of representation. The first results from the human need to bring the transcendent down into the immanent and look at it, to make that which is hidden in God available for men.[47] Actually, what we have here is an obvious religious desire to escape from the effort to find the transcendent God, who is placed above every ecclesiastical institution and can therefore never fully coincide with it.

The second cause for the traditional understanding of representation undoubtedly lies in the intention to bestow as much dignity as possible upon the office-bearer—placing him above any human critique—in contrast to those under him.[48]

The words of Jesus, as recorded in Mt. 23:2-12, are directed against both of these mistaken attitudes. He sharply condemns the custom of the Pharisees—which he specifically foresees as constituting a possible danger for his disciples—to have themselves called "Master," "Father," "Leader" and to arrogate this role to themselves in relationship to the people. Jesus insists that there is only one Father, only one Master and Leader and he rejects as illegitimate any kind of assumption of these predicates by any human being. This weakens and refutes the viewpoint still represented in the church today, that the "vertical-authoritative" elements must be emphatically manifested in the church and must not be "leveled off into the horizontal," for, it is held, the fulfillment of faith is dependent upon them.[49] Jesus' words, "You are all brothers" (Mt. 23:8), means that the one God and "Father in heaven" (cf. Mt. 23:9) will not be witnessed to in this world except by one who stands on equal footing with his fellowmen, does not exalt himself above them and is ready to serve them unpretentiously. (Cf. Mt. 23:11f.; and especially Mt. 5:14-16).

In contrast to the attempt rashly to place the office-bearer on the side of Christ and thus to identify him with Christ as over against the church—on whatever grounds the attempt is—it must be emphatically stated that only one is "head," "Lord," "bridegroom" of the church, the Christ raised to the right hand of God. (Cf. Eph. 4:4ff.; Eph. 5:23b.) He is Lord and head of the church not because he appeared in his historical existence as a male—such an idea betrays an unspiritual way of thinking—but rather because he is the God who became a human being,[50] who through his suffering and death won the church for himself and adopted it as his own "body." (Cf. Eph. 2:13ff.; Eph. 5:25f., 29; Acts 20:28.) "All life and growth, the whole 'building up' of the body," comes from him alone, the only head,[51] through the power of the spirit.[52] "From him the whole body is joined and knit together by every joint with which it is supplied, when each part is working properly, and thus makes for bodily growth . . ." (Eph. 4:16). The different offices of ministry in the church are spiritual gifts of grace (charisma) of the exalted Lord, which he has established for the building up of the church: "'Ascend on high . . . he gave gifts to men. . . .' And his gifts were that some should be apostles, some prophets, some evangelists, some pastors and teachers, for the equipment of the saints, for the work of the ministry, for building up the body of Christ" (Eph. 4:8, 11f.).[53] Those bearers of high office who have the gift of leadership (1 Cor. 12:28; Rom. 12:8; 1 Thess. 5:12) do not relinquish membership in the church any more than those members who have other gifts and tasks. They continue to be members and never take the place of the head, over against the "body." They are, to a certain extent, organs through whom—together with those who have other gifts[54]—the exalted Christ wants to lead and build his church, to make it a "holy priesthood"[55] (1 Peter 2:5, 9). Thus they stand vis-à-vis Christ in the position of servants, as many passages in the New Testament emphasize (e.g., Rom. 12:4f.; 1 Cor. 3:5ff, 4:1, 1 Peter 4:10f.; 2 Cor. 6:3ff.). *There is no other form of representation in the New Testament than that of service and obedience toward Christ*; representation never means to take the place of Christ as the head of the church—that is apparent from the very dissimilarity between head and member—or to play his role vis-à-vis the church, or even to be the imaged portrayal of the man Jesus.[56] The idea of such an imaged portrayal clearly betrays both an inability to think theologically, and the unspirituality and sexism of the traditional understanding of church office.

It may not be inappropriate in this connection to point out that sex is irrelevant for representation even according to the concept applicable in the sphere of church law. The abstraction from the concrete person to be represented has developed in this sphere to such an extent that the principle applies even to marriage, in which the sex of the partner obviously plays a decisive role: a partner who cannot be present for the ceremony is not directed to obtain a proxy of his or her own sex.[57] This example illustrates clearly what is involved in deputyship: a personal-spiritual act in the name of the one represented,[58] not a pictorial representation of the one represented. The will of the one who has himself represented is the only determinant of the action of his deputy.[59] As spiritual and personal act, representation in New Testament understanding—as different as it is in other ways from the juridical institution of deputyship[60]—is free from any linkage to sex. Fitness for official representation is grounded according to the witness of the New Testament on the endowment of men with grace for the task of administration and on the charisma of leadership or pastoral ministry—which is of course activated only by giving oneself in faith to Christ and by an inner bond of the office-bearer with him. It is true that the validity of official functions is independent of the inner attitude of the office-bearer, but a ministry of representation in the fullest sense is not possible without an existential act of faith,[61] which is true for every Christian and not only for church officials. The New Testament is referring specifically to oneness with Christ, when it talks about representation or witnessing for Christ in an official capacity. The classic passage often adduced is 2 Cor. 5:20, without however considering the context (vv. 14ff.), which precisely illustrates how divine grace is a prerequisite for representation:

> The love of Christ controls us, because we are convinced that one has died for all; therefore all have died. And he died for all, that those who live might no longer live for themselves but for him who for their sake died and was raised. . . . Therefore if any one is in Christ, he is a new creation; the old has passed away, behold the new has come. All this is from God, who through Christ reconciled us to himself and gave us the ministry of reconciliation; that is, God was in Christ reconciling the world to himself, not counting their trespasses against them, and entrusting to us the message of reconciliation. So we are ambassadors for Christ (ὑπὲρ Χριστοῦ,)[62] God making his appeal through us. We beseech you on behalf of Christ, be reconciled to God.

The inner connection between God's redeeming action for the apostle and the apostle's ministry for Christ, which is so clear in this passage, is rightly characterized by J. E. Belser as follows: ". . . God has given to them [i.e., the apostles] the ministry of reconciliation, after they had themselves already experienced reconciliation, so that what they have to proclaim is not a strange mystery but a happy one which had become their own."[63]

The words of Jesus to the seventy disciples whom he sent out, "He who hears you, hears me and he who rejects you, rejects me . . ." (Lk. 10:16)—often misused by being taken from their context and absolutized—are a promise whose effectiveness is likewise linked to the oneness of the disciples with their Lord as indispensable presupposition. The disciples stand under the command of their Lord: "Go your way; behold I send you out as lambs in the midst of wolves"[64] (Lk. 10:3). To the disciples who return after fulfilling their mission, who express their joy that the demons were subject to them in the name of the Lord, Jesus replies that the only ground for joy is the fact that they are forever united with God: ". . . Rejoice that your names are written in heaven" (Lk. 10:20). Chosen by God, freely accepted by men: this is what counts in the fruitful activity of those who work for the kingdom of God in particular office and commission. Office—or ordination—in and for itself by no means brings about the identity of the human word with the word of Christ referred to in Lk. 10:16 though this idea is expressed in the Constitution on the Church of Vatican II.[65] The message of the New Testament recognizes that among the office-bearers there may be shepherds not worthy of the name, who act like "thieves and robbers" to those entrusted to them (Jn. 10:1), or who do their tasks only because they are forced to do them and who are motivated by lust for gain and power. (Cf. 1 Peter 5:2f.) The promise of Jesus about the fruitfulness of his word cannot be true of them.

That only an attachment to Jesus bestows fitness and worthiness to a ministry of representation is shown with particular clarity in the calling of Simon Peter to the pastoral ministry (Jn. 21:15-17). Jesus directs the question to Peter three times, whether he loves him, whether he loves him more than the others. Jesus makes the transfer of the pastoral function to Peter dependent only on love to him. For Jesus is and remains the only true pastor (Jn. 10:11ff.), the "first and chief shepherd" (ρχιποιμήν; cf. 1 Peter 5:4), the sheep belong to him alone and the fact that he gives the apostle the "responsibility for their feeding," does not mean that he gives up "his rights of ownership of them."[66] Thus only those who are one—by means of faith and—with the one true shepherd are able to "feed" his "sheep" in the right sense and thus act as his representative to them. The office-bearer receives the power necessary to his task only by means of unconditional devotion to Christ and faith in him. In accordance with the New Testament message, the apostle is so fundamentally and exclusively directed to this preparation through the power of the Spirit (Acts 1:8) that beside it there can be no reliance on, and building on, the power of his own nature or of his own sex. (Cf. 2 Cor. 3:5f.; 10:3ff.; 1 Cor. 2:4f.; Col. 1:28f.) Indeed the apostle understands himself before Christ exactly as one who of himself is "weak" (cf. 2 Cor. 12:9f.; 1 Cor. 2:3; 4:10)—a self-understanding that obviously stands in opposition to the normal idea of the nature of the male.[67] He knows, however, that in confessing his own weakness he is strong (2 Cor. 12:10) because this attitude expects everything from God and "the power of God is made perfect in weakness" (2 Cor. 12:9). To become strong one must rely on "the grace that is in Christ Jesus" (2 Tim. 2:1; cf. 2 Cor. 4:7ff.) as alone exclusively and unconditionally effective.

But as long as church teaching and canon law, misunderstanding the fact that God in his freedom can bestow the charisma that belongs to ecclesiastical office on women just as well as on men, declare that the male sex of the ordinand is the indispensable presupposition for valid ordination and thus for the priestly vocation, support will doubtless be given to an unspiritual and unbiblical conception of ministry and the practice of ministry. This is all the more obvious as the position of women in secular society develops into that of full equality, and thus the exclusion of women from church positions is no longer accepted as in the early Christian times as an unchallenged matter of course. Instead of basing capacity for ministry on the power and spirit of God, the priest is more likely—in accordance with the one-sided male structure of office—to expect to have this capacity because of his masculinity, and thus to attribute to his sex an essential significance in the representation of Christ. Thus he runs the danger of largely missing the servanthood structure of his office, since he often takes over the role of the master, which is always accorded him as a male in our society and which actually rests on the suppression of women. He takes no account of the fact that this role is totally opposed to the attitude of Jesus.[68] (Cf. Lk. 22:25ff.) The extent to which genuine Christian understanding of the ministerial office and representation is impeded by the patriarchate—and the mistaken attitudes necessarily linked with it—is graphically evident in the following statement, which is by no means unique and which clearly characterizes the unequal evaluation of the sexes in the Catholic Church: The Church has,

> it is true, feminine and motherly traits but it is not women's business. Its founder is the eternal God and the most perfect Man, Jesus Christ. He did not found his church on volatile women but on the twelve male apostles. Women are excluded from the church regiment [!] and St. Paul writes: 'Women must keep silent in church' (1 Cor. 14:34). The divine

> power to forgive sins, to celebrate the mass and to mediate grace rests on the masculine shoulders of the apostles, the pope, the bishops, the priests. The church is founded on the hard, indestructible and storm-tossed rock—and men [males] are like rocks. Therefore the church is from the beginning and for all time men's business.[69]

If only to cleanse the conception of the ministry from this kind of unspiritual elements, it is necessary that admission to the priesthood be opened to women and in this way for the first time church office receive its full human dimension.

With this presupposition, the witness to Christ required of office-holders can be fulfilled in a more pure and perfect form.[70] Then in such a renewal of official structure, it will be seen that representation of Christ is not the result of (male) sex but rather of an inner transformation of human beings into the likeness of Christ through the power of the Spirit (cf. 2 Cor. 3:18), as the Galatians passage, 3:27f. testifies validly, once and for all: "As many of you as were baptized into Christ have put on Christ. There is neither Jew nor Greek, there is neither slave nor free, there is *neither male nor female*; for you are all one in Christ Jesus." Only when the office-bearer on the basis of his inner attachment to and union with Christ becomes transparent for him—in which case the office-bearer's sex has become irrelevant—is the word of Christ a reality: "He who hears you hears me" (Lk. 10:16). Yet even in regard to such a witness, based not on sex but on the power of Christ, the following words of H. Gollwitzer are worthy of consideration:

> His representation—i.e., Christ's representation for God—goes far beyond ours, precedes it, overtakes it, exceeds it, completes it and fulfills it. . . . He is present to those who are absent to us. He does not abandon those whom we abandon. His loving is greater than ours. Hope in his representation is the hope of our representation.[71]

Notes

1. Besides the works of Van der Meer and van Eyden quoted frequently in previous chapters of this book, see the following: Vincent Emmanuel Hannon, *The Question of Women and the Priesthood: Can Women be Admitted to Hold orders?* (London: G. Chapman, 1967); Mary Daly, *The Church and the Second Sex*, (New York: Harper & Row, 1968); J. Peters, "Women in Church Vocation," *Concilium* 34 (1968), 126-138; Ruud Johan Bunnik, *Das Amt in der Kirche. Krise und*

Erneuerung in theologischer Sicht, (Düsseldorf: Patmos-Verl., 1969), 140-147. In addition, the following may be mentioned from Protestant literature, which contains an abundance of material on the question of ordination of women: G. Heintze, "Das Amt der Pastorin," in *Evangelische Theologie* (hereafter cited as *EvTh*) 22 (1962): 509-535 , H. D. Wendland, O.H. v.d. Gablentz and W. Stählin, "Das geistliche Amt in der heutigen Kirche," *Quatember*, 27 (1962-1963):63-77; M. Barot, "Die Ordination der Frau: ein ökumenisches Problem," *Zusammen; Beiträge zur Soziologie und Theologie der Geschlechter*, Christine Bourbeck, ed., (Witten, Luther-Verlag, 1965), 329-337; Bertinetti, *Frauen im geistlichen Amt*; K. Klein, "Das Amt der Pastorin," *EvTh*, 26 (1966):96-109.

2. On this see the standard investigation by Per Erik. Persson, *Repraesentatio Christi. Der Amtsbegriff in der neuren römischkatholischen Theologie*, (Göttingen: Vandenhoeck & Ruprecht, 1966). (Persson does not undertake a conceptual differentiation between deputyship and "repraesentatio" since he considers them to be internally connected.)

3. See J. Pascher, "Die Hierarchie in sakramentaler Symbolik," in *Episcopus: Studien über das Bischofsamt*, Michael von Fulhaber, ed., (Regensburg: Gregorius-Verlag Vorm. Friedrich Pustet, 1949), 278-295, esp. 290-294; M. C. Vanhengel, "Die Rolle des der Priesters in der Symbolik der Sakramente," *Theologie der Gegenwart*, 9 (1966):137-144, esp. 137-139. Cf. also the text from the Ambrosiaster commentary on 1 Cor. 11:10 (*causa* 33, *questio* 5, c. 19 in Gratian): "A woman . . . does not have the power of speaking because the bishop holds the person of Christ. Therefore, as though before Christ the judge, she is thus before the bishop because he is the vicar of the Lord; she ought to be seen to be subservient because of original sin." *Corpus*, ed. Friedberg 1:1255f.

4. Cf. Persson, who gives many source references; Walter Kasper, "Amt und Gemeinde," in his *Glaube und Geschichte*, (Mainz, M. Grünewald 1970) 396, n. 24, points out the change in meaning of the concept *repraesentatio* from the first to the second millenium, from a "more symbolic-sacramental-actualist connotation to a more juridic-static connotation."

5. For instance in the encyclicals "*Mystici Corporis Christi*," (*AAS* 35, (1943), 193-248, esp. 200, 210f., 232) and "*Humani generis*," (*AAS*, 42, (1950), 561-577, esp. 568).

6. *AAS* 39, (1947), 556, n. 93; cf. also no. 84: "The priest acts for the people only because he represents Jesus Christ, who is head of all His members and offers Himself in their stead. . . . The people, on the other hand, since they in no sense represent the Divine Redeemer and are not a mediator between themselves and God, can in no way possess the sacerdotal power," *AAS*, 553f.; English text, *Encyclical Letter of his Holiness Pius XII On the Sacred Liturgy*, (Washington, D.C.: National Catholic Welfare Conference, 1948), 33.

7. *Ibid*., no. 40, *AAS* 538; *On the Sacred Liturgy*, 18.

8. *Ibid*., no. 42, AAS 539; *On the Sacred Liturgy*, 19.

9. *Ibid*., no. 68, AAS 548; *On the Sacred Liturgy*, 28. Many further references to this concept are given by Persson, 73ff., 115 with n. 80, 116f.

10. Pascher, "Die Hierarchie," 278-283.

11. See p. 122; Persson, 12 with n. 15.

12. Pascher, "Die Hierarchie," 282.

13. Cf. *ibid.*, 283.

14. Josef Pascher, *Die christliche Eucharistiefeier als dramatische Darstellung des geschichtlichen Abendmahles*, (München: M. Hueber 1958), 4; also by Josef Pascher, *Die Liturgie der Sakramente,* 3rd ed. (Münster: Aschendorffsche Verlagsbuchhandlung, 1961), 9. Similarly, Michael Schmaus, *Katholische Dogmatik*, 6th ed., (Munchen, Max Hueber, 1964) 4/1, 757. It is often said that the unity between Christ and priest is expressed in the recitation of the words of consecration, when the priest says, "This is my Body," not, "This is the Body of Christ." E.g., Matthias Premm, *Katholische Glaubenskunde. Ein Lehrbuch der Dogmatik*, (Freiberg: Herder, 1955), 3/1:26; similarly, Pascher, "Die Hierarchie," 295.

15. No. 198 (*AAS* 39, (1947), 592); Decree on the Ministry and Life of Priests, art. 11 (*AAS* 58, (1966), 1008; English text in Abbott, *Documents of Vatican II*, 555f.); Dogmatic Constitution on the Church, art. 20/21 (*AAS* 57, (1965), 23f.; English text in Abbott, *Documents of Vatican II*, 39ff.)

16. According to Persson, 121, "the customary ways of thinking" (about office and representation) appear in Semmelroth "in extraordinarily clear and concentrated formulation."

17. Otto Semmelroth, *Maria oder Christus*, 131; and his *Das geistliche Amt theologische Sinndeutung*, (Frankfurt am Main: Josef Knecht, 1958), 208 ("The meeting of the teaching office-holders of the church with the obedient congregation is, by virtue of Christ's presence, a representation of the revelation of God in Jesus Christ to the members of the congregation who receive the revelation and thereby imitate the obedient Mary.") The author expresses a similar opinion, though somewhat more cautiously—the comparison of the congregation to Mary is abandoned—in "Demokratie in der Kirche?" in *Martyria, Leiturgia, Diakonia; Festschrift für Hermann Volk, Bischof von Mainz, zum 65. Geburtstag*, Hermann Volk, Rudolf Haubst, and others, eds., (Mainz, Matthias-Grünwald-Verlag 1968), 406.

18. *Maria oder Christus?*, 99.

19. *Ibid.*, 149.

20. E.g., René Laurentin, *Marie, L'Église et le Sacerdoce; étude théologique*, (Paris, Nouvelles Éditions Latines, 1953), 2:74ff.: The church is said to have two aspects, it is "Jèsus-Christ rèpandu et communiquè" and "l'èpouse du Christ"; according to the first aspect, the church is masculine and is represented by men, while according to the second aspect it is essentially feminine—its prototype is Mary. Similarly, A. Wintersig, "Liturgie und Frauenseele," in Ecclesia orans: zur einfuhrung in den geist der liturgie, Ildefons Herwegen, ed., (Freiburg im Breisgau, Herder & Co., 1925), 16ff.

21. Engelbert Krebs, *Dogma und Leben: die kirchliche Glaubenslehre als Wertquelle für das Geistesleben*, (Paderborn: Bonifacius-Druckerei, 1925-1930), 1st and 2nd ed., (Paderborn, 1925), 5/2.:483f.; cf. also Georg Bichlmair, *Der Mann Jesus*, 2nd ed., (Vienna: Herder, 1948), 118: "Christ is the bridegroom, the

church his bride. As vicars and workers together with Christ, the apostles and their successors had to take a similar position toward the church. They were supposed to portray in allegorical form the one bridegroom of the church, and of course for this reason they had to be males." So argues Wintersig also, 18.

22. Michael Schmaus, *Katholische Dogmatik*, 5th ed., (München M. Hueber, 1957), 4/1:661. In the 6th ed. (1964), pp. 753f., this point of view—which is clearly based on the Aristotelian-Thomistic concept of the procreation process (cf. Meer, "Priestertum der Frau?", 143ff.)—is abandoned, but it is still maintained that only men are by nature suited to public functions, *Dogmatik*, 6th ed., 753.

23. E.g., G. Concetti, in Gertrude Heinzelmann, *Die getrennten Schwestern, Frauen nach dem Konzil*, (Zürich: Interfeminas-Verlag, 1967), 99 (". . . The role of mediator" belongs, "according to the will of God and Christ, to the male because of his preeminence and his natural qualifications for portraying in concrete forms the highest Mediator, which is Christ.") See also Alois Winklhofer, *Kirche in den Sakramenten*, (Frankfurt am Main, J. Knecht 1968), 227 ("Should he, the head, be portrayed in this concrete symbolization by a woman—contrary to the order of creation—a woman who is subject to man and not the 'head'? Church office follows the order of creation.") Remberger, "Priestertum der Frau?", 134f., simply grants to women the capability to represent Christ in the so-called universal priesthood. Cf. in addition C. Bamberg, "Die Aufgabe der Frau in der Liturgie," *Anima* 19 (1964):304-317; I. F. Gorres, "Über die Weihe von Frauen zu Priesterinnen," *Der Christliche Sonn*, 17, (1965):197-199.

24. Cf. Persson, 129f.

25. E.g., Krebs, Wintersig, Laurentin.

26. *Das geistliche Amt*, 27; and his *Maria*, 130, 146.

27. Wintersig, 18. A similar form of magnification of the position of the priest is given by Matthias Premm, *Katholische Glaubenskunde; ein Lehrbuch der Dogmatik*, (Vienna: Herder, 1951-1955), 3/2:389: "By the ordination of the priest the ordained one is lifted out of earthly spheres and stands before us like another Christ, as mediator between God and man in all religious concerns."

28. See pp. 180f.

29. In the *Pontificale Romanum*, (Regensburg: F. Pustet, 1888), 1:84, the formula used in the presentation of the rings is as follows: "Accept this ring, as a sign of faith in order that adorned with pure faith you safeguard inviolately the bride of God, namely the holy Church." (It is true that the formula does not use the expression "bride of the bishop" which was well known throughout the Middle Ages.) Concerning the origin and development of the ring symbol, see V. Labhart, *Zur Rechtssymbolik des Bishofsrings*, (Cologne, 1963).

30. See "J. Trummer, Mystisches im alten Kirchenrecht. Die geistige Ehe zwischen Bishof und Diözese," in *ÖAKR* 2 (1951): 62-75.

31. *Ibid.*, 66.

32. Cf. Semmelroth, *Maria oder Christus*, 149.

33. In fact the factor of visibility in representation of Christ plays a decisive role in the traditional understanding of church office. Cf. Persson, 22, 24 with n. 38. This visibility reaches its highest degree in the papal office: "Christ himself

acts in the actions of the pope. Christ appears in each of them, in the here and now. We can hear and see Christ himself in what the pope does. Yes, the pope plays the role of Christ. One can say of him, 'Personam Christi gerit (he manifests the person of Christ) . . . .'" The pope represents "in the visible world Christ, the Head of the church." (Schmaus, *Katholische Dogmatik*, 5th ed., 3/1:488.)

34. Thus, clearly, Bichlmair (see n. 21, above) and Concetti (see n. 23, above); similarly, too, Schmaus, *Katholische Dogmatik*, 6th ed., 4/1:753: "It is reasonable that a baptized person who serves as the instrument of Christ in a special way should also share in his natural individuality." Premm, 242f. says: "The priest is the image of the High Priest Christ, leader of the faithful, person of authority—all of which are things belonging essentially to the masculine sphere."

35. According to the encyclical of Pius XII, *Mediator Dei*, (*AAS* 39, (1947), 539) the boundary line drawn by the ordination of the priest between clergy and laity is just as firm as the boundary line drawn by baptism between Christians and non-Christians.

36. Decree on the Ministry and Life of Priests, art. 2 (*AAS* 58, (1966) 992); English text in Abbott, *Documents of Vatican II*, 535.

37. Dogmatic Constitution on the Church, art. 26 (*AAS* 57, (1965), 31); English text in Abbott, *Documents of Vatican II*, 50.

38. *Ibid*., art. 27 (*AAS* 57, (1965), 32); English text in Abbott, *Documents of Vatican II*, 51.

39. *Ibid*., art. 21 (*AAS* 57, (1965), 25); English text in Abbott, *Documents of Vatican II*, 41f.

40. *Ibid*., art. 27 (*AAS* 57, (1965), 33); English text in Abbott, *Documents of Vatican II*, 52.

41. *Ibid*., art. 20 (*AAS* 57, (1965), 24); English text in Abbott, *Documents of Vatican II*, 40.

42. Decree on the Ministry and Life of Priests, art. 7 (*AAS* 58, (1966), 1003); English text in Abbott, *Documents of Vatican II*, 549. A similar injunction is directed to all believers in the Decree on the Bishop's Pastoral Office in the Church, art. 16 (*AAS* 58, (1966), 680); English text in Abbott, *Documents of Vatican II*, 407ff.

43. See Decree on the Bishop's Pastoral Office in the Church, art. 16 (*AAS* 58, (1966), 679ff.); English text in Abbott, *Documents of Vatican II*, 406ff.

44. Cf. Persson, 90, 117.

45. Decree on the Bishop's Pastoral Office in the Church, art. 16 (*AAS* 58, (1966), 680); English text in Abbott, *Documents of Vatican II*, 407ff. Dogmatic Constitution on the Church, arts. 21, 28 (*AAS* 57, (1965), 24, 35); English text in Abbott, *Documents of Vatican II*, 40ff., 52ff.

46. See Persson, 101f., 117f.; F. Wulf, "Stellung und Aufgabe des Priesters in der Kirche nach dem zweiten Vatikanischen Konzil," *Geist und Leben*, 39 (1966), 48 ("In a few decades one may even judge that the image of the priest in Vatican II, especially in the decree on priests [cf. *ibid*., art. 9, on the relation of priests to laity, is still strongly influenced by paternalistic viewpoints.")

47. Cf. Semmelroth, *Das geistliche Amt*, 41 ("The clerical office . . . portrays the God whose people is the church and offers to the people a visible appearance of God, so that in meeting with him they may live as the people of God.")

48. A. M. Henry, "Obéissance commune et obéissance religieuse," Supplément de *La Vie Spirituelle* 6, (1953), 262, is rightly critical of such a basis for authority and obedience: "Toute théologie de l'obéissance dont l'insistance irait dans le sens d'une identification entre supérieur et autorité du Christ, resiquerait de compromettre gravement les valeurs religieuses et personnelles les plus fondamentales et les plus certaines." (quoted from Alois Müller, *Das Problem von Befehl und Gehorsam im Leben der Kirche; eine pastoraltheologische Untersuchung*, (Einsiedeln: Benziger, 1964) 126, n. 1). Müller likewise, pp. 125f., points to the negative consequences—for understanding obedience—of an identification of human authority with divine authority: "A doctrine of obedience should proceed from the difference, rather than from the similarity, existing between obedience to God and obedience to men." On this problem see also Kasper, 398; Persson, 50.

49. Thus W. Heinen, "Die Gestalten des Vaters und des Paternalen in der Lebengestaltung der Gesellschaft," *Jahrbuch des Instituts für christliche Sozialwissenschaften der Westfälischen Wilhelms-Universität Münster*, 6 (1965), 18: "The perpetuation of the status of son or of daughter in a universal fraternization contradicts the order of reality, if the vertical (hierarchical superiority or inferiority) is leveled out into the horizontal." Similarly, F. Gamillscheg in *Die Presse* (Jan. 18, 1965), 3: "The vertical-hierarchical-authoritative elements must work together in the church with the horizontal-fraternal elements, in order to preserve the cruciform pattern necessary for all Christians. . . . The conservatives, the 'Catholics on the right,' must provide for these vertical elements." (quoted by Wilfried Daim, *Progressiver Katholizismus*, (München, Manz 1967), 124). Daim writes against this view, 116ff., and also in "Rückkehr zur Brüderlichkeit," in *Kirche und Zukunft,* Wilfried Daim and Friedrich Heer, eds., (Vienna: Europa-Verlag, 1963): 11ff., where he refers to Mt. 23:8f. Daim thinks that church office can be subsumed under the "brother" concept and can be rewritten in its terms. So, too, W. Dirks, "Über die Stellung des Laien in der Kirche," in *Neues Denken in der Kirche.Standpunkte*. Max Lehner and August Hasler, ed., (Lucerne: Rex-Verlag, 1968), 207ff.

50. So, rightly, Daly, *The Church and the Second Sex*, 157.

51. Rudolf Schnackenburg, *Die Kirche im Neuen Testament: ihre Wirklichkeit und theologische Deutung, ihr Wesen und Geheimnis*, (Freiburg: Herder, 1961), 151f.

52. Cf. Schnackenburg, 152; H. Schürmann, "Die geistlichen Gnadengaben," in De Ecclesia; Beiträge zur Konstitution "Über die Kirche" des Zweiten Vatikanischen Konzils, Guillermo Baraúna, ed., (Freiburg: Herder 1966) 1:505.

53. Cf. Schnackenburg, 114, 152; Ritter and Leich, 68f.; Schürmann, 500. According to this passage, there can be no separationn between charismatic and official ministries; the fundamental charismatic structure of the church comprehends the clerical office. Cf. H. Küng, "The Charismatic Structure of the Church,"

in *Concilium*, 4, (1965): 41-61; Wilhelm Pesch, "Kirchlicher Deinst und Neues Testament," in *Zum Thema Priesteramt*, Wilhelm Pesch, ed., (Stuttgart: Verl. Katholisches Bibelwerk, 1970), 14f.

54. On this see Kasper, 402: "The charismatic structuring of the Christian congregation is not simply a product of the clerical office: it is not based dualistically on a polarity of office-congregation, but rather pluralistically on a fullness of charisma."

55. Cf. Schnackenburg, 25, 152; Ritter-Leich, 69, 72.

56. Representatives of such an understanding of office and deputyship have been named above, p. 206 with n. 21 and p. 209 with n. 33 and n. 34.

57. Cf. Anton Kradepohl, *Stellvertretung und kanonisches Eherecht*, (Bonn: Röhrscheid, 1939), 100, 143.

58. Cf. Mörsdorf, *Lehrbuch des Kirchenrechts*, 1:230.

59. Cf. Kradepohl, 7 (The voluntary action of the deputy must "conform to that of the one who empowers him.")

60. The difference is especially the result of the essential incongruity between the one to be represented (Christ) and the one who represents him, and therefore the concept representation is basically inadequate and should only be cautiously used in consideration of that fact. Cf. the discussion of Kasper, 396: "The concept of representation . . . contains no mystical or juridical identification with Christ but rather a differentiation. Precisely as the church, and in particular the office, completely disappears behind its mission and so makes itself insignificant, it is truly the epiphany of Christ." It seems to me that a further but similar differentiation from representation in the juridical sense consists in the fact that the office-holder does not in himself possess the competence to function as representative of Christ but rather Christ has in his grace bestowed that competence upon him.

61. See the noteworthy discussion of this in Karl Rahner, Kirche und Sakramente, (Freiburg: Herder 1960), 87-95.

62. Johannes Evangelist Belser, *Der zweite Brief des Apostels Paulus an die Korinther*, (Freiburg im Breisgau: Herder, 1910) 190, translates ὑπὲρ Χριοσοῦ as "in the place of Christ" (for this he refers to Mt. 10:40; he also finds support in 2 Cor. 5:15, where ὑπὲρ likewise has the meaning of "in the place of," according to Belser.) Similarly, Karl Prümm, *Diakonia pneumatos; der zweite Korintherbrief a als Zugang zur apostolischen Botschaft*, (Freiburg, Herder 1967),1: 345: " . . . This equation of the apostle with Christ in the decisive point of the final source of the commissioning is already established by verses 18 and 19 of 2 Cor. 5. This makes it possible with Chrysostom to attribute the same objective significance to 'for Christ' of v. 20 as to 'in the place of Christ.'" Against this view, Bauer, *Griechisch-deutsches Wörterbuch*, 1658, translates ὑπὲρ Χριοσοῦ (Cor. 5:20) as "as Christ's helper we beseech you."

63. Belser, 187. Similarly Adolf von Schlatter, *Paulus, der Bote Jesu: eine Deutung seiner Briefe an die Korinther*, (Stuttgart: Calwer Vereinsbuchhandlung, 1934), 565. " . . . Whoever is in Christ has God for himself. At the same time that Paul receives the divine love—since he is not living for himself—he is blessed with a ministry which, corresponding to that which had happened to him himself,

consists in his being the messenger of that divine will which creates reconciliation."

64. What is clearly pointed out here is the quite different style of living and living arrangements of the disciples, in comparison to their environment, which characterized the disciples and which necessarily led to a tense and dangerous situation for them. They could endure only by an unconditional trust in their Lord. Cf. Walter Grundmann, *Das Evangelium nach Lukas*, 2nd ed., (Berlin: Evangelische Verlagsanstalt 1961), 209. Cf. Dogmatic Constitution on the Church, art. 20 (*AAS* 57, 1965, 24; English text in Abbott, *Documents of Vatican II*, 39f.) P. Fransen makes a more exact differentiation in "Einige dogmatische Bemerkungen über das christliche Priestertum," in *Der Priester in einer säkularisierten Welt* (Informationsblatt des Instituts für europäische Priesterhilfe, 2, (1968), Heft 1/2), 46: he says that the hierarchy operates only in its sacerdotal task—particularly in the administration of the sacmments—"in persona Christi," but not in the exercise of jurisdictional authority. "The will of the hierarchy cannot be purely and simply equated with the divine will." Cf. Fransen, "(Heilige) Weihen," in *Sacramentum mundi. Theologisches Lexikon für die Praxis*, Karl Rahner, ed., (Freiburg: Herder 1967) 4:1281-1283. On this question see also Persson, 49f.

66. R. Schnackenburg, "Episkopos und Hirtenamt. Zu Apg. 20:28," in *Episcopus*, 80.

67. See Bichlmair, 216: "The man who is creative, ready for action, the man who works and gets things done, is an image and reflection of the creative God, who operates and governs with omnipotence." Also *ibid.*, 7, 127.

68. Daly, 146ff., refers to a faulty development of man in a patriarchy, corresponding to a lack of development of woman's personality; Luise Rinser, Unterentwickeltes Land Frau. Untersuchungen, Kritik, Arbeitshypothesen, (Würzburg: Echter-Verl., 1970), 23, 81f., 88, makes the same point.

69. H. Stadler, *Männergespräche*, 3rd ed. (Leutesdorf, 1961), 24. (The publication is provided with the imprimatur of the General Vicar of the diocese of Trier, Dr. Weins.) Similarly, Bichlmair, 11: "The Christian religion was established by a man. How should it not be a masculine affair? Twelve men were the first assistants of the man Jesus. He made men to be the pillars of the church. He called men to be priests and distributers of his sacraments. In the earliest succession men were the flag bearers of his kingdom. The first [!] places in the Catholic House of God are reserved for men." In connection with the fact that the existing patriarchal structure in the church is understood as divine directive, a higher evaluation of masculinity results, according to Karl Rahner, "Der Mann in der Kirche," in *Sendung und Gnade; Beiträge zur Pastoraltheologie*, Karl Rahner, ed., (Innsbruck: Tyrolia-Verlag 1959): The male has by nature he says, "a sensitivity for the transcendental purity of the religious" (304); the "transcendental, anonymous, indirect, silent side of religion is characteristic" of the male (305); the male is reticent to speak of holy things (306). It is a task peculiar to the male to bring into the church peacefulness, reasonableness, trustworthiness, sense of responsibility, clarity of intention (308). Somewhat the opposite qualities are

attributed to femininity by Rahner; although he is at pains to call them equally legitimate expressions of humanity—a hopeless undertaking since they are forms of human nature stunted by repression—he is obviously not able to give them equivalent evaluation. Note, for instance, his summons to a "manly Christianity." (296ff.) It is true that the author has separated himself from this extreme viewpoint in his more recent publications: see "Die Frau in der neuen Situation der Kirche," in *Theologisches Jahrbuch* (1966), 121-133. Appealing to the earlier Rahner work, a cliché-ridden description of the nature of the sexes and its effect on the church has been written by Hubertus Halbfas, (Jugend und Kirche; eine Diagnose, [Düsseldorf, Patmos-Verlag 1964], 205ff.); it clearly implies a denigration of women.

70. A similar conception is represented by J. Peters, 297f.: Office carried out and characterized only by men inevitably leads to a one-sided and deprived office and to the like injury to the church's transmission of grace. Thus a "humanizing of ecclesiastical office," its extension and enrichment, is definitively required and for this women must have their place in the ministry: "Together they [man and woman] must create a profile of the ministerial office and practice it together, so that it loses its one-sidedness [297]. . . . Humanity is whole only in the togetherness of man and woman and with this argument we wish to state that it is not only possible, it is also desirable, that women be admitted to the office. . . . The first question about the office-bearer must therefore not be, Must it be a man or can it also be a woman? but rather, How can we use the very best humanity for the transmission of divine grace?" (298). On the other hand, E. Gössmann "Die Frau als Priester?" (trans. into English, "Women as Priests?" in *Concilium*, 34, [1968], 115-125), does not recognize that the admission of women to the ministry can have, and will have, positive consequences for office and its structure—especially in cleaning out the patriarchal elements. She expects that the ministerial office itself without any help from women "will be renewed from within and in relation to the community;" only when that happens will it "make sense to extend the office to women" (291f.). This statement lacks a requisite objective understanding of organic development.

71. Helmut Gollwitzer, *Von der Stellvertretung Gottes. Christlicher Glaube in der Erfahrung der Verborgenheit Gottes*, (München, Ch. Kaiser, 1967), 147f.

Chapter 7

Equal Rights for Women in the Church Today: A Requirement of Justice and the Condition for Their Full Development and Cooperation

We may conclude as the result of our investigation that the legal sources which support canon 968 §1 (and the canons that are connected with it in content) imply a distinct concept of the essential and ethical inferiority of women; that the biblical passages—concerning the subordinate position of women—which in part lie at the basis of these sources have been shown by historical-critical exegesis to be conditioned by the times and thus not convincing; that, further, the argument resulting from the traditional understanding of office and representation—that women must be excluded from them—carries no weight. But, if these are our conclusions, we cannot rest content with them. For an objective treatment of the problem before us requires a consideration of the fact that this exclusion of women is not an item of merely theoretical significance but is a rule of law which considerably limits the freedom of women and therefore prevents the development of their person, to the detriment of church and society.

Of course one often hears the objection that by their very nature women do not show the aptitude requisite to church office and that consequently one cannot speak of depriving them of any freedom. Such an a priori affirmation, grounded in no facts of experience, is based on a dated and narrow conception of the nature of women, which, as the history of the women's movement shows, has repeatedly blocked the advance of women vocationally.[1] Among other implications, it is insinuated here that a woman is not qualified for public activity; a private and more passive role in society is more fitting for her; she does not have the capacity to direct and to lead, because she lacks the necessary objectivity and decisiveness; and her original place has always been the "hearth," not the altar.[2] In accordance with this kind of alleged feminine nature, woman is appointed a limited sphere of activity, which of course leaves no room for ecclesiastical position. Enlisting the principle of natural law, "to each his own," one finds justification in this way for such an attitude toward woman.[3] But it is obvious that use of this principle in the question before us must result, as in other social problems—e.g., in the question of slavery and in regard to blacks[4]—in arbitrary regulation contrary to justice. Certainly the nature of woman does not permit the kind of definition described above. It is recognized today, on the basis of sociological and ethnological research, that the differing male and female behavior patterns, which have been attributed to intrinsic and unchangeable characteristics, are dependent upon social and cultural conditioning and therefore changes may come about in the course of history:[5] In the past, especially, the traditional picture of woman was derived from her narrow sphere of activity (in the house, in the family), then anchored in the psychological and even in the metaphysical, and finally proclaimed as immutable feminine nature.[6] (If women sometimes confirmed this conception of their nature,[7] that is in no way a proof of the correctness of the conception, for as manipulated, unfree persons, women were and are very often not in the position to speak about themselves in an independent and competent manner.[8])

Thus, since according to the conclusions of modern sociological-anthropological research a description of the nature of womanhood, which would integrate all the individual distinguishing features of her sex, is impossible, a delimitation of the sphere of freedom belonging to woman is not practicable. This is true because "when one sex is dominant, no absolute sexual difference can be determined"[9] perhaps it never can be, since that which binds the sexes together—their humanness—always outweighs that which separates them.[10] Whenever such a delimitation of the sphere of freedom belonging to woman is undertaken, as in the case of exclusion from the church ministry, it arbitrarily violates the freedom and independence of her person—a serious injustice. Such an action shows clearly that despite all contrary asseveration, woman is not yet considered as a person equivalent to man and thus the derogatory opinion of woman—as it appeared in blatant form in the sources discussed in earlier chapters—continues.[11] The concept of "differentness" of woman, used to try to justify the deprivation of freedom, is employed as a cloak for the persisting denigration of woman.[12] The worth of a person is recognized and respected when he or she is granted full freedom, e.g., in the basic human right of vocational choice, or in the opportunity for free personal development.[13] Only so can one take into account the truth established in the creation, that human beings are created free, that they are characterized by knowledge of themselves and by self-possession, that they have the capability for self-determination.[14] This truth of creation is just as true for woman as for man. Because of her independent and self-responsible personhood, she has the same possibility and necessity as a man to "define" herself, to limit herself within the dimensions of full freedom,[15] to plan ahead for herself what vocation or life situation she wishes to choose. The same worth of person demands the same possibilities and conditions for the accomplishment of freedom, and as long as these are not forthcoming, necessary respect for the worth and freedom of her person is lacking and she is not yet released from the state of subjugation (*status subiectionis*).

But, looking more deeply, the claim of woman that the freedom of her person must be recognized also and exactly in the sphere of the church cannot be waived or revoked, because the will of God is that he should be unconditionally acknowledged by men and women in his sovereign freedom and power of dominion. As Lord and head of the church, Christ (God) bestows his manifold gifts and powers for the upbuilding of his body in an absolute freedom beyond the calculation of human beings; he whose spirit "apportions to each one individually as he will" (1 Cor. 12:11) is free and powerful to give to women as well as to men the special charisma for the ministry, along with other charisma.[16] Respect for this sovereign freedom and dominion of Christ (or God) demands that in the official church care will be taken, in obedience to its head and Lord, to provide for the full unfolding of the various charisma given by God for the upbuilding of the church. To hinder such unfolding would be disloyal to God's gifts of grace and therefore certainly culpable.[17] Ecclesiastical legality should thus be so formulated that women and men are granted a full and equal sphere of freedom, so that they may follow the call and claims of God, whatever these may be. So long as the official church in teaching and in legal regulations sets forth as normative the contention that God calls no woman to ministerial service, obstacles are autocratically placed against the working of the Spirit in the church.[18]

Therefore, if today Catholic women in increasing numbers are offended by this behavior on the part of responsible office-bearers in the church and by the disrespect for women which it expresses, and if these Catholic women speak out for equal positions with men, this is not in the last analysis a struggle for rights for rights' sake—not "the registration of a claim of human beings by human beings"—but rather a "testimony to the claim of God," and his rights, on human beings.[19] *Before anything else, equal rights present the presupposition that women can freely answer the claim of God and his call to them in its humanly unpredictable form and variety.*[20] Understood in this way, equal rights make possible the service of God in the sphere of the church and become at the same time the opportunity for the unfolding of the personhood of women.

Of course women who are awakened to a consciousness of their worth as persons (and with them every group discriminated against) are summoned and obliged to lay claim to those inherent rights which are signs of their worth as persons[21] and which should open to them possibilities for service and for assumption of responsibilities in the church. But exactly because of their disadvantaged position they are not able by themselves alone to advocate this concern and to bring it to successful conclusion. Thus justice and love require of those who have come to church offices and so to more influential position in the church on the basis of male sex—falsely considered as "higher"—that they help emancipate women from their oppressed situation and from the stunted humanity that has resulted from it. In such a way these leaders could assist women to receive at last the respect and the opportunities for development within the church that are due them.[22] There is, to be sure, only small evidence of the requisites for such assistance and the inner willingness to help. Yet certain changes are fortunately coming about in the viewpoint of the official church concerning equal rights for women in the secular realm: Long resisted in the church, this development is finally recognized as genuine progress in the history of mankind and ecclesiastical officials come forward to encourage it.[23] But only a beginning has been made, and hesitantly, in comprehending that a fundamental reform in the evaluation of women and in the position of women in the church is needed before the church can legitimately and credibly advocate a more humane treatment of women and a more worthy position for women in the secular world.[24] The persistent resistance of a majority of church officials to an equal place for women in the ecclesiastical sphere is doubtless a result of the men's "clubby" and antifeminist education by which many clerics have been profoundly conditioned so that they are simply not able to accept women as equal partners and to appreciate even faintly the values to be gained by admission of women to ministry in the church. How little they accept women as fellow human beings is shown by the fact that the clergy, by and large, are not shocked by the disadvantaged position of women in the church. They apparently think that the subordination of women accords with their nature, whereas an equalization of woman with man, which from pride of sex and struggle for ascendancy they resist, would be abnormal. It would be hard to persuade them that woman in her present situation lacks anything at all, not to speak of any injustice being done to her.

Although, on the one hand, woman has become a grievous victim of this kind of behavior on the part of clergy and men in general, it is also true, on the other hand, that woman must share the blame for this abuse and for her own situation. Out of convenience and insincerity[25] she has often acquiesced in her lowly and unworthy position and accepted an extensive paralysis of her self-respect as a human being, instead of taking on herself—a course requiring sacrifice and therefore avoided—to set limits to masculine sovereignty pretensions and thus assist men to be more humane.

It is not reasonable to expect, on the basis of the interdependent circumstances mentioned, that the official church alone can bring about removal of the far-reaching disturbances in relations between the sexes, with which the church today is especially burdened. Rather, a fundamental readiness for the emancipation of women and for the formation of life-styles involving partnership of men and women must be developed. Of course the resolute will to overcome in this way the anti-feminist tradition in the church must be respected and adopted by ecclesiastical authorities,[26] so that they themselves may be willing to integrate women into all areas of church life and ministry.

The renewal of the church—i.e., the maturation of its members into vital and convinced Christians, who only as such are able to dismantle structures and relationships in the church that are unworthy of human beings and thus to set an example to society—cannot be successful without the liberation of women as autonomous human beings conscious of their responsibilities, and without their active participation in the official ministry of the church.

Notes

1. See Josef Mörsdorf, *Gestaltwandel des Frauenbildes und Frauenberufs in der Neuzeit*, (München, M. Hueber, 1958), 288-290; Betty Friedan, *The Feminine Mystique*, (New York: Norton, 1963), 69-79; Mathilde Vaerting, *Wahrheit und irrtum in der Geschlechterpsychologie*, 2nd ed., (Weimar: E. Lichtenstein 1931), 242f.; B. J. Leclercq, *Familie im Umbruch*, 63, 66.

2. Thus Heinen, "Die Gestalten des Vaters," 22; see also 18 *et passim*. Also descriptions of the conservative picture of women, e.g., in Schüssler Fiorenza, *Der vergessene Partner,* 29ff., and Hermann Ringeling, *Die Frau zwischen Gestern und Morgen; der sozialtheologische Aspekt ihrer Gleichberechtigung*, (Hamburg: Furche-Verlag 1962), 22f.

3. Thus, e.g., in Krebs, 478; Schmaus, *Katholische Dogmatik,* 6th ed., 4/1:754; similarly in Premm, 3/2:243 ("Women are excluded from the priesthood not because they are inferior but because they are different; this difference points to the ministry of motherhood, which is a kind of hidden, unofficial priesthood.")

4. Cf. August M. Knoll, *Katholische Kirche und scholastisches Naturrecht: zur Frage der Freiheit*, (Vienna: Europa Verlang, 1962), 24ff.; Wilfried Daim, *Die kastenlose Gesellschaft*, (München: Manz 1960), 359f.

5. The following basic investigations—already partly cited—should be noted: Vaerting, *Wahrheit und irrtum*; Margaret Mead, *Male and Female, A Study of the Sexes in a Changing World*, (New York: W. Morrow, 1949); Sigrid Hunke, *Am Anfang waren Mann und Frau; Vorbilder und Wandlungen der Geschlechterbeziehungen*, (Hamm: Grote 1955), (e.g., 261: "That which we characterize as 'male' and 'female' is the product of our culture and cannot claim universal validity any more than the dogma of the polar antithesis of the sexes can do so"; or 264: "One must be careful not to confuse the historical and sociological qualities of the sexes with their essential nature."); H. Schelsky, *Soziologie der Sexualität*, (Hamburg: Rowohlt, 1962); Ringeling, *Die Frau zwischen Gestern und Morgen; The Potential of Woman: A symposium*, Seymour M. Farber and Roger H. L. Wilson, eds., (New York: McGraw-Hill Book Co., 1963); *The Development of Sex Differences*, Eleanor E Maccoby, ed., (Stanford, CA: Stanford University Press, 1966).

6. See Hunke, 251; Ringeling, 15, 33. When Gertrud von Le Fort, *Die ewige Frau; die Frau in der Zeit; die zeitlose Frau*, 19th ed., (Munich: Kösel-Verlag, 1960), brings the vocation of women within the formula, "mother and servant," the traditional role of woman is crystalized into a structure of nature; W. Trillhaas remarks about this: "Here a late bourgeois ideal is misinterpreted as Christian" (quoted from L. Preller, "Die benifstätige Frau als Glied der Gesellschaft," in Gesellschaft für Sozialen Fortschritt, *Die berufstätige Frau heute und morgen, Referate und Diskussionen auf einer Tagung der Gesellschaft für Sozialen Fortschritt über "Die berufstätige Frau heute und morgen" in Bad Godesberg am 3. Mai 1966*, (Berlin: Duncker u. Humblot, 1966), 50.

7. So e.g., Oda Schneider, *Vom Priestertum der Frau*, 2nd ed. (Vienna: Herder, 1937). (A passage from her book is used by Premm, 243, as evidence that

in his discussion of the exclusion of women from orders it is not a question of "male theology"; but Premm ignores the fact that the "evidence" is not "what women themselves say" but a recapitulation of "male theology," which is actually the result of women's lack of independence.) See also Ottilie Mosshamer, *Priester und Frau*, (Basel: Herder, 1961).

8. B. J. Leclercq, *Familie im Umbruch*, 61, freely admits this: "Everything that was publicly said was said by men. . . . Men view woman as spiritually inferior. She was good only for house-work, in which she had to serve men. . . . Since men unceasingly repeated all this and since they alone did the speaking, women believed it . . . "; any opposition was sharply condemned. Cf. also Vaerting, 14: "Women who are ruled over have the tendency in general to accept uncritically the views of men." (Also Vaerting, 46; Preller, 44, 50.)

9. Hunke, 264; and also Vaerting, 9: "We can only approach a solution of the problem of natural sex differences when both sexes grow up in exactly the same circumstances. But that can come about only when the full realization of equal rights of the sexes becomes a fact." Vaerting, 11, also rightly notes that: "The otherness of women, as it predominantly appears today, is not congenital but is rather the typical otherness that differentiates the ruled from the ruler." See also Ringeling, 35.

10. Vaerting, 17, has already noted this fact: "The results of scientific investigations during the last decades have shown a preponderant similarity of the sexes and only a small dissimilarity. In all cases the similarity of the sexes was greater than the dissimilarity. A large majority of men and women showed the same qualities, with only a small minority indicating differences. Those qualities usually designated as masculine were found in almost as many women as men, while those called feminine were found in almost as many men. The differences between individuals within the same sex was much greater than that between male and female." Also *ibid.*, 21; Ringeling, 33ff.

11. E.g., the investigations of Hans Anger, *Probleme der deutschen Universität; Bericht über eine Erhebung unter Professoren und Dozenten*, (Tübingen: Mohr (Siebeck) 1960), 451-500, have shown numerous proofs of this; cf. also chapter 5, n. 3 and chapter 6, n. 69.

12. Vaerting, 22f., makes a similar observation: "Although today the theory of the equal value of the sexes is recognized, as the result of advancing equal rights, the ancient cloven-foot of feminine inferiority very often appears in the presentations of the sex psychologists, because the male is always dominant." This statement is confirmed by an analysis of the various descriptions of feminine nature often advanced by theologians. Cf. Schüssler, 77f. That the thesis "equal but different" is actually camouflage for the persisting denigration of women (Vaerting, 14, has already criticized this thesis) is especially clear from the fact that the legal situation of women in the church has hardly changed from what it used to be—it is still, afterward as well as before, the consequence of their derogation.

13. Cf. the encyclical *Pacem in Terris* of John XXIII (*AAS* 55, [1963], 259ff.).

14. Ibid. (*AAS* 55, 259); J. B. Metz, "Freiheit," in *Handbuch theologischer Grundbegriffe* Heinrich Fries, ed., (Munich: Kösel-Verlag, 1962), 1:408; Karl Rahner, "Würde und Wert des Menschen," *Schriften zur Theologie*, (Einsiedeln: Benziger, 1955), 258f.

15. Cf. Metz, "Freiheit," 411.

16. According to biblical studies (e.g., of Gal. 1:15; Heb. 5:4ff.; Romans 12:6ff.; 1 Cor. 12:27ff.; Acts 6:3ff.), it is obvious that office presupposes God-given charisma, and thus office and charisma are not to be understood as two disparate entities independent of each other. Besides the literature indicated above (see chapter 6, n. 53), see J. Peters, "Women in Church Vocation," in *Concilium* 34 (1968), 137, and van Eyden, "Die Frau im Kirchenamt," 357.

17. See the Dogmatic Constitution of the Church, art. 12 (*AAS* 57, 1965, 16f.; English text in Abbott, *Documents of Vatican II*, 29f.); but here, characteristically, the discussion concerns only charisma not related to the ministerial office. But Hans Küng in *The Church*, (New York: Sheed & Ward), 19, says: ". . . This special commission, as much as the unasked and unanticipated gift of the Spirit, takes its origins from the grace of God who has freedom to call whom he wishes; the men who commission, as much as those who are commissioned, must be the willing tools of God."

18. Protestants have already clearly pointed out that such procedure is unacceptable and injurious to the church. Heintze, "Das Amt der Pastorin," 531ff., remarks: "We fall into the great danger of hindering the spirit of God when concern for the possible 'crossing of boundaries' by women and the possible infringement of 'masculine privileges' becomes for us stronger than gratitude for the great enrichment bestowed upon the church by the self-reliant ministry of women in partnership with men." (See also *ibid.*, 526f.) Discerning Roman Catholic theologians have also recently warned of this danger, e.g., Peters, 295: It is presumptuous to try to limit the spirit of God to a single sex. "Who knows whether we might not in this way partly extinguish it?" While numerous Protestant denominations have drawn the consequences consistent with this realization—admitting women to ordination—a practical implementation of such insight is still lacking in the Catholic Church.

19. Cf. Friedrich Karl Schumann, "Die Frage der Menschenrechte in der Sicht des christlichen Glaubens," Wort und Gestalt, gesammelte Aufsätze, (Witten-Ruhr: Luther-Verlag, 1956), 374. So too, P. Althaus, "Person und Persönalichkeit in der evangelischen Theologie," in Theodor Heckel, *Person und Recht; Vorträge gehalten auf der Tagung evangelischer Juristen, 1962*, (Munich: Evangelischer Presseverband für Bayern, 1962), 14: "The right of personhood is grounded in a moral obligation that comes from God. . . . By insisting on this human right, man gives honor to God."

20. Elisabeth Gössmann disregards this variety of charisma, with which women as surely as men are endowed, when she asks women "to forego rising above the laity" in order to help the laity to full development. (*Die Frau im Aufbruch der Kirche*, Michael Schmaus and Elisabeth Gössmann, eds., [Munich: M. Hueber, 1964], 119f.) It is true that she tones down this contention somewhat

in "Die Frau als Priester," English trans. in "Women as Priests?" *Concilium*, 34 (1968), 115-125. Apart from the fact that ministerial office is inaccurately described or at least very much misunderstood ("rising above"!), it is apparently presumed by Gössmann that women cannot be endowed with the charisma requisite for office—since the same request is not made of the male laity. Van Eyden, "Die Frau im Kirchenamt," 360, successfully refutes this standpoint when he remarks: "Why should we not strive to give women at the same time their rightful place in the lay apostolate and in ministerial office? As long as women are admitted to other areas of church life and an exception is made only in regard to the ministerial office, it is impossible to speak of any true recognition of their equality of position in the church. This reflects unfavorably on their position in the lay apostolate. . . . Certainly one would not draw the conclusion that all male laypersons remain such and none become priests."

21. Cf. the following statements by John XXIII in his encyclical *Pacem in Terris*: "The long-standing inferiority complex of certain classes because of their economic and social status, sex, or position in the State, and the corresponding superiority complex of other classes, is rapidly becoming a thing of the past. Today, on the contrary, the conviction is widespread that all men are equal in natural dignity; . . . for man's awareness of his rights must inevitably lead him to the recognition of his duties. The possession of rights involves the duty of implementing those rights, for they are the expression of a man's personal dignity. And the possession of rights also involves their recognition and respect by other people." (*The Encyclicals and Other Messages of John XXIII*, [Washington, D.C.: TPS Press, 1964], 337f.)

22. This opinion is also expressed in a letter to *Orientierung*, 32, (1968), 104f. from a woman theologian (Dr. theol. W.-E.) who remarks: "I turn to you because I think that support must come from the circle of priests and of men; for since we ourselves are not represented anywhere there is little we can do for ourselves. The situation here is like that in the race question. There too it is not sufficient that a white person has nothing against a black's receiving appropriate jobs, etc.; rather, he must be the one who helps blacks get what they should have."

23. This happened repeatedly in the second Vatican Council. See Luitpold Dorn and Georg Denzler, *Tagebuch des Konzils: die Arbeit der dritten Session*, (Nürnberg: J. M. Sailer, 1965), 265f. Heinzelmann, *Schwestern*, 71-83. The statements of the Council Fathers were brought together in the Pastoral Constitution on the Church in the Modern World, art. 9, 29 (*AAS* 58, 1966, 1031, 1049; Abbott, *Documents of Vatican II*, 206f., 227f.)

24. It is true that in Vatican II several interventions requested, beyond improvement of the position of women in the world, also an increased possibility for employment of women in the church. (See Heinzelmann, *Schwestern*, 71-74, 77-79; the written intervention of Archbishop Halinan of Atlanta is noteworthy for his advocacy of admission of women to the diaconate and to appointment to various commissions. *Ibid.*, 78f.) But the Council texts ignored these suggestions. The need for reform of the position of women in the church was seen more clearly in the second regular Bishops' Synod in Rome. While some bishops included in

their reform proposals (cf. Introduction, n. 3) the admission of women to ecclesiastical office—including that of the priesthood—such a possibility was sharply rejected by Cardinal Stipyj (Ukraine), who appealed to Scripture and church tradition (cf. *L'Osservatore Romano*, English ed., [November 11, 1971], 9). Despite express request by the Committee for Responsible Activity of Women in the Church (AFK), the German bishops in the Synod did not advocate integration of women into ecclesiastical office. (*Aktion* Information Letter of March 12, 1971.) When Cardinal Höffner (Cologne) was asked about his attitude toward the reform proposals of the Canadian Bishops' Conference (see Introduction, n. 3), he expressed a narrow view of women and their claim to free opportunities for self development. He thus strongly rejected the Canadian proposal: "Women's opportunities for apostleship in our church do not depend upon whether or not they can become priests." He said he did not see why the position of women in the church should be determined simply by the question of the priesthood; in the modern democratic state there are regulations which do not apply to both sexes. Besides, he said, it is not yet theologically clarified whether doctrinal questions do not prevent the ordination of women (*Publik*, no. 44, v. 29. 10, [1971], 13). In a letter of December 1969, to Cardinal Alfrink—occasioned by the approaching 5th meeting of the Dutch Pastoral Council in January, 1970—Pope Paul VI also declared against the admission of women to the priestly ministry. He objected to the fact that in the outlines and issues for discussion worked out for the meeting a critique was included concerning the thesis that only a man can become a priest (*AAS* 62, [1970], 67). The pope speaks similarly in a sermon on the occasion of the declaration of St. Teresa of Avila as Teacher of the Church: On the basis of an uncritical, biblicist scriptural interpretation he derives the exclusion of women from the "hierarchical functions of the teaching and priestly office" from the passage 1 Cor. 14:34 ("women should keep silence in the churches"). (*AAS* 62, [1970], 593). On the Corinthian passage see chapter 5, n. 158.

25. One can see to what degree this quality has impressed itself on the behavior of women—and still does so—in the common idea that insincerity is an element in women's character. E.g. Otto Weininger, *Geschlecht und Charakter; eine prinzipielle Untersuchung*, (Vienna: W. Braumüller, 1903), 355: "Women are not sincere in any phase of their lives." Other writers, however, see in this fact an intrinsic consequence of the repression and faulty education of women. E.g., Elizabeth Leigh Hutchins, *Conflicting Ideals; Two Sides of the Woman's Question*, (London: Murby, 1913), 30: "Girls are raised according to profoundly hypocritical ideals." Likewise Mary Wollstonecraft (quoted by Germaine Greer, *The Female Eunuch*, ([New York: Ballantine Books, 1971] 349). Women will have to put forth great moral effort to refute this injurious prejudice against them.

26. The Canadian bishops have been the first to take a stand for this, in their hearing and accepting the request of the Canadian Women's Associations concerning a reform of the valuation of women and the place of women in the church. (Cf. *Osservatore Romano*, English ed., (October 28, 1971), 5.

Bibliography

I. Lexicons, Handbooks and Dictionaries

Brechter, Heinrich, et. al., eds. *Das Zweite Vatikanische Konzil (LThK). Dokumente und Kommentare.* 3 vols. Freiberg: Herder, 1966-1968.

Fries, Heinrich, ed. *Handbuch theologischer Grundbegriffe.* 2 vols. Munich: Kösel-verlag, 1962.

Galling, Kurt, ed. *Die Religion in Geschichte und Gegenwart. Handwörterbuch für Theologie und Religionswissenschaft.* 6 vols. Tübingen: Mohr, 1957-1965.

Georges, Karl E. *Ausführliches lateinisch-deutsches Handwörterbuch.* Basel: B. Schwabe, 1962.

Gesenius, Wilhelm. *Hebräisches und aramäisches Handwörterbuch über das Alte Testament.* Leipzig: F. C. W. Vogel, 1921.

Hauck, Albert, ed. *Realencyklopädie für protestantische Theologie und Kirche*, 3rd ed. 24 vols. Leipzig: J. C. Hinrichs, 1896-1913.

Heumann, Hermann G. and Emil Secker. *Handlexikon zu den Quellen des römischen Rechts*, 10th ed. Graz: Akademische Druck-u. Verlagsanstalt, 1958.

Höfer, Josef and Karl Rahner. *Lexikon für Theologie und Kirche*, 2nd ed. 10 vols. Freiberg: Herder, 1957-1965.

Kittel, Gerhard, ed. *Theologisches Wörterbuch zum Neuen Testament.* Stuttgart: W. Kohlhammer, 1932-.

Klauser, Theodor, ed. *Reallexikon für Antike und Christentum.* Stuttgart: A Hiersemann, 1950-.

Naz, Rajesh K. *Dictionnaire de Droit Canonique.* Paris: Librarie Letouzey, 1935-1965.

Sleumer, Albert. *Kirchenlateinisches Wörterbuchi,* 2nd ed. Limburg: Gebrüder Steffen, 1926.

II. Sources

Achelis, Hans and Johannes Fleming. *Die syrische Didaskalia*. Leipzig: J. C. Hinrichs, 1904.

Acta Apostolicae Sedis, Commentarium officiale. Vatican City: Typis Polyglottis Vaticanis, 1909-.

Aegidius Bellamera. *Praelectiones in decretalium libros.* 6 vols. Lyon, 1548-1549.

———. *Remissorius, qui primus est tomus in duas partes dictus ad Commentaria in Gratiani Decreta.* 3 vols. Lyons: Apud Sennetonious fratres, 1550.

Antonius de Butrio. *In quinque libros decretalium commentaria.* 7 vols. Venice: Apud Juntas, 1578; reprinted Turin: Bottega d'Erasmo, 1967.

Boxler, Franz. *Die sogenannten Apostolischen Constitutionen und Canonen.* Kempton: Jos. Kösel, 1874.

Bruns, Hermann T., ed. *Canones Apostolorum et Conciliorum saeculorum IV. V. VI. VII.* Berlin: Reimer, 1839; reprinted Turin: Bottega d'Erasmo, 1959.

Codex Juris Canonici Fontes, cura et studio Emmi. Justiani Card. Serédi editi. Vol. 9 (Tabellae) Vatican City: Typis Polyglottis Vaticanis, 1939.

Codex Juris Canonici Pii X pontificus maximi iussu digestus. Vatican City: Typis Polyglottis Vaticanis, 1948.

Corpus Juris Canonici. Edited by Aemilius Freiberg. 2 vols. Leipzig: J. C. Hinrichs, 1879-1881; reprinted Graz: Akademische Druck-u. Verlagsanstalt, 1955.

Corpus Juris Canonici Gregorii Papae XIII. Lyon: I. A. Hvgvetan & G. Barbier, 1671.

Corpus Juris Civilis. Edited by Paulus Krueger, Theodore Mommsen and Rudolfus Schoell. 3 vols. Berlin: Werdmannsche Bundhandlung, 1904-1906.

Corpus scriptorum ecclesiasticorum latinorum. Vienna: C. Geroldi, 1866-.

Didascalia et Constitutiones Apostolorum. Edited by Franciscus X. Funk. Paderborn: Ferdinandi Schoeningh, 1905.

Duchesne, Louis, ed. *Le Liber Pontificalis*. Paris: E. de Boccard, 1866, Vol. 1.

Goffredus de Trani, *Summa super titulis decretalium*. Lyon, 1519; reprinted Aalen: Scientia Verlag, 1968.

Guido von Baysio, *Rosarium*. Strassburg: Johann Mentelin, 1473; reprinted Lyon, 1549.

Hinschius, Paulus, ed. *Decretales Pseudo-Isidorianae et Capitula Angilramni*. Leipzig: B. Tauchnitz, 1863; reprinted Aalen: Scientia Verlag, 1963.

Hostiensis (Henricus de Segusio). *Commentaria in quinque libros decretalium*. 5 vols. Venice: Apud Juntas, 1581; reprinted Turin: Bottega d'Erasmo, 1965.

———. *Summa Aurea*. Venice: Apud Iacobum Vitalem, 1574; reprinted Turin: Bottega d'Erasmo, 1963.

Huguccio, *Summa on the Decretum Gratiani*. (Manuscripts used: Munich, lat. 10247; Vatican lat. 2280)

Innocent IV (Sinibaldus Fliscus). *Apparatus in quinque libros decretalium*. Frankfurt, 1570; reprinted Frankfurt: Minerva, 1968.

Johannes Andreae. *Novella Commentaria in quinque libros decretalium*. 5 vols. Venice: Apud F. Fransicum 1581; reprinted Turin: Bottega d'Erasmo, 1963.

Mansi, Joannes D. *Sacrorum conciliorum nova et amplissima collectio*. Florence: A. Zatta, 1759-1798; reprinted Paris: H. Welter, 1901-1927.

Migne, Jacques-Paul. *Patrologiae cursus completus*. Latin series, 221 vols. Paris: Migne, 1878-1890. Greek series, 161 vols. Paris: Migne, 1857-1866.

Munier, Charles. *Les Statuta ecclesiae antiqua*. Paris: Presses universitaires de France, 1960.

Nicolaus de Tudeschis. *Lectura in decretales*. Lyon, 1534, Vols. 1-3. Venice: 1504, Vols. 4-5.

Paucapalea. *Summa über das Decretum Gratiani*. Edited by Johann F. Schulte. Gießen: E. Roth, 1890; reprinted Aalen: Scientia Verlag, 1965.

Petrus de Ancharano. *Commentaria in quinque libros decretalium*. 5 vols. Bologna: Apud societatem Typographiae Bononienis, 1581.

Raymund of Peñaforte. *Summa de poenitentia et matrimoni cum glossis Joannis de Friburgo*, Rome: Sumptibus Ioannis Tallini, 1503.

Roland Bandinelli. *Die Summa magistri Rolandi, nachmals Papstes Alexander III*. Edited by Friedrich Thaner. Innsbruck: Wagner, 1874; reprinted Aalen: Scientia Verlag, 1962.

Rufinus of Bologna. *Summa decretorum des Magister Rufinus*. Edited by Heinrich Singer. Paderborn: Ferdinandi Schoeningh, 1902; reprinted Aalen: Scientia Verlag, 1963.

Sicard of Cremona. *Summa decretorum*. (Manuscript used: Munich lat. 4555)

Stephan von Doornick (Stephanus Tornacensis). *Die Summa über das Decretum Gratiani.* Edited by Johann F. Schulte. Gießen: E. Roth, 1891; reprinted Aalen: Scientia Verlag, 1965.

Summa Parisiensis, The Summa Parisiensis on the Decretum Gratiani. Edited by Terence P. McLaughlin. Toronto: Pontifical Institute of Mediaeval Studies, 1952.

III. Studies

Bardenhewer, Otto. *Geschichte der altkirchlichen Literatur.* 5 vols. Freiberg: Herder, 1902-1932.

Beer, Georg. *Die soziale und religiöse Stellung der Frau im israelitischen Altertum*. Tübingen: Mohr, 1919.

Begrich, Joachim. Die Paradieserzählung. Eine literargeschichtliche "*Der Paradieserzählung. Eine literargeschichtliche Studie*," in *Gesammelte Studien zum Alten Testament*, W. Zimmerli, ed. Munich: C. Kaiser, 1964.

Bertinetti, Ilse. *Frauen im geistlichen Amt. Die theologische Problematik in evangelisch-lutherischer Sicht.* Berlin: Evangelische Verlagsanstalt, 1965.

Browe, Peter. *Beiträge zur Sexualethik des Mittelalters*. Breslau: Müller & Seiffert, 1932.

Brox, Norbert. *Die Pastoralbriefe*, 4th ed. Regensberg: Pustet, 1969.

Concetti, Gino. "La donna e il sacerdozio." *L'Osservatore Romano* 8-12 (November 1965): 89-101.

Daly, Mary. *Kirche, Frau und Sexus.* Freiberg: Herder, 1970.

Daniélou, Jean. "Le ministére des femmes dans l'Englise ancienne." *La maisoon-Dieu* 61 (1960): 70-96.

Duchesne, Louis. *Christian Worship, its Origin and Evolution. A study of the latin liturgy up to the time of Charlemagne,* 5th ed. London: Society for Promoting Christian Knowledge, 1956.

Eichrodt, Walther. *Theologie des Alten Testaments, Teil II/III*, 5th ed. Götingen: Vandenhoeck & Ruprecht, 1964

Eyden, R. A. J. van, "Die Frau im Kirchenamt. Plädoyer für die Revision einer traditionellen Haltung," *Wort und Wahrheit* 22 (1967): 350-362.

Feine, Hans E. *Kirchliche Rechtsgeschichte. Die katholische Kirche*, 4th ed. Cologne: Böhlau, 1964.

Friesen, Joseph. *Geschichte des Canonischen Eherechts bis zum Verfall der Glossenliteratur*, 2nd ed. Paderborn: F. Schöningh, 1893.

Funk, Jens. "Klerikale Frauen?". *Osterreichisches Archiv für Kirchenrecht* 14 (1963): 271-290.

Gillmann, Franz. "Weibliche Kleriker nach dem Urteil der Frühscholastik." *Archiv für Katholisches Kirchenrecht* 93 (1913): 239-253.

Gunkel, Hans. *Genesis*, 6th ed. Göttingen: Vandenhoeck & Ruprecht, 1964.

Haag, Herbert. "Die Themata der Südenfall-Geschichte." 101-111 in *Lex tua veritas*, edited by Heinrich Groß and Franz Mußner. Trier: Paulinas-Verlag, 1961.

———. "Die biblische Schöpfungsgeschichte heute," in *Evolution und Bibel*, edited by Herbert Haag, Adolf Haas, and Johannes Hürzeler. Freiberg: Herder, 1962.

———. "Die Komposition der Sündenfall-Erzählung." *Tübingen Quartalschrift* 146 (1966): 1-7.

Hefele, Karl J. *Conciliengeschichte*, 2nd ed. 9 vols. Freiberg: Herder, 1873-1890.

——— and Henri Leclercq. *Historie des conciles d'aprés les documents originaux*. Paris: A. LeClére, 1907-.

Heggelbacher, Othmar. *Vom romischen zum chistilichen Recht. Juristische Elemente in den Schriften des sog. Ambrosiaster.* Freiberg: Universitätsverlag, 1959.

Heilfron, Eduard. *Röminisches Rechtsgeschichte und System des römischen Privatrechts*, 7th ed. Mannheim: J. Bensheimer, 1920.

Heinisch, Paul. "Das Buch Genesis," in *Die Heilige Schrift des Alten Testamentes*, edited by Franz Feldmann and Heinrich Herkenne. Bonn: Hanstein, 1930.

Heinzelmann, Gertrude. *Wir schweigen nicht länger! Frauen äußbern sich zum II. Vatikanischen Konzil.* Zurich: Interfeminas-Verlag, 1964.

———. *Die getrennten Schwestern. Frauen nach dem Konzil.* Zürich: Interfeminas-Verlag, 1967.

Hinschius, Paul. *Das Kirchenrecht der Katholiken und Protestanten in Deutschland.* 5 vols. Berlin: Werdmannsche Bundhandlung, 1869-1893; reprinted Graz: Akademische Druck-u. Verlagsanstalt, 1959.

Hove, Alphonse van. *Prolegomena ad Codicem Juris Canonici*, 2nd ed. Rome: H. Dessain, 1945.

Hunke, Sigrid. *Am Anfang waren Mann und Frau. Vorbilder und Wandlungen der Geschlechterbeziehungen.* Hamm: Grote, 1955.

Jeremias, Joachim. *Jerusalem zur Zeit Jes. Eine kulturgeschichtliche Untersuchung zur neutestamentlichen Zeitgeschichte,* 3rd ed. Göttingen: Vandenhoeck & Ruprecht, 1962.

Jervell, Jacob. "Imago Dei. Gen 1,26f. im Spätjudentum," in *der Gnosis und in den paulinischen Briefen.* Göttingen: Vandenhoeck & Ruprecht, 1960.

Kalsbach, Adolf. *Die altkirchliche Einrichtung der Diakonissen bis zu ihrem Erlöschen.* Freiberg: Herder, 1926.

Kaser, Max. *Das römische Privatrecht.* 2 vols. Munich: Beck, 1955-1959.

Köhler, Ludwig. *Theologie des Alten Testaments*, 4th ed. Tübingen: Mohr, 1966.

Kuttner, Stephan. *Kanonistiche Schudlehre von Gratian bis auf die Dekretalen Gregors IX.* Vatican City: Biblioteca apostolica vaticana, 1935.

———. *Repertorium der Kanonistik (1140-1234). Prodromus corporis gloassarum I.* Vatican City: Biblioteca apostolica vaticana, 1937.

Leipoldt, Johannes. *Die Frau in der antiken Welt und im Urchristentum.* Leipzig: Koehlert & Amelang, 1954.

Loretz, Oswald. *Schöpfung und Mythos. Mensch und Welt nach den Anfangskapiteln der Genesis.* Stuttgart: Katholisches Bibelwerk, 1968.

Maassen, Friedrich B. *Geschichte der Quellen und der Litertur des canonischen rechts im Abendlande.* Graz: Leuschner & Lubensky, 1870; reprinted Graz: Akademische Druck-u. Verlagsanstalt, 1956, Vol. 1.

Meer, Haye van der. *Priestertum der Frau? Eine theologie-geschichtliche Untersuchung.* Freiberg: Herder, 1969.

Metz, René. "Le statut de la femme en droit canonique medieval." 59-113 in *Recueils de la Société Jean Bodin XII/2.* Brussels: Editions de la librairie encyclopédique, 1962.

———. "Recherches sur la condition de la femme selon Gratien." *Studia Gratiana XII* (1967): 377-396.

Mörsdorf, Klaus. *Lehrbuch des Kirchenrechts auf grund des Codex Juris Canonici.* 3 vols. Munich: F. Schöningh, 1961-1967.

Morant, Peter. *Die Anfänge der Menschheit. Eine Auslegung der ersten 11 Genesis-kapitel.* Lucerne: Räber & Cie, 1960.

Mundle, Wilhelm. *Die Exegese der paulinischen B riefe im Kommentar des Ambrosiaster.* Marburg: C. Schaaf, 1919.

Munier, Charles. *Les sources patristiques du droit de l'Eglise du VIIIe au XIIIe siécle.* Mulhouse: Salvator, 1957.

Muschalek, Herbert. *Urmensch-Adam. Die Herkunft des menschlichen Leibes in naturwissenschaftlicher und theologischer Sicht.* Berlin: Morus Verlag, 1963.

Mußner, Franz. *Christus, das All und die Kirche. Studien zur Theologie des Epheserbriefes.* Trier: Paulinas-Verlag, 1955.

Persson, Per Erik. *Repraesentatio Christi. Der Amtsbegriff in der neuren römischkatholischen Theologie.* Göttingen: Vandenhoeck & Ruprecht, 1966.

Peters, Jochen-Ulrich. "Die Frau im kirchlichen Dienst." *Concilium* 4 (1968): 293-299.

Phillips, Georg. *Kirchenrecht*, 3rd ed. Regensberg: Pustet, 1855; reprinted Graz: Akademische Druck-u. Verlagsanstalt, 1955, Vol. 1.

Plöchl, Willibald M. *Das Eherecht des Magisters Gratianus.* Leipzig: F. Deuticke, 1935.

———. *Geschichte des Kirchenrechts*, 2nd ed. 2 vols. Vienna: Herold, 1960-1962.

Premm, Matthias. *Katholische Glaubenskunde. Ein Lehrbuch der Dogmatik.* Freiberg: Herder, 1955.

Procksch, Otto. *Die Genesis*, 2nd ed. and 3rd ed. Leipzig: A. Deichert, 1924.

Rad, Gerald von. *Das Erste Buch Mose.* Göttingen: Vandenhoeck & Ruprecht, 1949.

Remberger, Franz. "Priestertum der Frau?" *Theologie der Gegenwart* 9 (1966): 130-136.

Renckens, Henricus. *Urgeschichte und Heilsgeschichte. Israels Schau in die Vergangenheit nach Gen. 1-3.* Mainz: Matthias-Grünewald-Verlag, 1959.

Ringeling, Hermann. *Die Frau zwischen gestern und morgen. Der sozialtheologische Aspekt ihrer Gleichberechtigung.* Hamburg: Fuche-Verlag, 1962.

Ritter, Adolf M. and Gottfried Leich. "Wer ist die Kirche/Amt und Gemeinde im Meuen Testament." *Der Kirchengeschichte und heute.* Göttingen: Vandenhoeck & Ruprecht, 1968.

Sägmüller, Johannes B. *Lehrbuch des katholischen Kirchenrechts*, 4th ed. Freiber: Herder, 1925, Vol. 1.

Schäfer, Karl H. *Die Kanonissenstifter im deutschen Mittelalter. Ihre Entwicklung und innere Einrichtung im Zusammenhang mit dem altchristlichen Sanktimonialentum.* Stuttgart: W. Kohlhammer, 1907; reprinted Amsterdam: P. Schippus, 1965.

———. "Kanonissen und Diakonissen." *Römische Quartalschrift für christliche Altertumskunde und für Kirchengeschichte* 24 (1910): 49-80.

Schaller, John. *Gen. 1.2 im antiken Judentum. Untersuchungen über Verwendung und Deutung der Schöpfungsaussagen von Gen. 1.2 im antiken Judentum.* Göttingen: Vandenhoeck & Ruprecht, 1961.

Schmidt, Werner H. *Die Schöpfungsgeschichte der Priesterschrift. Zur Überlieferungsgeschichte von Genesis 1,1-2,4a und 2,4b-3,24*, 2nd ed. Neukirchen-Vluyn: Neukirchener-Verlag des Erziehungsvereins, 1967.

Schüssler Fiorenza, Elisabeth. *Der vergessene Partner. Grundlagen, Tatsachen und Möglichkeiten der beruflichen Mitarbeit der Frau in der Heilssorge der Kirche.* Düsseldorf: Patmos Verlag, 1964.

Schulte, Johann F. *Die Geschichte der Quellen und Literatur des canonischen Rechts von Gratian bis auf die Gegenwart.* Stuttgart: W. Kohlhammer, 1875; reprinted Graz: Akademische Druck-u. Verlagsanstalt, 1956.

Schulz, Fritz. *Prinzipien des römischen Rechts, Vorlesungen.* Leipzig: Dunker & Humblot, 1954.

Schwegler, Theodor. *Die biblische Urgeschichte im Lichte der Forschung.* Munich: A Pustet, 1960.

Semmelroth, Otto. *Das geistliche Amt. Theologische Sinndeutung.* Frankfurt: J. Knecht, 1958.

———. *Maria oder Christus/Christus als Ziel der Marienverehrung.* Frankfurt: J. Knecht, 1954.

Sohm, Rudolf. *Institutionen. Geschichte und System des römischen Privatrechts,* 17th ed. München: Dunker & Humblot, 1923.

Stickler, Alphonse M. *Historia juris canonici latini.* Turin: Libraria Pontificium Anthenaeum Salesianum, 1950, Vol. 1.

Stier, Friedrich. "Adam." *Handbuch theologischer Grundbegriffe* 1:13-25.

Strach, Hermann and Paul Billerbeck. *Kommentar zum Neuen Testament aus Talmud und Midrasch.* 4 vols. Munich: Beck, 1922-1928.

Stutz, Ulrich. *Der Geist des Codex juris canonici. Eine Einführung in das auf Geheiß Papst Pius X. verfaßte und von Papst Benedikt XV. Erlassene Gesetzbuch der katholischen Kirche.* Stuttgart: F. Enke, 1918.

Thraede, Klaus. "Frau." *Reallexikon für Antike und Christentum,* 8 (1970): 197-269.

Vaerting, Marie. *Warheit und Irrtum in der Geschlechterpsychologie,* 2nd ed. Weimar: G. Braun, 1931.

Weber, Marianne. *Ehefrau und Mutter in dr Rechsentwicklung.* Tübingen: Mohr, 1907.

Weiß, Johannes. *Der erste Korintherbrief,* 10th ed. Göttingen: Vandenhoeck & Ruprecht, 1925.

Wendland, Heinz D. *Die Briefe an die Korinther*, 12th ed. Göttingen: Vandenhoeck & Ruprecht, 1968.

Westermann, Claus. *Genesis.* Neukirchen-Vluyn: Neukirchener-Verlag des Erziehungsvereins, 1966-.

Zscharnack, Leopold. *Der Dienst der Frau in den ersten Jahrhunderten der christlichen Kirche.* Göttingen: Vandenhoeck & Ruprecht, 1902.

Appendixes

Ida Raming

Appendix 1

"The Twelve Apostles Were Men . . ."

From *Orientierung* 56 (1992), 143-146; translated for www.womenpriests.org by Mary Dittrich and republished on the website with permission of the author and the editor of *Orientierung*. [The additions and revisions introduced into the original article by Ida Raming have been translated by Gary Macy]

Stereotypical Objections to the Ordination of Women and Their Deeper Causes.

Now that the question of "women in the Church" is getting widespread attention, and more and more women are able to learn from a range of publications about their position in the Church, the question of ordination of women to priestly office comes up with increasing frequency in talks with churchmen or in discussion groups. Nothing odd in that, for the credibility of the Church leadership in its relations with women depends in particular on its answer; one can deem this a test case. In spite of all the scientific enlightenment achieved in years past, specific objections to the ordination of women are still being raised by holders of higher ecclesiastical office.

What follows deals with these stereotypically repeated objections, and attempts to shed light on what may be their deeper psychological background.

Jesus Called Only Men to Be Apostles . . .

Most frequently, in discussions but also in popular scientific articles, the "twelve apostles" are wheeled in as apparently having been chosen by Jesus so as to make clear "for all time" that he wanted to exclude women form the Group of Twelve, the apostles, and the offices subsequently emanating—the priesthood and episcopate. This argument has already been refuted in numerous relevant articles and books,[1] so that we can limit ourselves to a resume of the counter arguments before revealing the true background of this pseudo-argument.

Contrary to traditionalist argumentation, it has long been made clear that Jesus, of necessity in accordance with the social structure of ancient Israel which was purely patriarchal, chose twelve men to represent the twelve tribes of Israel; these were also represented by tribal fathers (the sons of Jacob), this was to tally with the belief prevalent in antiquity that only men ranked as progenitors (cf. Gen. 35:23; Gen. 49:1-28).

In choosing the Twelve, Jesus wanted to show symbolically that *all Israel* was being addressed by his message and called to conversion. This symbolic action by Jesus was achieved in no way for exclusivity ("only men"), but had a manifestly *inclusive* character. This may be understood as an eschatological sign: "Jesus procedure is directed as the assembly of the new eschatological People of God in the nearby Kingdom of God,"[2] so he used the number twelve, a symbol understood by all Israelites. However, if the implication is that Jesus in doing this intended specifically to exclude women from the Group of Twelve, that is no less than a projection onto Jesus of the patriarchal attitude of today's ecclesiastical office-holders, and a perversion of his message of salvation to all Israel. In the Gospels not one word of Jesus can be found that would justify such an intention in the very least.

The New Testament tells us that the "Twelve" were sent forth by Jesus to proclaim the Good News of the Kingdom of God. Jesus himself and the Twelve preached in Israel's villages and towns, including the local synagogues. (Mk. 1:39; 6,1f; 6:6b-13, par.; Acts 13:5b and other texts). How could women assume or carry out such tasks in those days, when they were not even entitled to speak in the Synagogue? They could not bear public, official witness.

Against the background of the strictly patriarchal structure of Jesus' times, the only plausible interpretation thus seems to be that the attitude of Jesus and his associates in this regard can be sufficiently explained by "the cultural and social milieu of the period in which they acted, and had to act the way they did, without their behavior having normative meaning for all time"[3] Their practice has therefore no prescriptive meaning for the structures of a later church, no more than the fact that Jesus had chosen only Jews for the group of the Twelve.[4]

Jesus could not simply do away with the patriarchal, sociologically grown structures of his time. To expect that of him would amount to not taking really seriously the incarnation of God in Jesus. These preconditions and circumstances are ignored when Pope John Paul II declares, in support of his thesis, that "*In calling only men as his Apostles*, Christ acted *in a completely free and sovereign manner*. In doing so, he exercised the same freedom with which, in all his behavior, he emphasized the dignity and the vocation of women, without conforming to the prevailing customs and to the traditions sanctioned by the legislation of the time."[5]

Such a statement lacks, in my opinion, the requisite differentiation. For Jesus, dealings with individual women whom he meets, or who are among his disciples, are not on the same plane as *the appointment of the Twelve, which should be understood as a symbolic act*. In other words, Jesus did certainly infringe when dealing with women, the taboos and prejudices of these times (cf. John 4:27; Mk. 5:24b-34b and other texts); but he was unable to break through or conquer sociological and legally set contemporary structures (e.g., the exclusion of women from public speaking in the Synagogues and from bearing witness in court). In the same way he encountered and knew slavery as a sociological institution of these times, but neither scorned it nor fought it, although for its victims slavery meant sinking into being a material possession of the owner. According to the Gospels, Jesus did not see himself as a social reformer; he merely laid the foundations for the future structural reforms in church and society that emerge from his announcement of the reign of God.

More Recent Research on the Concept of Apostleship

Against the pseudo-argument with which we started, with its disregard of historical context, it has been contended that the definition "Twelve Apostles" (who were men) should be regarded as "a secondary narrowing of an initially far broader concept of apostolicity" . . . "In earliest times apostles are all who are solemnly and officially sent out, either by a community (cf. 2 Cor. 8:23; Ph. 2:25) or by the Risen One himself (cf. 1 Cor. 9:1; 15:7)"[6] Evidently women (cf. Rom. 16:7; Junia)[7] were also included in this larger group of apostles which, apart from the Twelve, numbered roaming missionary apostles (Rom. 16, 3; Prisca and Aquila are named as Paul's co-workers in the missionary field). The existence of female missionary apostles in the early church represents proof in tradition of the existence of female office holders—contrary to the traditional view that only men held ecclesiastical office. The "Declaration of the Congregation for the Doctrine of the Faith on the Question of Admitting Women to the Priesthood" (*Inter insigniores*, 1976) which argued along these lines and postulates that a straight line leads from the "Twelve Apostles" to the subsequent bishops and priests, is countered by the indication that "the transition from the concept of the apostle and of the Twelve to that of the priest (and bishop)" is too simply constructed "for it to comply with today's knowledge of the emergence of the early Church and its structures and organization."[8] According to these findings, Jesus "established no official priesthood," but sent out "disciples to proclaim the rule of God and appointed twelve of them to be eschatological witnesses for Israel (Matt. 19:28; par.; Lk. 22:29f). The formation and structuring of offices (episcopacy, presbyterate, and diaconate) was left to the developing Church."[9]

What follows from all this is that the "argument" cited at the beginning that Jesus knowingly and intentionally excluded women for all time from the grouping of Twelve and thus from the offices allegedly deriving from it (episcopacy and presbyterate) collapses once one differentiates when considering how the Church and its offices came to be. The Pontifical Biblical Commission also came to a similar conclusion, which had already been included in the preparation of the declaration *Inter insigniores*: "According to their judgment concerning the question of the biblical basis for the critical examination of the ordination of women priests," the majority of the members of the Biblical Commission had explained that Holy Scripture does not contain a prohibition against female priests and that the Christ's plan of salvation would not be transgressed or falsified by the admission of women's ordination.[10] Obviously the Congregation for the Doctrine of the Faith neither anticipated or desired these results, so that they wanted "to put a stop to . . . this trend" by their clarification.[11]

Deeper Grounds for the Position of the Magisterium

This clinging to a pseudo-argument shows only too clearly that it is not a matter of recognizing historical or scientific truth. Rather, such a stance merely conceals the deeply patriarchal, anti-feminine attitude which pleads the authority of Jesus and God because (today) it would be inopportune to come out openly against the admission of women to ecclesiastical office. And this patriarchal attitude prevents the message in Gal. 3:28 that "in Christ there is neither male nor female" from being taken seriously, for it means that in religion gender differences are entirely irrelevant. If it is cynically countered that this statement applies only before God and "in heaven," not on earth and in visible institutions, that again points to an extremely patriarchal hardening of the heart, a denial of the will of a God who seeks justice in his world ("Thy will be done on earth as it is in heaven"), a clinging to the false spirit of the "Old Adam" (Ep. 4:22) and blindness to the new spirit made present by the coming of the Kingdom in and with Jesus.

Against this the early Christian appeal rings out: "You must be clothed in the new self, which is created in God's image, justified and sanctified by the truth (Ep. 4:24)—"When one becomes a new creature in Christ, the old life has disappeared, everything has become new" (2 Cor. 5:17) and "As many of you as were baptized into Christ have clothed yourselves with Christ . . . there is no longer more male and female for all of you are one in Christ Jesus" (Gal. 3:27-28). So, to adhere to the patriarchal "gender order," to the dominance of men over women in the Church, means being insensitive to the action of the spirit of Christ and God in our times, delaying the dawning of the Kingdom of God, trying to stop it. Thus, if the powers of the "old Adam," the sin of patriarchy, are to be conquered in church and society, nothing less than a conversion of hearts to the will of God, to what is really meant by the Kingdom of God, is needed.

In this connection, however, we face an unavoidable question: Can men who are involved in a strongly hierarchical ecclesiastical system that gives priority to the principle of obedience before free decision of conscience really embrace such a conversion with all its consequences?

Since they have themselves surrendered their inner freedom to this closed hierarchical system or perhaps are unable to develop, they are convinced that only obedient men can be entrusted to hold ecclesiastical offices. So the closed system is perpetuated. Reforms, whether from above or below, are not desired and are blocked. Is then all hope for the liberation of the oppressed illusory?

In my opinion there is hope. Despite everything, I trust in God's Spirit, which "breathes where it will" (John. 3:8), that the oppressed, filled with faith in the irresistible power of the risen Christ, will rise up and commit themselves to a revolutionary shift.

The Weight of a Two-Thousand-Year-Old Tradition?

A tendency to stick to the handed down patriarchal gender relationship within the Church, in other words a refusal to rethink them, is evident in the often advanced argument concerning the ordination of women that "the weight of a two-thousand-year-old tradition"[12] precludes a change in the relevant rules. This implies that there is an unbroken chain of serious witnesses or documents in tradition, reaching from the very origins of the Church, indeed from Jesus himself, to our times. Psychologically the argument is pretty effective, for who can deny the force of so lasting a tradition? In such circumstances is it not pointless to press for the ordination of women?

To a great extent the authorities responsible use the apparently two-thousand-year-old tradition to justify postponing any change in the present status of women in the Church, if possible indefinitely. Rarely, or rather not at all, is this "two-thousand-year-old-tradition" given a close look. But on examination it turns out to be a collection of statements (e.g., quotations from the Church Fathers—genuine and bogus—papal decretals including some forgeries, synodal decisions). They agree in withholding from women liturgical ritual and pastoral function linked with ecclesiastical office, and in subjecting women to men.[13] The so-called witnesses to tradition,[14] among them specific Biblical passages and the texts from the patristic and the medieval theology upon which they depend, are based uniformly on the rational and even ethical preeminence of the male. This has been since confirmed through numerous relevant studies. A tradition, however, that is based on the discrimination against the woman due to the female sex can have no claim to validity.

In addition, this appeal to an allegedly continuous "two-thousand-year-old tradition" quite blots out striking examples of a *counter tradition*, friendly to woman; as well as the fact that women in the early Christian missionary movement worked as official co-workers (deaconesses, heads of domestic communities, female missionary apostles) (see Col. 4:15; 1 Cor. 16:19; Rom. 16:1-3; Rom. 16:7). In the course of consolidating the threefold offices (episcopacy, presbyterate, diaconate) women were already very early excluded from meaningful community service (e.g., 1 Tim. 2:11-15). Exercise of office by women was forbidden already in the NT and also in later sources (Church orders from the 3rd to 5th centuries, synodal decrees, Papal decretals) that to be sure implicitly witness the existence of women officeholders.[15] Moreover, tombstone inscriptions also indicate the existence of women officeholders in the early Church.[16] Contrary to the prevailing teaching in medieval sacramental theology that women, because of the inferiority of their sex, are not "able to be ordained," there was the opposing view of some theologians and canonists, who saw grounds for valid ordination in baptism and not in (masculine) sexual identity: "Anyone, after receiving baptism, whether man or woman, can be ordained" (*post baptismum quilibet potest ordinari*).[17] The absolute condition for valid ordination is, then, baptism alone and, of course, appropriate qualifications (charism) for diaconate or priesthood. Only this interpretation can pretend to agree with the good news of the gospel (Gal. 3: 27f).

To this countertradition also belong the *testimonies of women* who mourned their exclusion from the priestly office in the course of the centuries as shameful degradation (e.g., *Marie de Jars de Gournay,* 17th century) or who, even further, aspired to the priesthood based on their religious charisms (e.g., Therese of Lisieux, 1873-1897). Especially since the Second Vatican Council, the number of women has grown continually all over the world who declare their priestly vocation.[18] Since the Second Vatican Council, even on the local and universal church level, there has been manifold witnesses to a tradition divergent from that of the Vatican church leadership. Numerous national synods have passed resolutions in favor of the diaconate for women, some even in favor of the presbyterate. Bishops and Cardinals themselves speak out for this.[19]

To sum up: There can be no question of an unbroken monolithic two-thousand-year-old tradition on the exclusion of women from priesthood accepted unanimously by the church community. That, on the contrary, is tendentious fiction. There are countless, numerous documents which show that this tradition has been artificially preserved through decrees, repression and sanctions on the part of the Vatican church leadership. If they continue in this way, it would mean clinging to a misogyny that manifests itself in a special manner in the exclusion of women from the priesthood, and thus placing a stumbling block on the path of the movement from Vatican II towards a renewed Church of brothers and sisters.

Symbolism of Relation between the Sexes and Women's Ordination

In order to deepen and support the previous grounds from "scripture and tradition" the ecclesiastical teaching office seized on the argument from symbol, a kind of anthropological-metaphysical attempt at clarification. In this way the clarification *Inter insigniores* seeks to "illustrate this norm by showing the profound fittingness that theological reflection discovers between the proper nature of the sacrament of Order, with its specific reference to the mystery of Christ, and the fact that only men have been called to receive priestly ordination." To be sure, it was conceded that this kind of argument "is not a question here of bringing forward a demonstrative argument, but of clarifying this teaching by the analogy of faith."[20] However, this "argument from analogy" in the discussion about women's ordination acquired great prominence, so much so that one had the impression that it was decisive for the official Church. In this debate, Church leadership seized upon the anthropology of sex to decisively provide the ground for maintaining a purely male priesthood.

The argument from symbolism proceeded as follows: It appealed first to the Old Testament theme of "bridegroom and bride" which served to illustrate the intimate relation between Yahweh and the Israelite people; then in the New Testament (Eph. 5) the relation between Christ and the Church is applied analogously. Hence concludes the declaration *Inter insigniores*, "it must be admitted that, in actions which demand the character of ordination and in which Christ himself, the author of the Covenant, the Bridegroom, the Head of the Church, is represented, exercising his ministry of salvation," especially in celebration of the Eucharist, "his role must be taken by a man" since—so argues the declaration—"For Christ himself was and remains a man." The functioning of Christ in Eucharist can occur sacramentally only through a male priest.[21]

With this line of argument *Inter insigniores* harps back to the discussion of the early decades of the 20th century. Especially in liturgical studies the relation between officials and community was often described with the symbolism of Eph. 5 (Christ the bridegroom, Church the bride), even though the text deals only with marriage and not with Church structures.[22]

Against this argument from symbolism the following response must be made:

- Symbols are multivalent; they correspond to the frame of reference within which they function. That the theme Bridegroom/bride that in the Old Testament and Ephesians expresses a hierarchical preference is convincing only within a patriarchal society.[23] Human patterns of marriage undergo historical and societal change. The relation between Christ and the Church is also expressed in the NT through other symbols (vine and branches, hen and chicks, friends with one another, etc.). Symbols cannot provide absolute validity, since they are changeable, have multiple meaning and are conditioned by time. Above all, one cannot from them derive norms or Church laws.
- The basis for surrogate activity in the name and by the commission of Christ, e.g., official action *in persona Christi*—specifically in the celebration of Eucharist—is not the male sex of the officeholder. Such a view is in stark opposition to the New Testament gospel in which neither the maleness of Jesus nor the sex of officials have any specific religious meaning. "In sacramental theology *in persona Christi* pertains not to Jesus' sexuality but to the fact that Christ is the proper and originating dispenser of all the sacraments and the human minister is always only his personally representative instrument. In other words, speaking dogmatically, a priest is a priest because of his consecration not because of his sexual distinctiveness. What Christ does he does, not as a male, but as the God-man. Otherwise it would be unthinkable that a woman would baptize or (according to current Western theology) be a minister of the sacrament of marriage."[24] Each baptized person is on principle capable of all official activity in the name of and by the commission of Christ, independent of her or his sex, if she or he has been ordained and officially assigned.
- Contrary to Gal 3:28, through the argument from symbolism, the preference of men to women and consequently the hierarchical relation between the sexes in the sphere of ecclesiastical office is confirmed. As

"vicar" of the "bridegroom Christ," the "head of the Church," the priest has attached to him a role (respectively, it is claimed for him) which involves him in a "quasi-identification" that is contrary to the structure of the Church as a *communio*, that separates him from the rest of the Church, puts him symbolically on the side of Christ as "head of the Church" and indeed has him coincide with Christ. Thus the declaration *Inter insigniores*: "The priest alone has the power to celebrate the Eucharist, he not only possesses the power of office entrusted to him by Christ, but acts in the person of Christ when he takes the place of Christ and becomes his image when he speaks the words of Eucharistic consecration"[25]

• To justify the exclusion of women from priesthood, Pope John Paul II[26] stresses that we are dealing with the Church as a realm that is *sui generis*, that can in no way be compared with secular institutions that are subject to "purely human formulation." Claiming to guard the mystery dimension of the Church, the Pope has insisted, by using the image of 'Bridegroom (Christ)—bride (Church),' on a hierarchical ordering of the sexes in the Church. That has the result that Church and society are ever further distanced from one another, especially in the relationship of the sexes. John Paul's insistence on the "mystery character" of the Church—the Church as "the mystery of God's love manifested in human history"—will through an official structure shaped by male dominance and thereby through discrimination against women obscure rather than enlighten.

A Threat to Church Unity?

While the usual objections to the ordination of women were repeatedly refuted in decades past by cogent argument, the authorities stuck to their well-known negative attitude of disinclination to reform. In view of the conspicuous intellectual advances in this field, which makes repetition of the traditional positions look increasingly uncertain, the authorities have resorted to a last line of defense in appealing to the *unity of the Church* which could, supposedly, be threatened by the ordination of women.[27] For instance, one is told that on a worldwide basis—for by now the main focus of the Catholic Church is felt to be in the so-called Third World—the ordination would be unacceptable. In practice, such a stance would mean that the patriarchal structure of the Catholic Church would be preserved for a long time. That being so, this appeal to Church unity conceals in its essence a refusal to aim at or prepare a thorough, Gospel-guided change in the relationship between the sexes.

Challenging the presumptions of that argument, the first international conference for women's ordination in Dublin (June 29-July 1, 2002) with the motto "Now is the Time. A Celebration of Women's Call to a Renewed Priesthood in the Catholic Church" clearly demonstrated that the voices for the ordination of women in the Catholic Church come from *many countries and all the continents*. Representatives from 26 countries and 5 continents took part in the congress, in order with one voice to argue for women's ordination.[28]

In any case, serious reservation can be made with respect to the idea of Church unity. Does it mean a set of rules applicable to all Catholic Christians, despite differing ways of life and culture, despite the varying levels of knowledge and education deeply ingrained in Christendom in so many countries? An interpretation of unity as a rigid grip or fetter clearly denies the varying pastoral needs of people in different countries and stifles legitimate pluriformity within the Church.

So the principle of a rigid church unity becomes a "club" not infrequently used against the ordination of women, even in the ecumenical arena. For a few years now, the request concerning Protestant women pastors has been put in the World Council of Churches by the conservative, fundamentalist side that they should "sacrifice the ordination of women on the altar of the ecumenism!"[29] Such disrespect for the gifts which women pastors bring to the church announces itself through the impudence of wishing to establish the unity of the church "on the backs" of women!

The actual threat of the churches' unity lies, in my opinion, in the tension between fundamentalist-minded circles, on the one hand, that reject even urgently needed reforms in the church and this through their decisive influence on the Vatican church leadership seeking with all their powers to prevent it—and reform-oriented circles, on the other hand, for whom the principle *Ecclesia semper reformanda* is binding. This rift goes far deeper in endangering unity than that allegedly caused by the ordination of women. Refusal and advocacy of the ordination of women are, for the most part, only incidental expressions of both opposing movements.

Therefore, "unity in pluriformity" is the only principle applicable to the ordination of women that can claim validity. For only so can it be assumed that women with a priestly vocation and theological training, indeed all women, at last get justice in the Church, that their charisms are no longer suppressed by church law to the detriment of the entire Church, and that a stride towards a Church of brothers and sisters is taken. That Church, in helping the paths towards the life fulfillment of the Kingdom of God, would at last be the "city on a mountain," the "salt of the earth" (Mt. 5, 13-16).

Notes

1. See inter alia the following literature: Haye van der Meer, *Priestertum der Frau? Eine theologie-geschichtliche Untersuchung*, (Freiberg: Herder, 1969); Karl Rahner, "Priestertum der Frau?" *Stimmen der Zeit* 195 (1977): 291-201: Hans Küng and Gerhard Lohfink. "Keine Ordination der Frau?" *Theologische Quartalschrift* 157 (1977): 144-146; Elizabeth Schüssler Fiorenza, "The Twelve," in: "Women Priests, a Catholic Commentary on the Vatican Declaration," Leonard Swidler and Arlene Swidler, eds., *Women Priests. A Catholic Commentary on the Vatican Declaration*, (New York: Paulist Press, 1977), 114-122; Gerhard Lohfink, 'Weibliche Diakone in Neuen Testament' in *Die Frau im Urchristentum*, Josef Blank, Gerhard Dautzenberg, et al., (Freiburg im Breisgau: Herder, 1983), 320-338; Gertrud. Heinzelmann, *Die geheiligte Diskriminierung: Beiträge zum kirchlichen Feminismus*, (Bonstetten: Interfeminas, 1986), esp 194-200; *Einbeziehung der Frauen in das Apostolichen Amt. Entscheidung der Synode der Alt-Katholischen Kirche Deutschlands und ihre Begründung*, (no year) 11 ff; Ruth Albrecht, "Apostelin/Jüngerin" in *Wörterbuch der feministischen Theologie,* Elisabeth Gössmann, ed., (Gütersloh: Gütersloher Verlagshaus G. Mohn, 1991) 24-28; Ida Raming, 'Priestertum der Frau,' *ibid.* 328-330. The question of whether the choice of the Twelve was made by the historical Jesus or whether the group was a post-Resurrection institution, back-projected by the evangelists into Jesus' post-Resurrection life has elicited varying responses from exegetes; cf. the pro and contra arguments in the survey by Joachim Gnilka, *Das Evangelium nach Markus*, (Zürich [etc.]: Benziger, 1978), 141-143. Gnilka states on these dissenting views: "The arguments on this matter which are unlikely ever to reach agreement, have long been exchanged . . . The most satisfactory assumption is still that Jesus assembled the Twelve."

2. Gnilka, 143.

3. Rahner, 'Priestertum de Frau?' 299.

4. Although the affiliation to the Jewish people still had a religious meaning in the thought of Jesus, (e.g., See John 4:22; Mark 7:27 [par]), the early church soon disposed of this principle in the transmission of offices.

5. *Mulieris Dignitatem*, Apostolic Letter of August 15, 1988, n. 26. *Acta Apostolica Sedis* 80 (1988), 1653-1729. English translation *On the Dignity and Vocation of Women* (*Mulieris Dignitatem*), (Washington, D.C.: United States Catholic Conference, 1988).

6. Lohfink, 330.

7. On this, see Lohfink (with reference to B. Brooten), 327ff.

8. Thus Rahner, 295.

9. Lohfink 321f.

10. A. Ebneter, "Keine Frauen im Priesteramt," *Orientierung* 41 (1977): 25f. See also John R. Donahue, "A Tale of two Documents," in Swidler, *Women Priests*, 25-34, here 25.

11. Ebneter, 26.

12. Thus, e.g., Cardinal A. Sterzinsky (in an interview with the *Berliner Morgen Post*) *Münstersche Zeitung*, November 8, 1991; similarly Bishop R Lettmann, *Münstersche Zeitung*, November 16/17, 1991.

13. On this, see the literature in n. 1, also: Ida Raming, *The Exclusion of Women from the Priesthood: Divine Law or Sex Discrimination*, [edited above]; *ibid., Frauenbewegung und Kirche. Bilanz eines 25 jährigen Kampfes für Gleichberechtigung und Befreiung der Frau seit dem 2. Vatikanischen Konzil*, 2nd ed., (Weinheim: Dt. Studien Verlag, 1991).

14. For a critical study of this tradition, see Peter Hünermann, "Lehramtliche Dokumente zur Frauenordination. Analyse und Gewichtung," *Theologische Quartalschrift* 173 (1993): 204-218.

15. Cf. Giorgio Otranto: "Note sul sacerdozio femminile nell' Antichitá in margine a una testimonianza di Gelasio I" *Vetera Christianorum* 19 (1982) 341-360. A complete translation of Otranto's study into English by Mary Ann Rossi was published in the article "Priesthood, Precedent and Prejudice: On recovering the women Priests of Early Christianity, containing a translation from the Italian of 'Notes on the Female Priesthood in antiquity' by Giorgio Otranto," *Journal of Feminist Studies in Religion*, 7 (1991): 73-94 (in the opinion of the translator: "Otranto provides ample grounds for reconsidering the role of women in the priesthood of early Christianity. . . ." *ibid.*, 78).

16. See also Ute E. Eisen, *Amtsträgerinnen im frühen Christentum. Epigraphische und literarische Studien*, (Göttingen: Vandenhoeck & Ruprecht, 1996); English translation: *Women Officeholders in Early Christianity. Epigraphical and Literary Studies*, (Collegeville, MN: The Liturgical Press, 2000).

17. See Raming, *The Exclusion of Women from the Priesthood*, p. 95 above.

18. See also Ida Raming, Gertrud Jansen et. al., eds. *Zur Priesterin berufen. Gott sieht nicht auf das Geschlecht. Zeugnisse römisch-katholischer Frauen*, (Thaur: Druck-und Verlagshaus Thaur, 1998). In other countries there are similar publications with the testimonies of women who feel called to priestly ministry.

19. Cf. Gertrude Heinzelmann, *Die getrennten Schwestern. Frauen nach dem Konzil*, (Zürich: Interfeminas-Verlag, 1967), 66; A Jensen, "Diakonin," in: *Wörterbuch der feministichen Theologie*, 58-60 (further literature therein). Ida Raming, *Frauenbewegung und Kirche*, 37-61.

20. *Inter insigniores*, 5. The declaration of the Congregation for the Doctrine of the Faith on the admission of women to the priesthood, *Inter Insignores* is in *Acta Apostolica Sedis*, 69 (1977): 98-116. The English translation of *Inter Insignores* appeared in *Origins*, 6 (1977): 517-524 with commentary on pp. 524-531. The commentary has also been included as an appendix in Swidler, *Women Priests*, 319-337.

21. *Ibid.*

22. For a critical response to the metaphor of Bridegroom-Bride, see the dogmatic section of my dissertation, pp. 197-227 of the English edition above. Also John Wijngaards, *The Ordination of Women in the Catholic Church. Unmasking a Cuckoo's Egg Tradition*, (London: Mowbray, 2001).

23. Cf. Wolfgang Beinert, "Dogmatische Überlegungen zum Thema Priestertum der Frau," in *Frauenordination. Stand der Diskussion in der katholischen Kirche.* Walter Groß, ed., (München: E. Wewel Verlag, 1996), 64-82, here 74ff.

24. Beinert, "Dogmatische Überlegungen," 75.

25. *Inter insigniores*, 5. See also the official commentary on *Inter insigniores*: "Saying 'in the name and place of Christ' is not however enough to express completely the nature of the bond between the minister and Christ as understood by tradition. The formula *in persona Christi* in fact suggests a meaning that brings it closer to the Greek expression *mimema Christou*. The word *persona* means a part played in the ancient theatre, a part identified by a particular mask. The priest takes the part of Christ, lending him his voice and gestures." Swidler, *Women Priests*, 330. On the other hand, John Wijngaards (*The Ordination of Women*, 107-112), based on an analysis of the eucharistic words of institution, rightly emphasizes that the priest in the course of this prayer of Christ always speaks in the third person (". . . clearly as someone other than himself, even in the pronounciation of the words of consecration" [*ibid.*, 109]).

26. Address to the German bishops of November 15, 1991 in *L'Osservatore Romano*, November 21, 1991. English edition of *L'Osservatore Romano*, 47 (November 24, 1999): 5, 6.

27. Evidence of this attitude can be found in Raming, *Frauenbewegung*, 72 with n. 126 and 104 with n. 49.

28. See also Judith Stofer, "Die Mauer des Schweigens niederreißen. Der Vatikan und sein Widerstand gegen die Frauenordination: Mit Macht protestierten hunderte von Frauen und Männern in Dublin," *Publik-Forum,* 13 (2001): 32f..

29. See "Unterwegs in die Weite. Interview mit den drei Bischöfinnen: Maria Jepsen, Margot Käßmann und Bärbel Wartenberg-Potter," *Publik-Forum*, 11 (2001): 24-27, 26.

Appendix 2

A Definitive "No" to the Ordination of Women?

On Pope John Paul II's Apostolic Letter *Ordinatio Sacerdotalis*

Originally published in *Orientierung* 58 (1994): 190-193, translated for www.womenpriests.org by Mary Dittrich and republished on the website with permission of the author and the editor of *Orientierung*. [The addition and revision introduced into the original article by Ida Raming has been translated by Gary Macy.]

The Apostolic Letter *Ordinatio Sacerdotalis* dated 22 May 1994.[1] was intended by Pope John Paul II to deliver a binding magisterial decision against the admission of women to priestly ordination, which "is to be definitively held by all the Church's faithful" (n. 4). The Pope firmly opposes the view that the exclusion of women from priestly ordination has merely "a disciplinary force," and that this praxis may continue to be the subject of theological discussion. With this decree he counters the increasing querying of the magisterium's pronouncements on this subject, particularly since the introduction of female ordination in England's Anglican Church, so that "all doubt may be removed regarding a matter of great importance, a matter which pertains to the Church's divine constitution itself" (n. 4).

But can that be done quite so simply by Papal decree?

It is clear from the many and diverse critical reactions to the Papal pronouncement that the decision of the Papal teaching authority necessarily reaches its limit and remains ineffective insofar as it is based on theological ideas and thought processes which in no way can stand up to scientific theological examination. "Well-founded arguments running counter to the stance of the magisterium regarding the priestly ordination of women cannot be dismissed by applying authority"[2]—no matter how weighty. Nor will the semi-official commentaries[3] on the Apostolic letter published in the *L'Osservatore Romano* which easily exceed it in sharpness and relentlessness, be able to reverse the level of theological findings since then achieved.

Even More Binding?

The wording of intention of the semi-official presentational document are remarkable in that here, even more strongly than in the Apostolic letter itself, its compulsory nature is stressed. "No one, therefore, not even the Supreme Authority in the Church, can fail to accept this teaching" (on the reservation of priestly ordination to men only) "without contradicting the will and example of Christ himself, and the economy of salvation . . ." It is conceded that the Apostolic letter "is . . . not a new dogmatic formulation" but nevertheless the papal decision is viewed as quasi-dogmatic, for it is described as a "certainly true" doctrine,[4] withdrawn from free theological discussion and calling for "the full and unconditional assent of the "faithful." So as to make this ruling look like a divine command the author of the Commentaries does not hesitate to resort to intimidation by conscience, in that he stresses that "to teach the contrary" (to the Papal teaching) "is equivalent to leading consciences (of the faithful) into error," because the Papal declaration is

o the word of God and of obedience to the Lord on

Critical Comments on the Argumentation

Such truly inflationary use of metaphysically loaded terms (e.g., "Eternal Plan of God," "divine constitution of the Church," "course of Revelation," "Truth") characterizing the Apostolic Letter, but even more so the commentary, leads to the question of what this apparently "definitively binding" doctrine is based on.[5]

It is solely the fact (reported in the New Testament) that Jesus called only men into the group of the "Twelve," and that this practice of appointing only men as holders of office was retained by the Apostles when choosing their associates and successors in office (n. 2). So the Pope maintains that "also included in this choice were those who, throughout the time of the Church, would carry on the Apostles' mission of representing Christ the Lord and Redeemer." (n. 2) The doctrine on reserving priestly ordination to men "has been preserved by the constant and universal Tradition of the Church and firmly taught by the Magisterium in its more recent documents" (n. 4).

Summing up this explanation, the Pope draws the following conclusion: "that the Church has no authority whatsoever to confer priestly ordination on women" (n. 4).

A serious exegetical error in the Apostolic Letter already occurs in the interpretation of the Biblical facts quoted, especially the procedure of Jesus choosing the Twelve. Here a historical fact becomes the "perennial norm" (n. 2), and is even declared an essential part of the "Church's divine constitution itself" (n. 4); this is supported by the assertion that the appointment of the twelve men "was made in accordance with God's eternal plan: Christ chose those whom he willed, and he did so in union with the Father, 'through the Holy Spirit' (1:2), after having spent the night in prayer" (n. 2).

The various biblical passages quoted and the fact that the twelve men were chosen, by no means permit the conclusion that Jesus expressly wished to exclude women on account of their sex from the group of twelve and from the offices which would develop in the early Christian Church, and which were not instituted at all by him (!). For in the Gospels there is not one word uttered by Jesus which would justify in the very least such an intention! But this specific act of the will gets quite simply assumed as being within Jesus' procedure, or projected onto it.[6]

Against this, Jesus procedure should be viewed against the background of the social culture of those times. In necessary agreement with the social structure of the Israel of antiquity, which was definitely patriarchal (for instance women were excluded from public teaching in the synagogues and from acting as witnesses in court). Jesus chose twelve men as symbolic representatives of the twelve tribes of Israel, these being represented, again, in the Hebrew Bible only by founders of races (the sons of Jacob), so as to express symbolically that the whole of Israel was addressed by his message and called to conversion. The New Testament tells us that the "Twelve" were sent forth by Jesus to proclaim the Good News of the Kingdom of God. Jesus himself and the Twelve preached in Israel's villages and towns, including the local synagogues. (Mk. 1:39; 6,1f; 6:6b-13, par.; Acts 13:5b and similar texts). How could women assume or carry out such tasks in those days, when they were not even entitled to speak in the Synagogue?

They Could Not Bear Public, Official Witness

Against the background of the strictly patriarchal structure of Jesus' times, the only plausible interpretation thus seems to be that the attitude of Jesus and his associates in this regard can be sufficiently explained by "the cultural and social milieu of the period in which they acted, and had to act the way they did, without their behavior having normative meaning for all time."[7]

Jesus could not simply do away with the patriarchal, sociologically-grown structures of his time. To expect that of him would amount to not taking really seriously the incarnation of God in Jesus. These preconditions and circumstances are ignored when the Pope declares, in support of his thesis, that "when Christ appointed only men as his apostles he did that quite freely and independently. He did it with the same freedom with which in his whole behavior he stressed the dignity and mission of woman, without adhering to the customs prevailing and to the tradition sanctioned by the laws of that time."[8]

Such a statement lacks the requisite differentiation. For Jesus dealings with individual women whom he meets, or who are among his disciples, are not on the same plane as the appointment of the Twelve, which should be understood as a symbolic act. In other words, Jesus did certainly infringe when dealing with women, the taboos and prejudices of these times (cf. John 4:27; Mk. 5:24b-34b and similar texts); but he was unable to break through or conquer sociological and legally set contemporary structures (e.g., the exclusion of women from public speaking in the Synagogues and from bearing witness in court). In the same way he encountered and knew slavery as a sociological institution of these times, but neither scorned it nor fought it, although for its victims slavery meant sinking into being a material possession of the owner.

Disregard of Recognized Rules of Interpretation

So in its use of the Bible the Apostolic letter thus diverges in several ways from the standards and rules laid down in the Instruction of Papal Biblical Commission on the "interpretation of the Bible in Church," published in 1993.[9] No attention whatsoever is paid to the historical-critical method said therein to be dispensable. Indeed, the Apostolic letter clings to the fundamentalist approach, although this is expressly rejected by the Biblical Commission. Again, the Pope supports his decision with arguments '*e silento*' which "can never suffice as a firm basis for a finding."[10] Further weaknesses in the argumentation of the papal letter, which can only be mentioned here, are in the erroneous depiction of the development of ecclesial offices and of ecclesial tradition.[11]

Contrary to the assumption in the Apostolic Letter that there was one straight line descended from the Twelve, who are not the same as the group of Apostles which is broader and which evidently included women (cf. Rm. 16;7:Junia)—none of the later offices (bishopric, presbyterate and diaconate) was founded by Jesus. For "the shaping and structuring of offices—was left to the developing Church."[12] Over and above that, the reference to the apparently "constant and comprehensive tradition of the Church" (n. 4) regarding the "doctrine on the restriction of priestly ordination to men" (n. 4) by no means stands up to critical examination. This undifferentiated line of argument wholly suppresses both the fact that in the early Christian missionary movement women acted as official co-workers, and also strands of tradition in later times running counter to the Church's usual patriarchal praxis. First and foremost, though it disregards the fact that the apparently constant tradition of excluding women from priestly office rests on a highly impaired valuation of women. That can already be found in the later New Testament books (cf specially 1 Tim. 2:11-15); it got worse as the centuries passed and reached its sad culmination in the "Hammer of Witches." The so-called witnesses from tradition[13] which include certain biblical passages and texts based on them, both patristic and in medieval theology, are permeated by the preeminence of men by nature, often ethically too.

However, though the misogynist nature of this tradition has now come to light, especially since Vatican II, the Church leaders are still clinging to it with the negative concept of women, however much they try to obfuscate the way in which it is presented. Divergent opinions run up against repressive measures.[14]

Unconquered Misogyny

From all this it follows that none of the reasons adduced in the Apostolic Letter for excluding women from priestly ordination holds water. Basing on such arguments a definitive decision having the force of law, which excludes half the membership of the Church from priestly ordination and office on account of gender (cf c. 1024 *CIC*/83) is, frankly monstruous and a grave injustice. It clearly shows to what extent women are at the mercy of arbitrary patriarchal stances in the Roman Catholic Church.

The theological reasoning in the Apostolic Letter and other instruction of recent date, to which the Pope expressly refers (including *Inter Insigniores, Mulieris dignitatem*, *Catechism of the Catholic Church*, n. 1577) is in fact based on an unconquered misogyny. It is expressed by disappointing women and by allocating to them a dependent, subordinate role in the Church.

Critical observers (in the U.S.A.), both male and female, see linkage, both in time and in content, between the Apostolic Letter *Ordinatio Sacerdotalis* and Vatican politics in the forefield of the International Conference in Cairo on Population and Development (ICPD). The decisive rejection of artificial birth control by the Vatican is at the same time an attack on women's right of self-determination in sexual matters, and opposition to the growing importance of women and their requirements at this conference.[15] In both cases the intention is to maintain the patriarchal gender pattern.

In fact according to prescribed phraseology of the Vatican, this antiquated, unjust assignment of roles based on sex disguises the exclusion of women from the priesthood with the harmless labels "diversity" and "complementarity" of the sexes,[16] or it gets built up into mystical-religious categories such as "symbolic transparence of the corporeal" linked to the "mystery of the incarnation" (in context, that can only mean a link with the masculinity of Christ), or "a binding to the will of the Creator, and binding within the Church to the will of the Redeemer." And so it is pronounced indispensable.[17]

On the other hand, the call for equality for women in the priesthood on account of their human dignity gets discredited as an exteriorised, purely functional understanding of priestly office as "decision-making power," and as an ominous route to the purely "functional equivalence of sexes" and to the "abstract, sexless human being." And so it gets rejected.[18]

Of course, in this way the fundamental "data" that demand equality of the sexes and thus equal access to ecclesial office are entirely left out of consideration. These are the personal dignity of woman, her baptism and confirmation, her mystical bond with Christ as a member of the Church, the right to free choice of status (guaranteed in *CIC* c.219)[19] and, not least, the promise in Gal. 3:28 that "in Christ there are no more distinctions between male and female," which definitively revokes the unchristian preeminence of men, which is why, typically, it is not mentioned anywhere in the Apostolic Letter and the commentaries on it.

The Need to Turn Away from the Sin of Sexism

For the tradition of the church is therefore nothing less than an imperative renunciation of the antiquated assignment of gender roles and with it of the sin of the patriarchy if the leadership of the Church is not to petrify in the guise of "the old Adam" (Eph. 4:22) and block the dawning of the Kingdom of God in the Church. In positive terms that means turning to what according to Eph. 4:22 is meant by the Kingdom of God: "Put on the new self that has been created in God's way, in the goodness and holiness of the truth" and according to Gal. 3:27: "All baptised in Christ, you have all clothed yourselves in Christ, and there are no more distinctions between Jew and Greek, slave and free, male and female, but all of you are one in Christ Jesus."

Abolishment of all domination by some humans over others, by men over women, will finally light up fully the image of God and Christ in both sexes, so that the Easter message of liberation and renewal in Christ will at last apply to women too, who will no longer be cheated out of it.

This Papal pronouncement should spur (Catholic) women into firm and courageous opposition to any disadvantage based on their sex. They should insist upon the unrestricted recognition within the Church of their person and of their image in God, and also of their religious vocation, including one to the priesthood. For in the words of John Paul II "women themselves have the duty to demand respect for their nature as persons, not descending to any form of complicity with what demeans their dignity."[20] The struggle for full recognition of their personal dignity must be undertaken by the women themselves. But feeling and establishing what conflicts with their dignity must be left, even by the Pope, to women themselves. Not as in his last Apostolic Letter when he wanted to do their thinking for them and tell them what to do. Then the point of the pope concerning Mary's singular calling as "mother God and mother of the church," who however nevertheless "received neither the mission proper to the Apostles," is not useful as proof that "the non-admission of women to priestly ordination cannot mean that women are of lesser dignity, nor can it be construed as discrimination against them," and denies how Mary was under the identical patriarchal laws as were the other women of her people (n. 3). For the rest, Mary's religious calling and meaning as mother of Jesus Christ, insofar she is not misinterpreted and deformed by an anthrocentrically stamped Mariology, by no means speaks against the priesthhod of a woman—in the present![21]

Through the Apostolic writing *Ordinatio Sacerdotalis* women are definitely denigrated—their dignity and rights as members of the church are disregarded in a major way. This signifies a challenge for all Catholic women. For the sake of their dignity they are called to fight for their liberation. The movement for the entire liberation of women in the Catholic Church has in fact to be mainly conducted by themselves. But it needs the firm solidarity of right-thinking men if it is to succeed and help the Church to a fundamental renewal.

Notes

1. *Acta Apostolica Sedis*, 86 (1994): 546-549 with commentary in the English edition of *Osservatore Romano,* 22/1343 (1994): 1-2 and in *Origins*, 24 (1994): 49-52 with commentary on pp. 52-3 and comments by U.S. bishops on pp. 53-58. The declaration of the Congregation for the Doctrine of the Faith on the admission of women to the priesthood, *Inter Insignores* is in *Acta Apostolica Sedis*, 69 (1977): 98-116. The English translation of *Inter Insignores* appeared in *Origins*, 6 (1977): 517-524 with commentary on 524-531.

2. Ulrich Ruh, "Lehramt in Abseits?" *Herder Korrespondenz* 48, (1994): 325ff, here 327; Peter Hünermann, "Schwewiegende Bedenken. Eine Analyse des Apostolischen Schreibens *Ordinatio Sacerdotalis*," *Herder Korrespondenz* 48 (1994): 406-410.

3. Cf. *Herder Korrespondenz,* 48, (1994): 356ff and also n. 1 above.

4. This wording leads one to suspect that it is a circumlocution of the term "infallible," which is avoided in the Apostolic Letter. Cf. Archbishop R. Weakland "I note that the Holy Father has avoided the word 'infallible.'" *Origins* 24 (1994): 55f. The clarification of the degree of consent in the comments already heralds, in my opinion, the shortly thereafter published *Responsum ad dubium* (October 28, 1995) of the Congregation for the Doctrine of the Faith in which it is declared, that the teaching contained in *Ordinatio Sacerdotalis* belongs to the deposit of faith, has been declared by the church's "infallible" magesterium and demands therefore "full definitive assent"; furthermore the Congregation points this out in advance of the Apostolic letter *Ad tuendam fidem* (May 18, 1998); for a fuller discussion, see Introduction, above p. xix-xxx. English edition in *Origens*, 28/8 (1998): 113, 115-16; commentary by Cardinal Ratzinger, 116-119.

5. In the following observations my sources include: Karl Rahner "Priestertum, der Frau?" *Stimmen der Zeit* 102 (1977): 291-301; Ruth Albrecht, entry on "Apostelin/Jüngenin," *Wörterbuch der feministischen Theologie*, Elisabeth Gössmann, ed., (Gütersloh: Gütersloher Verlagshaus G. Mohn, 1991), 24-28; Ida Raming, "Die zwölf Apostel waren Männer . . . ," Orientierung, 56 (1992): 143-146 (translated above); the relevant articles in *Theologisch Quartalschrift* 173 (1993) on the subject of ordination for women. Cf. also the opinion of the Biblical Commission dated June/July 1976, in which a 12 to 5 majority vote recorded that on the basis of New Testament writings, the ordination of women is not excluded. The text of this finding is in *Women Priests. A Catholic Commentary on the Vatican Declaration*, Leonard Swidler and Arlene Swidler, eds., (New York: Paulist Press, 1977), 338-346.

6. According to the commentary on the Apostolic Letter (cf. n. 1), "not only words but also deeds (of Jesus) are sources of Revelation and become words in the living memory of the Church." One notices, however, that only such "deeds" as sustain the patriarchy in the Church are declared to be "sources of Revelation" and norms, Jesus' healing methods (e.g., Jn. 9:6) are not assessed in this way.

7. Rahner, 299.

8. *Acta Apostolicae Sedis* no. 80 (1988). The text is repeated verbatim in the Apostolic Letter *Ordinatio Sacredotalis*, n. 2.

9. Cf. Herbert Haag, "Bilanz eines Jahrhunderts. Ein Lehrschreiben der päpstlichen Bibelkommission" *Orientierung*, 58 (1994): 129-132; Ruh, 327.

10. Haag, 131.

11. Further comments on this in Raming, "The Twelve Apostles," above p. 241ff.

12. Gerhard Lohfink, "Weibliche Diatone in Neuen Testament" *Die Frau im Urchristentum*, Josef Blank, Gerhard Dautzenberg and others, (Freiburg im Breisgau: Herder, 1983), 320-338, esp 322.

13. A critical examination of the tradition is found inter alia in Peter Hünerman, "Lehramtliche Dokumente zur Frauenordination, Analyse und Gewichtung" *Theologische Quartalschrift*, 173 (1993): 204-218; Ida Raming,

Der Ausschluss der Frau vom priesterhchen Amt—gottgewollte Tradition oder Diskriminierung? (Cologne-Vienna: Böhlau Verlag, 1973).

14. More on this in Ida Raming, *Frauenbewegung und Kirche. Bilanz eines 25 jährigen Kampfes für Gleichberechtigung und Befreiung der Frau seit dem 2. Vatikanischen Konzil*, 2nd ed., (Weinheim: Dt. Studien Verlag), 1991, esp. 40-61.

15. See article by D. von Drehle. "Population Summit has Pope worried. Vatican fears Advocacy of Reproductive Rights" *The Washington Post*, 16 (June 1994).

16. Apart from many quotations in Vatican pronouncements recently, see again John Paul II's address on the dignity and mission of the Christian woman in *L'Osservatore Romano* 24 (1994): 1ff. [English edition of *L'Osservatore Romano*, 26/1347 (1994): 11.]

17. Thus remarkably often in the explanatory article on the Apostolic Letter *Ordinatio Sacerdotalis* by J. Ratzinger: "Die Kirche kann nicht machen, was sie will," *Rheinischer Merkur*, 22, vol. 3 (June 1994): 27 and 30; now too, amplified by a body of comment in *Internationale Katholische Zeitschrift* 23 (1994): 337-345.

18. Ratzinger, 27 and 30.

19. Cf. Ida Raming: "Ungenutzte Chancen für Frauen im Kirchenrecht. Widersprüche im *CIC*/1983 und ihre Konsequenzen," *Orientierung* 58 (1994): 68ff.

20. Address on the dignity and mission of the Christian woman, *L'Osservatore Romano,* 24 (1994): 17 [English edition of *L'Osservatore Romano*, 26/1347: 11].

21. See also Wolfgang Beinert, "Dogmatische Überlegungen zum Thema Priestertum der Frau," in *Frauenordination. Stand der Diskussion in der katholischen Kirche*, Walter Groß, ed., (München: E. Wewel Verlag, 1996), 64-82, esp. 76f (Where "the theologians and mystics . . . have reflected on the mother of Christ and her role in salvation history, the idea of the priesthood of Mary has immediately suggested itself . . . "); also John Wijngaards, *The Ordination of Women in the Catholic Church*, (London: Mowbray, 2001), 156-163.

Appendix 3

Women Reject Discrimination and Disenfranchisement in the Church

The Formation and Development of the Women's Ordination Movement in the Roman Catholic Church in Europe.

Published originally in *Orientierung* 65 (2001): 75-79, 86-91, revised version of earlier article in French published in *Feminist Perspectives on History and Religion; Feministische Zugänge zu Geschichte und Religion; Approches féministes de l'histoire et de la religion*, Angela Berlis and Charlotte Methuen, eds., (Peeters, Louvain, 2000), 225-240. Translated by Bernard Cooke).

As a most important experience of Church politics the Second Vatican Council exercises an authoritative influence on theological discussion within the Roman Catholic Church and beyond—and that still after almost forty years since its inception. Numerous theological discussions deal with the interpretation and reception of the conciliar decrees, scholarly publications document and analyze the overall conduct of the Council from the view of underlying sources.[1] This process is by no means closed. Clearly influenced by the reactionary political climate of the Church at that time, reflection focused specially on the ecclesiology of the Council. Introduced by the Constitution on the Church, *Lumen gentium*, the biblically grounded view of the Church as "people of God"—prior to all the distinctions in diverse functions, offices and roles—can rightly be judged to have a programmatic, future oriented character.[2] Only seldom is attention drawn to women who are half of "the people of God," only very late with deliberate voice (in the background), but in no case with decision-making power, were women able to influence the Council's proceedings. Until the third session of the Council (September 1964) women were completely absent,[3] and even then only a small group were admitted as simply auditors without any right to vote. Even less noticed in this context was the initiative begun by European women, before and during the Council, to clearly identify this severe discrimination on the basis of (female) gender and to confront the purely male ecclesial assembly with the demand for an appropriately contemporary role for and appreciation of women in the Church, i.e., for their admission to diaconate and priesthood.

The pioneering effort of women in the context of the Second Vatican Council should therefore be highlighted in the following, so that recollection of what occurred in the ecclesiastical milieu of that time may guard us against historical writing about the Council being done only from a male perspective.

What is valid for the Churches of other Christian denominations which already recognize women's ordination and women's equality is also valid for the Roman Catholic Church. It is, first of all, not men in the Church who prepared for and opened up the advance of women to ecclesial offices—in many cases they hindered it—but women themselves began it. They questioned their oppressed position in the Church and demanded as Christians the full membership which belonged to them as believers, and baptized and strove for their religious vocation to unrestricted access to service and office in the Church.[4]

Which women stood at the beginning of the women's ordination movement in the Roman Catholic Church? What reaction did they encounter from men and women? Were they able in the course of the Council's session and thereafter to "move something," some positive resonance, or even achieve progress? To answer these obvious questions the following remarks come from the viewpoint of one who has been an engaged witness.

Given these limits, the whole development during and after the Council will not be recalled in detail, but it will deal with some distinctive processes. The presentation concentrates primarily on happenings in Europe, especially in Switzerland and Germany, since the first impetus for women's ordination was fostered by women in these countries and only then took hold and strengthened in other countries (especially in the U.S.A.).[5]

The Image of Woman before the Council

Officially and publicly formulated for the first time at the beginning of the 1960s by Roman Catholic women,[6] the question of their ordination was characterized by an image of woman determined by the idea of her subordinate role, of her servitude and her inferiority. The results of the oppression of millions of Christian women were still omnipresent, in particular in the Catholic world that was marked by these traditions. The demand for subordination of women to men in marriage, family and society was substantiated in official church statements with corresponding biblical support based on the ancient "household laws" (see, e.g., Col. 3:18-41; Eph. 5:22-6:9) and propagated as the divine order: "God himself has placed woman under this authority in the order of nature and of grace."[7] Even if, after the Second World War, official ecclesial documents avoided repeatedly demanding the submission of the woman to the man in marriage, the family, and society, the description of women's nature and duties—in contrast to men's—was still visibly influenced by the idea of men's domination over women. So, Pius XII declared in 1956 that there exists between the sexes "an absolute equality at the level of fundamental personal values," but that there are "different functions" and therefore also "different right and needs." By virtue of Gen 1:28 woman would not be excluded from any sphere of human activity, but this is true "always in a fashion subordinate to the functions that are dictated by nature to be primary."[8] The primary functions are motherhood and care of the family. Consequently the fundamental feminine characteristics would be spouse and mother—in the religious realm, vowed religious and virgin. A modern woman exercising a profession in secular society and whose range of activity is constantly broadening, such does not fit into the view of

Catholic officials. Rather, they consider this "degenerate," not in conformity with women's vocation.

First Conciliar Petition for Women's Ordination

It was in this climate, prevalent in a large part of the Roman Catholic world, that a first claim for the ordination of women was officially formulated. During the preparation for Vatican II (1962-1965) the Swiss jurist Gertrud Heinzelmann (deceased in September 1999) sent a detailed petition to the preparatory commission (May 1962). "The first and only conciliar petition sent during the preliminary phase, it confronted the Church with the intolerable situation of women dictated by tradition, and demanded equality at every level of ecclesial life."[9] In accordance with the intention of John XXIII, who called the Council, the Council should strive vigorously for dialogue with the modern world and endeavor for an *aggiornamento*. Heinzelmann's petition pursued this intention: "The Church should have pursued the confrontation it desired, not only with the Englightenment but also engaged the Women's Movement in its cultural, legal and social context."[10]

At the beginning of the 1960s the theme "women and Church" did not yet exist. This was manifest in the discussion in "Soundings about the Council" in the magazine *Wort and Wahrheit* (Herder 1961). Among the eighty-one persons interviewed there were only five women. Of these, one did not wish to deal with the women's question, others did not even mention it. Only one, Erika Weinzierl-Fischer (Vienna), called for a revision of the system of scholastic thought maintaining that "the status of women in the Church today is still determined by the depreciating view of woman that is rooted in Thomas Aquinas' *Summa theologica*."[11] The claim of equality of the sexes in the Church was completely ignored. For Gertrud Heinzelmann this triggered her action. As a Catholic woman jurist fighting for many long years for women's rights in Switzerland, she knew only too well the influence of the Church's pernicious and antifeminist norms on the whole of society during research for her dissertation on the topic of Church-State legal relations.[12] She had been shocked by the misogynist statements of Church Fathers and teachers and she had assembled a large collection of texts of Thomas Aquinas with her critical commentary, to which she referred in the composition of her conciliar petition.

Her petition contained a critical confrontation with the ontic subordination of women in the view of Thomas Aquinas (influenced by Aristotelian presuppositions), a view that enjoyed special authority in the official Church. From positive Thomist statements about the spiritual nature of humans and about the sacraments in general, Gertrud Heinzelmann argued in principle to the possibility and implementation of women's ordination. Having done this, she hoped that "if the burden of medieval doctrine pertaining to the nature of women is formally rejected by the official Church, the path to the priesthood of women will be open —this on the basis of purified Thomist teaching, the philosophy of human nature properly understood."[13] Following the first publication of her text in the bulletin of the Frauenstimmrechtsverein of Zurich, *Die Staatsbuergerin* (July/August 1962) she was convinced "That she had taken an irreversible step. At least a future council would have to remember that already in the past, even prior to Vatican II, someone had reclaimed for women full equality and access to the ordained ministry."[14] Thanks to the journalistic support of Placidus Jordan, OSB, correspondent of the NC News Services of the National Conference of Bishops of the U.S.A. and council *peritus* for the American bishops, Heinzelmann's petition had a wide circulation, not only in the circles of the Council Fathers, particularly among the U.S. bishops, but also in many countries.[15]

The Debate Continues

As one might expect, the quick circulation of this petition aroused heated reactions.[16] The author was subjected to injurious attacks, to jokes and sarcasm—especially in some Swiss journals. On the other hand, positive reactions showed "that the views of a large number of persons concerned about the same problem were simultaneously moving in the same direction."[17] It was in this way that the first contacts originated with German women theologians. Beginning in 1959, one of them, Josefa Theresia Münch, had addressed to the Vatican several demands in writing (not published) regarding revision of canon law (canon 968 §1 *CIC*/1917) that excluded women from sacramental ordination.[18] At the beginning of the 1960s the students of the theological faculty of Münster—first Iris Müller, joined shortly by Ida Raming—questioned the motives for the exclusion of women from ordination and priestly ministry, reflection that provided the basis of their later conciliar petition (1963). Through several detours the text of Gertrud Heinzelmann fell into their hands. Consequently the three theologians met together in Münster in 1963. In the same year, Rosemary Lauer, professor of philosophy at St. John's University in New York, got information about this conciliar petition. She published several articles about "Women and the Church" in the well-known review *Commonweal* and provided an English translation of Gertrud Heinzelmann's text for the American press.[19]

These publications came to the attention of Mary Daly. At the time she was studying Catholic theology at the University of Fribourg, where she was the first American graduate (in 1964). At the time a doctorate in Catholic theology was not yet available to a woman studying in the U.S.A. Mary Daly contacted Gertrud Heinzelmann and in a letter to the editor of *Commonweal* (Feb. 14, 1964) acknowledged being ashamed for herself and for all women who "are aware of the semi-human status of women in the Church but have nevertheless remained silent." "Like a prophecy and a promise" she foresaw a flood of books about "women and the Church."[20]

Contacts among these six women resulted in a book in English and German, published in 1964 by Gertrud Heinzelmann, *We Won't Keep Silent Any Longer! Women Speak Out to Vatican Council II.* (*Wir schweigen nicht langer!*).[21] In addition to Gertrud Heinzelmann's text, it contained the conciliar petitions of Josefa Theresia Münch, Iris Müller and Ida Raming, along with articles of Rosemary Lauer and Mary Daly. It also contained resolutions of the St. Joan's International Alliance,[22] an international organization of Catholic women who during the Second Vatican Council held gatherings of delegates in 1963 and 1964 and had spoken out for admission of women to the diaconate and presbyterate, the participation of women in the commissions of the Council and for broader reforms, e.g., for abolishing Church laws that discriminated against women.

This volume presented for the first time a critical analysis of the various biblical and doctrinal justifications for the exclusion of women from priesthood; in conclusion it reclaimed the absolute equality of women in the ecclesiastical institutions of the Roman Catholic Church. Moreover, it insisted on a revision of liturgical texts that were deeply marked by masculine language. This publication notably stimulated public debate about the ordination and ministry of women. In Europe a number of commentaries dealt with it, as did articles in the press that pronounced for or against the claims expressed in the book.[23]

Pacem in Terris: Human Rights for Women

Already before publication of the book, the Pope of the Council, John XXII, had through his encyclical *Pacem in Terris* (1963) given the developing women's movement, still invisible within the Church, strong support. The central theme of this teaching document[24] is that the unconditioned recognition of the personal dignity of each human, which is grounded in the divine image of women and men, is the presupposition for an orderly human living together in truth, justice, peace and freedom. From the nature of humans, i.e., out of their human worth, are given inalienable rights and obligations, independent of sex, race, economic or social location. For the first time in a Papal teaching document was woman asserted to be the subject and bearer of human rights. John XXIII esteemed the women's movement as an observable "sign of the times"—women's movement is for the first in the history of the Papacy judged positively "Since women are becoming ever more conscious of their human dignity, they will not tolerate being treated as mere material instruments, but demand rights befitting a human person both in domestic and in public life." Clearly, this statement did not yet lead to a conclusion about the position of women in the Church. Subsequent declarations were not limited to women, even in the ecclesial domain, for human dignity is *one*, equal between both sexes and founded in the "equality in the one human, rational nature, that rules out the subordination of women due to her gender"[25]—their recognition cannot and may not be something restricted to the profane sphere: "Human beings have the right to choose freely the state of life which they prefer, and therefore the right to set up a family, with equal rights and duties for man and woman, and also the right to follow a vocation to the priesthood or the religious life." This principle takes as its basis that "every human being has the right to respect for his person." "For, if a man becomes conscious of his rights, he must become equally aware of his duties. Thus he who possesses certain rights has likewise the duty to claim those rights as marks of his dignity, while all others have the obligation to acknowledge those rights and respect them."

Did these words of John XXIII, together with the conciliar petitions that had been circulated through the journalistic efforts of Placidus Jordan, have some positive influence on the Council's proceedings relative to reforming the status of women?

Women in the Council

On October 11, 1962 the Council opened, and it was as a purely male gathering. Already at the first German-speaking press conference the theologian Josefa Theresia Münch posed the justified and provocative question whether women would be invited to the Council. "The reaction was embarrassment, indignation and laughter. Finally the director of the German press center, Bishop Kampe, responded half-pleasantly, half-jokingly 'Women also will be at Vatican III.'"[26] However, no male laity were present at the Council's beginning so that paradoxically during the first session of the Council the commission for the Council, which was responsible for the decree on the lay apostolate, worked totally without any lay input. For the first time, in the Council's second session, in September 1963, thirteen laymen were invited as auditors.[27] One of the Canadian bishops [Carter of Sault St. Marie] expressed—in looking back—his regret that laity were officially consulted "too little and too late." The Canadian bishops overall were prominent for their advocacy of declericalizing the decree on the laity.[28]

In order for women as completely neglected members of the Church to come to the Council's attention, a special initiative was required. It was the Belgian Cardinal Leo Suenens, who (in the second session, on October 22, 1963) as the first of the Council Fathers, in his notable speech on the charismatic dimension of the Church, took account of the total absence of women at the Council. He proposed that "the number and universality of lay faithful should be increased and that women also should be invited as auditors"—and with some irony remarked "Women . . . who, if I am not mistaken, make up half of humanity."[29] Although the intervention of the Belgian Cardinal was received by the Council very favorably and truly caused a sensation,[30] it did not initiate any real change, of course, a propos relations with women, half of the Church membership. That was clear from the mild response of Church leadership to the proposal. A few women indeed were, at the beginning of the third session (September 1964) by decree of Pope Paul VI, admitted as auditors.[31] By the end of the Council their number had increased to twenty-three (laywomen and women religious). Three of the auditors, among them Sister Luke Tobin, at that time president of the Conference of Women Religious in the U.S.A. and the Australian Rosemary Goldie, executive secretary of the standing committee of the International Congress for the Lay Apostolate (COPECIAL) were admitted to the Council's commissions that were working on the final draft of the documents on the lay apostolate and on

"The Church in the Modern World."[32] These auditors were given right to speak but no voting rights, even when the matter concerned them. These rules prevailed also for male auditors, though four of them held prepared speeches in the Council hall. This possibility was not granted to the women. In solidarity with their sisters, the auditors proposed that at least one of the interventions should be made by a laywoman. They found considerable support from several Cardinals. However, their efforts were fruitless; the proposal was rejected as "premature."[33] So the few lay auditors had very little influence during the last session of the Council on the drafting of the documents mentioned above. Their presence had merely "a symbolic significance."[34] For the laymen who had participated in the commissions, it was extremely difficult to make a real contribution to the drafting of the decrees, since the work schedule of the Council was already fixed. At best they were able to have some influence in gatherings of the Council Fathers or on one of the influential *peritus*.[35] Because of their inferior position in the Church, women were excluded from the process of the passage of the binding documents of the Council. In any event, proposals for reform of their position were only indirectly entertained.

References to "The Women's Question" in the Conciliar Documents

Despite this notable restriction, the few references of the Council to the theme of women in society and Church did not occur without the influence of the women auditors.[36] It resulted in the following basic passages that have a programmatic, demanding character.

In the pastoral constitution *Gaudium et spes* [n. 29] the fundamental equality of all humans and the resultant recognition of human rights was stressed: "Since all men possess a rational soul and are created in God's likeness, since they have the same nature and origin, have been redeemed by Christ and enjoy the same divine calling and destiny, the basic equality of all must receive increasingly greater recognition. True, all men are not alike from the point of view of varying physical power and the diversity of intellectual and moral resources. Nevertheless, with respect to the fundamental rights of the person, every type of discrimination, whether social or cultural, whether based on sex, race, colour, social condition, language or religion, is to be overcome and eradicated as contrary to God's intent. For in truth it must still be regretted that fundamental personal rights are still not being universally honoured. Such is the case of a woman who is denied the right to choose a husband freely, to embrace a state of life or to acquire an education or cultural benefits equal to those recognized for men." In similar fashion the constitution on the Church *Lumen gentium* [n. 32, 2] stresses the equality and unity of all members of "God's people," the Church. "Therefore, the chosen People of God is one: one Lord, one faith, one baptism;" sharing a common dignity as members from their regeneration in Christ, having the same filial grace and the same vocation to perfection; possessing in common one salvation, one hope and one undivided charity. There is, therefore, in Christ and in the Church no inequality on the basis of race or nationality, social condition or sex, because "there is neither Jew nor Greek: there is neither bond nor free: there is neither male nor female. For you are all 'one' in Christ Jesus." (Gal. 3:28; Col. 3:11)

The essential agreement of these passages with the earlier encyclical of John XXIII *Pacem in Terris* in relation to human rights as a norm and their application to women is unmistakable. As the biblical basis for human rights Gal. 3:28 (overcoming of division between men and women in Christ) is cited. However, although these programmatic clarifications do relate to and speculate about overcoming the difficult *inner-Church* discrimination against women, their exclusion from all ordained office on the grounds of female gender has meant that no reforms have resulted from them. Indeed not once was there any prospect of this. At most a reform of the place of women as laity came to the attention of the Council Fathers, though without any precision. "Since in our times women have an ever more active share in the whole life of society, it is very important that they participate more widely also in the various fields of the Church's apostolate." (Decree on the Apostolate of the Laity "*Apostolicam actuositatem*," n. 9).

From all this it is clear that the Second Vatican Council reached a "reconciliation" with the democratic, liberal principles of secular society, but at the same time excluded these principles from the "inner realm" of the Church. So, the statements of the Council supporting the civil rights of women, not the reform of their place in the Church,[37] since women as equal members of the Church—with expression of full recognition of their personal dignity as human and Christian and of their unrestricted equal rights in the Church—remained beyond the perspective of almost all the Council Fathers. This is clear—and to feminine sensibilities unbearably clear—from the language and metaphors of the Council documents. Often the language is about "sons of the Church" and "brothers" when the reference is to *all* the members of the Church—to "sons of God" (e.g.,

Lumen gentium, ns. 2, 3, 11, 14) . "The Christian man, conformed to the likeness of that Son Who is the firstborn of many brothers, received "the first-fruits of the Spirit" . . . Christ has risen, destroying death by His death; He has lavished life upon us so that, as sons in the Son, we can cry out in the Spirit: 'Abba, Father!'" (*Gaudium et spes*, n. 22). Challenge to this view of human salvation, envisaged "as the drama of a purely male world"[38] and confrontation with the concrete concerns of women, their sisters, occurred in only a few interventions of some bishops.[39] Specially notable was the written intervention of Archbishop Paul Hallinan (Atlanta, U.S.A.) which was presented in October 1965, during the fourth session: It proposed, not only that women should exercise the offices of lectors and acolytes at Mass but that the office of deacon should be opened to women; further that women should participate in the study of theology and in the revision of the Code of Canon Law.[40] Despite the considerable publicity, particularly influenced by Council *peritus* Placidus Jordan (who circulated the collected Council petitions of women among the American bishops), his effort which occurred just before the end of the Council, could no longer lead to success.[41] The intervention was not possible earlier, since the discussion about women's active participation in the Mass, especially their vocation to the diaconate or priesthood, first occurred in the course of the Council, not least because of a private petition to the Council which was published in the book *We won't keep silent any longer! Women speak out to the Second Vatican Council* that had worldwide influence.[42]

Reaction to *We Won't Keep Silent Any Longer!*

All this helped give prominence to the theme "Women and the Church." Several articles appeared in reaction to the book *We won't keep silent any longer!* that advanced this feminist initiative.[43] Conservative elements in the Vatican launched an attack against the efforts to open up the priesthood to women. Soon after the end of the Council, with explicit reference to *We won't keep silent*, of course without reference to bibiliographical notes, *L'Osservatore Romano* published a series of articles on the theme "Woman and the Priesthood."[44] The author was the traditionalist Franciscan Gino Concetti. From his introductory remarks it became already clear that the effort for the ordination of women was not only regarded at the Vatican with mistrust, but in a disparaging way was being judged as erroneous: "The climate of zealous efforts that emerged from and accompanied the Second Vatican Council had among numerous other initiatives let that one stand out which aimed to draw the attention of responsible hierarchy to the extension of the priestly office to women . . . Very shortly the theme was taken up in Protestant circles. Since 1948 there has existed research by a commission of experts of the World Council of Churches." In response, Concetti attacked a publication of the World Council of Churches "On the question of ordaining women" (1964) as worthless because of its groundless argumentation. Concetti continued "Similar efforts have come from a few circles of Catholic women who forwarded their votes and resolutions to the preparatory commission of the Vatican." Shortly thereafter, the same circle published a book in German and English entitled *We won't keep silent any longer!* "Some theologians had not neglected to ally themselves, more or less prudently, with the female chorus. Even some qualified theologians were among them—how when in this matter the Church had already since the earliest period of Christianity had given a final and unchangeable answer . . . ." There followed a sharp rejection to the priesthood of women that— without any critical analysis of current scholarship—relied on a gathering of texts from tradition which supported the subordination of women to men and according to Concetti finally went back to institution by Jesus Christ himself. His conclusion: "Christ could have chosen women if he had wished . . . and raised them to priestly dignity. He did not do this, not because he was respecting some human tradition of his culture, but because he honored the order of creation and the plan of salvation, both of which involved the superiority of man, of the old Adam and the new Christ."[45]

"Coming out of the heated discussion of the Council Fathers . . . the widely circulated viewpoint in the article of Concetti was presented as a quasi-authoritative statement," reported Monsignor George Higgins of the bishops' central office in the U.S.A. with the observation that "the *Osservatore Romano* does not have any binding doctrinal force. . . . Efforts for publishing a reply in *Osservatore* was on the way, but did not come through." An article in response was eventually written by a woman journalist and published in the German edition of *L'Osservatore* but completely mutilated, any reference to Gertrud Heinzelmann's book *We won't keep silent any longer!* or to the priesthood of women was omitted.[46]

However, it was not only male theologians who were opposed to the ordination of women; there were also women, like Ida Friederike Görres in her article "Über die Weihe von Frauen zu Priesterinnen."[47] It was a veritable diatribe against women, their ambitious nature eager for power, would be unsuited for sacerdotal ministry which belongs only to men, the sole adequate symbol of "the spouse," Jesus Christ, because they possessed the same sexual identity. It was with considerable pain that Josefa Theresia Münch published her response in the review *Der christliche Sonntag*.[48]

Based on the irreconcilable positions of the two authors, a lively discussion ensued.[49]

But traditionalist women were not the only ones to manifest their opposition; there were also women with theological formation, as e.g., Elizabeth Gössmann.[50] In her book *Das Bild der Frau heute*,[51] published in 1962, she had remarked "Sensible women, having an accurate understanding of their place in the people of God would never have the idea that they lack anything or that they face a barrier because they cannot receive the sacrament of Orders."[52] In a later essay, "Das Ringen der Frau um ihr Selbstverständis" (1964)[53] she nuanced this statement, referring to women engaged in spiritual guidance and catechetics, "who in their work alongside those possessing the sacerdotal function are constantly conscious of their sad exclusion." All told, she did not reach any conclusion favorable to the ordination of women. Later Gertrud Heinzelmann[54] will pass judgment on this behavior that was inconsequential in her eyes, but widespread in the 1960s. "While recognizing that the traditionalist arguments advanced against women's access to ecclesial functions are not insurmountable when dealing with history or exegesis, she prefers nevertheless to keep women in the ranks of the laity because 'for the first time in the Church's history this can expand fully.'" As for her "professional projects," "the claim to parity seemed most inopportune."[55]

The Debate after the Council

In the post-conciliar period the debate about "women and the Church" moved into university circles. Here, even more than elsewhere, an outstanding pioneering work was necessary that would prepare the ground for acceptance of a reform of women's position in the Church. The situation of Catholic theology in the University of Münster was thoroughly typical of the climate that prevailed in faculties of theology at the beginning of the 1960s: Teaching was exclusively the domain of men, all of them priests. In their courses they generally conveyed an image of women that was completely out of date, a figure in the background, inept in politics, in the natural sciences, and of course incapable of priesthood and preaching. Biblical texts where woman was only "the glory of man"

(1 Cor. 11:7) and should during the liturgical instruction remain completely silent (1 Tim. 2:12). Dogmatic treatises offered women marriage or consecrated virginity as life options. Men engaged in study enjoyed a liberty of choice incomparably greater. It was clear that the complete range of ecclesial functions was open to them equally.

From the beginning of the 1960s the degreed theologian Iris Müller, then a student, publicly contested the discriminatory practices regnant in graduate programs. As a convert theologian, coming from Protestantism, with the aim of becoming a woman pastor, she discerned, much more clearly than Catholics who were accustomed to adapting, to what extent the university climate in Roman Catholic circles was retrograde and sexist. Later she wrote "What I learned in courses concerning the role of women . . . appeared very shocking to me. So, I went to the professor of ecumenical theology. To my question about the reasons for blocking women from ordination he gave an answer that shook me profoundly. His argument was: Since a man cannot give birth, he had by way of compensation the privilege of being able to approach the altar, while a woman had the privilege of maternity."[56] Clearly, this kind of justification could not convince Iris Müller; it served only to reinforce her rebellion against the sexist structures of the Church with its religious pretensions. Her heartfelt critique, however, brought her serious personal cost. She was threatened, for example, with the loss of her stipend, upon which she urgently depended as a refugee from East Germany.[57] And in the context, she could not hope for any solidarity on the part of the other Catholic theological students.

As a friend and colleague of Iris Müller, I (Ida Raming) noticed the signs of her material and spiritual distress. I understood perfectly well her pain, a concrete result of the oppression of women in the Roman Catholic Church, since I had myself suffered from the lack of liberty in my life up to then, shaped as it had been by ecclesiastical norms. How often I had felt women's exclusion from priestly functions solely because of their female sex![58] Because of this sad personal experience of a woman in the Church, I felt myself called to devote my life to attempting to overcome these sexist ecclesiastical structures that focused principally on the exclusion of women from ordained ministry.

With this objective in mind, I succeeded even before the end of Vatican II in convincing the professor of canon law and the history of law, Peter-Joseph Kessler, to direct my thesis on the exclusion of women from the priesthood and its historical-dogmatic foundations. In the context of that period this was completely exceptional, because professors strived

—with rare exceptions—to prove their loyalty to the ecclesiastical teaching authority. To carry on my research I had available only a very few specialized works. There was only one typewritten thesis dealing with the priesthood of women that was critical and analytic: The work of Haye van der Meer, S. J., written under the direction of Karl Rahner. It was a study that Rahner did not wish to have published before the end of the Council to avoid reprisal from the ecclesiastical teaching authority.[59] Finally, this thesis appeared in 1969 with the title *Priestertum der Frau? Eine theologiegeschichtlieche Untersuchung.* (*Women priests in the Catholic Church? A theological-historical investigation*)[60] It dealt with an approach critical of exegetical, historical-dogmatic and doctrinal justifications for excluding women from priesthood that arrived at the conclusion that all the traditional arguments lacked foundation and could not justify any notion that it was by divine law. It is worth noting that van der Meer did not express a definite opinion regarding women's ordination to the priesthood. It was a question he left open. Moreover—a significant fact, he adopted an attitude that was ambiguous, even scornful of women who actually aspired to ordination.[61]

During the winter of 1969 and 1970 my thesis was accepted by the theological faculty of the University of Münster and published in 1973 under the title *Der Ausschluss der Frau vom priestlicher Amt—Gottegewollte Tradition oder Diskriminierung?*[62] (*The Exclusion of Women from Priestly Ministry—a Tradition Conforming to the Will of God or Discrimination?*) Publication encountered numerous difficulties because Catholic editors refused to publish it. Finally I was able to have it published by an editor without confessional ties, the Boehlau-Verlag (Cologne-Vienna).

Compared to the thesis of van der Meer, my study arrived at a more definite conclusion. On the basis of numerous sources from the early Church and the Middle Ages (notably the *Corpus Iuris Canonici*) I was able to demonstrate that the exclusion of women from priesthood rested on the idea of their ontological and ethical inferiority. The foundations of this idea were based on certain biblical texts—notably Gen. 2 and 3 dealing with the creation of woman from the "side" of the man and her so-called "original sin"—and their reception and interpretation by the Church Fathers and in Church regulations. In the dogmatic section of my dissertation, I took issue with the traditional understanding of priesthood in which the necessarily male character was declared a hindrance for women's ordination. I was able to demonstrate to the contrary that a conception of priesthood oriented to statements about community and ministry throughout the bible is open to active cowork by women.

In the years following the publication of this work and continuing even today, in response to these explicit results, the dissertation and its author have endured many attacks, largely from misogynist and conservative circles. There was also the attempt to suffocate the work by passing over it in silence. But these methods of repression were finally thwarted thanks to positive reactions that the thesis received abroad.[63]

The two theses, that of Haye van der Meer and mine, were translated and published in the U.S.A.[64]—an eloquent sign of the growing interest that this issue was arousing outside Europe. Parallel to these scientific efforts (and to the two mentioned texts) the 1960s and the beginning of the 1970s saw the appearance in Europe of several works moving in the same direction, e.g., those of Elizabeth Schüssler, Tina Govaart-Halkes, Sr., Vincent E. Hannon, Mary Daly and Placidus Jordan.[65] These books—a more popular style—touched the sensibilities of other levels of the Catholic population. Even members of traditional Catholic women's associations were led to question the conventional image of the role of women circulated by the Church.

Synods on the Place of Women within the Church

The growing sensitizing and the dissemination of information about the unfavorable situation of women in the Roman Catholic Church initiated by the publications mentioned as well as by other media (film, revues) did not fail to have impact on official ecclesiastical agencies. They finally found themselves constrained to deal with the issue of women at the heart of the Church. The post-conciliar phase of the discussion was shaped by various synods of Roman Catholic bishops as well as by some national synods (in Europe and elsewhere) in which the ordination of women played a role.

So, the majority of the participants in the pastoral council of the Netherlands in 1970 declared themselves in favor of women's ordination.[66] There had been extensive preparation for this by St. Willibroard Vereinigung. This organization of women and men had quickly taken up the petition for women's ordination (diaconate and presbyterate) at the Second Vatican Council and supported it through publications.[67] Other European national synods did not express as progressive a view[68] being content to support a vote for the diaconate of women, e.g., the "1972" pastoral synod of Switzerland that adopted a resolution in favor of the diaconate for women and agreed to further studies about their sacerdotal ministry. The synods of the bishops of the Federal Republic of Germany (1971-1975) took similar decisions.

Faced with all these efforts, both scientific and synodal, in favor of women's ordination, the forces resolved to maintain the status quo organized within the Roman Catholic Church.

The pontificate of Pope Paul VI saw the appearance of the first official document (1977) opposing the admission of women to sacerdotal ministry, the declaration of the Congregation for the Doctrine of the Faith *Inter insigniores*.[69] It aroused negative reaction in the entire world, criticisms coming not only from associations of Catholic women but from theological circles and even from certain members of Roman authorities (the Biblical Commission and the Secretariat for Christian Unity) who felt themselves excluded from the preparation of the document.

During the pontificate of John Paul II, other harsher statements have condemned the ordination of women, the apostolic letter *Ordinatio sacerdotalis* (1994) on sacerdotal ministry being reserved to men and the *Responsum ad dubium* (1995) of the Congregation for the Doctrine of the Faith. Its prefect, Cardinal Joseph Ratzinger responded to doubts about the doctrine contained in the apostolic letter *Ordinatio sacerdotalis* declaring that the doctrine (sacerdotal ministry being reserved to men) had an infallible character.[70]

Despite these increasingly virulent statements coming from the Vatican, numerous pastoral conferences have been held in several European dioceses in which access of women to the diaconate and further discussion concerning ordination to priesthood have been advocated.[71]

Worldwide Linkage of the Women's Ordination Movement[72]

Very aware that confronted with an all-powerful patriarchal-clerical hierarchy, isolated women could never effect reforms, several feminist organizations have sprung up within the Church, especially since Vatican II (in Europe and elsewhere). Likeminded groups in several countries and continents formed the network "Women's Ordination Worldwide" (WOW) in 1996 to agitate openly for women's ordination and consequently the full and equal rights of women in the Church.

With the motto "Now is the Time: A Celebration of Women's Call to a Renewed Priesthood" representatives of WOW gathered in Dublin, Ireland (from June 29 to July 1, 2001) for the First International Conference for Women's Ordination. Participants came from twenty-six countries and five continents, three hundred fifty women and about forty men. They produced eleven resolutions, joining themselves to efforts for the advancement of women called to ordained positions (diaconate and presbyterate) in the Roman Catholic Church and committed themselves not to be deterred on the way to this goal by any Vatican repression or prohibitions.[73]

Remembrance as a Guard against Forgetting

Recalling the beginnings and gradual development of the women's movement since the Second Vatican Council helps not only to remember things that had been forgotten and/or bring to light things not previously known, but it can also provide renewed inspiration for present day efforts at reforming Church structures that are still inimical to women

As we look back on the almost forty years since the beginning of the Council, it is clear that out of the first initiatives of a few women in Europe, motivated by their striving for fuller recognition of women's personal worth and their vocation to spiritual office in the Church, a worldwide movement for the ordination of women has come to be. Numerous reform groups and personalities as well as Church synods in several countries have advanced the movement and supported it, despite all the repressive measures and "definitive" prohibitions of women's ordination by the highest official level of the Church.

Reception and acceptance of Papal pronouncements against women's ordination will not succeed—all signs point to this. Stronger than all these centralized efforts inimical to women, the spiritual reality proclaimed in Gal. 3:28 will prevail: "All you who have been baptized have put on Christ. There is no longer Jew nor Greek, neither slave nor free, neither male nor female; for you are all one in Christ Jesus."

The barriers between Jew and Gentile, as well as between slave and free, have in the course of time been overcome. This has been linked with the recognition of human rights—*apart from sex*—to the basic principles of democratic states; this has also involved the right of women to freely choose their calling and their state in life. Contrariwise, the responsible officials of the Roman Catholic Church, against the "signs of the times" and to the shame of the Church still maintain with all their strength the traditional hierarchical-patriarchal structures, so that women remain dominated, forgotten and without rights. This constitutes a grave scandal and an immense loss of credibility for the Christian community. With its structures weighed down by the sin of sexism the Roman Catholic Church can in no way lay claim to being the one true Church of Christ.[74] It is this goal to which all reform-minded fellow members, not only of the Catholic Church but also of the other Christian Churches should be committed. To help translate the biblical passage "in Christ . . . there is no discrimination between women and men" (Gal. 3:28) into the structures of the Church without restriction, and so in the power of God's Spirit to break down the last wall—that between men and women in the Roman Catholic Church. That is an unrecognized condition for the democratizing and renewing of the Church.[75]

Notes

1. See the following: *Die Rezeption des Zweiten Vatikanischen Konzils*, Hermann J. Pottmeyer, et al., eds., (Düsseldorf: Patmos Verlag, 1986), (with essays by Guiseppe Alberigo, Jean-Pierre Jossua and others); *Geschichte des Zweiten Vatikanischen Konzils (1959-1965)*, Giuseppe Alberigo and Klaus Wittstadt, eds., (Mainz: Grünewald, 1997-) in Italian and German versions, Otto Hermann Pesch, *Das Zweite Vatikanische Konzil (1959-1965) Vorgeschichte, Verlauf, Ergebnisse, Nachgeschichte*, (Würzburg: Echter, 1994). Gunnel Vallquist, *Das zweite Vatikanische Konzil*, (Nürnberg: Glock und Lutz 1966).

2. Cf. Christian Duquoc, "An Active Role for the People of God in Defining the Faith of the Church," *Concilium*, 180/4 (1985): 73-81; Dietrich Wiederkehr, "'Volk Gottes': theologische und kirchliche Hausaufgaben nach Vaticanum II," *Diakonia* 23 (1992): 295-303; Herbert Vorgrimler, "Die Volk-Gottes-Theologie des Zweiten Vatikanischen Konzils und die Folgen 30 Jahre 'danach,'" *Bibel und Liturgie*, 66 (1993): 67-72.

3. That was true also of the preparatory period before the Council, cf. Alberigo and Wittstadt, *Geschichte*: "Obviously, no women, lay or vowed religious, were members of the commissions" (201). Given the estimation and status of women in the Roman Catholic Church one understands that this was the case but who took offense at the word "obviously"? Even though there was criticism from many quarters that laity had no part in the preparation for the Council (*ibid.*, 201 with notes), that was in the context of men's participation.

4. In the following remarks, restricted because of space, I will confine myself to the beginning and general development of the women's ordination movement

in the Roman Catholic Church in Europe. Treatment of all the Christian churches could only be realized in a more extensive project. The following literature may permit a review of women's ordination in other churches: Andrea Bieler, *Darum wagt es, Schwestern—zur Geschichte evangelischer Theologinnen in Deutschland*, (Neukirchen-Vluyn: Neukirchener, 1994); Dagmar Herbrecht, Ilse Härter, et al., eds., *Der Streit um die Frauenordination in der Bekennenden Kirche: Quellentexte zu ihrer Geschichte im Zweiten Weltkrieg*, (Neukirchen-Vluyn: Neukirchener, 1997) (Evangelical); Jacqueline Field-Bibb, *Women towards priesthood: Ministerial Politics and Feminist Praxis*, (Cambridge; New York: Cambridge University Press, 1991); Susan Dowell and Jane Williams, *Bread, Wine, and Women. The Ordination Debate in the Church of England* (London: Virago Press 1994) (Methodist and Anglican); Urs von Arx, "Die Debate uber die Frauenordination in den Altkatholischen Kirchen der Utrechter Union," *Gleichstellung der Geschlechter und die Kirchen: ein Beitrag zur menschenrechtlichen und ökumenischen Diskussion*, Denise Buser and Adrian Loretan, eds., (Freiburg, Schweiz: Universitätsverlag, 1999), 165-211; Angela Berlis,"The Ordination of Women: A Test Case for Conciliarity," *Concilium* 35 (1999): 77-84 (Old Catholic); Elisabeth Behr-Sigel, *Le ministère de la femme dans l'Eglise*, (Paris: Editions du Cerf, 1987), English translation, *The Ministry of Women in the Church*, (Redondo Beach, Calif.: Trabuco Canyon, CA: Oakwood Publications; Distributed by Source Books, 1991); Thomas Hopko, (ed.), *Women and the Priesthood*, (Crestwood, N.Y.: St. Vladimir's Seminary Press, 1999). Cf. also the survey of literature in Haye van der Meer, *Priestertum der Frau? Eine theologiegeschichtliche Untersuchung* (Freiberg: Herder, 1969), 197-213. Also the listing of literature on women and (priestly) ministery in *Zur Priesterin berufen. Gott sieht nicht auf das Geschlecht. Zeugnise römisch-katholischer Frauen*, Ida Raming, Gertrud Jansen, Iris Müller, Mechtilde Neuendorff (eds.), (Thaur: Druck- und Verlagshaus Thaur, 1998), 248-255.

5. Cf. also *Women Priests. A Catholic Commentary on the Vatican Declaration*, Leonard Swidler and Arlene Swidler, eds., (New York: Paulist Press, 1977), S. L. Swidler designates the petition of Gertrud Heinzelmann (1962) as the beginning of the debate about the ordination of women; see also Carmel Elizabeth McEnroy, *Guests in Their Own House: The Women of Vatican II* (New York: Crossroad Pub. Co., 1996), 40f., 223, 270.

6. In the wake of the secular women's movement, after the opening of university studies and the political franchise for women, the place of women in the Catholic Church and their advancement to the diaconate, seldom to priesthood, was treated by a few women in the 1920s and 1930s. Among others were the authors Hildegard Borsinger, *Rechtsstellung der Frau in der katholischen Kirche*, (Borna-Leipzig: RNB, 1930), Edith Stein, *Beruf des Mannes und der Frau nach Natur- und Gnadernordnung*, (1932); *ibid.*, *Frauenbildung und Frauenberufe*, (München: Schnell & Steiner, 1956), 169-171; Josephine Mayer, *Hochland*, 36 (1938/1939): 107, which focused on the diaconate. Finally, inferior instruction in the historical critical exegesis (forbidden until 1943!) and developments subsequent to World War II soon silenced these few voices. More detailed

information in: Ida Raming, *Frauenbewegung und Kirche. Bilanz eines 25 jährigen Kampfes für Gleichberechtigung und Befreiung der Frau seit dem 2. Vatikanischen Konzil,* 2nd ed., (Weinheim: Dt. Studien Verlag, 1991), 38 ff.; Friederike Kukulla, "Der Streit um den Diakonat der Frau—Zur Entwicklung vor dem II Vatikanischen Konzil," *Diakonat: ein Amt für Frauen in der Kirche—ein frauengerechtes Amt?* Peter Hünermann, ed., (Ostfildern: Schwabenverlag, 1997), 304-308.

7. Pius XII, *Das Ideal der christlichen Ehe. Ansprachen an Braut- und Eheleute*, Luzern 1946, 195, 197; English translation, Pius XII, *Moral Questions Affecting Married Life: Addresses given October 29, 1951 to the Italian Catholic Union of midwives and November 26, 1951 to the National Congress of the Family Front and the Association of Large Families*, (Washington, D.C.: National Catholic Welfare Conference, 1951). More recent Papal descriptions and images of woman in Raming, *Frauenbewegung*, 22-24.

8. Cited in Raming, *Frauenbewegung*, 24.

9. Gertrud Heinzelmann, *Die geheiligte Diskriminierung: Beiträge zum kirchlichen Feminismus*, (Bonstetten: Interfeminas, 1986), 90.

10. *Ibid.*, 96

11. *Ibid.*, 109, 112.

12. The dissertation was entitled *Das grundsätzliche Verhältnis von Kirche und Staat in den Konkordaten*, (Aarau: Sauerländer, 1943).

13. Heinzelmann, *Diskriminierung*, 97.

14. *Ibid.*, 112.

15. On P. Jordan as a person and his work, cf. Heinzelmann, *ibid.*, 114 ff.

16. Heinzelmann, *Diskriminierung*, 115-121.

17. *Ibid.*, 90.

18. Cf. Raming, *Priesterin*, 53, 64f.

19. Heinzelmann, *Diskriminierung*, 122f.

20. *Ibid.*, 123.

21. Published by Interfeminas Press, Zurich, which Gertrud Heinzelmann had founded, since no Roman Catholic Press was willing to publish it!

22. On this organization cf. Heinzelmann, *Diskriminierung*, 216 ff.

23. Cf. Heinzelmann, *ibid.*, 130ff. with the relevant notes.

24. Encyclical of Pope John XXIII, April 11, 1963: *Pacem in Terris*. The encyclical stands as a Catholic charter of human rights. A convenient English translation is *Pacem in Terris: Encyclical Letter "Peace on Earth,"* (New York: Paulist Press, 1982). The citations here are taken from this first part, n. 41 and 15, 12 and 44 respectively.

25. See Helmut Hoping, "Der Ausschluss von kirchlichen Weiheamtern aufgrund des Geschlechts. Ein kirchlicher Modernitätskonflikt," in Buser and Loretan, *Gleichstelllung*, 38-51; here 38.

26. Heinzelmann, *Diskriminierung*, 121. See also the report of J. Th. Münch in Raming, *Priesterin*, 66f.; McEnroy, *Guests*, 14: "Th. Münch put the question to provoke thinking about it."

27. Rosemary Goldie, "La participation des laïcs aux travaux du Concile Vatican II," in *Revue des sciences religieuses*, 62 (1988): 1, 55-73. In all, twenty-nine men were invited as auditors.

28. According to Goldie, 67 and n. 27 the Canadian bishops criticized the continuance of the sin of sexism (*peccatum clericalismi*) in the decree on the laity.

29. *Konzilsreden*, Yves Congar and Hans Küng, eds. (Einsiedeln Benziger, 1964), 28, English translation, *Council speeches of Vatican II* , Yves Congar and Hans Kung, eds, (Glen Rock, N.J.: Paulist Press, 1964); P. Xavier Tilliette, *Etudes*, (June, 1965): 824 coined the expression, *le sexe inexistant* in this context for the approach to women within the Catholic Church—that is for the total omission and silence of women; see also Gertrude Heinzelmann, *Die getrennten Schwestern. Frauen nach dem Konzil*, (Zürich: Interfeminas-Verlag, 1967), 10ff.

30. *Tagebuch des Konzils. Die Arbeit der zweiten Session*, Wolfgang Seibel and Luitpold Dorn, eds., (Nürnberg, J. M. Sailer 1964), 92, English edition, *Council Daybook, Vatican II, session 1-4*, Floyd Anderson, ed., (Washington, D.C. National Catholic Welfare Conference 1965-1966). The suggestion by Cardinal Suenens was supported by the Greek-Catholic Archbishop Hakim, but was greatly deprecated by conservative bishops, especially by the Italians (McEnroy, 35, 39). Sneering, misogynist comments about the attempt by Cardinal Suenens, the "paladin of ecclesiastical Neo-feminism," were also not lacking in the Italian right wing press (*Il Borghese*, [October 31, 1963]). The editor of the London *Tablet* reported: "I had hoped in the near future to be included among the Lay Auditors at the Council, but now it seems as though my wife will be beat me to it." [Editor: For an English account of these incidents, see Xavier Rynn, *The Second Session: The Debates and Decrees of the Vatican Council II, September 29 to December 4, 1963*, (New York: Farrar, Straus & Company, 1964), 117-118.]

31. Cf. *Tagebuch des Konzils: die Arbeit der dritten Session*, Luitpold Dorn and Georg Denzler, eds., (Nürnberg, J. M. Sailer, 1965), 431; *Tagebuch des Konzils, Vierte Session*, Wolfgang Seibel, Luitpold Dorn and Georg Denzler (Nürnberg, J. M. Sailer, 1966), 398 ff. where the names and functions of the women auditors are detailed. English edition, *Council Daybook, Vatican II, session 1-4*. They were predominantly religious women and the heads of women's associations. The experience of these auditors is described in the documented monograph of McEnroy.

32. Cf. Rosemary Radford Ruether, "The Place of Women in the Church," *Modern Catholicism: Vatican II and After*, Adrian Hastings, ed., (London: New York: SPCK; Oxford University Press, 1991), 260-266; here 261.

33. Cf. G. Heinzelmann, *Schwestern*, 5; Goldie, 65.

34. So, in compliance with Paul VI's invitation (September 8, 1964) inviting women as observers, cf. McEnroy, 43ff., Sister Maria Brüning, superior of the Ursulines in Dorsten and head of the German Religious Superiors, with Sister Juliane of the Poor Servants of Jesus, were invited as the first German observers. They conceded that there were too few women to permit women's independent contributions in theological debates. (*KIPA* [December 12, 1964], 674; cited by Heinzelmann, *Diskriminierung*, 159, n. 44).

35. Cf. Goldie, 69.

36. According to Radford Ruether, 261, the presence of the women auditors did actually influence the insertion of the remarks about discrimination against women and about their human rights. Also Goldie, 72.

37. Cf. Radford Ruether, 262.

38. Convincingly argued by Heinzelmann, *Schwestern*, 32.

39. Noteworthy were the interventions of Bishops Coderre (Quebec, Canada), Frotz (Cologne, Germany), Malula (Leopoldville, Congo) documented by Heinzelmann, *Schwestern*, 71-79

40. Cf. Heinzelmann, *Schwestern*, 78 ff. This book is, as far as I know, the only publication immediately after the Council which documented and appraised the event of the Council from a feminist viewpoint. See also *Diskriminierung*, 138.

41. On Archbishop Hallinan's intervention cf. Heinzelmann, *Diskriminierung*, 138; *Schwestern*, 20. Because of the closure of debate, the intervention was never discussed but it belongs to the acts of the Council.

42. Heinzelmann, *Schwestern*, 20.

43. References in Heinzelmann, *Diskriminierung*, 131 with n. 35. Specially noteworthy are the articles of J. A. van Eyden in Dutch periodicals.

44. *L'Osservatore Romano* of November 8, 9, 11 and 12, 1965. German translation in Heinzelmann, *Schwestern*, 89-101. Her critical remarks, 23 ff.

45. Cited by Heinzelmann, *Schwestern*, 99.

46. Heinzelmann, *Diskriminierung*, 139 ff.

47. *Der christliche Sonntag* of June 20, 1965. The article of I. F. Görres appeared also in English translation in *Herder Correspondence*, July 1966, but without the response of J. T. Münch.

48. "Sollen die Frauen in der Kirche schweigen?" *Der christliche Sonntag*, August 15, 1965 and "Katholishce Priesterinnen?" *ibid.*, October 10, 1965.

49. Cf. Heinzelmann, *Diskriminierung*, 132.

50. Heinzelmann, *Diskriminierung*, 132-135 from which the accompanying bibliographical references and citations are drawn.

51. (Düsseldorf: Haus der Katholischen Frauen, 1962.)

52. Elizabeth Gössmann, *Bild der Frau*, 111, n. 24.

53. *Die Frau im Aufbruch der Kirche*, Michael Schmaus and Elisabeth Gössmann, eds., Theologische Fragen heute, vol. 5, (München, M. Hueber, 1964), 119.

54. Heinzelmann, *Diskriminierung*, 133.

55. While Gössmann in 1968 ("Women as Priests?" *Concilium*, 34 (1968): 115-125) had harshly criticized the pioneering effort of women in "Wir schweigen nicht langer" (1964)—she recognized the fact that by its influence on the ordination of women it had drawn attention to the call of women to priesthood and had also drawn attention to the basic rights of women to free vocational choice within the Church, based on her own research into the history of the discrimination against women, she had revised her earlier view regarding statements about women's ordination in Christian tradition. Cf. *Warum keine Ordination der Frau? Unterschiedliche Einstellungen in den christlichen Kirchen*, Gössmann, Elisabeth

and Dietmar Bader, eds., (München: Schnell & Steiner, 1987), 9-25 ("It is the responsibility of theology today as the present-day bearer of tradition, to draw attention to the fact that the presupposition for not ordaining women are not conclusive. A conclusion drawn from false presuppositions is as false as they are.") *ibid.* 23.

56. Raming, *Priesterin*, 49ff.

57. *Ibid.* 47-51. For a detailed account of her difficult and repressed human situation cf. Gerburgis Feld and Dagmar Henze, (eds.) *Wie wir wurden, was wir sind: Gespräche mit feministischen Theologinnen der ersten Generation*, (Gütersloh: Gütersloher Verlagshaus, 1998), 60-67; here 62f.

58. Cf. Raming, *Priesterin*, 78-87.

59. Rahner's relevant comment: "It's a shame that one has to leave so many things on ice." In Herlinde Pisssarek-Hudelist, "Die Bedeutung der Sakramententheologie Karl Rahners für die Diskussion um das Priestertum der Frau," Herbert Vorgrimler, (ed.) *Wagnis Theologie: Erfahrungen mit der Theologie Karl Rahners*, (Freiburg: Herder, 1979), 427 and n. 38. See also Heinzelmann, *Diskriminierung*, 128.

60. *Quaestiones disputatae*, 42 (Freiburg: Herder, 1969), The original title was "Theologische Uberlegungen uber die Thesis: 'subiectum ordinationis est solus mas'" (Innsbruck, 1962).

61. Cf. Heinzelmann, *Diskriminierung*, 147.

62. The subtitle was *Eine rechtshistorisch-dogmatische Untersuchung der Grundlagen von Kanon 968 § 1 des Codex Iuris Canonici* (Köln: Böhlau, 1973).

63. Among others, Professors Yves Congar, Rene Metz (both in France) and Leonard Swidler (U.S.A.), the latter of whom was responsible for the publication of the thesis in America.

64. The book of Haye van der Meer was published in 1973 (Temple University Press, Philadelphia) and mine in 1976 (Scarecrow Press, Metuchen, NJ).

65. Worth mentioning are Elizabeth Schüssler, *Der vergessene Partner, Tatsachen und Möglichkeiten der beruflichen Mitarbeit der Frau in der Heilsorge der Kirche*, (Dusseldorff: Patmos 1964); Tine Govaart-Halkes, *Storm no de stilte. De plaats van den vrouw in de Kerk*, (Utrecht: De Fontein 1964); Sister Vincent Hannon, *The Question of Women and Priesthood*, (London: Chapman, 1967); Mary Daly, *The Church and the Second Sex*, (London: Chapman, 1968); Placidus Jordan, *Die Töchter Gottes. Zum Thema Frau und Kirche*, (Frankfurt a.M.: Joseph Knecht, 1973); Joan Morris, *Against Nature and God. The History of Women with Clerical Ordination and the Jurisdiction of Bishops*, (London: Mowbrays, 1973). Out of the increasing number of journal articles the following are important to mention: Josef Funk, "Klerikale Frauen?" *Österreichisches Archiv für Kirchenrecht*, 14 (1963): 271-290; René van Eynden, "Die Frau im Kirchenamt: Plädoyer für die Revision einer traditionellen Haltung," *Wort und Wahrheit*, 22 (1967): 350-362; Jan Peters, "Is there Room for Women in the Functions of the Church?" *Concilium*, 4 (1968): 126-138; Joan Brothers, "Women in Ecclesial Office," *Concilium*, 8 (1972): 109-122.

66. Cf. *Herder-Korrespondenz*, 24, (1970): 57, 130.

67. The group published, for example, listings of current literature on the theme "Women and Church." Leadership in the group was exercised particularly by René J. A. van Eyden and Katharina Halkes.

68. See the overview in Raming, *Frauenbewegung*, 41 ff.

69. Cf. Raming, *ibid.*, 43-50.

70. For the official Church document along with a critical analysis, cf. *Frauenordination. Stand der Diskussion in der katholischen Kirche,* Walter Groß, ed., (München: E. Wewel Verlag, 1996).

71. For a detailed account cf. Dorothea Reininger, *Diakonat der Frau in der Einen Kirche: Diskussionen, Entscheidungen und pastoral-praktische Erfahrungen in der christlichen Ökumene und ihr Beitrag zur römisch-katholischen Diskussion*, (Ostfildern: Schwabenverlag, 1999), especially 50-55.

72. The various European and non-European organizations are described in Raming, *Priesterin*, 237-247. Also in Iris Müller and Ida Raming. Aufbruch aus männlichen "Gottesordnungen." Reformbestrebungen von Frauen in christlichen Kirchen und im Islam, (Weinheim: Dt. Studien Verlag, 1998), 53-64. Finally, for details reviewing the reform initiatives of these groups, Raming, "Frauen suchen Antworten. Reaktionen auf frauenfeindliche Blockaden," *Orientierung*, 64 (2000): 100-103, 111-114.

73. Cf. Judith Stofer, "Die Mauer des Schweigen niederreissen," *Publik-Forum*, 13 (2001): 32 ff.; For conference reports, text of the speeches and the resolutions, see www.wow2001.org.

74. Cf. Congregation for the Doctrine of the Faith, *Declaration Dominus Iesus On the Unicity and Salvific Universality of Jesus Christ and the Church*; English version in *Origens*, 30/14 (2000): 209, 211-219; commentary, 220-222.

75. So I disagree with the often stated position of Herbert Haag, that by the ordination of women the "two tiered structure" (clergy—layperson) of the church will be "further cemented" and therefore the demand of the priestly ordination of women is not wise; thus recently in *Nur wer sich ändert, bleibt sich treu: Für eine neue Verfassung der katholischen Kirche*, (Freiburg: Herder, 2000). In opposition, Christine Duquoc, "Die Reform des Priesterstandes," in Pottmeyer, *Rezeption*, 369-383, sees in the Vatican declarations against the the ordination of women "an ideological justification of the status quo," a "blockade of the church administration" concerning a reform of the priestly office. The "limit, that regulates the access to the priest-service," (exclusion of women, exclusion of the married), determines from the start "the possible framework of reform"; because "in the Roman Church no societal and legal circumstances are allowed to be introduced that could prejudice the hierarchical structure" (382).

Appendix 4

Updated Bibliography for Women and Priestly Office

(For the years 1974 to 2001 in chronological order)

Note: This bibliography contains mainly literature by Roman Catholic authors; and in this sense does not seek to be complete. For further literature as well as other Christian confessions on the topic of women's ordination, refer to the following bibliographies:

1. Kendall, Patricia A. *Women and the Priesthood. A Selected and Annotated Bibliography*. Philadelphia, Phil.: Committee to Promote the Cause of and to Plan for the Ordination of Women to the Priesthood, 1976.

2. Morgan, John H. and Teri Wall. *The Ordination of Women: A Comprehensive Bibliography (1960-1975)*. Wichita, Kan.: Institute on Ministry and the Elderly, 1977.

3. Langeley, Wendell E., S. J. and Bernard and Jermann Asen. "Women and the Ministerial Priesthood: An Annotated Bibliography." *Theology Digest* 29: 4 (1981): 329-342.

4. Zimmermann, Marie and Jean Schlick. *The Woman in the Church: International Bibliography, 1975-1982. RIC Supplement 70-71.* Strasbourg: Cerdic Publications, 1982.

5. Women's Ordination Conference (WOC), *Women and Priesthood: A Bibliography, Compiled and Selectively Annotated by the Women's Ordination Conference.* Fairfax, Va: The Conference, 1995.

6. Lienemann, Wolfgang. *Bibliographie zur Frauenordination.*, Internet: www.theol.unibe.ch/pdf/Frauenordination.WLienemann.pdf

7. Wijngaards, John, *Women's Ordination Catholic Internet Library.* Internet: www.womenpriests.org

1973/1974

Heyer, Robert J., ed. *Women and Orders.* New York: Paulist Press, 1974.

King, J. A. "The Ordination of Women to the Priesthood." *Theology* 78 (1974): 142-147.

Morris, Joan. *Against Nature and God. The History of Women with Clerical Ordination and the Jurisdiction of Bishops.* London: Mowbrays, 1973.

1975

Carroll, Elizabeth. "Women and Ministry." *Theological Studies* 36 (1975): 660-687.

Donnelly, Dorothy H. "Women-Priests—Does Philadelphia Have a Message for Rome?" *Commonweal* 102 (1975): 206-210.

Hamilton, Michael P. and Nancy S. Montgomery, eds. *The Ordination of Women: Pro and Con.* New York: Morehouse-Barlow Co., 1975.

Lakeland, Paul. *Can Women Be Priests. Ordination of Women in Ecumenical Perspective.* Cork: The Mercier Press, 1975.

Meyer, Eric C. "Are There Theological Reasons Why the Church Should not Ordain Women Priests?" *Review for Religious* 34 (1975): 957-967.

Raming, Ida. "Frau und kirchliche Ämter." in *Diaconia Christi. Dokumentation,* edited by Internationales Diakonatszentrum Freiburg, 10 (1975): 24-28.

1976

Bouyer, Louis. *Mystère et ministères de la femme*. Paris: Aubier Montaigne, 1976.

Bruce, Michael and Gervase E. Duffield, eds. *Why not? Priesthood and the Ministry of Women: A Theological Study*. Abington, Pa.: Marcham Manor Press, 1976.

Gardiner, Anne Marie, ed. *Women and Catholic Priesthood. An Expanded Vision*. New York: Paulist Press, 1976.

Küng, Hans. "Thesen zur Stellung der Frau in Kirche und Gesellschaft." *Theologische Quartalschrift* 156 (1976): 129-132.

Micks, Marianne and Charles P. Price. *Towards a New Theology of Ordination. Essays on the Ordination of Women*. Sommerville, MA: Hadden & Company Ltd., 1976.

Neumann, Johannes. "Die Stellung der Frau in der Sicht der katholischen Kirche heute." Theologische Quartalschrift 156 (1976): 111-128.

Radford, Rosemary R. "Frau und kirchliches Amt in historischer und gesellschaftlicher Sicht." *Concilium* 12 (1976): 17-23.

Raming, Ida. "Die inferiore Stellung der Frau nach geltendem Kirchenrecht." *Concilium* 12 (1976): 30-34.

Schüssler Fiorenza, Elisabeth "Die Rolle der Frau in der urchristlichen Bewegung." *Concilium* 12 (1976): 3-9.

1977

Coridin, James A., ed. *Sexism and Church Law*. New York: Paulist Press, 1977.

Ebneter, Albert. "Keine Frauen im Priesteramt." *Orientierung* 41 (1977): 25f.

Frieling, Reinhard. "Rom gegen Frauenordination. Belastung für die Ökumene." *Lutherische Monatshefte* 16 (1977): 130f.

Hünermann, Peter. "Roma locuta—causa finita? Zur Argumentation der vatikanischen Erklärung über die Frauenordination." *Herder Korrespondenz* 31 (1977): 206-209.

Küng, Hans and Gerhard Lohfink. "Keine Ordination der Frau?" *Theologische Quartalschrift* 157 (1977): 144-146.

Rahner, Karl. "Priestertum der Frau?" *Stimmen der Zeit* 195 (1977): 291-301.

Sekretariat d. Dt. Bischofskonferenz, ed. *Erklärung der Kongregation für die Glaubenslehre zur Frage der Zulassung der Frauen zum Priesteramt*. Bonn: Sekretariat d. Dt. Bischofskonferenz, 1977.

Swidler, Leonard and Arlene Swidler, eds. *Women Priests. A Catholic Commentary on the Vatican Declaration.* New York: Paulist Press, 1977.

Weger, Karl-Heinz. "Endgültig keine Ordination der Frau?" *Orientierung* 41 (1977): 64-67.

Wijngaards, John. *Did Christ Rule Out Women Priests?* Great Wakering: Mayhew-McCrimmon, 1977.

1978

Bläser, Peter. "Liturgische Dienste und die Ordination von Frauen in nichtkatholischen Kirchen." *Liturgisches Jahrbuch* 28 (1978): 155-169.

Coyle, John K. "The Fathers on Women's Ordination." *Eglise et Théologie* 9 (1978): 51-101.

di Noia, Joseph. "Women's Ordination: Can the Debate Be Revived?" *New Black Friars* 59 (1978): 488-497.

Ferder, Fran. *Called to Break Bread?: A Psychological Investigation of 100 Women Who Feel Called to Priesthood in the Catholic Church.* Mt. Ranier, MD: Quixote Center, 1978.

Hemperek, Piotr. "The Catholic Church and the Ordination of Women." *Roczniki teologiczno-kanoniczne* 25 (1978): 33-44. (English summary)

Stuhlmueller, Carroll, ed. *Women and the Priesthood: Future Directions*. Collegeville, MN: The Liturgical Press, 1978.

1979

Pissarek-Hudelist, Herlinde. "Die Bedeutung der Sakramententheologie Karl Rahners für die Diskussion um das Priestertum der Frau." 417-434 in *Wagnis Theologie. Erfahrungen mit der Theologie Karl Rahners*, edited by Herbert Vorgrimler. Freiburg: Herder, 1979.

Raming, Ida. "Gleichwertig—aber andersartig. Zu einem üblichen Argumentationsschema gegen das Priestertum der Frau." *Orientierung* 43 (1979): 218-221.

Singles, Donna. "The Case of Women in the Church: Objection Sustained." *Concilium* 15 (1979): 71-79.

1980

Brennan, Margaret. "Women and Men in Church Office." *Concilium* 16 (1980): 107-109.

Parvey, Constance F., ed. *Ordination of Women in Ecumenical Perspective.* Commission on Faith and Order. Geneva: World Council of Churches, 1980.

———. *Ordination of Women in Ecumenical Perspective: Workbook for the Church's Future.* Geneva: World Council of Churches, 1980.

Reichle, Erika. "Frauenordination aus ökumenischer Sicht. Ein Bericht über eine Tagung." *Ökumenische Rundschau* 29 (1980): 89-96.

1981

Bébère, Marie-Jeanne. "L'ordination des femmes." *Lumière et vie* 30 (1981): 90-102.

Gemeinsame römisch-Katholische-Evangelisch-Lutherische Kommission, ed. *Das geistliche Amt in der Kirche.* Paderborn: Verlag Bonifatius-Druckerei, 1981.

Légrand, Hervé and Jorge Vikström. "Die Zulassung der Frau zum Amt." 102-126 in *Das geistliche Amt in der Kirch,* edited by Gemeinsame römisch-Katholische-Evangelisch-Lutherische Kommission. Paderborn: Verlag Bonifatius-Druckerei, 1981.

1982

Brooten, Bernadette and Norbert Greinacher, eds. *Frauen in der Männerkirche.* München: Kaiser, 1982.

Hauke, Manfred. *Die Problematik um das Frauenpriestertum vor dem Hintergrund der Schöpfungs-und Erlösungsordnung.* Paderborn: Verlag Bonifatius-Druckerei, 1982.

Warkentin, Marjorie. *Ordination. A Biblical-Historical Overview.* Grand Rapids, Mich.: Eerdmans, 1982.

1983

Nientiedt, Klaus. "Verdrängte Weiblichkeit. Zur Stelllung der Frau in der Kirche." *Herder Korrespondenz* 37 (1983): 573-578.

Puza, Richard. "Zur Stellung der Frau im alten und neuen Kirchenrecht." *Theologische Quartalschrift* 163 (1983): 109-122.

1984

"Die Ordination der Frau in Lutherischen Kirchen. Ergebnisse einer Umfrage des Lutherischen Weltbundes." *LWB-Dokumentation* 18 (1984): 1-39.

Doyle, Eric. "The Question of Women Priests and the Argument *In Persona Christi*." *Irish Theological Quarterly* 37 (1984): 212-221.

Pree, Helmuth. "Mann und Frau im neuen Kirchenrecht." *Diakonia* 15 (1984): 107-112.

Raming, Ida. "Damit auch Frauen Priester werden . . . Die Women's Ordination Conference streitet für mehr Rechte der Frauen in der Kirche." *Publik-Forum* 13:10 (1984): 26f.

Schelkle, Karl H. "'Denn wie das Weib aus dem Mann ist, so auch der Mann aus dem Weib' (1 Kor. 11, 12). Zur Gleichberechtigung der Frau in Neuen Testament." *Diakonia* 15 (1984): 85-90.

1985

Jensen, Anne. "Wie patriarchalisch ist die Ostkirche? Frauenfragen in der orthodoxen Theologie." *Una Sancta* 40 (1985): 130-145.

Oeyen, Christian. "Frauenordination: Was sagt die Tradition wirklich?" *Internationale Kirchliche Zeitschrift* 75 (1985): 97-118.

Parvey, Constance F., ed. *Die Gemeinschaft von Frauen und Männern in der Kirche*. Neukirchen-Vluyn: Neukirchener Verlag, 1985.

Ruh, Ulrich. "Anglikanische Entscheidung für die Frauenordination." *Herder Korrespondenz* 39 (1985): 12f.

1986

Heinzelmann, Gertrud. *Die geheiligte Diskriminierung: Beiträge zum kirchlichen Feminismus*. Bonstetten: Interfeminas, 1986.

Oeyen, Christian. "Priesteramt der Frau? Die altkatholische Theologie als Beispiel einer Denkentwicklung." *Ökumenische Rundschau* 35 (1986): 254-266.

Ruh, Ulrich. "Anglikaner: Streit um Frauenordination und Glaubensfragen." *Herder Korrespondenz* 40 (1986): 361f.

Wijngaards, John. *Did Christ Rule Out Women Priests?*, 2nd ed. Essex: McCrimmons, 1986.

Women Priests, Obstacles to Unity? Documents and Correspondence Rome and Canterbury 1975-1986. London: Catholic Truth Society, 1986.

1987

Beinert, Wolfgang, ed. *Frauenbefreiung und Kirche: Darstellung—Analyse—Dokumentation*. Regensburg: F. Pustet, 1987.

Bührig, Marga. "Wenn Frauen Heilige sein können, warum können sie nicht auch Priesterinnen sein?" *Reformatio* 36 (1987): 331-334.

Gössmann, Elisabeth and Dietmar Bader, eds. *Warum keine Ordination der Frau? Unterschiedliche Einstellungen in den christlichen Kirchen*. München: Schnell & Steiner, 1987.

Hauke, Manfred. "Das Weihesakrament für Frauen—eine Forderung der Zeit?" *Forum Katholische Theologie* 3 (1987): 119-134.

Kaufmann, Ludwig. "Auf dem Weg zur Teilhabe." *Orientierung* 51 (1987): 144.

Martin, John H. "The Injustice of Not Ordaining Women: A Problem for Medieval Theologians." *Theological Studies* 48 (1987): 303-316.

Rosato, Philip J. "Priesthood of the Baptized and Priesthood of the Ordained." *Gregorianum* 68 (1987): 215-265.

Vögtle, Anton. "Frauen und Ämter in der frühen Kirche." *Christ in der Gegenwart* 39 (1987): 389f., 397f., 405f.

1988

"Ein Plädoyer für die Frau im kirchlichen Amt. Die Enzyklika 'Mulieris dignitatem' über die Würde der Frau." *Imprimatur* 21 (1988): 322-324.

Lissner, Anneliese. *Zur Gleichheit berufen: Entwurf des "Frauen"—Hirtenbriefes der Katholischen Bischofskonferenz der USA.* Oberursel: Publik-Forum, 1988.

Nürnberg, Rosemarie. "'Non decet neque necessarium est, ut mulieres doceant.' Überlegungen zum altkirchlichen Lehrverbot für Frauen." JAC 31 (1988): 57-73.

Osborne, Kenan B. *Priesthood: A History of the Ordained Ministry in the Roman Catholic Church.* New York: Paulist Press, 1988.

Raming, Ida. "Frauenordination. Fortschritt auf dem Weg zur Befreiung der Frau in der katholischen Kirche." *Schlangenbrut* 22 (1988): 10-14.

Raske, Michael. "Warum dürfen Frauen nicht Priester werden?" *Katechetische Blätter* 113 (1988): 886-895.

Wojciechowski, Tadeusz. "Könnte eine Frau katholischer Prester sein?" *Analecta Cracoviensia* 20 (1988): 299-308.

1989

"Beschuß der 49. ordentlichen Bistumssynode der Altkatholiken zur Frauenordination." *Ökumenische Rundschau* 38 (1989): 333.

"Die Stellung der Frau in der Orthodoxen Kirche und die Frage der Ordination von Frauen. Abschlußbericht einer Interorthodoxen Theologischen Konsultation." *Una Sancta* 44 (1989): 252-260.

Field, Barbara, ed. *Fit for this Office. Women and Ordination.* Melbourne: Collins Dove, 1989.

Gössman, Elisabeth. "Außerungen zum Frauenpriestertum in der christlichen Tradition." 304-321 in *Freiburger Akademiearbeiten 1979-1989*, edited by Dietmar Bader. München: Schnell & Steiner, 1989.

Raming, Ida. *Frauenbewegung und Kirche. Bilanz eines 25 jährigen Kampfes für Gleichberechtigung und Befreiung der Frau seit dem 2. Vatikanischen Konzil.* Weinheim: Deutscher Studien Verlag, 1989.

Trapp, Daniel J. *The Discussion of the Ordination of Women to the Priesthood among Roman Catholics in the United States 1977-1987.* Rome: Graziani, 1989.

1990

"'Gleiche Würde'—aber keine gleichen Rechte. Stellungnahme der Frauengruppe Maria von Magdala zum Apostolischen Schreiben Johannes Pauls II. Mulieris Dignitatem." 46-51 in *Es gibt nicht mehr Mann und Frau . . . (Gal. 3,28)*, edited by Initiative Gleichberechtigung für Frauen in der Kirche, 1990.

Raming, Ida and Iris Müller. "Testfall 'Frauenordination.' Amtskirchliche Positionen und ihre Widelegung." 13-18 in *Es gibt nicht mehr Mann und Frau . . . (Gal. 3,28)*, edited by Initiative Gleichberechtigung für Frauen in der Kirche, 1990.

Raming, Ida. "Frauen in der Kirche." *Stimmen der Zeit* 115 (1990) 415-426.

1991

Behr-Seigel, Elisabeth. *Le minstère de la femme dans L'Eglise.* Paris: Editions du Cerf, 1987. English translation: *The Ministry of Women in the Church*, Redondo Beach, Calif. 1991.

Raming, Ida. *Frauenbewegung und Kirche. Bilanz eines 25 jährigen Kampfes für Gleichberechtigung und Befreiung der Frau seit dem 2. Vatikanischen Konzil*, 2nd ed. Weinheim: Dt. Studien Verlag, 1991.

1992

Baumert, Norbert. *Frau und Mann bei Paulus. Überwindung eines Mißverständnisses.* Würzburg: Echter, 1992.

Geldbach, Erich. "Frauenordination: Dienst an der Ökumene?" *Materialdienst des Konfessionskundlichen Instituts Bensheim* 43 (1992): 103-107.

Kirchenamt der Evangelischen Kirche in Deutschland, ed. *Frauenordination und Bischosfamt: eine Stellungnahme der Kammer für Theologie.* Hannover: Kirchenamt der Evangelischen Kirche in Deutschland, 1992.

Raming, Ida. "'Die zwölf Apostel waren Männer. . . .' Stereotype Einwände gegen die Frauenordination und ihre tieferen Ursachen." *Orientierung* 56 (1992): 143-46.

1993

Armstrong, Karen. *The End of Silence: Women and the Priesthood.* London: Fourth Estate, 1993.
"Frauenordination (volume theme)." *Theologische Quartalschrift* 173 (1993): 161-264.
Jensen, Anne. "Christusrepräsentation, kirchliche Ämter und Vorsitz bei der Eucharistie. Zur heutigen *relecture* einer frühchristlichen Tradition." *Freiburger Zeitschrift für Philosophie und Theologie* 40 (1993): 282-297.
Légrand, Hervé. "Traditio Perpetuo Servata? The Non-Ordination of Women: Tradition or Simply Historical Fact?" *One in Christ* 29 (1993): 1-23.
Müller, Iris. "Priesteramt—für Männer eine Ehre—für Frauen ein Tabu." 37–43 in *Keine Frau schweige in der Kirche!*, edited by Initiative Gleichberechtigung für Frauen in der Kirche, 1993.
Ohme, Heinz. "Die orthodoxe Kirche und die Ordination von Frauen. Zur Konferenz von Rhodus vom 30. Oktober bis 7. November 1988." *Ökumenische Rundschau* 42 (1993): 52-65.
Schießl, Johanna. "Priestertum der Frau." *Stimmen der Zeit* 211 (1993): 115-122.

1994

"*Apostolische Schreiben*, von Papst Johannes Paul II. Über die nur Männern vorbehaltene Priesterweihe (*Ordinatio Sacerdotalis*) vom 22.5.1994." 3-7. Bonn, 1994.
"*Das Apostolische Schreiben Ordinatio Sacerdotalis*, vom 22.5.1994. Wortlaut—Stellungnahmen—Reaktionen." *Klerusblatt* 74 (1994): 147-151.
"Gott ist in Christus Mensch, nicht Mann geworden. Zur Ablehnung der Frauenordination in dem vatikanischen Schreiben über die Priesterweihe." *Ökumenische Rundschau* 43 (1994): 332f.
"Keine Priesterweihe von Frauen. Das Apostolische Schreiben Ordinatio Sacerdotalis mit den Erläuterungen im 'Osservatore Romano.'" *Herder Korrespondenz* 48 (1994): 355-358.
Antón, Angel. "'Ordinatio Sacerdotalis.' Algunas reflexiones de 'gnoseiología teológica.'" *Gregorianum* 75 (1994): 723-742.
Beinert, Wolfgang. "Priestertum der Frau. Der Vorhang zu, die Frage offen?" *Stimmen der Zeit*, 212 (1994): 723-738.
Brunelli, Lucio and Andrea Tornielli. "Frauen als Priester. Der Fall ist abgeschlossen." *30 Tage* 30:6 (1994): 10-13.

Byrne, Lavinia. *Women at the Altar—The Ordination of Women in the Roman Catholic Church.* London: Mowbray, 1994.

Cullinane, Peter J. Bishop. "A Pastoral-Theological Reflection on Pope John Paul II's Apostolic Letter Concerning Ordination to the Priesthood." *Australasian Catholic Record* 71 (1994): 465-474.

Geldbach, Erich. "Endgültiges Nein Roms zur Priesterweihe von Frauen." *Materialdienst des Konfessionskundlichen Instituts Bensheim* 45 (1994): 65-67.

Hälbig, Klaus W. "'Er hat sie durch sein Blut gereinigt.' Zur Frage der Frauenordination im Horizont sakramentalen Denkens." *Internationale Katholische Zeitschrift Communio* 23 (1994): 345-359.

Hünermann, Peter. "Schwerwiegende Bedenken. Eine Analyse des Apostolischen Schreibens *Ordinatio Sacerdotalis*." *Herder Korrespondenz* 48 (1994): 406-410.

Jensen, Anne. "Ist Frauenordination ein ökumenisches Problem? Zu den jüngsten Entwicklungen in den anglikanischen, altkatholischen und orthodoxen Kirchen." *Internationale kirchliche Zeitschrift* 84 (1994): 210-228.

Nientiedt, Klaus. "Bischofskonferenz: Spannungen nehmen zu." *Herder Korrespondenz* 48 (1994): 549-551.

Raming, Ida. "Endgültiges Nein zum Priestertum der Frau? Zum Apostolischen Schreiben Johannes Pauls II. *Ordinatio Sacerdotalis*." *Orientierung* 58 (1994): 190-193.

———. "Ungenutzte Chancen für Frauen im Kirchenrecht. Widersprüche im *CIC*/1983 und ihre Konsequenzen." *Orientierung* 58 (1994): 68-70.

Ratzinger, Joseph. "Grenzen kirchlicher Vollmacht. Das neue Dokument von Papst Johannes Paul II. Zur Frage der Frauenordination." *Internationale Katholische Zeitschrift* 23 (1994): 337-345.

Ruh, Ulrich. "Die Würfel sind gefallen. In der Kirche von England empfingen erstmals Frauen die Priesterweihe." *Herder Korrespondenz* 48 (1994): 176-180.

———. "Lehramt im Abseits?" *Herder Korrespondenz* 48 (1994): 325-327.

Seibel, Wolfgang. "Priestertum der Frau." *Stimmen der Zeit* 212 (1994): 577f.

St. Pierre, Simone M. *The Struggle to Serve: The Ordination of Women in the Roman Catholic Church.* Jefferson, N.C.: McFarland, 1994.

Waldrond-Skinner, Sue. *Crossing the Boundary. What Will Women Priests Mean?* London: Mowbray, 1994.

1995

Dulles, Avery. "Tradition Says No." *The Tablet* 249 (1995): 1572-1573.

Gleeson, Gerald. "The Status of the Church's Teaching that Ordination is Reserved to Men Alone." *The Australasian Catholic Record* 73 (1995): 286-294.

Hauke, Manfred. "'*Ordinatio Sacerdotalis.*' Das päpstliche Schreiben zum Frauenpriestertum im Spiegel der Diskussion." *Forum Katholische Theologie* 11 (1995): 270-298.

Küng, Hans. "Das Nein zur Frauenordination—unfehlbar! Anti-Priesterinnen-Dekret des Vatikans stellt Theologen vor Entscheidung." *Süddeutsche Zeitung* 2:12 (1995): 10.

Laurien, Hanna-Renate. *Abgeschrieben? Plädoyer für eine faire Diskussion über das Priestertum der Frau.* Freiburg: Herder, 1995.

McSorley, Harry. "Ecclesial Communio, Reception, and the Apostolic Letter of Pope John Paul II. 'Ordinatio Sacerdotalis.'" *Communion et Réunion* (1995): 389-401.

Raming, Ida. "Priesteramt für Frauen: Eine Forderung der Gerechtigkeit und Anerkennung ihres Christseins." *Katechetische Blätter* 120 (1995): 296-299.

Reynolds, Philip R. "Scholastic Theology and the Case Against Women's Ordination." *Heythrop Journal* 36 (1995): 249-285.

Sullivan, Francis A., S. J. "Guideposts from Catholic Tradition. Infallibility Doctrine Invoked in Statement against Ordination by Congregation for the Doctrine of Faith." *America* 173 (December 9, 1995): 5-6.

1996

Bébère, Marie-Jeanne. "L'ordination des femmes dans L'Eglise catholique: Les decisions du magistère." *Revue de droit canonique* 46 (1996): 7-20.

Catholic Theological Society of America. "Tradition and Women's Ordination: A Question for Criteria." *Origins* 26 (1996): 556-564.

Eisen, Ute E. *Amtsträgerinnen im frühen Christentum. Epigraphische und literarische Studien.* Göttingen: Vandenhoeck & Ruprecht, 1996. English translation: *Women Officeholders in Early Christianity. Epigraphical and Literary Studies.* Collegeville, Minn.: The Liturgical Press, 2000.

Ferme, Brian E. "The Response of the Congregation for the Doctrine of Faith to the Dubium Concerning the Apostolic Letter 'Ordinatio Sacerdotalis': Authority and Significance." *Periodica* 85 (1996) 689-727.

Field-Bibb, Jacqueline. "Praxis versus Image: Women Towards the Priesthood in the Roman Catholic Church." *Concilium* 32 (1996): 81-89.

Gaillardetz, Richard R. "Infallibility and the Ordination of Women." *Louvain Studies* 21 (1996): 3-24.

Gössman, Elisabeth. "Die 'Braut Kirche' und der Priester als 'Bräutigam.' Rom und das neue Exempel männlicher Macht. Zum Verbot der Priesterweihe von Frauen." *Frankfurter Rundschau* 5:2 (1996): 12.

Groß, Walter, ed. *Frauenordination. Stand der Diskussion in der katholischen Kirche.* München: E. Wewel Verlag, 1996.

Hafner, Felix and Denis Buser. "Frauenordination via Gleichstellungsgesetz? Die Anwendbarkeit des Gleichstellungsgesetzes auf die Dienstverhältnisse in der römisch-katholischen Kirche." *Aktuelle Juristische Praxis* (1996): 1207-1214.

Haustein, Jörg. "Unfehlbar, aber nicht unwiderrufbar? Zum Diskurs um die Ablehnung der Frauenordination." *Materialdienst des Konfessionskundlichen Instituts Bensheim*, 47 (1996): 21f.

Joubert, Jacques. "L'ordination des femmes et le dépot de la foi. A propos d'une 'résponse' de la Congrégation pour la doctrine de la foi." *Revue de droit canonique* 46 (1996): 29-36.

Lüdecke, Norbert. "Also doch ein Dogma? Fragen zum Verbindlichkeitsanspruch der Lehre über die Unmöglichkeit der Priesterweihe für Frauen aus kanonistischer Perspektive." *Trierer Theologische Zeitschrift* 105 (1996): 161-121.

Nientiedt, Klaus. "Eine weitere Etappe. Zur Priesterweihe von Frauen bei den deutschen Altkatholiken." *Herder Korrespondenz* 50 (1996): 352-355.

Raberger, Walter. "'Ordinationsfähigkeit' der Frau? Anmerkungen zum Thema 'Frauenpriestertum.'" *Theologisch-praktische Quartalschrift* 144 (1996): 398-411.

Raming, Ida. "Für die Rechte der Frauen in der Kirche. Eindrücke und Überlegungen zur Women's Ordination Conference 1995." *Orientierung* 60 (1996): 54-57.

Ruprecht, Sabine u. Arndt. "Frauenordination in der Kirche von England. Ein Bericht." *Pastoraltheologie* 85 (1996): 190-195.

Sullivan, Francis A., S. J. *Creative Fidelity: Weighing and Interpreting Documents of Magisterium.* New York: Paulist Press, 1996.

Vobbe, Joachim, ed. "Geh zu meinen Brüdern." *Vom priesterlichen Auftrag und Amt der Frauen in der Kirche. Brief des Bischofs an die Gemeinden des Katholischen Bistums der Alt-Katholiken.* Bonn: Kath. Bistum der Alt-Katholiken in Deutschland, 1996.

1997

"Frauenordination und Tradition. Stellungnahme der 'Catholic Theological Society of America.'" *Herder Korrespondenz* 51 (1997): 414-419.

Professorenkollegium der Bonner Katholisch—Theologischen Fakultät, ed. *Projekttag Frauenordination.* Alfter: Borengässer, 1997.

Rigl, Thomas. "Kontext und Begründung der Frauenordination in der Kirche von England." *Catholica* 51 (1997): 3-31.

Schwarz, Roland. "Verbieten Bibeltexte die Frauenordination?" *Diakonia* 28 (1997): 167-173.

1998

Gössman, Elisabeth. "Women's Ordination and the Vatican." *Feminist Theology* 18 (1998): 67- 86.

van Lunen Chénu, Marie-Thérèse. "Human Rights in the Church: a non-right for women in the Church." *Human Rights. The Christian Contribution* (July, 1998).

Müller, Iris and Ida Raming. *Aufbruch aus männlichen "Gottesordnungen." Reformbestrebungen von Frauen in christlichen Kirchen und im Islam.* Weinheim: Dt. Studien Verlag, 1998.

Raming, Ida, Gertrud Jansen et. al., eds. *Zur Priesterin berufen. Gott sieht nicht auf das Geschlecht. Zeugnisse römisch-katholischer Frauen.* Thaur: Druck- und Verlagshaus Thaur, 1998.

1999

The Non-Ordination of Women and the Politics of Power. Concilium 35, n. 3. Elisabeth Schüssler Fiorenza and Hermann Häring, eds. Maryknoll, NY: Orbis Books, 1999.

Berlis, Angela. "The Ordination of Women: A Test Case for Conciliarity." *Unanswered questions. Concilium* 35, n. 1. Christoph Theobald and Dietmar Mieth, eds. Maryknoll, NY: Orbis Books, 1999: 77-84.

Buser, Denise and Adrian Loretan, eds. *Gleichstellung der Geschlechter und die Kirchen. Ein Beitrag zur menschenrechtlichen und ökumenischen Diskussion.* Freiburg: Universitätsverlag Freiburg Schweiz, 1999.

Müller, Gerhard L., ed. *Der Empfänger des Weihesakraments. Quellen zur Lehre und Praxis der Kirche, nur Männern das Weihesakrament zu spenden.* Würzberg: Echter, 1999.

2000

Bock, Wolfgang and Wolfgang Lienemann, eds. *Frauenordination. Studien zu Kirchenrecht und Theologie*, 3. vol. Heidelberg: FEST, 2000.

Macy, Gary. "The Ordination of Women in the Early Middle Ages." *Theological Studies* 61 (2000): 481-507.

Müller, Gerhard L. *Priestertum und Diakonat. Der Empfänger des Weihesakramentes in schöpfungstheologischer und christologischer Perspektive.* Freiburg: Herder, 2000.

Raab, Kelley A. *When Women Become Priests.* New York: Columbia University Press, 2000.

Raming, Ida. "Frauen suchen Antworten. Reaktionen auf frauenfeindliche Blockaden." *Orientierung* 64 (2000): 100-103, 111-114.

2001

Raming, Ida. "Frauen gegen Diskriminierung und Entrechtung. Entstehung und Entwicklung der Frauenordinationsbewegung in der katholischen Kirche Europas." *Orientierung* 65 (2001): 75-79, 86-91.

Wijngaards, John. *The Ordination of Women in the Catholic Church. Unmasking a Cuckoo's Egg Tradition.* London: Mowbray, 2001.

Winter, Miriam T. *Out of the Depths. The Story of Ludmila Javorova, Ordained Roman Catholic Priest.* New York: Crossroad Publishing Co., 2001.

Index

About the Author and Editors

Ida Raming, Ph.D. is a pioneer of the women's ordination movement, who, together with Dr. Iris Müeller, drew up a published submission to the Second Vatican Council in 1963, challenging the exclusion of women from the priesthood. She received her doctorate in theology from the University of Münster in 1970, and her thesis was published in Germany in 1973. Dr. Raming's thesis was translated into English and published by Scarecrow Press in 1976 under the title *The Exclusion of Women From the Priesthood: Divine Law or Sex Discrimination*?

For several years, Dr. Raming held an academic post in the department of theology at the University of Münster. She later taught in gymnasiums in Münster and Emsdetten. Dr. Raming has taught philosophy, education, theology and German. From 1984 until 1993, she served as an advisory member to the feminist theology section of the international theological journal, *Concilium*, and held several lectureships at theological colleges. Dr. Raming has published numerous books and articles in the area of the history and theology of women, especially on the theme of the role and value of women in the Roman Catholic Church. On June 29, 2002, she was one of the seven women who were ordained to the Roman Catholic priesthood, an ordination subsequently rejected by the Roman Catholic hierarchy.

Bernard Cooke, Ph.D. is a prominent U.S. theologian who has served as president of both the College Theology Society and the Catholic Theological Society of America and received from the latter its John Courtney Murray award. Following doctoral studies at the Institut catholique de Paris, where he obtained the doctorate in 1956, he has taught theology at

Marquette, Boston College, Loyola of New Orleans, Santa Clara, Holy Cross (Worcester), Gonzaga, Incarnate Word (San Antonio) and San Diego Universities in the U.S. and the Universities of Windsor and Calgary in Canada. He has lectured widely in the U.S. and abroad. He is the author of more than twenty books and numerous articles, many of them dealing with sacramental ritual.

Gary Macy, Ph.D., is currently a professor in the Department of Theology and Religious Studies at the University of San Diego. He received both his bachelor's and his master's degrees from Marquette University where he specialized in historical and sacramental theology. He earned his doctoral degree in Divinity from Cambridge University in 1978. In 1991 and 1992, Dr. Macy was a Herodotus Fellow at the Institute for Advanced Studies at Princeton. Dr. Macy has published three books on the history of the Eucharist, *Theologies of the Eucharist in the Early Scholastic Period, The Banquet's Wisdom: A Short History of the Theologies of the Lord's Supper* and most recently, *Treasures from the Storeroom: Essays on Medieval Religion and the Eucharist.* He has published and lectured extensively on medieval theology and religious practice and has received four national awards for his books and articles.

This journal is a personal process I've used to keep my dreams and goals top of mind and in focus…it's literally how I started today and every day for the last several years. I think it's a major contributing factor for why I've achieved the success I have: an online community of millions, becoming a #1 New York Times Bestselling author, building a multi-million dollar company and brand with only a high school diploma under my belt – and more impressive than all of them – a thriving marriage and four kids who are (mostly) kind, well adjusted members of society. Truthfully, I never imagined I'd have my own journal (with a snazzy name!) but over the last several years any time I showed a glimpse of my morning routine on social media thousands of people would respond with questions.

Why do you journal? How do you know what to write down?

Where did you get that notebook? Can you teach me how to do this?

So, like with most everything we've created as a company, this idea came from a direct ask from our online family and even though we had no idea how we'd pull it off (also a hallmark of our business!) I did know how helpful daily, intentional focus could be. There is so much power in setting your intentions every day. There is so much power in focusing on the *outcome* you're after instead of the to-do list you have in your mind.

This practice was born out of frustration. I was tired of starting and stopping my goals over and over again. I wanted a habit that would help me see them through to completion. In the past, whenever I set out to change my life for the better (like at the New Year or right before a big birthday) I tended to get really fired up and tried to improve everything at once. Have you ever done that? January would roll around and I'd be like, "OK, I'm starting a diet and writing the next great American novel and working on my marriage and I'm finally going to get my dog to stop pulling on the leash!" And the thing is, for a few days, I'd kill it! But then life would happen and one ball would drop and then another and suddenly I was right back where I started only now I was beyond discouraged. I speak about this process in my book *Girl, Stop Apologizing* and I highly recommend that as a companion for this journal if you want to go into more detail on goal-setting and how to take actionable steps, but the impetus for this daily practice in my life was that I couldn't understand how I could start out so strong and determined only to watch my drive fizzle and fade in no time flat. The worst part was that whenever I failed to achieve my goals or gave up (again) I would mentally berate myself for not being able to achieve big things. It's only now that I understand that it wasn't that my goals were too big, it's that there were too many.

There were too many priorities, too many things to keep track of. I got overwhelmed easily and couldn't keep up with it all which robbed me of whatever motivation I had started with.

When everything is important, nothing is important.

So I narrowed my focus. I went all-in, super hard on one thing and the results were exponential!

I found success –both personally and professionally– when I learned to focus, and focus requires choosing *one goal.* It's hard for many people to commit to only one area of attention when they're passionate about growth. They think they've got to do it all and be it all to see massive change. What they don't realize is that achieving a goal is like water coming into a harbor. When the tide rises in the harbor, all the boats rise.

This amazing thing happens when you start to grow in one area of your life: other areas improve right along with it. If you drop a handful of pebbles into a lake, you'll move the water around a bit. If you drop a boulder into a lake— meaning, if you put all your energy into one area— the impact is incredible. The ripple effects of that choice spread out in all directions.

For clarity's sake, I'd like to mention that it's very possible to grow in multiple areas of your life once you've achieved success in one area and established it as a habit. For instance, I am able to maintain my health and fitness regimen while pursuing a new goal because health and fitness are habits in my life now. But, if I had tried to conquer them simultaneously or attempted to take them on while starting my company, let's say, I wouldn't have been successful.

The question then becomes, how do you decide? How do you pick the right thing to focus on next? Well, if you're me, you narrow it down using a process I used to call 10,10,1.

Like most things in life I figure out something that works for me and, when pressed to explain it, I write it out and give it a snappy title. See: my entire publishing career.

Ten years.
Ten dreams.
One goal.

Who do you want to be in ten years? What are the ten dreams that would make that vision a reality for you? Which one of those dreams are you going to turn into a goal and focus on next? For clarity's sake, let me explain the difference between a dream and a goal. A dream is an idea that you have. A dream is something you think about or obsess over. A dream is something you fantasize about coming true. You might have a dream to get into shape. It becomes a goal when you sign up for a half marathon and join a running club and start racking up the miles. A goal, is when you stop hoping for your dreams and actually start working toward them.

A goal is a dream with its work boots on.

Here's how this process works:

You, Ten Years From Now

Have you ever thought about what the *best version* of you is like? Many of us imagine great things happening but very few people spend the time to imagine –in vivid detail— what their best self would be like. If we were at one of my conferences I'd take you through a full visualization exercise and ask you to close your eyes and dream about the best version of you. For today's purposes, you've got to keep reading so keep your eyes open and maybe try meditating on this later. Imagine that a decade of time has gone by, and you are living your best possible ideal for yourself and your life. Dream big! Don't put any restriction on it. Don't overthink it; just allow yourself to envision the most magnificent possible future version of yourself. A decade in the future, what is the very best version of yourself doing? What does she look like? How does he go about his day? How does she speak to people she loves? How is she loved in return? What kind of clothes do you wear? What kind of car do you drive? Are you a great cook? Do you love to read? Do you love to run? Get as specific as you possibly can. Where do you go on vacation? What's your favorite restaurant to eat at now that your life is different? What kind of food do you consume? What does it feel like to go throughout your day?

Are you optimistic? Are you encouraging to others? After a decade of working on yourself and growing as a person, how much joy is there in your life? Who's in your life? What's your week like? How do you treat people? How do they treat you?

Let your dreams run absolutely wild. Are you happy? Are you energetic? Are you driven? Do you feel ambitious? What's your relationship like with your family members? Do you own a home, and what does it look like? Do you have kids, do you have a family, are you married? What's the best of the best?

Now go bigger!

What's a bigger version of the best version of you living every day in the best state that you know how to be? What do you do for work? What is the highest value that your future self holds? Is it family, is it loyalty, is it growth? Be as specific as you can be. See it like a movie in your mind.

Now, without a second of judgement or overthinking it, I want you to write down everything that you just thought of as fast as you can. I don't want you to forget any of it; I want that future version of you to be seared inside your brain.

The best version of me is...
When I'm at my best, I…

Don't hold back. This is not the time to think it through or tell yourself to slow down. This is not the time for realistic; this is the time to think as big as you can possibly go. You've got two pages to fill up with words and sentences or even pictures and doodles that will help you visualize the future you.

Get to work!

In Ten Years, I Will Be...

In Ten Years, I Will Be...

Dang! That future version of you sounds awesome and I want to take a moment to acknowledge you for writing all those hopes and ideas down. Very few people have the courage to ever put their desires into substance and I'm proud of you for calling your shot. Hopefully, this exercise helped you paint a clear picture in your mind of a lot of different awesome things your future self can take part in. Personally, I like to do this once or twice a year and create a vision board (like in fifth grade when you glue a bunch of magazine clippings to poster paper), so I've got a visual to go along with my mental imagery.

That is the first step; that's you in ten years.

Now here is how you narrow it down.

Ten Dreams

Turn your ten years into ten dreams. The ten dreams are the things that if they came true, they would make your vision a reality. So, if you saw a future that was completely financially free, maybe your dreams would be things like making a six-figure salary, getting completely out of debt, etc. But maybe your future dream self is also healthy and happy and energetic. Add becoming a marathon runner and vegetarian to the mix. The important thing is, again, to be specific. The list of dreams is how that future vision manifests for you.

Often, when we do this, we come up with more than ten, but it's essential to narrow it down. Focus matters, remember? Choose ten dreams that, if they were to come true, would make your future-self real.

Now here's the key to the start today journal: use the prompts as a daily practice to write down those ten dreams… but you have to write them as if *they've already happened.* I do this every day of my life, because I want the repetition to instill in my head and my heart where my focus should be.

I write them as if they've already happened, because I read once that your subconscious focuses on what you give it. So if you tell yourself (and your subconscious), "I'm going to make a million dollars," you don't end up focusing on the goal but on the words "going to." It's just another to-do list for your brain. You didn't give it direction. You didn't ask your mind to help you figure out how. You only told it that you were *going to do* something, which isn't especially powerful no matter how big a goal you set for yourself. After all, you create to-do lists all the time. What makes this something your brain should take notice of? What if instead you told yourself, "I have a million dollars in the bank"? That's specific. That's an outcome. That's a direction to head. "Going to" is something in the future. "Have" is present tense, which means your subconscious starts focusing on how to make that real *right now.*

Some items on my list are things that I want to achieve; other items are things I can accomplish every day.

"I am an exceptional wife."

That one is on my list. I write it down every day as a reminder of who I am and who I want to be. When I imagine my future best self, she's still drunk in love with my husband Dave. In the future he's still my best friend, and we still can't keep our hands off each other. Only now we look so much fresher, because all our kids are older and we don't have to change diapers or wake up with a teething baby.

I'm careful with the words I write down too. I don't use the word *good.* I don't use the word *great.* I use the word *exceptional.* When I write that sentence about being an exceptional wife every day, I have to ask myself what I did today that made me exceptional. It's a simple prompt to move me into action. It reminds me to text my husband and tell him how hot he looked in those pants or how much I love him or how much I appreciate what a good dad he is. That wouldn't happen if I didn't have the prompt reminding me who I want to be.

Another item on my list? *I am a New York Times Bestseller.* I wrote this for years and years. I wrote it with my first book and my third and my fifth and each time I was discouraged when I didn't make the list… but then, I had pages and pages of me reminding myself where I was going. It worked as the inertia I needed to stand back up and try again and again. It wasn't until my sixth book and over a decade of dreaming about it that I finally made that dream a reality and even though it took years, every single day I reminded myself where I was headed.

Take a moment and brainstorm dreams… all kinds of dreams. Look at your vision of who you want to be ten years from now and write down all of the things that would be true if that was your reality. You don't need to narrow it down to ten things just yet, just brainstorm and fill up the pages with possibilities!

Dreams That Will Make My Vision A Reality...

Dreams That Will Make My Vision A Reality...

Now that you have a bunch of ideas, narrow it down to the ten that matter most. The ten dreams that are most affective to get you where you want to go. Don't worry about getting these perfect—my dreams have remained the same but the way I wrote them down has changed as I've learned in more detail what I want and how to pursue it. For now, just decide on the ten dreams you're going to commit to at the start of this journey.

These should be the kind of dreams that light your heart on fire just to write them down and also make you a little nervous. These are the kind of things that if other people saw your list they'd be like, "That girl has lost her mind! Who does she think she is?!" But guess what, these aren't dreams for the naysayers… these aren't dreams for anyone else, these are the things you want for your life and nobody else gets an opinion here.

Not even that snarky voice in the back of your mind that likes to remind you to slow down and be cautious and play it small. Tell that voice to shut it! Let your heart decide which ten dreams are best, not your brain.

Now list them on the next page.

Ten Dreams I Made Happen *yes I know you didn't make them happen YET, but the point is to write them as if you have!

1.

2.

3.

4.

5.

6.

7.

8.

9.

10.

One Goal

The next step is narrowing your focus down to one goal. 10, 10, 1. Ten years becomes ten dreams becomes one goal. Your dream is your ideal; it becomes a goal when you actively begin to pursue it.

The ten dreams, even though they're maybe more focused than you've ever been are still too broad. We've got to narrow it down to one thing. So I want you to ask yourself right now, what is one goal— one thing you can do— that will get you closer to the ten-years-from-now version of yourself the fastest. What is the one goal out of the ten you just finished identifying that you can work on this quarter?

To achieve a goal, you need to make sure you have clarity on two things:

1. What are the specifics?
2. How will you measure your progress?

"I want to lose weight" is not specific. Do you want to lose two pounds or a hundred pounds? That's specific.

"I want a body-fat percentage of 24%."

"I want to save $5,000."

Those are specific goals that you can measure against.

"I want to do better with my finances." That's garbage. You're already setting yourself up for failure, or you're setting up to give yourself credit for work without making measurable progress. Paying cash for my latte instead of using a credit card could be considered "doing better on my finances," but where is it getting you? If your goal was something along the lines of "I want to save $5,000," you wouldn't have a latte at all.

Your goal also needs to be *measurable*. You have to be able to judge whether you're making progress or getting closer to where you want to be. A lot of people also say that a goal has to have a time limit, but I don't like that for goals because I feel like it sets you up for failure. If you tell yourself you've got to be in shape by the end of February and then you get to mid February and you haven't done it, you beat yourself up. The intention here is that working on your ideal self is a lifelong process to become who you were meant to be. Lifelong processes don't have a time limit. All that matters is that you have consistency. We're not looking for perfection; we're looking for habit and that's why this journal is a practice for every day.

So everyday, you're going to start your day using the journal prompts to remind you of who you want to be. I like to take five to ten minutes each day to meditate or pray on the things I'm grateful for. Taking a few minutes to mentally list out my blessings gets me in a great headspace. From a place of gratitude we see so much possibility in front of us.

So get grateful, and then use the prompts to set your intention. Write down ten dreams every day as if they've already happened and finish with one big, incredible goal that will get you there fastest. Now that you know where you're truly headed you can build your action plan and to-do list about the results that you want and the direction that you're headed!

START TODAY

DATE:

Today I Am Grateful For:

1. ____
2. ____
3. ____
4. ____
5. ____

Ten Dreams I Made Happen:

1. ____
2. ____
3. ____
4. ____
5. ____
6. ____
7. ____
8. ____
9. ____
10. ____

The Goal I Am Going To Achieve First:

Show us how you *start today* on Social! – #StartTodayJournal

START TODAY

DATE:

Today I Am Grateful For:

1. ______

2. ______

3. ______

4. ______

5. ______

Ten Dreams I Made Happen:

1. ______

2. ______

3. ______

4. ______

5. ______

6. ______

7. ______

8. ______

9. ______

10. ______

The Goal I Am Going To Achieve First:

START TODAY

DATE:

Today I Am Grateful For:

1. ______________________________
2. ______________________________
3. ______________________________
4. ______________________________
5. ______________________________

Ten Dreams I Made Happen:

1. ______________________________
2. ______________________________
3. ______________________________
4. ______________________________
5. ______________________________
6. ______________________________
7. ______________________________
8. ______________________________
9. ______________________________
10. ______________________________

The Goal I Am Going To Achieve First:

Show us how you *start today* on Social! – #StartTodayJournal

START TODAY

DATE:

TODAY I AM GRATEFUL FOR:

1. __________
2. __________
3. __________
4. __________
5. __________

TEN DREAMS I MADE HAPPEN:

1. __________
2. __________
3. __________
4. __________
5. __________
6. __________
7. __________
8. __________
9. __________
10. __________

THE GOAL I AM GOING TO ACHIEVE FIRST:

START TODAY

DATE:

TODAY I AM GRATEFUL FOR:

1. ____________________
2. ____________________
3. ____________________
4. ____________________
5. ____________________

TEN DREAMS I MADE HAPPEN:

1. ____________________
2. ____________________
3. ____________________
4. ____________________
5. ____________________
6. ____________________
7. ____________________
8. ____________________
9. ____________________
10. ____________________

THE GOAL I AM GOING TO ACHIEVE FIRST:

Show us how you *start today* on Social! – #StartTodayJournal

START TODAY

DATE:

TODAY I AM GRATEFUL FOR:

1. ______________________
2. ______________________
3. ______________________
4. ______________________
5. ______________________

TEN DREAMS I MADE HAPPEN:

1. ______________________
2. ______________________
3. ______________________
4. ______________________
5. ______________________
6. ______________________
7. ______________________
8. ______________________
9. ______________________
10. ______________________

THE GOAL I AM GOING TO ACHIEVE FIRST:

START TODAY

DATE:

Today I Am Grateful For:

1. ____________________
2. ____________________
3. ____________________
4. ____________________
5. ____________________

Ten Dreams I Made Happen:

1. ____________________
2. ____________________
3. ____________________
4. ____________________
5. ____________________
6. ____________________
7. ____________________
8. ____________________
9. ____________________
10. ____________________

The Goal I Am Going To Achieve First:

Show us how you *start today* on Social! – #StartTodayJournal

START TODAY

DATE:

TODAY I AM GRATEFUL FOR:

1. __________
2. __________
3. __________
4. __________
5. __________

TEN DREAMS I MADE HAPPEN:

1. __________
2. __________
3. __________
4. __________
5. __________
6. __________
7. __________
8. __________
9. __________
10. __________

THE GOAL I AM GOING TO ACHIEVE FIRST:

START TODAY

DATE:

Today I Am Grateful For:

1. ______________________
2. ______________________
3. ______________________
4. ______________________
5. ______________________

Ten Dreams I Made Happen:

1. ______________________
2. ______________________
3. ______________________
4. ______________________
5. ______________________
6. ______________________
7. ______________________
8. ______________________
9. ______________________
10. ______________________

The Goal I Am Going To Achieve First:

Show us how you *start today* on Social! – #StartTodayJournal

START TODAY

DATE:

TODAY I AM GRATEFUL FOR:

1. ______
2. ______
3. ______
4. ______
5. ______

TEN DREAMS I MADE HAPPEN:

1. ______
2. ______
3. ______
4. ______
5. ______
6. ______
7. ______
8. ______
9. ______
10. ______

THE GOAL I AM GOING TO ACHIEVE FIRST:

START TODAY

DATE:

TODAY I AM GRATEFUL FOR:

1. __________
2. __________
3. __________
4. __________
5. __________

TEN DREAMS I MADE HAPPEN:

1. __________
2. __________
3. __________
4. __________
5. __________
6. __________
7. __________
8. __________
9. __________
10. __________

THE GOAL I AM GOING TO ACHIEVE FIRST:

Show us how you *start today* on Social! – #StartTodayJournal

START TODAY

DATE:

TODAY I AM GRATEFUL FOR:

1. ______________________
2. ______________________
3. ______________________
4. ______________________
5. ______________________

TEN DREAMS I MADE HAPPEN:

1. ______________________
2. ______________________
3. ______________________
4. ______________________
5. ______________________
6. ______________________
7. ______________________
8. ______________________
9. ______________________
10. ______________________

THE GOAL I AM GOING TO ACHIEVE FIRST:

START TODAY

DATE:

Today I Am Grateful For:

1. ___
2. ___
3. ___
4. ___
5. ___

Ten Dreams I Made Happen:

1. ___
2. ___
3. ___
4. ___
5. ___
6. ___
7. ___
8. ___
9. ___
10. ___

The Goal I Am Going To Achieve First:

START TODAY

DATE:

TODAY I AM GRATEFUL FOR:

1. ______
2. ______
3. ______
4. ______
5. ______

TEN DREAMS I MADE HAPPEN:

1. ______
2. ______
3. ______
4. ______
5. ______
6. ______
7. ______
8. ______
9. ______
10. ______

THE GOAL I AM GOING TO ACHIEVE FIRST:

START TODAY

DATE:

Today I Am Grateful For:

1. __________
2. __________
3. __________
4. __________
5. __________

Ten Dreams I Made Happen:

1. __________
2. __________
3. __________
4. __________
5. __________
6. __________
7. __________
8. __________
9. __________
10. __________

The Goal I Am Going To Achieve First:

Show us how you *start today* on Social! – #StartTodayJournal

START TODAY

DATE:

TODAY I AM GRATEFUL FOR:

1. ______
2. ______
3. ______
4. ______
5. ______

TEN DREAMS I MADE HAPPEN:

1. ______
2. ______
3. ______
4. ______
5. ______
6. ______
7. ______
8. ______
9. ______
10. ______

THE GOAL I AM GOING TO ACHIEVE FIRST:

START TODAY

DATE:

Today I Am Grateful For:

1. __________
2. __________
3. __________
4. __________
5. __________

Ten Dreams I Made Happen:

1. __________
2. __________
3. __________
4. __________
5. __________
6. __________
7. __________
8. __________
9. __________
10. __________

The Goal I Am Going To Achieve First:

Show us how you *start today* on Social! – #StartTodayJournal

START TODAY

DATE:

TODAY I AM GRATEFUL FOR:

1. __________
2. __________
3. __________
4. __________
5. __________

TEN DREAMS I MADE HAPPEN:

1. __________
2. __________
3. __________
4. __________
5. __________
6. __________
7. __________
8. __________
9. __________
10. __________

THE GOAL I AM GOING TO ACHIEVE FIRST:

START TODAY

DATE:

Today I Am Grateful For:

1. ______________________
2. ______________________
3. ______________________
4. ______________________
5. ______________________

Ten Dreams I Made Happen:

1. ______________________
2. ______________________
3. ______________________
4. ______________________
5. ______________________
6. ______________________
7. ______________________
8. ______________________
9. ______________________
10. ______________________

The Goal I Am Going To Achieve First:

Show us how you *start today* on Social! – #StartTodayJournal

START TODAY

DATE:

Today I Am Grateful For:

1. ________________________________
2. ________________________________
3. ________________________________
4. ________________________________
5. ________________________________

Ten Dreams I Made Happen:

1. ________________________________
2. ________________________________
3. ________________________________
4. ________________________________
5. ________________________________
6. ________________________________
7. ________________________________
8. ________________________________
9. ________________________________
10. ________________________________

The Goal I Am Going To Achieve First:

START TODAY

DATE:

Today I Am Grateful For:

1. ____________________
2. ____________________
3. ____________________
4. ____________________
5. ____________________

Ten Dreams I Made Happen:

1. ____________________
2. ____________________
3. ____________________
4. ____________________
5. ____________________
6. ____________________
7. ____________________
8. ____________________
9. ____________________
10. ____________________

The Goal I Am Going To Achieve First:

Show us how you *start today* on Social! – #StartTodayJournal

START TODAY

DATE:

Today I Am Grateful For:

1. ______________________________
2. ______________________________
3. ______________________________
4. ______________________________
5. ______________________________

Ten Dreams I Made Happen:

1. ______________________________
2. ______________________________
3. ______________________________
4. ______________________________
5. ______________________________
6. ______________________________
7. ______________________________
8. ______________________________
9. ______________________________
10. ______________________________

The Goal I Am Going To Achieve First:

START TODAY

DATE:

TODAY I AM GRATEFUL FOR:

1. __________
2. __________
3. __________
4. __________
5. __________

TEN DREAMS I MADE HAPPEN:

1. __________
2. __________
3. __________
4. __________
5. __________
6. __________
7. __________
8. __________
9. __________
10. __________

THE GOAL I AM GOING TO ACHIEVE FIRST:

Show us how you *start today* on Social! – #StartTodayJournal

START TODAY

DATE:

TODAY I AM GRATEFUL FOR:

1. __________
2. __________
3. __________
4. __________
5. __________

TEN DREAMS I MADE HAPPEN:

1. __________
2. __________
3. __________
4. __________
5. __________
6. __________
7. __________
8. __________
9. __________
10. __________

THE GOAL I AM GOING TO ACHIEVE FIRST:

START TODAY

DATE:

TODAY I AM GRATEFUL FOR:

1. ____________________
2. ____________________
3. ____________________
4. ____________________
5. ____________________

TEN DREAMS I MADE HAPPEN:

1. ____________________
2. ____________________
3. ____________________
4. ____________________
5. ____________________
6. ____________________
7. ____________________
8. ____________________
9. ____________________
10. ____________________

THE GOAL I AM GOING TO ACHIEVE FIRST:

Show us how you *start today* on Social! – #StartTodayJournal

START TODAY

DATE:

TODAY I AM GRATEFUL FOR:

1. ____________________
2. ____________________
3. ____________________
4. ____________________
5. ____________________

TEN DREAMS I MADE HAPPEN:

1. ____________________
2. ____________________
3. ____________________
4. ____________________
5. ____________________
6. ____________________
7. ____________________
8. ____________________
9. ____________________
10. ____________________

THE GOAL I AM GOING TO ACHIEVE FIRST:

START TODAY

DATE:

Today I Am Grateful For:

1. __________
2. __________
3. __________
4. __________
5. __________

Ten Dreams I Made Happen:

1. __________
2. __________
3. __________
4. __________
5. __________
6. __________
7. __________
8. __________
9. __________
10. __________

The Goal I Am Going To Achieve First:

Show us how you *start today* on Social! – #StartTodayJournal

START TODAY

DATE:

TODAY I AM GRATEFUL FOR:

1. ______
2. ______
3. ______
4. ______
5. ______

TEN DREAMS I MADE HAPPEN:

1. ______
2. ______
3. ______
4. ______
5. ______
6. ______
7. ______
8. ______
9. ______
10. ______

THE GOAL I AM GOING TO ACHIEVE FIRST:

START TODAY

DATE:

TODAY I AM GRATEFUL FOR:

1. __________
2. __________
3. __________
4. __________
5. __________

TEN DREAMS I MADE HAPPEN:

1. __________
2. __________
3. __________
4. __________
5. __________
6. __________
7. __________
8. __________
9. __________
10. __________

THE GOAL I AM GOING TO ACHIEVE FIRST:

Show us how you *start today* on Social! – #StartTodayJournal

START TODAY

DATE:

Today I Am Grateful For:

1. ____________________
2. ____________________
3. ____________________
4. ____________________
5. ____________________

Ten Dreams I Made Happen:

1. ____________________
2. ____________________
3. ____________________
4. ____________________
5. ____________________
6. ____________________
7. ____________________
8. ____________________
9. ____________________
10. ____________________

The Goal I Am Going To Achieve First:

START TODAY

DATE:

Today I Am Grateful For:

1. ____________________
2. ____________________
3. ____________________
4. ____________________
5. ____________________

Ten Dreams I Made Happen:

1. ____________________
2. ____________________
3. ____________________
4. ____________________
5. ____________________
6. ____________________
7. ____________________
8. ____________________
9. ____________________
10. ____________________

The Goal I Am Going To Achieve First:

Show us how you *start today* on Social! – #StartTodayJournal

START TODAY

DATE:

Today I Am Grateful For:

1. ________________________________
2. ________________________________
3. ________________________________
4. ________________________________
5. ________________________________

Ten Dreams I Made Happen:

1. ________________________________
2. ________________________________
3. ________________________________
4. ________________________________
5. ________________________________
6. ________________________________
7. ________________________________
8. ________________________________
9. ________________________________
10. ________________________________

The Goal I Am Going To Achieve First:

START TODAY

DATE:

TODAY I AM GRATEFUL FOR:

1. ______________________
2. ______________________
3. ______________________
4. ______________________
5. ______________________

TEN DREAMS I MADE HAPPEN:

1. ______________________
2. ______________________
3. ______________________
4. ______________________
5. ______________________
6. ______________________
7. ______________________
8. ______________________
9. ______________________
10. ______________________

THE GOAL I AM GOING TO ACHIEVE FIRST:

Show us how you *start today* on Social! – #StartTodayJournal

START TODAY

DATE:

TODAY I AM GRATEFUL FOR:

1. __________
2. __________
3. __________
4. __________
5. __________

TEN DREAMS I MADE HAPPEN:

1. __________
2. __________
3. __________
4. __________
5. __________
6. __________
7. __________
8. __________
9. __________
10. __________

THE GOAL I AM GOING TO ACHIEVE FIRST:

START TODAY

DATE:

Today I Am Grateful For:

1. ____________________
2. ____________________
3. ____________________
4. ____________________
5. ____________________

Ten Dreams I Made Happen:

1. ____________________
2. ____________________
3. ____________________
4. ____________________
5. ____________________
6. ____________________
7. ____________________
8. ____________________
9. ____________________
10. ____________________

The Goal I Am Going To Achieve First:

START TODAY

DATE:

Today I Am Grateful For:

1. ______
2. ______
3. ______
4. ______
5. ______

Ten Dreams I Made Happen:

1. ______
2. ______
3. ______
4. ______
5. ______
6. ______
7. ______
8. ______
9. ______
10. ______

The Goal I Am Going To Achieve First:

START TODAY

DATE:

Today I Am Grateful For:

1. ______________________________
2. ______________________________
3. ______________________________
4. ______________________________
5. ______________________________

Ten Dreams I Made Happen:

1. ______________________________
2. ______________________________
3. ______________________________
4. ______________________________
5. ______________________________
6. ______________________________
7. ______________________________
8. ______________________________
9. ______________________________
10. ______________________________

The Goal I Am Going To Achieve First:

Show us how you *start today* on Social! – #StartTodayJournal

START TODAY

DATE:

TODAY I AM GRATEFUL FOR:

1. ________________________________
2. ________________________________
3. ________________________________
4. ________________________________
5. ________________________________

TEN DREAMS I MADE HAPPEN:

1. ________________________________
2. ________________________________
3. ________________________________
4. ________________________________
5. ________________________________
6. ________________________________
7. ________________________________
8. ________________________________
9. ________________________________
10. ________________________________

THE GOAL I AM GOING TO ACHIEVE FIRST:

START TODAY

DATE:

Today I Am Grateful For:

1. ______
2. ______
3. ______
4. ______
5. ______

Ten Dreams I Made Happen:

1. ______
2. ______
3. ______
4. ______
5. ______
6. ______
7. ______
8. ______
9. ______
10. ______

The Goal I Am Going To Achieve First:

Show us how you *start today* on Social! – #StartTodayJournal

START TODAY

DATE:

TODAY I AM GRATEFUL FOR:

1. ___
2. ___
3. ___
4. ___
5. ___

TEN DREAMS I MADE HAPPEN:

1. ___
2. ___
3. ___
4. ___
5. ___
6. ___
7. ___
8. ___
9. ___
10. ___

THE GOAL I AM GOING TO ACHIEVE FIRST:

START TODAY

DATE:

TODAY I AM GRATEFUL FOR:

1. __________
2. __________
3. __________
4. __________
5. __________

TEN DREAMS I MADE HAPPEN:

1. __________
2. __________
3. __________
4. __________
5. __________
6. __________
7. __________
8. __________
9. __________
10. __________

THE GOAL I AM GOING TO ACHIEVE FIRST:

Show us how you *start today* on Social! – #StartTodayJournal

START TODAY

DATE:

Today I Am Grateful For:

1. __________
2. __________
3. __________
4. __________
5. __________

Ten Dreams I Made Happen:

1. __________
2. __________
3. __________
4. __________
5. __________
6. __________
7. __________
8. __________
9. __________
10. __________

The Goal I Am Going To Achieve First:

START TODAY

DATE:

Today I Am Grateful For:

1. __________
2. __________
3. __________
4. __________
5. __________

Ten Dreams I Made Happen:

1. __________
2. __________
3. __________
4. __________
5. __________
6. __________
7. __________
8. __________
9. __________
10. __________

The Goal I Am Going To Achieve First:

Show us how you *start today* on Social! – #StartTodayJournal

START TODAY

DATE:

TODAY I AM GRATEFUL FOR:

1. ______
2. ______
3. ______
4. ______
5. ______

TEN DREAMS I MADE HAPPEN:

1. ______
2. ______
3. ______
4. ______
5. ______
6. ______
7. ______
8. ______
9. ______
10. ______

THE GOAL I AM GOING TO ACHIEVE FIRST:

START TODAY

DATE:

Today I Am Grateful For:

1. ______________________________
2. ______________________________
3. ______________________________
4. ______________________________
5. ______________________________

Ten Dreams I Made Happen:

1. ______________________________
2. ______________________________
3. ______________________________
4. ______________________________
5. ______________________________
6. ______________________________
7. ______________________________
8. ______________________________
9. ______________________________
10. ______________________________

The Goal I Am Going To Achieve First:

Show us how you *start today* on Social! – #StartTodayJournal

START TODAY

DATE:

TODAY I AM GRATEFUL FOR:

1. ______________________________
2. ______________________________
3. ______________________________
4. ______________________________
5. ______________________________

TEN DREAMS I MADE HAPPEN:

1. ______________________________
2. ______________________________
3. ______________________________
4. ______________________________
5. ______________________________
6. ______________________________
7. ______________________________
8. ______________________________
9. ______________________________
10. ______________________________

THE GOAL I AM GOING TO ACHIEVE FIRST:

START TODAY

DATE:

Today I Am Grateful For:

1. ______
2. ______
3. ______
4. ______
5. ______

Ten Dreams I Made Happen:

1. ______
2. ______
3. ______
4. ______
5. ______
6. ______
7. ______
8. ______
9. ______
10. ______

The Goal I Am Going To Achieve First:

Show us how you *start today* on Social! – #StartTodayJournal

START TODAY

DATE:

TODAY I AM GRATEFUL FOR:

1. ______________________
2. ______________________
3. ______________________
4. ______________________
5. ______________________

TEN DREAMS I MADE HAPPEN:

1. ______________________
2. ______________________
3. ______________________
4. ______________________
5. ______________________
6. ______________________
7. ______________________
8. ______________________
9. ______________________
10. ______________________

THE GOAL I AM GOING TO ACHIEVE FIRST:

START TODAY

DATE:

TODAY I AM GRATEFUL FOR:

1. ____________________
2. ____________________
3. ____________________
4. ____________________
5. ____________________

TEN DREAMS I MADE HAPPEN:

1. ____________________
2. ____________________
3. ____________________
4. ____________________
5. ____________________
6. ____________________
7. ____________________
8. ____________________
9. ____________________
10. ____________________

THE GOAL I AM GOING TO ACHIEVE FIRST:

Show us how you *start today* on Social! – #StartTodayJournal

START TODAY

DATE:

TODAY I AM GRATEFUL FOR:

1. ______________________
2. ______________________
3. ______________________
4. ______________________
5. ______________________

TEN DREAMS I MADE HAPPEN:

1. ______________________
2. ______________________
3. ______________________
4. ______________________
5. ______________________
6. ______________________
7. ______________________
8. ______________________
9. ______________________
10. ______________________

THE GOAL I AM GOING TO ACHIEVE FIRST:

START TODAY

DATE:

Today I Am Grateful For:

1. ______
2. ______
3. ______
4. ______
5. ______

Ten Dreams I Made Happen:

1. ______
2. ______
3. ______
4. ______
5. ______
6. ______
7. ______
8. ______
9. ______
10. ______

The Goal I Am Going To Achieve First:

Show us how you *start today* on Social! – #StartTodayJournal

START TODAY

DATE:

Today I Am Grateful For:

1. ______
2. ______
3. ______
4. ______
5. ______

Ten Dreams I Made Happen:

1. ______
2. ______
3. ______
4. ______
5. ______
6. ______
7. ______
8. ______
9. ______
10. ______

The Goal I Am Going To Achieve First:

START TODAY

DATE:

Today I Am Grateful For:

1. ____
2. ____
3. ____
4. ____
5. ____

Ten Dreams I Made Happen:

1. ____
2. ____
3. ____
4. ____
5. ____
6. ____
7. ____
8. ____
9. ____
10. ____

The Goal I Am Going To Achieve First:

START TODAY

DATE:

Today I Am Grateful For:

1. ______
2. ______
3. ______
4. ______
5. ______

Ten Dreams I Made Happen:

1. ______
2. ______
3. ______
4. ______
5. ______
6. ______
7. ______
8. ______
9. ______
10. ______

The Goal I Am Going To Achieve First:

START TODAY

DATE:

Today I Am Grateful For:

1.
2.
3.
4.
5.

Ten Dreams I Made Happen:

1.
2.
3.
4.
5.
6.
7.
8.
9.
10.

The Goal I Am Going To Achieve First:

Show us how you *start today* on Social! – #StartTodayJournal

START TODAY

DATE:

TODAY I AM GRATEFUL FOR:

1. ______________________________
2. ______________________________
3. ______________________________
4. ______________________________
5. ______________________________

TEN DREAMS I MADE HAPPEN:

1. ______________________________
2. ______________________________
3. ______________________________
4. ______________________________
5. ______________________________
6. ______________________________
7. ______________________________
8. ______________________________
9. ______________________________
10. ______________________________

THE GOAL I AM GOING TO ACHIEVE FIRST:

START TODAY

DATE:

Today I Am Grateful For:

1. ______
2. ______
3. ______
4. ______
5. ______

Ten Dreams I Made Happen:

1. ______
2. ______
3. ______
4. ______
5. ______
6. ______
7. ______
8. ______
9. ______
10. ______

The Goal I Am Going To Achieve First:

Show us how you *start today* on Social! – #StartTodayJournal

START TODAY

DATE:

TODAY I AM GRATEFUL FOR:

1. ____
2. ____
3. ____
4. ____
5. ____

TEN DREAMS I MADE HAPPEN:

1. ____
2. ____
3. ____
4. ____
5. ____
6. ____
7. ____
8. ____
9. ____
10. ____

THE GOAL I AM GOING TO ACHIEVE FIRST:

START TODAY

DATE:

Today I Am Grateful For:

1.
2.
3.
4.
5.

Ten Dreams I Made Happen:

1.
2.
3.
4.
5.
6.
7.
8.
9.
10.

The Goal I Am Going To Achieve First:

Show us how you *start today* on Social! – #StartTodayJournal

START TODAY

DATE:

TODAY I AM GRATEFUL FOR:

1. __________
2. __________
3. __________
4. __________
5. __________

TEN DREAMS I MADE HAPPEN:

1. __________
2. __________
3. __________
4. __________
5. __________
6. __________
7. __________
8. __________
9. __________
10. __________

THE GOAL I AM GOING TO ACHIEVE FIRST:

START TODAY

DATE:

Today I Am Grateful For:

1. ______
2. ______
3. ______
4. ______
5. ______

Ten Dreams I Made Happen:

1. ______
2. ______
3. ______
4. ______
5. ______
6. ______
7. ______
8. ______
9. ______
10. ______

The Goal I Am Going To Achieve First:

Show us how you *start today* on Social! – #StartTodayJournal

START TODAY

DATE:

Today I Am Grateful For:

1. ____________________
2. ____________________
3. ____________________
4. ____________________
5. ____________________

Ten Dreams I Made Happen:

1. ____________________
2. ____________________
3. ____________________
4. ____________________
5. ____________________
6. ____________________
7. ____________________
8. ____________________
9. ____________________
10. ____________________

The Goal I Am Going To Achieve First:

START TODAY

DATE:

Today I Am Grateful For:

1. ______
2. ______
3. ______
4. ______
5. ______

Ten Dreams I Made Happen:

1. ______
2. ______
3. ______
4. ______
5. ______
6. ______
7. ______
8. ______
9. ______
10. ______

The Goal I Am Going To Achieve First:

Show us how you *start today* on Social! – #StartTodayJournal

START TODAY

DATE:

Today I Am Grateful For:

1. ______________________________
2. ______________________________
3. ______________________________
4. ______________________________
5. ______________________________

Ten Dreams I Made Happen:

1. ______________________________
2. ______________________________
3. ______________________________
4. ______________________________
5. ______________________________
6. ______________________________
7. ______________________________
8. ______________________________
9. ______________________________
10. ______________________________

The Goal I Am Going To Achieve First:

START TODAY

DATE:

Today I Am Grateful For:

1. __________
2. __________
3. __________
4. __________
5. __________

Ten Dreams I Made Happen:

1. __________
2. __________
3. __________
4. __________
5. __________
6. __________
7. __________
8. __________
9. __________
10. __________

The Goal I Am Going To Achieve First:

Show us how you *start today* on Social! – #StartTodayJournal

START TODAY

DATE:

Today I Am Grateful For:

1. ______
2. ______
3. ______
4. ______
5. ______

Ten Dreams I Made Happen:

1. ______
2. ______
3. ______
4. ______
5. ______
6. ______
7. ______
8. ______
9. ______
10. ______

The Goal I Am Going To Achieve First:

START TODAY

DATE:

Today I Am Grateful For:

1. ______
2. ______
3. ______
4. ______
5. ______

Ten Dreams I Made Happen:

1. ______
2. ______
3. ______
4. ______
5. ______
6. ______
7. ______
8. ______
9. ______
10. ______

The Goal I Am Going To Achieve First:

Show us how you *start today* on Social! – #StartTodayJournal

START TODAY

DATE:

Today I Am Grateful For:

1. ______________________
2. ______________________
3. ______________________
4. ______________________
5. ______________________

Ten Dreams I Made Happen:

1. ______________________
2. ______________________
3. ______________________
4. ______________________
5. ______________________
6. ______________________
7. ______________________
8. ______________________
9. ______________________
10. ______________________

The Goal I Am Going To Achieve First:

START TODAY

DATE:

TODAY I AM GRATEFUL FOR:

1. ____________________
2. ____________________
3. ____________________
4. ____________________
5. ____________________

TEN DREAMS I MADE HAPPEN:

1. ____________________
2. ____________________
3. ____________________
4. ____________________
5. ____________________
6. ____________________
7. ____________________
8. ____________________
9. ____________________
10. ____________________

THE GOAL I AM GOING TO ACHIEVE FIRST:

Show us how you *start today* on Social! – #StartTodayJournal

START TODAY

DATE:

TODAY I AM GRATEFUL FOR:

1. ______________________________
2. ______________________________
3. ______________________________
4. ______________________________
5. ______________________________

TEN DREAMS I MADE HAPPEN:

1. ______________________________
2. ______________________________
3. ______________________________
4. ______________________________
5. ______________________________
6. ______________________________
7. ______________________________
8. ______________________________
9. ______________________________
10. ______________________________

THE GOAL I AM GOING TO ACHIEVE FIRST:

START TODAY

DATE:

Today I Am Grateful For:

1. __________
2. __________
3. __________
4. __________
5. __________

Ten Dreams I Made Happen:

1. __________
2. __________
3. __________
4. __________
5. __________
6. __________
7. __________
8. __________
9. __________
10. __________

The Goal I Am Going To Achieve First:

Show us how you *start today* on Social! – #StartTodayJournal

START TODAY

DATE:

TODAY I AM GRATEFUL FOR:

1. ______________________________
2. ______________________________
3. ______________________________
4. ______________________________
5. ______________________________

TEN DREAMS I MADE HAPPEN:

1. ______________________________
2. ______________________________
3. ______________________________
4. ______________________________
5. ______________________________
6. ______________________________
7. ______________________________
8. ______________________________
9. ______________________________
10. ______________________________

THE GOAL I AM GOING TO ACHIEVE FIRST:

START TODAY

DATE:

Today I Am Grateful For:

1. ______
2. ______
3. ______
4. ______
5. ______

Ten Dreams I Made Happen:

1. ______
2. ______
3. ______
4. ______
5. ______
6. ______
7. ______
8. ______
9. ______
10. ______

The Goal I Am Going To Achieve First:

Show us how you *start today* on Social! – #StartTodayJournal

START TODAY

DATE:

Today I Am Grateful For:

1. ______________________________
2. ______________________________
3. ______________________________
4. ______________________________
5. ______________________________

Ten Dreams I Made Happen:

1. ______________________________
2. ______________________________
3. ______________________________
4. ______________________________
5. ______________________________
6. ______________________________
7. ______________________________
8. ______________________________
9. ______________________________
10. ______________________________

The Goal I Am Going To Achieve First:

START TODAY

DATE:

Today I Am Grateful For:

1. ______
2. ______
3. ______
4. ______
5. ______

Ten Dreams I Made Happen:

1. ______
2. ______
3. ______
4. ______
5. ______
6. ______
7. ______
8. ______
9. ______
10. ______

The Goal I Am Going To Achieve First:

Show us how you *start today* on Social! – #StartTodayJournal

START TODAY

DATE:

TODAY I AM GRATEFUL FOR:

1. ______________________________
2. ______________________________
3. ______________________________
4. ______________________________
5. ______________________________

TEN DREAMS I MADE HAPPEN:

1. ______________________________
2. ______________________________
3. ______________________________
4. ______________________________
5. ______________________________
6. ______________________________
7. ______________________________
8. ______________________________
9. ______________________________
10. ______________________________

THE GOAL I AM GOING TO ACHIEVE FIRST:

START TODAY

DATE:

Today I Am Grateful For:

1. ______
2. ______
3. ______
4. ______
5. ______

Ten Dreams I Made Happen:

1. ______
2. ______
3. ______
4. ______
5. ______
6. ______
7. ______
8. ______
9. ______
10. ______

The Goal I Am Going To Achieve First:

Show us how you *start today* on Social! – #StartTodayJournal

START TODAY

DATE:

TODAY I AM GRATEFUL FOR:

1. ____________________
2. ____________________
3. ____________________
4. ____________________
5. ____________________

TEN DREAMS I MADE HAPPEN:

1. ____________________
2. ____________________
3. ____________________
4. ____________________
5. ____________________
6. ____________________
7. ____________________
8. ____________________
9. ____________________
10. ____________________

THE GOAL I AM GOING TO ACHIEVE FIRST:

START TODAY

DATE:

Today I Am Grateful For:

1. ____________________
2. ____________________
3. ____________________
4. ____________________
5. ____________________

Ten Dreams I Made Happen:

1. ____________________
2. ____________________
3. ____________________
4. ____________________
5. ____________________
6. ____________________
7. ____________________
8. ____________________
9. ____________________
10. ____________________

The Goal I Am Going To Achieve First:

Show us how you *start today* on Social! – #StartTodayJournal

START TODAY

DATE:

TODAY I AM GRATEFUL FOR:

1. ____________________
2. ____________________
3. ____________________
4. ____________________
5. ____________________

TEN DREAMS I MADE HAPPEN:

1. ____________________
2. ____________________
3. ____________________
4. ____________________
5. ____________________
6. ____________________
7. ____________________
8. ____________________
9. ____________________
10. ____________________

THE GOAL I AM GOING TO ACHIEVE FIRST:

START TODAY

DATE:

Today I Am Grateful For:

1. ____
2. ____
3. ____
4. ____
5. ____

Ten Dreams I Made Happen:

1. ____
2. ____
3. ____
4. ____
5. ____
6. ____
7. ____
8. ____
9. ____
10. ____

The Goal I Am Going To Achieve First:

Show us how you *start today* on Social! – #StartTodayJournal

START TODAY

DATE:

TODAY I AM GRATEFUL FOR:

1. __________
2. __________
3. __________
4. __________
5. __________

TEN DREAMS I MADE HAPPEN:

1. __________
2. __________
3. __________
4. __________
5. __________
6. __________
7. __________
8. __________
9. __________
10. __________

THE GOAL I AM GOING TO ACHIEVE FIRST:

START TODAY

DATE:

Today I Am Grateful For:

1. __________
2. __________
3. __________
4. __________
5. __________

Ten Dreams I Made Happen:

1. __________
2. __________
3. __________
4. __________
5. __________
6. __________
7. __________
8. __________
9. __________
10. __________

The Goal I Am Going To Achieve First:

Show us how you *start today* on Social! – #StartTodayJournal

START TODAY

DATE:

TODAY I AM GRATEFUL FOR:

1. ______

2. ______

3. ______

4. ______

5. ______

TEN DREAMS I MADE HAPPEN:

1. ______

2. ______

3. ______

4. ______

5. ______

6. ______

7. ______

8. ______

9. ______

10. ______

THE GOAL I AM GOING TO ACHIEVE FIRST:

START TODAY

DATE:

Today I Am Grateful For:

1. ____________________
2. ____________________
3. ____________________
4. ____________________
5. ____________________

Ten Dreams I Made Happen:

1. ____________________
2. ____________________
3. ____________________
4. ____________________
5. ____________________
6. ____________________
7. ____________________
8. ____________________
9. ____________________
10. ____________________

The Goal I Am Going To Achieve First:

Show us how you *start today* on Social! – #StartTodayJournal

START TODAY

DATE:

TODAY I AM GRATEFUL FOR:

1. ____________________
2. ____________________
3. ____________________
4. ____________________
5. ____________________

TEN DREAMS I MADE HAPPEN:

1. ____________________
2. ____________________
3. ____________________
4. ____________________
5. ____________________
6. ____________________
7. ____________________
8. ____________________
9. ____________________
10. ____________________

THE GOAL I AM GOING TO ACHIEVE FIRST:

START TODAY

DATE:

TODAY I AM GRATEFUL FOR:

1. __________
2. __________
3. __________
4. __________
5. __________

TEN DREAMS I MADE HAPPEN:

1. __________
2. __________
3. __________
4. __________
5. __________
6. __________
7. __________
8. __________
9. __________
10. __________

THE GOAL I AM GOING TO ACHIEVE FIRST:

START TODAY

DATE:

TODAY I AM GRATEFUL FOR:

1. ______________________________
2. ______________________________
3. ______________________________
4. ______________________________
5. ______________________________

TEN DREAMS I MADE HAPPEN:

1. ______________________________
2. ______________________________
3. ______________________________
4. ______________________________
5. ______________________________
6. ______________________________
7. ______________________________
8. ______________________________
9. ______________________________
10. ______________________________

THE GOAL I AM GOING TO ACHIEVE FIRST:

START TODAY

DATE:

Today I Am Grateful For:

1. ______________________________
2. ______________________________
3. ______________________________
4. ______________________________
5. ______________________________

Ten Dreams I Made Happen:

1. ______________________________
2. ______________________________
3. ______________________________
4. ______________________________
5. ______________________________
6. ______________________________
7. ______________________________
8. ______________________________
9. ______________________________
10. ______________________________

The Goal I Am Going To Achieve First:

Show us how you *start today* on Social! – #StartTodayJournal

START TODAY

DATE:

TODAY I AM GRATEFUL FOR:

1. ______________________________
2. ______________________________
3. ______________________________
4. ______________________________
5. ______________________________

TEN DREAMS I MADE HAPPEN:

1. ______________________________
2. ______________________________
3. ______________________________
4. ______________________________
5. ______________________________
6. ______________________________
7. ______________________________
8. ______________________________
9. ______________________________
10. ______________________________

THE GOAL I AM GOING TO ACHIEVE FIRST:

START TODAY

DATE:

Today I Am Grateful For:

1. __________
2. __________
3. __________
4. __________
5. __________

Ten Dreams I Made Happen:

1. __________
2. __________
3. __________
4. __________
5. __________
6. __________
7. __________
8. __________
9. __________
10. __________

The Goal I Am Going To Achieve First:

Show us how you *start today* on Social! – #StartTodayJournal

START TODAY

DATE:

TODAY I AM GRATEFUL FOR:

1. ____________________
2. ____________________
3. ____________________
4. ____________________
5. ____________________

TEN DREAMS I MADE HAPPEN:

1. ____________________
2. ____________________
3. ____________________
4. ____________________
5. ____________________
6. ____________________
7. ____________________
8. ____________________
9. ____________________
10. ____________________

THE GOAL I AM GOING TO ACHIEVE FIRST:

START TODAY

DATE:

TODAY I AM GRATEFUL FOR:

1. __________
2. __________
3. __________
4. __________
5. __________

TEN DREAMS I MADE HAPPEN:

1. __________
2. __________
3. __________
4. __________
5. __________
6. __________
7. __________
8. __________
9. __________
10. __________

THE GOAL I AM GOING TO ACHIEVE FIRST:

Show us how you *start today* on Social! – #StartTodayJournal

START TODAY

DATE:

TODAY I AM GRATEFUL FOR:

1. ______________________________
2. ______________________________
3. ______________________________
4. ______________________________
5. ______________________________

TEN DREAMS I MADE HAPPEN:

1. ______________________________
2. ______________________________
3. ______________________________
4. ______________________________
5. ______________________________
6. ______________________________
7. ______________________________
8. ______________________________
9. ______________________________
10. ______________________________

THE GOAL I AM GOING TO ACHIEVE FIRST:

START TODAY

DATE:

Today I Am Grateful For:

1. __________
2. __________
3. __________
4. __________
5. __________

Ten Dreams I Made Happen:

1. __________
2. __________
3. __________
4. __________
5. __________
6. __________
7. __________
8. __________
9. __________
10. __________

The Goal I Am Going To Achieve First:

START TODAY

DATE:

TODAY I AM GRATEFUL FOR:

1. ____________________
2. ____________________
3. ____________________
4. ____________________
5. ____________________

TEN DREAMS I MADE HAPPEN:

1. ____________________
2. ____________________
3. ____________________
4. ____________________
5. ____________________
6. ____________________
7. ____________________
8. ____________________
9. ____________________
10. ____________________

THE GOAL I AM GOING TO ACHIEVE FIRST:

START TODAY

DATE:

Today I Am Grateful For:

1. ________________________________
2. ________________________________
3. ________________________________
4. ________________________________
5. ________________________________

Ten Dreams I Made Happen:

1. ________________________________
2. ________________________________
3. ________________________________
4. ________________________________
5. ________________________________
6. ________________________________
7. ________________________________
8. ________________________________
9. ________________________________
10. ________________________________

The Goal I Am Going To Achieve First:

Show us how you *start today* on Social! – #StartTodayJournal

START TODAY

DATE:

TODAY I AM GRATEFUL FOR:

1. ______
2. ______
3. ______
4. ______
5. ______

TEN DREAMS I MADE HAPPEN:

1. ______
2. ______
3. ______
4. ______
5. ______
6. ______
7. ______
8. ______
9. ______
10. ______

THE GOAL I AM GOING TO ACHIEVE FIRST:

START TODAY

DATE:

TODAY I AM GRATEFUL FOR:

1. __________
2. __________
3. __________
4. __________
5. __________

TEN DREAMS I MADE HAPPEN:

1. __________
2. __________
3. __________
4. __________
5. __________
6. __________
7. __________
8. __________
9. __________
10. __________

THE GOAL I AM GOING TO ACHIEVE FIRST:

Show us how you *start today* on Social! – #StartTodayJournal

START TODAY

DATE:

TODAY I AM GRATEFUL FOR:

1. ______
2. ______
3. ______
4. ______
5. ______

TEN DREAMS I MADE HAPPEN:

1. ______
2. ______
3. ______
4. ______
5. ______
6. ______
7. ______
8. ______
9. ______
10. ______

THE GOAL I AM GOING TO ACHIEVE FIRST:

START TODAY

DATE:

TODAY I AM GRATEFUL FOR:

1. ______________________________
2. ______________________________
3. ______________________________
4. ______________________________
5. ______________________________

TEN DREAMS I MADE HAPPEN:

1. ______________________________
2. ______________________________
3. ______________________________
4. ______________________________
5. ______________________________
6. ______________________________
7. ______________________________
8. ______________________________
9. ______________________________
10. ______________________________

THE GOAL I AM GOING TO ACHIEVE FIRST:

Show us how you *start today* on Social! – #StartTodayJournal

START TODAY

DATE:

TODAY I AM GRATEFUL FOR:

1. ______________________________
2. ______________________________
3. ______________________________
4. ______________________________
5. ______________________________

TEN DREAMS I MADE HAPPEN:

1. ______________________________
2. ______________________________
3. ______________________________
4. ______________________________
5. ______________________________
6. ______________________________
7. ______________________________
8. ______________________________
9. ______________________________
10. ______________________________

THE GOAL I AM GOING TO ACHIEVE FIRST:

START TODAY

DATE:

Today I Am Grateful For:

1. __________
2. __________
3. __________
4. __________
5. __________

Ten Dreams I Made Happen:

1. __________
2. __________
3. __________
4. __________
5. __________
6. __________
7. __________
8. __________
9. __________
10. __________

The Goal I Am Going To Achieve First:

Show us how you *start today* on Social! – #StartTodayJournal

START TODAY

DATE:

TODAY I AM GRATEFUL FOR:

1. ______________________________
2. ______________________________
3. ______________________________
4. ______________________________
5. ______________________________

TEN DREAMS I MADE HAPPEN:

1. ______________________________
2. ______________________________
3. ______________________________
4. ______________________________
5. ______________________________
6. ______________________________
7. ______________________________
8. ______________________________
9. ______________________________
10. ______________________________

THE GOAL I AM GOING TO ACHIEVE FIRST:

START TODAY

DATE:

Today I Am Grateful For:

1. ______
2. ______
3. ______
4. ______
5. ______

Ten Dreams I Made Happen:

1. ______
2. ______
3. ______
4. ______
5. ______
6. ______
7. ______
8. ______
9. ______
10. ______

The Goal I Am Going To Achieve First:

Show us how you *start today* on Social! – #StartTodayJournal

START TODAY

DATE:

TODAY I AM GRATEFUL FOR:

1. ____________________
2. ____________________
3. ____________________
4. ____________________
5. ____________________

TEN DREAMS I MADE HAPPEN:

1. ____________________
2. ____________________
3. ____________________
4. ____________________
5. ____________________
6. ____________________
7. ____________________
8. ____________________
9. ____________________
10. ____________________

THE GOAL I AM GOING TO ACHIEVE FIRST:

START TODAY

DATE:

Today I Am Grateful For:

1. ______
2. ______
3. ______
4. ______
5. ______

Ten Dreams I Made Happen:

1. ______
2. ______
3. ______
4. ______
5. ______
6. ______
7. ______
8. ______
9. ______
10. ______

The Goal I Am Going To Achieve First:

Show us how you *start today* on Social! – #StartTodayJournal

START TODAY

DATE:

TODAY I AM GRATEFUL FOR:

1. ____________________

2. ____________________

3. ____________________

4. ____________________

5. ____________________

TEN DREAMS I MADE HAPPEN:

1. ____________________

2. ____________________

3. ____________________

4. ____________________

5. ____________________

6. ____________________

7. ____________________

8. ____________________

9. ____________________

10. ____________________

THE GOAL I AM GOING TO ACHIEVE FIRST:

START TODAY

DATE:

Today I Am Grateful For:

1. ______________________________
2. ______________________________
3. ______________________________
4. ______________________________
5. ______________________________

Ten Dreams I Made Happen:

1. ______________________________
2. ______________________________
3. ______________________________
4. ______________________________
5. ______________________________
6. ______________________________
7. ______________________________
8. ______________________________
9. ______________________________
10. ______________________________

The Goal I Am Going To Achieve First:

Show us how you *start today* on Social! – #StartTodayJournal

START TODAY

DATE:

TODAY I AM GRATEFUL FOR:

1. ______________________________
2. ______________________________
3. ______________________________
4. ______________________________
5. ______________________________

TEN DREAMS I MADE HAPPEN:

1. ______________________________
2. ______________________________
3. ______________________________
4. ______________________________
5. ______________________________
6. ______________________________
7. ______________________________
8. ______________________________
9. ______________________________
10. ______________________________

THE GOAL I AM GOING TO ACHIEVE FIRST:

START TODAY

DATE:

TODAY I AM GRATEFUL FOR:

1. ______
2. ______
3. ______
4. ______
5. ______

TEN DREAMS I MADE HAPPEN:

1. ______
2. ______
3. ______
4. ______
5. ______
6. ______
7. ______
8. ______
9. ______
10. ______

THE GOAL I AM GOING TO ACHIEVE FIRST:

Show us how you *start today* on Social! – #StartTodayJournal

START TODAY

DATE:

TODAY I AM GRATEFUL FOR:

1. ______________________________
2. ______________________________
3. ______________________________
4. ______________________________
5. ______________________________

TEN DREAMS I MADE HAPPEN:

1. ______________________________
2. ______________________________
3. ______________________________
4. ______________________________
5. ______________________________
6. ______________________________
7. ______________________________
8. ______________________________
9. ______________________________
10. ______________________________

THE GOAL I AM GOING TO ACHIEVE FIRST:

START TODAY

DATE:

Today I Am Grateful For:

1. ______
2. ______
3. ______
4. ______
5. ______

Ten Dreams I Made Happen:

1. ______
2. ______
3. ______
4. ______
5. ______
6. ______
7. ______
8. ______
9. ______
10. ______

The Goal I Am Going To Achieve First:

Show us how you *start today* on Social! – #StartTodayJournal

START TODAY

DATE:

TODAY I AM GRATEFUL FOR:

1. ______
2. ______
3. ______
4. ______
5. ______

TEN DREAMS I MADE HAPPEN:

1. ______
2. ______
3. ______
4. ______
5. ______
6. ______
7. ______
8. ______
9. ______
10. ______

THE GOAL I AM GOING TO ACHIEVE FIRST:

START TODAY

DATE:

Today I Am Grateful For:

1. ______
2. ______
3. ______
4. ______
5. ______

Ten Dreams I Made Happen:

1. ______
2. ______
3. ______
4. ______
5. ______
6. ______
7. ______
8. ______
9. ______
10. ______

The Goal I Am Going To Achieve First:

Show us how you *start today* on Social! – #StartTodayJournal

START TODAY

DATE:

TODAY I AM GRATEFUL FOR:

1. ____________________
2. ____________________
3. ____________________
4. ____________________
5. ____________________

TEN DREAMS I MADE HAPPEN:

1. ____________________
2. ____________________
3. ____________________
4. ____________________
5. ____________________
6. ____________________
7. ____________________
8. ____________________
9. ____________________
10. ____________________

THE GOAL I AM GOING TO ACHIEVE FIRST:

START TODAY

DATE:

Today I Am Grateful For:

1. __________
2. __________
3. __________
4. __________
5. __________

Ten Dreams I Made Happen:

1. __________
2. __________
3. __________
4. __________
5. __________
6. __________
7. __________
8. __________
9. __________
10. __________

The Goal I Am Going To Achieve First:

Show us how you *start today* on Social! – #StartTodayJournal

START TODAY

DATE:

TODAY I AM GRATEFUL FOR:

1. ____________________
2. ____________________
3. ____________________
4. ____________________
5. ____________________

TEN DREAMS I MADE HAPPEN:

1. ____________________
2. ____________________
3. ____________________
4. ____________________
5. ____________________
6. ____________________
7. ____________________
8. ____________________
9. ____________________
10. ____________________

THE GOAL I AM GOING TO ACHIEVE FIRST:

START TODAY

DATE:

Today I Am Grateful For:

1. __________
2. __________
3. __________
4. __________
5. __________

Ten Dreams I Made Happen:

1. __________
2. __________
3. __________
4. __________
5. __________
6. __________
7. __________
8. __________
9. __________
10. __________

The Goal I Am Going To Achieve First:

Show us how you *start today* on Social! – #StartTodayJournal

START TODAY

DATE:

TODAY I AM GRATEFUL FOR:

1. __________
2. __________
3. __________
4. __________
5. __________

TEN DREAMS I MADE HAPPEN:

1. __________
2. __________
3. __________
4. __________
5. __________
6. __________
7. __________
8. __________
9. __________
10. __________

THE GOAL I AM GOING TO ACHIEVE FIRST:

START TODAY

DATE:

Today I Am Grateful For:

1.
2.
3.
4.
5.

Ten Dreams I Made Happen:

1.
2.
3.
4.
5.
6.
7.
8.
9.
10.

The Goal I Am Going To Achieve First:

Show us how you *start today* on Social! – #StartTodayJournal

START TODAY

DATE:

Today I Am Grateful For:

1. ______
2. ______
3. ______
4. ______
5. ______

Ten Dreams I Made Happen:

1. ______
2. ______
3. ______
4. ______
5. ______
6. ______
7. ______
8. ______
9. ______
10. ______

The Goal I Am Going To Achieve First:

START TODAY

DATE:

Today I Am Grateful For:

1. ______
2. ______
3. ______
4. ______
5. ______

Ten Dreams I Made Happen:

1. ______
2. ______
3. ______
4. ______
5. ______
6. ______
7. ______
8. ______
9. ______
10. ______

The Goal I Am Going To Achieve First:

Show us how you *start today* on Social! – #StartTodayJournal

START TODAY

DATE:

TODAY I AM GRATEFUL FOR:

1. __________
2. __________
3. __________
4. __________
5. __________

TEN DREAMS I MADE HAPPEN:

1. __________
2. __________
3. __________
4. __________
5. __________
6. __________
7. __________
8. __________
9. __________
10. __________

THE GOAL I AM GOING TO ACHIEVE FIRST:

START TODAY

DATE:

TODAY I AM GRATEFUL FOR:

1. ______________________________
2. ______________________________
3. ______________________________
4. ______________________________
5. ______________________________

TEN DREAMS I MADE HAPPEN:

1. ______________________________
2. ______________________________
3. ______________________________
4. ______________________________
5. ______________________________
6. ______________________________
7. ______________________________
8. ______________________________
9. ______________________________
10. ______________________________

THE GOAL I AM GOING TO ACHIEVE FIRST:

Show us how you *start today* on Social! – #StartTodayJournal

START TODAY

DATE:

Today I Am Grateful For:

1. ______________________________
2. ______________________________
3. ______________________________
4. ______________________________
5. ______________________________

Ten Dreams I Made Happen:

1. ______________________________
2. ______________________________
3. ______________________________
4. ______________________________
5. ______________________________
6. ______________________________
7. ______________________________
8. ______________________________
9. ______________________________
10. ______________________________

The Goal I Am Going To Achieve First:

START TODAY

DATE:

Today I Am Grateful For:

1. ______
2. ______
3. ______
4. ______
5. ______

Ten Dreams I Made Happen:

1. ______
2. ______
3. ______
4. ______
5. ______
6. ______
7. ______
8. ______
9. ______
10. ______

The Goal I Am Going To Achieve First:

Show us how you *start today* on Social! – #StartTodayJournal

START TODAY

DATE:

Today I Am Grateful For:

1. ______________________
2. ______________________
3. ______________________
4. ______________________
5. ______________________

Ten Dreams I Made Happen:

1. ______________________
2. ______________________
3. ______________________
4. ______________________
5. ______________________
6. ______________________
7. ______________________
8. ______________________
9. ______________________
10. ______________________

The Goal I Am Going To Achieve First:

START TODAY

DATE:

Today I Am Grateful For:

1. ______________________________
2. ______________________________
3. ______________________________
4. ______________________________
5. ______________________________

Ten Dreams I Made Happen:

1. ______________________________
2. ______________________________
3. ______________________________
4. ______________________________
5. ______________________________
6. ______________________________
7. ______________________________
8. ______________________________
9. ______________________________
10. ______________________________

The Goal I Am Going To Achieve First:

Show us how you *start today* on Social! – #StartTodayJournal

START TODAY

DATE:

TODAY I AM GRATEFUL FOR:

1. ____________________
2. ____________________
3. ____________________
4. ____________________
5. ____________________

TEN DREAMS I MADE HAPPEN:

1. ____________________
2. ____________________
3. ____________________
4. ____________________
5. ____________________
6. ____________________
7. ____________________
8. ____________________
9. ____________________
10. ____________________

THE GOAL I AM GOING TO ACHIEVE FIRST:

START TODAY

DATE:

Today I Am Grateful For:

1. ______
2. ______
3. ______
4. ______
5. ______

Ten Dreams I Made Happen:

1. ______
2. ______
3. ______
4. ______
5. ______
6. ______
7. ______
8. ______
9. ______
10. ______

The Goal I Am Going To Achieve First:

Show us how you *start today* on Social! – #StartTodayJournal

START TODAY

DATE:

TODAY I AM GRATEFUL FOR:

1. __________
2. __________
3. __________
4. __________
5. __________

TEN DREAMS I MADE HAPPEN:

1. __________
2. __________
3. __________
4. __________
5. __________
6. __________
7. __________
8. __________
9. __________
10. __________

THE GOAL I AM GOING TO ACHIEVE FIRST:

START TODAY

DATE:

Today I Am Grateful For:

1. ______
2. ______
3. ______
4. ______
5. ______

Ten Dreams I Made Happen:

1. ______
2. ______
3. ______
4. ______
5. ______
6. ______
7. ______
8. ______
9. ______
10. ______

The Goal I Am Going To Achieve First:

Show us how you *start today* on Social! – #StartTodayJournal

START TODAY

DATE:

TODAY I AM GRATEFUL FOR:

1. ______
2. ______
3. ______
4. ______
5. ______

TEN DREAMS I MADE HAPPEN:

1. ______
2. ______
3. ______
4. ______
5. ______
6. ______
7. ______
8. ______
9. ______
10. ______

THE GOAL I AM GOING TO ACHIEVE FIRST:

START TODAY

DATE:

Today I Am Grateful For:

1. ____________________
2. ____________________
3. ____________________
4. ____________________
5. ____________________

Ten Dreams I Made Happen:

1. ____________________
2. ____________________
3. ____________________
4. ____________________
5. ____________________
6. ____________________
7. ____________________
8. ____________________
9. ____________________
10. ____________________

The Goal I Am Going To Achieve First:

Show us how you *start today* on Social! – #StartTodayJournal

START TODAY

DATE:

TODAY I AM GRATEFUL FOR:

1. __________
2. __________
3. __________
4. __________
5. __________

TEN DREAMS I MADE HAPPEN:

1. __________
2. __________
3. __________
4. __________
5. __________
6. __________
7. __________
8. __________
9. __________
10. __________

THE GOAL I AM GOING TO ACHIEVE FIRST:

Hey you did it! Congratulations! You made it to the end of your Start Today journal and for many of you that may be the first time you've ever consistently written down your dreams and goals every day. Or at least as many times necessary to fill up these pages.

Have you ever heard that saying about how if you can do something consistently for 30 days it becomes a habit and if you can do it for 90 days it becomes a way of life? Well there are 135 daily prompts in this book so I hope you haven't just found a new habit, I hope you've changed your life and your day around intentionally reaching for the best version of yourself and practicing gratitude.

The point of this practice is to keep yourself crystal clear about where you're headed in the future and to remind yourself every day where your focus needs to be right now. Some of my goals were accomplished in a couple of months, other goals took years to achieve but I truly believe the reason I've been so successful is that I stayed focused and I stuck with it. So stick with it! Keep fighting for the life you are meant to live. Keep looking for solutions. Keep arming yourself with knowledge. Keep your eyes on your own work (just like you did during a math test in 6th grade!) don't worry about what she's doing or what he's accomplishing— you're not living their life, you're not running their race. This is your dream, your goal, your future…put your head down and get back to work!

xo, Rach

Concept By: Rachel Hollis
@msrachelhollis | www.thehollisco.com

Cover Artist: Katrina Perkins
@khousdesign | www.khousdesign.com

Produced In Toronto, Canada By:
The Time of Day Calendar Inc.
@timeofdaycalendar | www.timeofdaycalendar.com

ISBN: 1-897334-21-4